Village Values

Negotiating Identity, Gender, and Resistance in Urban Russian Life-Cycle Rituals

VILLAGE VALUES

NEGOTIATING IDENTITY, GENDER, AND RESISTANCE IN URBAN RUSSIAN LIFE-CYCLE RITUALS

JEANMARIE ROUHIER-WILLOUGHBY

Bloomington, Indiana, 2008

SLAVICA

ISBN 978-0-89357-353-9

Library of Congress Cataloging-in-Publication Data

Rouhier-Willoughby, Jeanmarie, 1961-
    Village Values : negotiating identity, gender, and resistance in contemporary Russian life-cycle rituals / Jeanmarie Rouhier-Willoughby.
        p. cm.
    Includes bibliographical references and index.
    ISBN 978-0-89357-353-9
    1. Rites and ceremonies--Soviet Union. 2. Soviet Union--Social life and customs. 3. Rites and ceremonies--Russia (Federation) 4. Russia (Federation)--Social life and customs. 5. Life cycle, Human. I. Title.

GT2402.S65R68 2008
306.40947--dc22

2008042815

Slavica Publishers
Indiana University
2611 E. 10th St.
Bloomington, IN 47408-2603
USA

[Tel.] 1-812-856-4186
[Toll-free] 1-877-SLAVICA
[Fax] 1-812-856-4187
[Email] slavica@indiana.edu
[www] http://www.slavica.com/

This book is dedicated to my parents, Bill and Helen Rouhier, who taught me to love ritual and who opened the door to Russia for me. Пусть земля будет им пухом.

Развитие новой обрядости всемерно способствует становлению и укреплению советского образа жизни, совершенствованию взаимоотношений людей на производстве, в семье и в быту […] исключают всякую возможность проповеди насилия, секса и прочих уродливых примет буржуазного образа жизни. (The development of a new ritualism enables the institution and strengthening of the Soviet way of life to its utmost, the perfection of mutual relations of people in production, in the family and in daily life […] they exclude any possibility for the propagation of violence, sex, and other abnormal tokens of the bourgeois way of life).

—V. A. Rudnev, *Sovetskie prazdniki, obriady, ritualy*

The family is founded on love and families are the cells that make up the state.

—Valentina in *Women's Decameron*, by Iulia Voznesenskaia

Для существования же общества требуется, чтобы новые поколения включались в процесс социализации, и это делает семью необходимо для него. Признавая и уважая семью, общество стремится осуществлять над ней контроль […]. Семья существует постольку, поскольку стремится к автономии […]. (For a society to exist it must ensure that new generations are included in the process of socialization, and this makes the family necessary to it. While recognizing and respecting the family, a society strives to exert control over it […]. The family exists only so long as it strives for autonomy […]).

—I. A. Razumova, *Potaennoe znanie sovremennoi russkoi sem'i*

Contents

Acknowledgments

I could not have completed this project without the help of a myriad of people. First and foremost, I owe a huge debt to the people I interviewed, who were willing to share both tales of pain and of joy with a foreign researcher. Their tolerance, helpfulness, and innumerable kindnesses epitomize the fabled Russian soul. Although I cannot name them all here, each has a place in my heart. Special thanks go to the teachers in the Vladimir KORA program, to the students in my folklore class at Novosibirsk State University, and to Marina Kamasheva and Nadezhda Pivkina and their families for their friendship and support during the writing of this book. All researchers are also dependent on the good graces of granting institutions. This research was funded by support from the Fulbright-Hays Association and from the University of Kentucky.

I would like to thank James Bailey and my colleagues at the University of Kentucky Karen Petrone and Monica Udvardy, all of whom provided me with invaluable commentary on the book as it evolved. Susan Janecek assisted with much needed, eagle-eyed editorial comments on the draft. I am also indebted to all those who have commented on my papers, articles, and grant proposals related to this project, including Natalie Kononenko, Galina and Bob Rothstein, Michele Rivkin-Fish, Faith Wigzell, Anne Ingram, Snejana Tempest, and Laura Olson. My gratitude goes to the anonymous reviewers of this book as well, for their insights and careful assessment of the manuscript. Any errors in this work are entirely my own.

I wish to express my appreciation also to those who have not only helped with my research, but who have contributed in many other ways to the success of my work. The professors in the English Department at Novosibirsk State University welcomed me into their community and saw me through the Siberian winter. My University of Kentucky colleagues Cynthia Ruder and Gerald Janecek have been supportive in countless ways and have made coming to work a pleasure over the last fourteen years. My Russian colleagues Mikhail Lobanov, Ekaterina Belousova, Sergei Nekliudov, Yelena and Sergei Minyonok, and Vera Kuznetsova have all have advised me and helped with logistics and materials during this project. The librarians at the University of Kentucky performed miracles and never tired of my requests for help and materials, no matter how far afield. My siblings Dan Rouhier and Chelle Melzer and my dear friends Suzanne Morgan, Betty Trotter, Patricia Hayward, Ed and Deb Flaga, Anna Voskresenskaia, Marina and Charles

Lyon, and Mark and Amy Pitton have cheered me on and given me the confidence to pursue this project to the end. Valentina I., Polina and Vadim D., and Olga V. opened their homes to me during my research trips to Moscow. Klara S. fed me and buoyed my spirits with her stories. Natalia Turner spent hours transcribing my interview tapes. The students in my Russian Folklore classes at the University of Kentucky listened patiently as I endlessly recited stories about my research and provided input on the material I collected; particular thanks go to my research assistants John Rucker and Adam Recktenwald. Last, but certainly not least, I would like to thank my husband Wes Rouhier-Willoughby, for his patience, good humor, and endless love and support, you deserve the big plate.

Note: All translations from my interviews and other sources are my own except as noted in the bibliography. I have used the Library of Congress transliteration system for Russian expressions and names.

Chapter 1

Introduction to the Question

Project Genesis

This project began in a St. Petersburg apartment in the summer of 1995, while I was visiting a family whose son was studying to be a doctor. He and his wife were in the midst of their three internship rotations (roughly described as general practice/internal medicine, obstetrics/gynecology and pediatrics). I inquired what specialization they might choose. The husband said that he would not specialize in obstetrics, as that was women's work. His wife agreed and thought that precisely for that reason, she might become a doctor of obstetrics and gynecology. I was struck by this comment; it seemed strange that this particular field would be singled out as women's work, since most doctors in Russia were (and are) women.[1] In essence, the entire profession of physician in Soviet Russia was "women's work." Why then would this young man specifically state that obstetrics was different from the other fields of specialty? I began to wonder if there might not be a connection between the role of women as healer and midwife in nineteenth-century village life (see Glickman 1991 and Listova 1989, 1992 for discussion) to the contemporary urban attitude that women were the best candidates to be physicians, and particularly obstetricians/gynecologists.

I asked my Russian friends (all lifelong urban residents) whether they had had a female or a male obstetrician for their delivery. Overwhelmingly they answered that they were treated by female physicians. While this response in and of itself is not surprising, given the large percentage of female doctors in Soviet and post-Soviet Russia, I was struck by the number who added that men are not suited to being obstetricians. It seemed to me that this attitude, so markedly different from that in the United States, might well have been inherited from the nineteenth-century village. Men were generally excluded from the delivery, which was the purview of women healers. I was

---

[1] As of 1975, 72 percent of doctors were women (Ryan 1978, 42). Sacks (1976, 97) notes that 91 percent of all medical personnel were women in 1970. As Rivkin-Fish (2005, 26) notes, the percentage of women was even higher among obstetricians.

surprised to hear this conservative, "folk" attitude expressed by urban professional people, particularly in the face of assiduous Soviet attempts to root out
both nineteenth-century values and ritual practices. I had imagined that the
Soviet officials had indeed destroyed folk culture after sixty years, just as my
informants all insisted. Repeatedly they would ask why I wanted to interview
them, since, as they often said, "we have no folklore. You need to go to a village for that." This view of the folk as village inhabitants and of lore as their
exclusive possession is the result of ideology about folklore as a discipline,
both in the former Soviet Union and in Western Europe and the United States
(for a discussion of these issues, see Olson 2004 and Bronner 1998). Nevertheless, contemporary folklorists have broadened their investigations not only
to urban groups, but to those defined by profession, age, gender, hobby or
class, as well as ethnicity and region (whether rural or urban). In essence,
every group may potentially be defined as "folk." since they all may possess
folklore, defined by Sims and Stephens (2005, 8) as

> informally learned, unofficial knowledge about the world, ourselves,
> our communities, our beliefs, our cultures and our traditions, that is
> expressed creatively through words, music, customs, actions,
> behaviors and materials. It is also the interactive, dynamic process of
> creating, communicating, and performing....

This study will examine how the "informally learned, unofficial" beliefs of
urban Russians from the 1950s to the present day have interacted and conflicted with the official norms of the government throughout this period.

    When I began this project, it was extremely difficult for an outsider to
gain admittance to the maternity hospital. As a result, direct observation of
birth procedures was impossible in the early stages of my research. Therefore,
I began my study by interviewing women about their birth experiences. I limited my informants to women, since no men were allowed into the delivery
room until after 1990.[2] As I interviewed people, I learned a great deal about
both medical practices surrounding birth in Russia and about related folk
material. In the course of four collecting trips between 1995 and 2001, I discovered that the rituals were changing rapidly in the face of post-Soviet Western influences. A system that had retained its essential form for fifty years
needed to be documented before it was lost entirely. At the same time, since
life-cycle rituals form an interconnected whole and share a symbolic network,
I realized that I should not limit my research to birth alone. Weddings and funerals were also undergoing a shift after the fall of the Soviet Union, and the
changes in all three rituals reflected other significant social shifts. Thus I dedi-

---

[2] Note that even among my informants who had children after 1990, only one man
was present in the delivery room, even when it was possible for a father to attend the
birth.

cated three additional visits between 2002 and 2004 to collecting information on wedding and funeral rituals as well. However, in this case my informants included both men and women, since both sexes were active participants in the rituals under consideration. My data show that many nineteenth-century folk values have survived into the modern world, despite the Soviet authorities' attempts to eradicate them, both for their religious content and for the fact that they represented an "unenlightened" period in Russian history. However, as with all types of folklore, rituals are not static. While nineteenth-century practices may have survived, these three rituals have evolved over time into a multi-faceted system which conveys both folk beliefs and the belief systems of Soviet and post-Soviet Russian society. I quickly learned that my initial goal to study only folk practices and their evolution must be revised. I needed to investigate these rituals as a microcosm of Soviet and post-Soviet society to understand not only the ritual structure and symbols conveyed, but also the people who celebrated them and whose roles in society these ceremonies defined.

The Soviet Ritual Complex

The rituals we will study provide us with an insight into how multiple strains of Russian culture from the October Revolution to the present have managed to coexist and evolve. All three rituals I examined exhibit traces of the nineteenth-century rural folk behaviors considered to be essential for proper transition into a new social status. In addition, they feature Soviet practices, some of which have continued to the present day despite significant social changes since the fall of the Soviet Union in the early 1990s. Finally, they show how ideas and behaviors from Western Europe and America were adopted into the Soviet and post-Soviet belief system. This trend had already begun in the nineteenth century in cities, but became a significant social issue within the context of Soviet socialist ideology and again after the collapse of the Soviet Union. The material borrowed from the Western tradition varies widely and cannot always be pinpointed to a single source; nor can it be categorized as a single type of material. The borrowings relevant to our discussion include: ritual behaviors commonly found in Europe and the United States (such as the wearing of a formal white gown at a wedding or placing flowers at a funeral service); capitalist or consumerist ideology (primarily conspicuous consumption and the concern for economic status); and finally science and technology (particularly in the area of childbirth, but not exclusively). In sum, these rituals provide a microcosm of the social influences that every Russian faced throughout Soviet history and now faces in the post-Soviet world. As one would expect, the meanings about family life and social roles contained within these various belief systems are not always consonant with each other. Nevertheless, they were melded into a series of rituals which form what I will

call the Soviet ritual complex.[3] However, this study will not be limited to Soviet ritual from the 1950s to the 1990s, but will examine how rituals are
changing in the post-Soviet world in response to the crisis engendered by
socio-political upheaval. These rituals allow us to better understand the social
conflicts faced by Russian citizens throughout this time period, since the
rituals help to cope with such stresses, provide a means for resistance to governmental hegemony and themselves help create socio-cultural categories. As
the rituals change, we can see evidence of different attitudes in the society
toward what it means to be a member and what values are most important at
a given juncture in history.

A Note on "The West"

In his illuminating study *Inventing Eastern Europe: The Map of Civilization on
the Mind of the Enlightenment*, Larry Wolff (1994) argues that Churchill's iron
curtain seemed like a natural boundary because it was part of the European
intellectual tradition on both sides of the "divide." He (4) concludes that

> the distinction is older than Churchill and the Cold War, but it is by
> no means a matter of time immemorial, undiscoverably ancient. It
> was not a natural distinction, or even an innocent one, for it was pro-
> duced as a work of cultural creation, of intellectual artifice, of ideo-
> logical self-interest and self-promotion.... It was Western Europe that
> invented Eastern Europe as its complementary other half in the eight-
> eenth century, the age of Enlightenment. It was also the Enlighten-
> ment, with its intellectual centers in Western Europe, that cultivated
> and appropriated to itself the new notion of "civilization," an eight-
> eenth-century neologism, and civilization discovered its complement,
> within the same continent, in shadowed lands of backwardness, even
> barbarism.

However, we would be mistaken if we concluded that the boundary was akin
to a one-way mirror. Wolff (360) asserts that "the invention of Eastern Europe
was a subtly self-promoting and sometimes overtly self-congratulatory event
in intellectual history, whereby Western Europe also identified itself and af-
firmed its own precedence," as a result of which they look at their eastern

---

[3] Note that some of the features discussed in this work about the nature of Soviet ritual
may also apply to other post-socialist countries in Eastern Europe. Indeed, I have received comments to that effect to papers I have presented on this material from citizens of the former Yugoslavia and Ukraine. When I assert that this is a Soviet ritual
complex, I recognize that it may be a broader phenomenon of the socialist world.
However, I do not have the data available on urban rituals in those countries to make
such a definitive conclusion here.

brethren as inhabitants of "an ambiguous space, in a condition of backward-ness, on a relative scale of development." In consequence of this powerful and influential conception of Europe's natural dichotomy, Wolff (373) illustrates how "the intellectuals of Eastern Europe have had to respond to the imposed images and formulas devised in Western Europe."

Certainly the Slavophile-Westernizer debate is evidence of this intellec-tual current within Russia itself. Slavophiles looked to Russia as an entity dis-tinct (and sometimes) superior to the Western nations. They turned to native Russian traditions, including folklore and the Orthodox Church, to establish a distinct Russian national identity, so that its culture would play a central role in what Rabow-Edling (2006, 7) calls "the core of Europe." While, as Rabow-Edling notes (37, 73), the concern for the imitation of the non-native cultural forms and values underlay the general call for national "enlightenment" to solve the conundrum of national Russian culture, these two groups had "di-verging views of the meaning and implementation of such an enlighten-ment." Westernizers considered their country to be culturally backward, a condition that could only be changed by its own enlightenment through the educated elite, not by the masses (Rabow-Edling 74–79). The key, from the Westernizers' point of view, was not slavish imitation of the West, but the introduction of humanistic values (often associated with Enlightenment phi-losophy), so that Russia could join "civilization" (Rabow-Edling 97–98). Rabow-Edling (8) argues that the Slavophile movement emerged from the same concern for this "dual crisis of identity." In contrast to the Westernizers, however, they saw enlightenment as a means to enact "social change" in na-tional identity, not through the state and political developments, but through spiritual enlightenment and national cultural unity among all classes (Rabow-Edling 136–37).

This conflict between the views on Russia's path of national and Euro-pean culture had existed at least since the time of Peter the Great's Western-izing reforms, which formed the basis of the "identity crisis" noted above. Wolff (1994, 373) has argued that the dichotomous view of Europe was en-hanced by Western attitudes toward Russia as backward which native intel-lectuals either adopted or attacked. Rabow-Edling (2006, 45, 50) remarks that Russian intellectuals certainly viewed themselves as part of the European tra-dition and, as a result, they also accepted the "backwardness" of their society. While the Slavophiles objected to this contention, they recognized that this perception had to be changed to ensure that Russia took its rightful place in the world. Regardless of their position on the matter, there is no doubt that these philosophical arguments about Russia's national culture and the divide between it and the West have long stood as fundamental questions in the minds of Russians from all walks of life.

These issues did not fade away with the advent of the Soviet Union. Not only were many of the ideals of the USSR based on the communist ideas of Marx and Engels, but its espousal of scientific materialism was inherited from

Western intellectuals as well. Throughout the Soviet period, the government (and its people) contrasted the West with the East, the lands behind Churchill's renowned iron curtain. This "great divide" was certainly enhanced by the lack of direct exposure to the West. Yurchak (2006, 159) discusses his conception of the "Imaginary West" from the 1950s to 1980s in the Soviet Union as follows: "this concept was disconnected from any 'real' abroad and located in some unspecified place—over there (*tam*), with them (*u nikh*), as opposed to with us (*u nas*)—and although references to it were ubiquitous, its real existence became dubious." As a folklorist and cultural theorist, I do not suggest that the West is a monolithic entity that should be viewed as a single unit, any more than the "East" should be. However, the "West" and "Western" practices and ideals, which by this time also included and indeed featured the United States in a prominent role, were treated in just such a way by Soviet people in all walks of life for much of their history (and to some extent, even in the post-Soviet period, as we will see). Thus, for the purposes of this book, material in rituals adopted or rejected from this mythical "West" is used to approximate this term as viewed through this lens of the Soviet Russians themselves during the period under consideration.

Rituals in Soviet History

When the Bolsheviks took power after the October Revolution in 1917, they brought with them a vision of society that would overturn the remnants of the tsarist government that had ruled Russia for centuries. Their vision for their nation, designed ultimately to bring about a communist state based on the ideas of Engels and Marx, was not limited to political transformation, but was also accompanied by sweeping social changes. This social policy included calls for the elimination of the "backwardness" of Russia, specifically conservative folk beliefs and religion (including rituals themselves); the institution of equal rights for women, not only in the professional world, but also in the family unit, through access to divorce, property rights and abortion and the elimination of the patriarchy; and the creation of a classless society where all were equal and where workers were as valued as the "elite." All of these aspects of social policy played an influential role in ritual development throughout the entire Soviet period, as we will see. As Stites (1989, 41) notes in *Revolutionary Dreams*, "utopianism accompanied every phase of Soviet history up to the early 1930s when Stalin came to power." Thus, while these early ideals of the Bolshevik revolution were officially espoused throughout the duration of Soviet rule, the authorities did not always maintain the same attitude toward them as they had in the first two decades of the USSR's existence. For example, while the right to abortion was eliminated under Stalin in 1936 and only reinstated in 1955, the Soviet government never abandoned its commitment to equal rights for women in all official documents and in the constitution. As a result of these policy shifts, there was often a disconnect between the ideals and the reality of the Soviet state, one that is reflected in the attitude toward rituals themselves.

Lane (1981) and Petrone (2000) have shown that the Soviet Union used ritual to foster social and political identity within the country. Hobsbawm (1983b, 263–65) argues that this approach to ritual is not uncommon, particularly in states faced with cultural revolution, since they need new methods to establish a national political identity. Lane (3) notes that "ritual has become an important means to structure and maintain power relations in Soviet society." It encouraged value-consensus in the face of social conflict (Lane 13). At the same time, as Petrone (2–3) observes, discourse in the Soviet Union was not unitary. While the USSR "tried to promote legitimacy and authority" through its rituals, the voices of those performing them also were heard, voices that could "express alternative, unofficial, and subversive viewpoints." Petrone concludes (205) that

> Soviet officials designed celebrations to provide a template for ideal Soviet identities and behaviors, but they could not control the way the audiences actually perceived the celebrations. Celebrations thus contributed to the formation of both official Soviet identities and unofficial and individual points of view.

The rituals under consideration here are evidence of this phenomenon as well. While the state was sending a series of messages about the family and how to act in society as a parent/child, spouse or widow(er), the people involved in the ritual had their own agendas, i.e., their own system of "folk" beliefs. They accepted some views endorsed by Soviet ideology, but, given the public/private distinction and the gulf between the family and the state (discussed in more detail below), they also reinterpreted messages or created their own to ensure that individual family traditions were passed on. In this way, Soviet Russian citizens used ritual as a means both to *conform* to state ideals they found consonant with their norms, but also to *resist* them. In essence, they were able to forge an identity independent of the Soviet government's ideal for the family.

Although it recognized that rituals could be used as a tool to mold its citizens, the Soviet Union had an uneasy relationship with them nevertheless. They represented a past the Soviet state longed to forget and indeed to recreate, since it was associated with religion as well as with the backwardness of village life. Yet rites served as an effective means for the government to restructure the society. At first, the rituals they created were consonant with the utopian ideals Stites outlines, and represented their intention to remake society entirely. However, once Stalin took power, the left-leaning radicalism of the early Soviet period was replaced by a desire to establish a stable Soviet identity that would preserve the state's power. This view of the family and the rituals used to create it, foster it, and shape it lasted through the Brezhnev era and even into the post-Soviet period to some extent. In consequence of these policy changes, the state developed the new profession of "ritual specialist" in the 1960s, whose charge was to devise rituals consonant with the Soviet Union's ideals (Lane 26).

While ritual specialists also dealt with yearly cycle and public rituals, the focus here will be on their work for smaller groups in life-cycle rituals. Ritual specialists, such as Rudnev (1979), Mar'ianov (1976a, 1976b), Sukhanov (1976), Ugrinovich (1975), Zagradskaia (1980, 1981), Leitsadu (1982, 1983), and Krasovskaia (1980), were trained philosophers (and propagandists). They enlisted the help of folklorists, including such noted names as Putilov and others, to draw on the "correct" Russian tradition and to make the rituals more consonant with people's experience. They produced not only books that defended the introduction of rituals into Soviet society, but also articles for club and registry office workers on how to organize life-cycle rituals, particularly weddings and naming ceremonies for newborns. Their primary task was to legitimate ritual in the face of the earlier, anti-ritual policy. They did so by connecting it to *dukhovnye tsennosti* 'spiritual values', namely values associated not with religion but with work, family, sport, and art (Mar'ianov 1976a, 3). Ritual, then, was another creative outlet that allowed citizens to develop their aesthetic and moral sense, as well as to show their ties to their ancestors, to teach youth and to promote the unity and ideals of Soviet society by strengthening the family (Mar'ianov 1976a, 6–12; Sukhanov 6, 24–25, 55; Ugrinovich 20; Rudnev 22).

However, ritual specialists did not recognize that ritual is an organic, complex event that changes over time. They viewed rituals as fixed entities designed to convey the proper symbolic messages, not as innovative, evolving, and creative forms (Ugrinovich 1975, 39). Nevertheless, for ritual to convey important symbolic meanings to participants, it must be adaptable to their circumstances. Hobsbawm (1983a, 3) argues that if ritual becomes prescribed and static, then it is subject to becoming bureaucratic routine and loses its effectiveness as a tool for society. As a result, ritual specialists were often dismayed that people did not conform to their ideals of family and social morality as espoused by the rituals they had devised. Ugrinovich, for example, decries (153) both the *vykup* 'buying of the bride' and 'stealing' of the bride traditions at wedding receptions, since they have no place in a society characterized by gender equality. In addition, he (150) criticizes excessive drinking, particularly at weddings. Folklorists describing contemporary wedding rituals are also critical of "inappropriate" behaviors. Listova (1993, 41) was also not pleased with the *vykup* or, somewhat oddly, with the tradition of having the groom, with the help of his witness and friends, retrieve the key to the bride's apartment from a three-liter jar filled with water or juice by drinking the liquid without spilling any of it. In essence, they either did not understand or wished to control common ritual processes related to excess and breaking of social norms. More importantly, they failed to grasp that ritual participants were agents, not passive recipients, who would inevitably take possession of these rites to establish their own identities within family and society.

Another dilemma for ritual specialists was that many of the rituals they wanted to introduce had connections to the religious life that they wanted to eliminate. They believed, in some cases correctly (for more on this issue see chapter 2), that if the state introduced its own rituals, then religious rituals would fall by the wayside (Ugrinovich 1975, 108). At the same time, by introducing their own versions of rituals traditionally associated with religion (e.g., baptism, weddings, and funerals), they left the way clear for continuing religious observations at home. Despite their arguments that folk ritual was not truly associated with Orthodoxy, since many ritual behaviors were inherited from pre-Christian agrarian belief,[4] and that folk rituals were anti-establishment and expressed dissent with Orthodox Russian society, the ties between Orthodoxy and folk practices were still clear well into the twentieth century (Rudnev 1979, 7ff.; Mar'ianov 1976a, 6–7; Sukhanov 1976, 5, 55). In fact, some of my non-Orthodox informants rejected folk wedding and funeral practices precisely because they perceived them to be associated with Christianity. The ritual specialists themselves recognized this dilemma. Sukhanov (54) notes that some aspects of Soviet rituals may look religious, as in the naming ceremony where two people who seemingly acted as godparents would participate, but that they served a completely different function in Soviet society. He (201) concludes that ritual specialists need to explain how the new rituals are different from the old ones, so that people would not be drawn back into their faith. Soviet ritual specialists hoped that their new rites would instill the values of communist morality, in lieu of religious principles, and strengthen the family unit with the life-cycle rituals they created (Mar'ianov 14; Sukhanov 45; Ugrinovich 44). They were most successful in this regard with the wedding. They succeeded here for several reasons; firstly, legal marriage was a state affair, and church weddings were not recognized, so that the Soviets controlled the rite exclusively. Secondly, the institution of the wedding palace allowed for a formal, public celebration, which had been frowned upon early in the Soviet period. Since there was no other means to have such a celebration, couples embraced the opportunity offered to them.

In the case of naming and funerary rituals, the Soviets made fewer inroads into the creation of truly secular rites. While it could make a marriage official, no law could prevent a child from being named or a person from dying. Since these events did not require a public, legal ceremony, it was more difficult to divest them of their religious content. A child received a name af-

---

[4] In order to deal with the issue that paganism was also a religious belief system, ritual specialists took the attitude that such remnants or resurrections of folk belief were outmoded superstitions that had been converted to amusing practices without any religious functions (Sukhanov 1976, 68).

ter registration of a birth at the *otdel zapisi aktov grazhdanskogo sostoianiia* or ZAGS, the Soviet registry office that recorded births, marriages, divorces, and deaths. The public Soviet naming rite designed to replace baptism never really caught on among the populace as a whole. In fact, baptism was still fairly widespread, as the ritual specialists (and some of my informants) reported (Rudnev 1979, 119; Ugrinovich 1975, 108, 124–26, 143). Funerary ritual was especially problematic, since it was tied to religious tenets about life after death. Therefore, although ritual specialists were charged with developing a more effective Soviet civil funeral dedicated to the memory of the dead, which also allowed for people to feel ties to the collective to assuage their grief, it was never totally "Sovietized." While the state did issue a death certificate and organized civil burials, the core of the ritual was in the family home, where religious ritual could not be prevented so easily. Therefore, the Soviet state was unable to co-opt baptism and funerals in the same way that they did weddings.

An additional factor to consider was the role of religion in the ceremonies themselves. Unlike the other rituals, weddings had also come to be disassociated from religious belief over time. Russians no longer viewed one's salvation as dependent on religious consecration of marriage.[5] In contrast, a person's soul was in jeopardy if (s)he was not baptized (from the Christian point of view only, of course) or buried with at least some aspects of a religious ceremony. As a result, the degree of Soviet, folk, religious and indeed Western elements in the rituals varied. Each rite must be examined in detail to tease out the role these various sources for ritual acts play in them. Since none of my informants took part in a Soviet-era naming ceremony, we will focus on traditional and Soviet practices during pregnancy and delivery in the discussion of the rituals of childbirth. However, the examination of funerals and weddings will feature both Soviet and "folk" elements as part of the entire ritual, although the wedding had much more well-developed and elaborate Soviet content than burial practices did.

The Soviet Family and Gender Roles

Life-cycle rituals in the nineteenth-century Russian village were primarily the purview of women. Women were the most important celebrants not only in birth, but in weddings and funerals as well (nineteenth-century village rituals and women's role in them will be discussed in more detail in chapter 2). Since the rituals helped to define roles in the domestic sphere, which women dominated, it is not surprising to find women in this role. In normal circumstances

---

[5] In fact, there is evidence that in the nineteenth-century village it was not the church ceremony but rather the reception that was the most important component of the wedding. In some cases, the ceremony actually occurred after the reception (and even consummation) of the marriage (Worobec 1995, 162).

it was perhaps their only source of significant social power within patriarchal village life (a woman might have become head of a household and have represented the family in the *mir* 'village community' publicly, but that was a rare occurrence). The centrality of women to life-cycle ritual carried on into the Soviet period, not only because it conformed to cultural expectations from the traditional folk point of view, but because people viewed their family life as an oppositional (private) space to the Soviet institutions of the collective and the workplace. Gal and Kligman (2000, 51–52) assert that people were, of course, not truly divided into two parts, but were participants in both public and private life. However, this concept "came to represent a stable reality to which they referred," and thus "it enabled people to differentiate between a trustworthy, private, familial 'we' who could rely on one another and an untrustworthy public 'they' who were in charge of the state." Women, who controlled the private space of the family (Edmondson 1996, 105; Verdery 1996, 70), became responsible for preserving practices perceived as threatened by Soviet life (as we will see below in our discussion of rituals) because without them core family traditions would be lost. As a result, women functioned as culture bearers not only because it conformed to the Russian worldview for them to do so, but because they were the center of the private family space in the Soviet Union. [6]

The family was the place where essential folk (and religious) beliefs were preserved, so that despite the best intentions of ritual specialists, Soviet rituals took on a life of their own. Citizens saw Soviet society as a threat to the folk traditions as a whole and to family traditions in particular. My evidence for this claim comes from my informants themselves. They often talked about what they had lost as a result of the Soviet authorities' attack on religion and folk practice. One woman, for example, reported that she really tried to honor the dead, but that her generation had lost so much being raised as atheists that she did not know how to do it properly. Another proudly said that she knew how to celebrate the spring holiday of *Semik* because her grandmother had taught her, even though the Soviet government had destroyed all these traditions. Certainly, restrictions on baptism, particularly to members of the older generation, were a threat to one's soul, but also to the proper celebration of the birth of child; as a result, many grandmothers baptized their grandchildren secretly.

Life-cycle rituals in the Soviet period not only conveyed folk and religious ideology, which many families tried to preserve, but also strengthened the family itself. Strengthening the family, of course, was a goal of Soviet theo-

---

[6] Other factors that played a role in women as "culture-bearers" were war deaths and lower life expectancy among men, as Olson (2004, 51, 179–83) has discussed. Verdery (1996, 65) also notes that older women maintained more control over the family due to the earlier retirement age for women, childcare responsibilities (for grandchildren), and their help with other household tasks for adult children.

rists, but they could not prevent people from co-opting rituals as a means to escape socialist norms. The family might indeed become stronger, but not always in service of the USSR. Rather, it used its new-found strength to serve its own ends, some of which supported the Soviet state and its ideals, others of which did not. The Soviet authorities recognized that traditional family mores often directly contravened standards of behavior they had established after the Revolution. As a result, they tried to influence and control the family as much as possible through multiple means, from popular culture and propaganda to classes in school. One significant method for achieving the goals of molding the family into one consonant with state ideals was the Soviet ritual complex itself (discussed in more detail in chapters 3–5).

Certainly every contemporary civil society has placed its stamp on rituals and aims to control the family, to some extent, e.g., through birth certificates and wedding licenses. What is distinctive about the Soviet situation is that there was an official ideology that underlay the rituals they devised. Even as the society became less totalitarian after Stalin's death in 1953, people read the practices in rituals as an attempt to make them conform to Soviet ideology about family life, which was ultimately perceived as inimical to the family itself. We will now turn our attention to the changing Soviet ideas on gender roles and the family, ideas which are essential to an understanding of life-cycle rituals throughout the period under consideration.

Just as the Soviet Union had originally attacked the bourgeoisie and glorified workers and peasants, it also thought that the family should be restructured. The revolutionaries accepted this contention because for them the family represented patriarchal and outmoded bourgeois values. Early Soviet social theorists expected, as Goldman (1993, 1–3) describes, that the family would "wither away" and that

> household labor would be transferred to the public sphere. The tasks performed by millions of individual unpaid women in their homes would be taken over by paid workers in communal dining rooms, laundries, and childcare centers. Women would be freed to enter the public sphere on an equal basis with men ... marriage would become superfluous.

However, these revolutionary goals did not take into consideration the social or personal consequences of the state assuming the role of "family;" nor did they truly consider how gender roles might be remade. Kukhterin (2000, 71) argues that the destruction of the patriarchy and the church was not truly designed to liberate women: "rather, the aim was to enlarge the public sphere at the expense of the private, in an attempt to render individuals more amenable to state control."

It was assumed that women would still perform domestic chores, not that both women and men would take part in all types of household labor equally

(Goldman 1993, 11–12). At the same time, the Soviet Union was faced with a dilemma. To eliminate marriage altogether (although some argued for it) would mean that the religious institutions could still claim some authority within an atheistic society, because they could still perform wedding ceremonies that would give them social clout (1993, 55–56). The solution to ceding such power to religious entities was to ensure that the state controlled both marriage and divorce; civil ceremonies became the only legal means to marry in 1917 (1993, 49). However, while the state did control the institution of marriage, it tried to downplay the ceremony itself, which took place in small offices without any ritual trappings that could threaten revolutionary ideals (Timasheff 1946, 193). The marriage and economic policies of the Soviet Union, which strongly promoted work outside the home,[7] without any attempt at restructuring traditional attitudes toward gender roles, of course resulted in the infamous "double burden" for women (Goldman 1993, 130). Marriage, however, did not die out, as expected, but came to be seen as an essential component of Soviet social stability as people became concerned about juvenile delinquency, the abandonment of women and children to poverty as a result of lax divorce laws without child support provisions, and low birthrates that resulted from the breakdown in the family and marriage (1993, 97, 217, 288).

Women had entered the workforce from the revolutionary period on, but Goldman (2002, 71) concludes that the real breakthrough came when the first five-year plan was adopted in 1928; "women entered all sectors of the economy, but the largest number went into industry. Within a short time, they assumed significant roles in industries long dominated by men, transformed the gender composition of the workforce, and subverted older lines of sex segregation." However, integration of the workforce was not to last, and an official policy that genderized various portions of the labor force was instituted in December 1930. Goldman (2002, 163) notes that "planners retrieved various versions of their 'female labor' plans and compiled a long list of jobs that were to be filled either primarily or exclusively by women. Covering fifteen pages, the lists carved out entire sectors of the economy and industry as preserves of female labor." As a result, Goldman (2002, 283) asserts that "the feminization of light industry and service jobs … in the industrialized Soviet economy bore a striking resemblance to the sex segregation that marked its Western capitalist counterparts." Thus, while the Soviet authorities espoused equality in the workforce, they also created a system in which certain jobs,

---

[7] Even women who wanted to stay home were not realistically able to, since the family could not survive without two incomes. Thus, women were officially encouraged to work both to ensure that the Soviet Union would meet its production quotas and also to illustrate the gender equality that the Soviet Union was said to have achieved. In essence, they were forced to work due to economic and political circumstances beyond their control.

often the most prestigious and better paid, were "masculine," while others were "feminine." As such, they carved out jobs that were suited to "natural" traits exhibited by women and men on the basis of their innate biological characteristics. The concept of "natural biological differences" not only played an important role in the workplace, but in the family as well, as we will see below.

Zdravomyslova and Temkina (2005, 98) assert that gender policy in the Soviet Union can roughly be divided into three periods: the Bolshevik era from the 1917 revolution to the early 1930s; the Stalinist conservative backlash to the mid-1950s; and finally, the program until the fall of the Soviet Union, which was designed to solve the "demographic crisis." Ashwin (2000b, 9) disagrees with this assessment of the attitude toward the family in the Stalinist period:

> The undermining of tradition was to be followed by a period of transformation, in which institutions such as the family would be reconstituted along communist lines.... This means that the supposed "resurrection" of the family in the Stalin era should not be viewed as a conservative retreat which curtailed the revolutionary potential of the 1920s. Rather, what occurred was an attempt to recreate the family as a specifically *Soviet* family, which, instead of serving as a "conservative stronghold of the old regime," would become a functional unit in the new polity ... the regime accepted the family, but only in its reconstituted form as the primary cell of Soviet society. This implied that citizens—while allowed to remain in families—had to be constantly reminded that their primary duty was to the state.

As a result, the Soviet Union under Stalin focused on a return to "traditional" family as a means to maintain social stability as well as in response to the revolutionary tradition of recreating the notion of family itself (see discussion above with regard to Soviet *dukhovnye* 'spiritual' values).

Even if the family was recreated into a new entity, it still was essential that women value their traditional roles as mothers to provide additional workers for the future state (Goldman 1993, 333; Hyer 1996, 111). Therefore, the Soviet Central Executive Committee outlawed abortion in 1936 (Goldman 1993, 241). However, the birthrate did not increase as expected; women were working outside the home and were facing the difficulty of balancing two separate lives (1993, 293). Hyer (112) describes the Soviet dilemma as follows: "women have been required for economic production, but at the same time increased fertility has been promoted; status has been derived through participation in social production, yet having children has also been glorified." The 1936 law that banned abortion also initiated the return to "family values." That is, new mothers received stipends and bonuses for having many children; maternity leave was extended for urban women (*kolkhoznitsy* 'female farm workers' did not get maternity leave); it also provided additional social services, such as more maternity clinics, daycares, and milk kitchens (Goldman 1993, 291). Goldman (1993, 336) argues that this law "offered women a tacit bargain. It broadened both state and male responsibility for the family, but in exchange it demanded that women assume the double burden of work and motherhood. The idea that the state would assume the functions of the family was abandoned." However, Stites (1978, 390) forcefully concludes that

> by any reasonable standards of judgment, including post-Stalinist Soviet ones, the effect of the reaction was to take away from Soviet women more than it gave them. In a number of mutually reinforcing ways, it tended to draw a line between the sexes and their respective roles which was wider and more visible than anything previously known in revolutionary imagery.

The next step in this process of remaking the family and shifting the attention to "traditional" gender roles within it was the creation of Soviet rituals that reflected these new views of the family. Thus in 1944 the Supreme Soviet, in Article 30 of its resolution on motherhood, called for ceremonial registration of births and weddings (Zhirnova 1980, 82).[8] While the resolution did initiate the process of creating Soviet rituals, the postwar economic situation did not allow for elaborate celebrations in any case. Real progress came only in the late 1960s, when the economy had improved, and ritual specialists had made progress on designing new Soviet life-cycle rituals. This development coincided with an even greater push for "family values." Trends initiated under Stalin to reinforce the family not only endured throughout the Soviet period, but were strengthened under later political regimes, from Brezhnev's *zastoi* through Gorbachev's *perestroika*.[9] Shlapentokh (1984, 1989), Buckley (1996), Ilic (1996), Field (1988), and Attwood (1990, 1996) discuss the importance of the family to Soviet society at various points from the 1970s to the 1990s. In the early years of this period, of course, the Soviet rituals themselves were being actively developed and promoted in an effort to strengthen the family.

Attwood traces the concern of Soviet theorists to the "masculinization" of Soviet women (citing Yankova 1975, 1978 and Kharchev 1979, 1981). She contends that the concern for the masculinization of women does not extend to

---

[8] The 1920s also saw an interest in the creation of Soviet ritual and elimination of older forms (see Stites 1989, 109ff.). The rituals created during this period were primarily officious and tedious revolutionary proclamations that did not receive much support from the people as a result (Sukhanov 1976, 184–85; Ugrinovich 1975, 115–16).

[9] Note that Putin's announcement in the spring of 2006 about governmental plans designed to increase the birthrate and support the family are a continuation of this trend over ten years into the post-Soviet period.

the feminization of men. That is, men who do domestic work, according to Attwood's reading of Soviet sociological literature (1990, 125), are not seen to be transformed by it in the same way that women are by their professional life and "masculine" roles. However, Verdery (1996, 65) and Kukhterin (2000, 78) claim that men did suffer, since their traditional authority within the family was undercut by the Soviet system. Kay (2002, 53) observes that from the 1970s on "discussions in the national media lamented the detrimental effect on marital relations and stable families purportedly caused by excessively self-confident and liberated, 'masculine' women and weak, 'effeminate' men." Nevertheless, as Kiblitskaia (2000, 91–92) points out, the Soviet-era Russian man still considered himself to be the breadwinner and head of the household, even if his wife worked; this role was reinforced by Soviet ideology as well as by the fact that men consistently earned more for their labor than women, despite laws mandating equal pay for all. Regardless of the concern that men had lost their "natural" role in the family, they seemingly perceived it differently to a great extent. As Ashwin (2000b, 18) concludes: "the paradoxical legacy of the Soviet era can be seen as strong, independent women who nevertheless ended up doing all the housework, and weak, 'feminine' men who none the less had the autonomy to relax, drink and escape the domestic arena," e.g., to capitalize on their public role as "patriarchs." The rituals under consideration here (particularly birth and marriage) helped to establish these contradictory gender roles within Soviet Russian society.

Most importantly, throughout Soviet history, theorists such as Posadskaia (1991, 139), Shlapentokh (1989, 3, 13, 164–65; 1984, 73), Verdery (1996, 94) Duffy (2000, 220), and Marody (1993, 859, 861) all argue that the family, however defined, became the bastion against the state within socialist society. Therefore, while the state was encouraging families to become stronger, in order to solve some of the state's own problems, at the same time people saw the family as a place where people were freed from the demands of the state itself. Not unexpectedly, the family rituals under consideration here also reflect this view. While the Soviets perceived ritual to be a normative means to control the family (see Ugrinovich 1975, 40), the families looked at ritual as one means to escape from Soviet mores and to convey their own values. As Boym (1994, 11, 29, 88) discusses, *byt* 'daily life' became the enemy of private life in the Soviet Union; it contrasted with one's spiritual being or "real" life. She particularly cites the example of obtaining a single-family apartment after living in a communal one, which had been common in the early Soviet period. This step encouraged people to take refuge within the family group and to forge a sense of independence. Because the Soviet state deemphasized individualism, the family space became a place where citizens could express themselves openly.

Shlapentokh (1984, 25) notes that a stable family is important to a totalitarian state, which the government recognized and thereby tried to foster through its family policies and propaganda. However, because the family can become a refuge from the state and espouses a set of values that may not correspond to state ideology, it is potentially a dangerous entity. One example of this attitude in fiction is Voznesenskaia's *Women's Decameron* (1986), in which ten women in a maternity ward discuss their lives, attitudes toward family, men and the Soviet state. In this private (feminized) space these women, even the Soviet party apparatchik, are more open in their criticism of the government and its policies. The Soviet government recognized both aspects of the family and attempted to mold it as much as possible to avoid such conflicts. Verdery (1996, 61ff.) discusses how the state tried to usurp family power by taking on traditional family roles itself. It functioned as a "father" by doling out goods to its citizens like an allowance and bestowing rewards; it functioned as a "mother" by providing services to nurture and protect the family. The government also attempted to achieve this goal by controlling ritual itself. Ultimately, as both Verdery (66) and Shlapentokh (1989, 165–66) argue, the state could not control the family (or, I would argue, its rituals) completely, especially given the post-Stalinist trend for the family to be viewed as a refuge from state/public demands.

According to Field (1998, 600), this trend for conservatism in women's social and familial roles reached its peak in the 1960s. Khrushchev recognized that "in order to work hard and to commit themselves whole-heartedly to the fulfillment of government priorities, Soviet people could not be distracted by family discord, unruly passions, and narrow personal interest." Ilic (1996, 230–31) attributes the rise in flex time and part-time work, shorter work days, and longer maternity leaves during Khrushchev's and Brezhnev's rule to the emphasis on increasing the birthrate and returning women to their traditional roles as mothers. Buckley (1996, 216) describes similar propaganda from the Brezhnev era, which focused on women's return to the home, an increase in the birthrate, and a reduction in juvenile crime. These attitudes sparked an interest in communist morality, which promoted good workers as well as stability in one's personal life (602). One response was a strengthening of ritual, not only to reinforce women's traditional role within Russian society, but also to strengthen the family and institute the aforementioned communist morality (see Ugrinovich 1975, 40ff. for a discussion). As a result, divorce was discouraged, since it interfered with work, and public involvement in private matters, such as "marital relations and sexual behavior was justified, even necessary in some instances" (Field 604).

Psychologists also became involved with the pro-family movement of the 1960s and 1970s in socialist Russia. They began to describe both typical "male" and "female" behaviors in children. A core part of the argument was that women differed from men biologically, as noted above in the discussion of "(fe)male" professions. Therefore, their failure to advance in the workplace was due not to discrimination, but to their biological personality and physical traits.[10] Women, within this framework, are not designed for the competition of the workplace and primarily focus their attention on their families. Attwood (1990, 164) argues that these attitudes stem from the belief that the Soviet Union had provided "complete equality of opportunity for men and women, so different choices of profession or position must be due to nature." Therefore, in 1984 pedagogues and psychologists introduced a course in high schools that focused on male and female roles in marriage and the family (Attwood 1990, 184). This class was the result of a recognition within the Soviet Union of what Attwood (1990, 185) describes as "a clash between the new ideology, which is based on the separation of male and female roles and personal traits, and an operational ideology, which assumes at least a theoretical equality and comradeship between sexes." The course was designed to strengthen the evolving ideology about gender roles and reinforce family values, reduce the number of abortions and divorces, increase family size, and push women toward a domestic role.[11]

These issues were revisited during Gorbachev's tenure as Soviet leader. He also emphasized women's domestic roles through shorter work days, longer holidays, and early retirement (Filtzer 1996, 216; Ilic 1996, 230; Attwood 1990, 12). However, as Attwood (1996, 277) observes, most of these attempts did not succeed, since daily life during *perestroika* became harder on women; due to rationing, inflation, and shortages they did not have the luxury of giving up their jobs.[12] Propaganda, the anti-Soviet backlash, and indeed some actual data on family life simultaneously led to the perception of the family as an entity that had been irrevocably harmed by Soviet behaviors. Attwood (1996, 255) states that

> from the middle of the 1970s, Soviet writers were arguing that women's high level of involvement in the workforce has led to a distortion both of female and male personality. Women had been forced to

---

[10] One doctor I interviewed, Natalia R., concurred, "We think that a doctor then will be more valuable namely if he is a man. In practice it turns out that way, because, in the first place, a woman gives birth to children, and she very often takes maternity leave, she often takes sick days, since the children get sick, everyone has gone through this.... And in connection with this and generally somehow it is thought that a man will be a more valuable doctor, he will give more of his effort to work than a woman.... And in practice I know everyone, who is working and where, and really men have achieved more than women."

[11] One woman who attended school in the 1970s in Krasnodar described how girls were expected to cook for class and perform other domestic chores, while boys went outside and did work on the school grounds; thus even if there was no class espousing traditional gender roles, teachers conveyed these ideals to their pupils.

[12] They did, however, suffer disproportionately through layoffs; during the Gorbachev era 70–80 percent of those laid off were women, so that even if they did not choose to return to the family, they were forced to by the economic crisis (Attwood 1996, 256).

develop personality traits more appropriate to the workplace than the home.... Men were robbed of the traditional masculine role of bread-winner and became weak, apathetic and alcoholic.

While these attitudes toward gender difference and family structure arose in the 1970s, as noted above, they reached fruition in the Gorbachev period, when people blamed the Soviet system for the destruction of the traditional ways of life and all that had been "good" about Russia. Even the Russian feminist Posadskaia (1991, 138), in an interview with Molyneux, argued that "gender relations were so deformed by the society we had...." There was also a backlash against feminism in all the former socialist states, since it was associated with the Soviet worldview that had broken down the family structure (see Duffy 2000; Marody 1993; Szabo 2006 for a discussion of this issue).

Eastern European feminists often remark on the dilemmas faced within society during the Soviet period with regard to gender equality and the family. In her interview with Molyneux, Posadskaia (1991, 134) states that

> one of the problems is that the solving of the so-called women's question under socialism never actually happened. The idea was that women's emancipation would occur through their mass incorporation into social production, and the "socialization" of domestic labour, while the Party worked at changing people's attitudes. But some of these aims did not get translated into policy.

As a result, Posadskaia concludes, women had "very narrow life perspectives, and hard lives." Marody (1993, 855–57) also asserts that despite evidence to the contrary, she never felt discriminated against in her professional life in Poland; rather, she understood that the differences between men and women professionally were based on biology rather than on social policy.[13]

As the period of *perestroika* came to an end, and the Soviet Union collapsed, the conception of family structure and gender relations was necessarily adjusted as well. Since the Soviet Union and its policies were blamed for

---

[13] A mathematician (mother of two) who came of age in the 1960s responded as follows to my questions on these issues: "My opinion is that our men are lazier. As a rule, they do not participate in housekeeping, in raising children. It was thought that a woman should do all that. And women bore all of that without complaint.... Girls were admitted to institutions of higher learning in various majors, they were enrolled if they did well on exams, just like the guys. In some institutions of higher learning, where few boys applied, and there were lots of girls, they preferred to take men, under the condition that they had identical scores on exams. There were, and probably are specializations where they don't take girls, to be a pilot, for example. But girls were even admitted there, if they had a very strong desire. I think that our men do not respect women, but that women have an overdeveloped sense of duty to family, children."

the "destruction" of the family, there has been a shift in the attitudes toward
how a family should be constructed and indeed perceived over the last fifteen
years. Gal and Kligman (2000, 69) discuss this issue:

> But today, nostalgic memory often constructs the communist-era fam-
> ily as autonomous from the corruption of the state and politics. The
> private household continues to be valued as the place where people
> live their honest, authentic, and meaningful lives. In the communist
> era the danger was understood to be the intrusiveness of the state;
> now it is more often the uncertainty and untrustworthiness of state
> action and the insecurity of markets and employment.

Even though this attitude toward the family persists, the family situation in
Russia is a complex one, influenced, according to Ashwin (2000b, 18), by the
same three sources as the life-cycle rituals themselves: Soviet policy, folk tradition, and Western ideas. As Rands Lyon (2007, 26) argues:

> The impact of Soviet *egalitarian* policies and rhetoric has not dissolved
> with the collapse of the Communist Party and its ideology ... a Post-
> Soviet backlash has not crowded the Soviet icons of sexual equality or
> of the woman-worker completely off the shelves of available gender
> role models. Few women are interested in giving up work altogether,
> and Russian men rarely exercise the kind of patriarchal authority in
> the home that they claim in survey responses to uphold....

While neotraditional views of the family may be at the forefront, the reality of
post-Soviet life is that the economy generally requires both parents to work.
Zdravomyslova and Temkina (2005, 110) argue that the difference for women
is that

> [i]n the post-Soviet version the duties of the "working mother" are
> not a civil obligation. The privatisation of motherhood and the re-
> moval of parenthood from the sphere of civic duties are combined
> with personal choice for women. The duty to participate in social
> production has been replaced by an economic need to provide for
> one's family, which has necessitated a more active role for women in
> the sphere of paid work.

Even in families where this is not the case, women often choose to work outside the home, as Rands Lyon (2007, 31) observes. My own informants echoed
this sentiment; they, both men and women, have accepted the Soviet-era
egalitarian model regarding work, and they find some meaningful avenue for
self-expression in professional life, regardless of economic circumstances.

Certainly, theorists who argue for the multivalent nature of gender identity in contemporary Russia have made some interesting points about family life and gender relations. However, my data support the claim that these issues are still strongly influenced by familiar tenets of Soviet-era (and indeed pre-Soviet Russian) attitudes. Both Kay (1997, 93–94) and Johnson and Robinson (2007b, 3) concur with this assertion. Kay describes the situation as follows:

> Superficially it appears that there has been a complete reversal of what went before: the Soviet ideal of strong working women has been thrown out and replaced with models of femininity, domesticity and maternity. Dip a little deeper below the surface, however, and we see that things are not so different ... a great many of the policies and attitudes given official backing today are firmly rooted in traditions from the Soviet period.

The Russian state itself continues to support many of the same attitudes about gender and the family that the Soviet government held for over seventy years. Khasbulatova (2005, 314), in her study of gender politics from 1917 to the present, notes that the post-Soviet era has been characterized by a policy of official gender equality, beginning with the first post-Soviet Russian constitution of 1993. Certainly, she demonstrates (315–30) that these goals are not always met in reality, just as they were not under Soviet rule. Nevertheless, the post-Soviet Russian government has at its core many of the same ideals as its predecessor. Nor has it abandoned, despite some claims to the contrary, its dedication to upholding the family. In the spring of 2006, as *The New York Times* reported on May 11, Putin called for a plan to improve the demographic situation: "among his proposals were one-time cash grants to mothers upon the birth of a second child, extended maternity leave benefits and a graduating scale of cash and day-care subsidies as a woman has more children."[14] In addition, the government has continued to pass laws that "protect" pregnant women, including one in 1996 that gave them days off from work for checkups and increased the length of maternity leave (Khasbulatova 337). As we will see in our study of life-cycle rituals throughout this period, attitudes toward gender roles and the family (and the

---

[14] Note that regional authorities have also attempted to raise the birthrate and support the family through similar incentives. In 2005 Sergei Morozov, governor of the Ulyanovsk region, declared September 12 to be Conception Day. Couples are allowed to take that day off from work to have sex, with an eye to producing "patriot" babies on June 12, Russia's Constitution Day. According to the August 14, 2007 edition of *The Guardian* (http://www.guardian.co.uk/worldlatest/story/0,,-6849496,00.html), "couples who 'give birth to a patriot' during the June 12 Festivities win money, cars, refrigerators and other prizes."

state's role in them) have played a significant role in (Soviet) Russian life from the 1950s to the present day.

The Nature of Life-cycle Rituals

Arnold van Gennep in his classic study *The Rites of Passage* (1960, 3) discusses the fact that human life

> comes to be made up of a succession of stages with similar ends and beginnings: birth, social puberty, marriage, fatherhood, advancement to a higher class, occupational specialization, and death. For every one of these events there are ceremonies whose essential purpose is to enable the individual to pass from one defined position to another which is equally well defined.

The four most prevalent life-cycle rites are birth, adulthood initiation, marriage, and funerals. However, life-cycle rites may also include much less common rituals such as elevation to kingship or gang initiation, as Turner describes in *The Ritual Process* (1969). According to structuralists, life-cycle rituals are designed to mark changes in social status as well as to release one from the bonds of social convention. Turner (95) concludes that after the ritual the initiate "must behave in accordance with certain customary norms and ethical standards binding on incumbents of social position." Bourdieu (1991, 115) takes a different view. Building upon Van Gennep's ideas, he states that one must consider the neglected "*social* [italics original] function of ritual and the social significance of the boundaries of limits which the ritual allows one to pass over or transgress in a lawful way." He argues that it is necessary to consider how the rite of passage (or in his terms, rite of institution), creates a marked distinction between people: "the distinctions that are the most efficacious socially are those which give the appearance of being based on objective differences.... None the less, as is very clear in the case of social classes, we are always dealing with continua ... due to the fact that different principles of differentiation produce different divisions that are never completely congruent." Baiburin (1993, 5) also builds upon structuralism in his theory of ritual as performance; he notes that "every society, being concerned about its wholeness, develops a system of social codes (programs) of behavior which are prescribed to its members." These codes help to ensure, according to Baiburin (1993, 17), that the society will continue to replicate its values, which is consonant with structuralist thought and also with one of the purposes of ritual outlined above. However, his argument centers on the performative force of rituals and is more in keeping with how people themselves view the rituals they practice. Baiburin (1993, 39) argues that life-cycle rituals also serve to ensure that the transitional figures of the child, wedding couple, and the deceased are properly incorporated into society or removed from it; without such rituals a person is not truly "born," "married," or "dead." Although the ritual itself may vary widely, it carries with it a significant social force, a construct for membership in the group, as Bourdieu also contends in *Language and Symbolic Power*. In sum, rituals create a social reality that seems natural; importantly, it is the ritual (and its agents) that create this reality through negotiation with social institutions and norms.

Western specialists on ritual, who emerged from the structuralist tradition, operate with certain assumptions about ritual as a device for social programming and control. McManus, for example, argues that the primary function of a ritual is to transmit a society's values to ritual participants symbolically (McManus 1979, 241ff.). Burns and Laughlin (1979, 249–50) conclude that ritual helps to maintain "social relationships and social structure" as well as establish a means of social control. While one can certainly find evidence for the fact that ritual attempts to achieve these goals, they are but one facet of the function of life-cycle rituals, which help participants not only learn about their new roles, but adjust to them psychologically and in fact, create them. In addition, rituals allow for public acknowledgment of social change for all involved, including initiates, relatives, and friends, i.e., the community is allowed to adjust to the social shifts in roles and to celebrate or grieve together. In essence, ritual establishes a state of affairs through the agentive powers of its performers.

Ritual, in Tolstoi's (1995, 168) view, is a cultural text that can be read like any text, and is used to establish meaning within the society. While ritual vocabulary may be repeated in many ceremonies, the text in each ritual is not the same and must be considered within the cultural context and the goal of the ritual. Humphrey and Laidlaw (1994, 265) object to this argument of ritual as a text akin to a language. Rather, they conclude that ritual may have symbolic meaning, but that the meanings are not inherent in the acts themselves, but are brought to bear by the participants from a wide variety of experiences. Therefore, interpreting a ritual as a single decisive text is problematic and does not take into account the variable attitudes the participants themselves have toward ritual and its meaning (213). They argue (227) that the key to their understanding of rituals is that the performers are willing to give up their intentionality as actors in society and enter into the ritual mode (89). Once they have entered into the ritual, participants find that ritual acts are "'apprehensible', waiting to be acted out in different modes and given symbolic meaning by the celebrants." This argument is consistent with Levi-Strauss (1981, 668), when he asserts that ritual acts are separate from any kind of mythological commentary related to meaning. Certainly there may be accompanying texts devised by religious or other authorities that contribute meaning to ritual acts, but these meanings are not inherent in the action themselves and are often difficult to read from the acts performed. Rather, they stem from a large number of social scripts and experiences that occur outside of the ritual itself (Humphrey and Laidlaw 180, 190ff.). This view of ritual is particularly enlightening in the Soviet Russian context, since, as noted above, the ritual theorists were trying to espouse a single view of family and social membership. As we will see in our discussion of these rituals, people brought to bear their own interpretations that the Soviet government could not control. Ideas about the life cycle and the family's role within it derived from multiple sources and individual experiences.

Ritual thus can be viewed as a normative device or a text, but it functions on many layers, from the institutional to the private, individual level. While certain messages about behavioral norms may be built into a ritual, how the participants receive and interpret them may vary widely. Structuralist theory does not allow for such "dissonance" within the group celebrating a ritual. Turner's analysis of the rituals in *The Ritual Process* (1969) is unitary; he views them as a totality that does not allow for variation. Similarly, he makes some significant claims about the power of ritual to remove an individual from the confines of social norms and to reduce tension and resentment as a result of these norms. However, ritual does not necessarily remove social tension. It may, in fact, create it for some participants. Nor does it truly eliminate the rules that we live by in our daily lives in every case. The bacchanalian atmosphere of Mardi Gras in New Orleans may be one example of such extreme license, but not every ritual exhibits the same degree of freedom from social prescriptions. Thus while these theorists can inform the study of rituals broadly, I will primarily rely on various contemporary theories, including the theory of practice, theories of identity creation, and theories of resistance, to gain an insight of how these rituals function within (Soviet) Russian society.

Practice theory, as Bourdieu (1977, 1990) conceived of it, seeks to remove ritual from the rigidity of structuralism and its single reading of ritual removed from the social context and identity. Bourdieu (1977, 114) argues that

> understanding ritual practice is not a question of decoding the internal logic of a symbolism but of restoring its practical necessity by relating it to the real conditions of its genesis, that is, to the conditions in which it functions, and the means it uses to attain them, are defined. It means, for example, reconstituting ... the significance and functions that agents in a determinate social formation can (and must) confer on a determinate practice or experience, given the practical taxonomies which organize their perception.

In this passage Bourdieu outlines for us the goal of this study: to illustrate how contemporary Russian life-cycle rituals create social reality on the basis of various taxonomies, in our case norms espoused by the Soviet government and society and by the family. Bourdieu (1990, 95) describes his view of ritual practice as follows: "forlorn attempts to act on the natural world as one acts on the social world, to apply strategies to the natural world that work on other men ... that is, strategies of authority and reciprocity, to signify intentions, wishes, desires or orders to it, through performative words or deeds, which make sense without any signifying intention." Practice theory treats the people in rituals as agents of creation. They are not simply performing acts that they are expected to do (although social pressure certainly is a factor), but rather are themselves performing a rite that helps to establish a state of affairs in the real world. This significant factor in ritual practice is one that the government's ritual specialists failed to grasp. They did not understand that while ritual may be created to establish a set of norms, the people within the ritual are free to establish their own version of those norms through the ritual itself. Bell (1997, 82) notes that "practice theory today seems to offer greater opportunity to formulate the more subtle ways in which power is recognized and diffused, interpretations are negotiated, and people struggle to make more embracing meanings personally effective." From this perspective, Ortner (1989, 11–18) discusses ritual as a circular process: ritual agents both modify and reproduce the organization of social structures, and yet their actions are also restricted by these same social structures. Practice theory will allow us to examine this circularity in terms of (Soviet) Russian life-cycle rituals and how the agents, both those who created the rituals and those who performed them, negotiated, used, and resisted political and social power structures. The issue we will address in this book is not only how ritual creates reality, but how the agents manipulate ritual to resist and negotiate power within the culture.

As a result, this study of ritual will focus on resistance, manipulation, and negotiation of identity and power within the (Soviet) Russian social structure. Foucault (1984, 173) describes power relations in the modern state as follows:

> this power is not exercised simply as an obligation or a prohibition on those who "do not have it"; it invests them, is transmitted by them and through them; it exerts pressure on them, just as they themselves in their struggle against it, resist the grip it has on them. This means that these relations go right down into the depths of society ... they are not univocal; they define innumerable points of confrontation, focuses of instability, each of which has its own risks of conflict, of struggles, and of an at least temporary inversion of the power relations.

This concept of power relations, whereby the "powerless" enable the social hierarchy as they resist it and attempt to manipulate it, plays an essential role in the understanding of (Soviet) Russian ritual. Yurchak (2006) argues convincingly that the Soviet Union cannot accurately be reduced to a dichotomous society of the people versus the government. He contends that resistance is not an accurate characterization of Soviet society. At the same time, he cites (101) a series of deceptive practices that Komsomol members used precisely to resist certain aspects of the government's demands. Such acts are consonant with Scott's analysis (1985) of Malay society. These Malay peasant farmers, like the urban Russians in this study, relied on a variety of resistance strategies to achieve their ends within the social hierarchy. Scott (xvii) describes this process as " a struggle over the appropriation of symbols, a struggle over how the past and present shall be understood and labeled, a struggle to identify causes and assess blame, a contentious effort to give partisan meaning to local history." This description not only applies to the Malay situation he studied, but also to the (Soviet) Russian one.

The rituals, as noted above, are a locus of negotiation about meaning, social constructs and power relations; in short in Comaroff's terms (1985, 196), ritual is "a struggle for the possession of the sign." I do not suggest that Soviet Russian society can be simplified, as Yurchak criticizes in other studies of the USSR, to a conflict between two diametrically opposed sides. Rather, I intend to show that, like the Malays Scott studied and the Bedouins in Abu-Lughod's 1986 monograph, (Soviet) Russians both enabled and undermined social structures. They were not solely sullen, disaffected people who wanted to bring the government down; rather they regarded (and still do) many Soviet-era values as positive, valuable forces in their lives. However, that does not mean that resistance was not part of their society. The rituals were one arena (of many) that allowed for the performance of social identity, a place where both resistance and acceptance manifested themselves and people created reality and identities based upon a complex range of social forces. As we will see, as social structures change in post-Soviet Russia, these rituals have adapted with them. They continue to reflect the variable worldviews of their performers and the world that they create through their ritual practice.

Data Collection

My data on contemporary urban ritual practices come from two major sources: ninety-six interviews with urban Russians[15] ranging in age from nineteen to seventy-five, and photographic and home video records (primarily of weddings, but not exclusively). I also will refer to the rituals as depicted in popular culture (films and novels) of the period and to my observations of weddings at the ZAGS and of birth procedures at maternity hospitals I visited. The majority of informants are representatives of the professional middle class, including teachers and professors, accountants, medical professionals, insurance agents, engineers, computer specialists, and other white-collar workers. There were also a few representatives from the working class, i.e., factory workers and hairdressers, or from the upper class, specifi-

---

[15] My informants included one Belarusian, one Bashkir, one Mordvin, and one Tatar. Note that additional informants did not want to be recorded, but were willing to discuss their experiences informally. These conversations bring the total number of informants for this project to over one hundred.

cally wealthy business people. Most hold a degree from some institution of higher education, i.e., an institute or university; a small percentage completed only high school or attended a technical school. They are all residents of Russia and were raised in the following cities: Moscow, St. Petersburg, Novosibirsk, Khabarovsk, Krasnodar, Cheboksary, Chita, Samara, Perm', Voronezh, Vladimir, Sergeev Posad, Kazan, Ufa, Suzdal', Ekaterinburg, Tver', Tomsk, Noril'sk, and Nizhnii Novgorod. Some informants had also lived in cities in former Soviet republics, such as Gomel', Tashkent, Semipalatinsk, and Ashkhabad, before moving to Russia. They were primarily areligious or Orthodox, but I also interviewed two Jews and two Muslims (one had converted to Orthodoxy). I also spoke with medical personnel and ZAGS (registry office) workers to get a professional perspective on the rituals. Informants will be referred to by their first name and first initial of their last name to preserve their anonymity. This informant pool provides a valuable cross-section of urban, professional Soviet Russian society. While it might also be informative to study working-class people or elites (*nomenklatura*) in more depth, I have chosen to concentrate on the educated "middle class."[16] They form the most populous group in Russian cities and can convey a sense of typical rituals during the period under consideration. In addition, they were the beneficiaries of the best Soviet educational and propaganda systems, so that if folk material exists among this group, it is evidence of its persistence and importance to social identity. My group of interviewees also represents a wide geographic range, since informants come from European Russia, the Urals, and Siberia (both the western and eastern portions of that region) as well as from some former republics. In addition, the cities represented include the three largest as well as mid-size regional centers and less populous ones. The variety of cities will enable us to see how widespread the behaviors under consideration were and what regional variations may have existed.

The middle class developed into a historically important group for the Soviet state after World War II. As Bushnell (1980) and Dunham (1976) have shown, they were key to the success of the system, providing a cohesive group that advanced political and workplace ideals. Bushnell (187, 195) asserts that they held society together and were the firmest supporters of Soviet principles. The process of creating the middle class and transforming it into the heart of Soviet society came at Stalin's instigation. Dunham (14) reports that Stalin desired to maintain the status quo, to move from a "revolutionary bolshevik force" to a "conservative establishment." The key to Stalin's goals

---

[16] The term "middle class" is problematic within the Soviet system, which was purportedly a classless society. Thus, while classes of sort did exist, they are not parallel to the classes of a capitalist society. I am using this term since it has already been used in historical literature to refer to this group, namely by Dunham (1976) and Bushnell (1980). Within the Soviet system it is contrasted to the *rabochie* 'workers' and the *nomenklatura* 'party elite'.

was finding a group of hard-working individuals to help strengthen the government and recreate the society after the devastation of the war. According to Dunham (17), in order to get the middle class on board, Stalin took advantage of its desire for "material incentives—housing, consumer goods, luxuries, and leisure time." Boym, in her discussion of this period, notes that the acquisition of material goods served also "to justify and disguise the legitimation of social inequality, special privileges, and spacious private housing, allocated to the Stalinist elite" (1994, 9). The middle class, who received these rewards, became the center of the Soviet universe. Since they feared to lose their power and the resulting perquisites, they imposed Stalinism on the populace (Dunham 132). In order to achieve these ends, Stalin had to make the pursuit of bourgeois goals acceptable. Dunham (42–46) observes that the popular literature of the time highlighted comfort, "the trappings of femininity," and the "luxury" of new Moscow apartments.[17] During this period, *kul'turnost'* 'degree of culture' became distinct from *kul'tura* 'culture'. Dunham (22) defines the former as "a mere program for proper conduct in public ... *kul'turnost'* represents ... a refurbished, victorious, conservative force in Soviet postwar life.... Its special function is to encode the proper relationship between people and through their possessions and labels; between mores and artifacts...." However, as Bushnell (185–86) and Shlapentokh (1989, 62) report, the middle class eventually abandoned its faith in the material rewards the government promised. They did not believe that the gap in the standard of living between the USSR and the capitalist societies in the West was likely to close, which enabled the spread of the black market. At the same time, they still supported Soviet ideals. Thus their attitudes toward society (and the rituals they participated in) reflect the conflicts between the materialistic and idealistic sides of Soviet life, as we will see.

These (Soviet) Russian urban life-cycle rituals are multi-faceted, sociocultural events that have evolved as the society itself has changed. They exhibit features not only of village folk rites, despite Soviet attacks on ritual generally in the early years of the Soviet Union, but of Western consumerist and Soviet practices as well. Chapter 2 will provide an overview of village rituals from the central region of the country. While many of these behaviors may be retained, nevertheless they may be radically reinterpreted by urbanites and thus convey different meanings than their village counterparts. Chapters 3–5 will focus on the nature of the Soviet ritual complex in the middle class from the post-war period to 1990 and on how folk, Western, and Soviet elements combined and interacted within these celebrations. Chapter 6 examines these rituals in the post-Soviet era and how they reflect a changing

---

[17] One Muscovite who lived in the city during the period Dunham describes reported to me that stores in post-war Moscow were full of goods on the shelves, seemingly in an effort to display not only recovery from the war, but also the positive nature of materialism. Ironically, she said, no one had the money to actually purchase these items.

view of social identity. Chapter 7 will provide an overview of the Soviet ritual complex as a whole.

This book is designed not only for folklorists who want to understand the nature of Soviet ritual and its changes throughout the twentieth century, but also for social scientists and cultural specialists more broadly. I hope to provide a perspective on Soviet life that has been little studied, because Soviet specialists in the field typically have not considered urban ritual to be worthy of consideration. If ritual was studied at all (given the Soviet reluctance to acknowledge that potentially religious, non-Soviet rituals were occurring on its soil), theorists focused on village practices. However, examination of urban rituals can provide us with a deeper understanding of the conflicts and stresses people faced as they attempted to find their place in society. Ethnographic studies such as this one complement the work of economists, political scientists, sociologists, and literary specialists striving to comprehend the complexity of Soviet and post-Soviet urban society.

Chapter 2

Nineteenth-Century Life-Cycle Rituals

It is not the goal of this book to provide a detailed examination of nineteenth-century life-cycle rituals in the Russian village. Abundant material is already available in both English and Russian on the practices. For broad overviews in English, see Tian-Shanskaia 1998 and Sokolov 1950; in Russian, see Aleksandrov et al. 2003, Zelenin 1991, and Kabakova 2001. There are also sources on individual rituals in both languages, including Ransel 2000 and Nekliudov 2001 on birth; Worobec 1995, Reeder 1975, and Zorin 2001 on weddings; and Warner 2000 and Nosova 1999 on funerals. However, a brief overview of the ritual behaviors will help define what remained viable into the twentieth century and beyond. I would argue that despite Soviet attacks on folk and religious rituals (Lane 1981, 23), the practices that survived were preserved because they were defining elements of significant social categories. Without them, Russians would not have been able to establish the nature of essential cultural roles and identities, which, as I have discussed, is one goal of any life-cycle ritual. An additional complication in outlining these rituals, of course, is the nature of folk practice. That is, we cannot simply describe a single nineteenth-century ritual, since it did not exist. Folklore by its very nature is characterized by regional variation, and Russia is a vast country. Therefore, I will present some common features of the three rituals as celebrated in villages in the central region of the country in the late nineteenth century. I have chosen the central region as the base for the rituals described below, since it is where Moscow is located; in the Soviet period it was Moscow, as the center of the state, that determined the nature of these rituals.

Childbirth in the Nineteenth-Century Central Russian Village[1]

Pregnancy and birth were shrouded by aversive practices in the nineteenth-century village of the central region of the country. In general, the pregnancy itself was concealed as long as possible (Dobrovol'skaia 2001, 94). In essence,

---

[1] Portions of the material on birth in this chapter and the next previously appeared in article form in *Slavic and East European Journal*. They are reprinted here by gracious permission of the editor.

the practice of secrecy and isolation during both pregnancy and delivery protected the mother and child from evil forces. Ramer notes that "pregnancy
itself was considered a particularly vulnerable time for a woman, and parturi-
tion even more so. One of the great fears was that a stranger would 'give her
the evil eye' (*sglazit' ee*), causing harm to her child" (1992, 228). Similar assertions that the isolation of the birth process was essential for the protection of
the mother and child are found in other studies as well (Ransel 2000, 124; Listova 1992, 125; Baiburin 1997, 7; Kabakova 2001, 65). Even when pregnancy
became obvious, it was not discussed openly, for fear of inviting harm to the
woman or the child. Secrecy could be maintained due to the design of peasant
dress, which was loosely fitting and concealed weight gain for a considerable
period of time. Within the veil of secrecy, the pregnant woman was limited in
the type of work she could do in order to protect her; it was unwise for her to
do work that might involve working with yarn or thread (weaving, for example, might result in the child's umbilical cord choking it) or with sharp instru-
ments (Kabakova 209). Looking at fire might cause a birth mark on the child;
a sudden fright that caused her to touch her belly would result in a spot on
the child; looking at horrifying sights (people, animals, or objects) could result
in her child being deformed; stepping on a crooked object could make the
child a hunchback; if she walked over or stepped on a dog or cat, the child
could be born with a hairy patch, and so on (Naumenko 2001, 24–26; Anashkina 2001, 208–09). Listova (2003, 503) also cites some of these beliefs: "She
could not sit on a stone or labor would be difficult, step over a rope or the
child would get tangled in the umbilical cord, step over a yoke or the child
would be hunchbacked, push away cats or dogs or the newborn would have
'a dog's old age,' bristles on its skin, etc." In other words, the expectant
mother had to be protected both from people who might send the evil eye her
way and from all manner of natural phenomena and daily occurrences. She
had the awesome burden of observing all these taboos, so that her child
would be born healthy.

Isolation and secrecy were also favored for the delivery itself, as Zelenin
(1927/1991, 319) observes:

> the woman giving birth assiduously hides the approach of labor and
> labor itself; there exists a strong conviction that labor pains will be
> that much stronger, the more people who learn about the delivery as
> it occurs. They conceal this especially assiduously from unmarried
> women, especially from old maids, and also from cunning or evil
> people, who could cause harm (*spoil, give the evil eye, and the like*).

Russian women in the northern and central portions of the country generally gave birth in the bathhouse.[2] The bathhouse was the ideal place for a delivery both practically and symbolically. From a practical point of view, it was warm and had an abundant source of water. In addition, symbolically, it preserved secrecy, since it was distant from the house. It also kept the house from being tainted by the birth process itself. The place where a birth took place was off limits until purified by a priest. Isolation was also intended to make the labor easier, because, as noted above, the more people who knew about the birth, the more difficult it would be. As a result, women often gave birth alone, and a midwife was called in only after the baby had been born (Listova 1992, 125; Ransel 2000, 126). Kabakova (2001, 69) describes the role of the midwife as follows:

> If the participation of the husband was not required, then the presence of a midwife was desirable and even required for first births and in the case of complications. Her participation in the post-partum period was particularly important, when she took care of the mother and the newborn and took upon herself all the ritual aspects of the affair.

However, given the trend toward isolation of the delivery for the protection of the mother and child, even the midwife was a potential threat to them and therefore often was not summoned until after the child was born.

Listova states that the *povitukha* 'midwife' was the most important figure in the childbirth process (1992, 128–29). When present, she not only delivered the child, according to Listova (1989, 142), but also "she was able to perform necessary procedures, from the point of view of the population, for the child and the mother, accompanying them with magical acts" both during and after the delivery. Her duties were numerous in this regard. She gave instructions to the family, if necessary, about how to behave to avoid the evil eye during delivery and afterwards. She ensured that the mother unbraided her hair and untied all her clothing (to loosen the womb symbolically) and removed any chains or rings (to prevent the child from being choked by the umbilical cord). In addition, to speed the delivery, she opened all the doors in the bathhouse (and possibly the family house, including the stove). In some particularly difficult cases, she might even order that someone go ask for the iconostasis gates to be opened in the church. She (and the mother-to-be) recited incantations, particularly to the Virgin Mary or to Saint Solomonida[3], to help speed

---

[2] Of course, there were situations in which a mother was working in the fields and could not reach the bathhouse in time and delivered on the spot (Tian-Shanskaia 1993, 10; Kabakova 2001, 66; Zelenin 1927/1991, 319).

[3] Also called Solomonia and Sofia, she was a noble woman married to Prince Vasily Ivanovich in 1505. She was childless, so her husband forced her into the Pokrov con-

and ease the labor (Naumenko 2001, 34–36; Baranov 2001, 22, 24; Zelenin 1927/1991, 320). Vlaskina (2001, 67) cites some of these incantations:

> In the charms personages from Christian mythology (the Mother of God, the Savior, grandmother Solomonida) were not only called upon as witnesses and as helpers, but were also called as direct actors to assist with the delivery: "Feodorov Mother of God, release one soul, allow another one into the world" (city Konstantinovsk; village Prisalsky), "Grandmother Solomonida, come, help our laboring woman" (villages Ternovskoi, Kolundaevsky)....

In addition to performing symbolic acts to help the delivery along, the midwife also instructed the mother how to behave during the delivery and treated the child after it was born, by shaping its head, cutting the umbilical cord, and bathing and swaddling it for the first time (Listova 1989, 145). She delivered the afterbirth and said charms to stop the bleeding (or offered some rudimentary medical treatments, such as herbal medicines, for the same purpose). Her ritual power was so impressive that, as Listova (1989, 148–49) discusses, she could baptize the child if it looked as though it would not survive until a priest arrived:

> [T]he midwife[4] baptizes the child in a domestic way, for this she takes "holy water," and adds plain water to it in a normal plate. After that she pours it over the child three times and says after each time: "In the name of the Father, in the name of the Son, in the name of the Holy Spirit. Amen," and she gives the child a name.... [A]fter the revolution baptism of the child by the midwife spread even more with the destruction of churches ... if the child lived, the priest completed the ritual without immersing the child in water and he pronounced the name the midwife had given.

Contact with the spirit world was laden with power, resulting in a liminal status for all those involved in the ritual. Therefore, on the third day after birth all those who were present at the birth underwent a hand-washing ritual, accompanied by incantations, to purify them; there was often a ritual steaming in the bathhouse for the mother as well (Zelenin 1927/1991, 325; Listova 2003, 506, 510). In some cases, this ritual was only required of the

---

vent in Suzdal' where she was said to perform miracles. Miraculous cures were also attributed to her gravesite.

[4] The word used here is "grandmother," but it refers to the midwife, who was often called *babushka*, lit. 'little woman.' As a result of her actions on behalf of the child, she became a family member and was accorded with a kinship term. See Listova (1989, 159–60) for a discussion of these relationships.

mother and midwife. The midwife performed this ritual washing for herself and for the mother (and the other women, if necessary) (Listova 1992, 131; Anashkina 2001, 204). She often received linens, particularly towels, or clothing and bread from the mother as a form of payment for her help during the delivery (Anashkina 204; Ransel 2000, 126; Zelenin 326). Dobrovol'skaia (2001, 100) cites one informant with regard to "paying" the midwife: "They used to give her shawls. She can't take money. She has a gift." Once the ritual bath was completed, the mother was free to return to the house, which usually occurred after three days' isolation with the baby (in the bathhouse or other outbuilding). In many cases, the midwife remained in the household to watch over the child and work in the woman's place (Glickman 1991, 159). While this purification ritual was an important one, it was not the last one that the mother was to undergo. The ritual washing described only allowed the mother to return to the family home, i.e., to the human realm, after her contact with the spirit world. She was still considered to be impure for at least forty days after childbirth until she was blessed by a priest (Worobec 1995, 187; Ransel 2000, 178). During this period, the new mother abstained from sexual relations with her husband, remained in the house, performed only limited household work, and could not attend church services. Baranov (2001, 21) cites a wide range of limitations on the mother and child's behavior during this period:

> The woman who has given birth: "For six weeks a woman who has given birth is considered to be half-dead, 'unclean,' she cannot pick up an icon, light the icon lamp, go to church until she has 'taken the prayer'; They didn't let her go into the bathhouse … the barn or to the well for 6 weeks." The newborn: "the child cannot been shown to outsiders before six weeks"; "Once the child is bathed, they pour water over him everyday for six weeks"; "For 6 weeks the mother feeds him only with her own milk."

The forty-day period was a particularly dangerous time for both mother and child, who were most susceptible to the evil eye during that time (Baiburin 1997, 8).

There is some variance in when the christening occurred; Listova (2003, 689) states that it depended on several factors:

> If the child was ill, if circumstances allowed, they christened him on the day of his birth. But the tradition of christening on the third day after birth was much more common in the European portion of Russia. The ritual of christening newborns was preserved among Old Believers among the confessions that had priests, but the sacrament was performed more often than not on the eighth day after birth.

The midwife's participation not only in the birth itself, but in the christening as well, was essential for the child to be healthy and to thrive. Listova (1992, 133–34) observes that the midwife was

> the mistress of ceremonies for a considerable number of ritual (nonecclesiastic) and nonritual actions.... She bathed and swaddled the child before christening, said parting words to the godparents, received the christened child from the godparents, ... often accompanying all of these procedures with incantations.

Most importantly, she blessed the child with charms before the assembled guests, so that the child would be acknowledged by the entire village (Listova 1992, 134–35). Without her involvement at this stage, there was no guarantee that the child would live to adulthood or be a respected member of the adult community. As a result, it was important that a midwife be of excellent character, since her behavior influenced the child's fate. Village midwives were usually post-menopausal widows who had borne children (Kabakova 2001, 69–70; Listova 1989, 149). Zelenin (1927/1991, 319) describes the ideal candidate: "a midwife is without fail an elderly woman who has had her own children; preference is given to respected widows and generally to those women who lead a moral life that is above reproach." Listova (1989, 146) also notes that they should not be confused with those who use magic, such as witches or sorcerers, but should be "god-fearing women."

It was generally at the christening that the midwife was remunerated for her services. The assembled family and other guests did not pay her for attendance at the birth, since midwives could not refuse to help a woman in labor even if no payment was offered (Listova 1992, 132; Naumenko 2001, 32). Recall also that she had already received gifts from the mother for her help with childbirth. At the baptismal feast the midwife was paid for the *babina kasha* (midwife's porridge) or other food items that she had brought to the christening (Listova 1992, 134–35). In some areas, as Anashkina (2001, 204) documents, the midwife might bring her porridge soon after birth rather than to the christening:

> For her help the midwife also received money, but at another time, during the performance of another ritual: treating to "midwife's porridge." For the first few days after the child's birth, women—friends, neighbors (only one at a time)—visited the mother and brought presents "for the little tooth" (for the newborn)—a pie, or a pot of porridge, or a cup of grain along with their congratulations.

In these ways the community recognized the contribution of the midwife and significance of her role in the child's well-being. The christening meal also allowed the community to recognize the infant publicly for the first time. The good will of the assembled guests ensured good fortune for the child as well as established their role in his or her upbringing.

These behaviors illustrate not only the importance of secrecy to protect the mother and her child, but the significance of the midwife and community to the child's welfare. The postpartum period was a particularly vulnerable time for the woman and the infant, and the community rallied to prevent any harm to them. Similarly, the community, represented first by the midwife and then by the rest of the village present at the christening party, assumed responsibility for the child's welfare. Similar acts were characteristic of both the wedding and funeral rituals as well, which relied on community involvement and protection for their success.

Weddings in the Nineteenth-Century Central Russian Village

As with birth rituals, weddings were also characterized by regional variation; in fact, there are more variations in this life-cycle ritual than in any of the three under consideration. Funerals and birth shared many commonalities across the Russian territory, but weddings varied widely. Nevertheless, there are some common factors that weddings shared; the exact order of the events and duration may have varied, but many ritual acts were repeated.[5] The wedding of the central region of Russia in the nineteenth century was characterized by both a mourning period[6] before the wedding service and a happy period after the wedding service and/or on the second day (Kabakova 2001, 186; Zelenin 1927/1991, 342). In central Russian cities at the time of the revolution the mournful portions had already been largely replaced by the happy elements, which have formed the basis for the contemporary urban wedding.

Generally speaking, the nineteenth-century Russian wedding was an economic bond between two families. Many of the preliminary ritual actions involved negotiations between the families; generally the groom's family picked a bride for him, so that the matches were based not on love, but on the ability of the woman to be a good worker (Makashina 2003, 473). Zorin (2001, 48–49) provides a detailed description of the issues involved in choosing a bride:

> The groom's parents gave exceptionally high significance to the economic status of the bride's parents, at family councils the degree of their wealth, their ability to run a household, the industriousness of

---

[5] For a description of the ritual acts and their exact order in various regions of Russia, see Kargin (2000, 1: 26–32).

[6] The mourning period was generally restricted to the bride and/or her representatives (married sisters, for example, who echoed the bride's laments), since she was losing her *volia* 'will, freedom' upon marriage (Baiburin 1993, 68).

family members were discussed.... They found out whether they had "useless, good-for-nothing" people: drunks, lazy people, etc. They considered the social position of the bride's family and other villagers' opinion of it. They estimated the amount of the dowry, the possibility for help in the organization of the wedding by [her] relatives. At family councils the personal characteristics of the bride were also discussed. Most importantly, they valued girls that had the ability to perform women's work, had a talent for handiwork—spinning, weaving, sewing, knitting, etc.—and also were physically capable and healthy. Secondarily, they considered such traits as "meekness," "obedience," and "respect," that is, characteristics which, given the intrafamilial conditions of the time, could ensure that the family had "peace" and a normal work life.

A young man could, of course, suggest a possible match to his parents, as Zorin notes, but ultimately, the parents determined whether to accept her or another choice. Once his parents had made their decision, they sent a matchmaker (*svakha* if a woman, *svat* if a man), to the woman's home. Makashina (475–76) describes the various options for picking a matchmaker:

> After the bride had been chosen, the groom's parents turned to the choice of the matchmaker (man or woman). The choice of matchmakers was a serious matter. They would say: "chose not a bride, but a matchmaker." They were usually the groom's spiritual parents—godfather or godmother. Or one of his relatives—uncle, aunt, a married brother or sister, the senior brother-in-law. Sometimes the groom's father or both of his parents served as matchmakers. But it was considered to be most prestigious to send someone from one's village who was known for artful speech ("who had a sharp tongue"), or a *matcher*—a smart, lively woman who was known for her eloquence and ability to arrange marriages.

The matchmaker, wearing clothing that indicated hi(s)her purpose (e.g., female matchmakers would wear felt boots, even in summer, and be covered with a large shawl), would enter the home and would begin the matchmaking with a series of ceremonial phrases, such as "you have the goods, we have the buyer" or "you have the chicken, we have the rooster." Only then did (s)he reveal the groom's identity and begin the proposal; (s)he and the woman's parents ate a meal and (s)he left. Generally, (s)he returned after a few days for the parents' answer, often with the groom and his parents (Zorin 2001, 53; Ananicheva and Samodelova 1997, 87).

If the bride's parents agreed, they and the *svakha* set a date for the *osmotr* or viewing of the groom's home, belongings, and farm by the bride's family

(Makashina 2003, 478; Ananicheva and Samodelova 1997, 164).[7] Zorin (1981, 74) describes the *osmotr* as follows:

> the "viewing of the homesteads" usually took place two or three days after receiving preliminary agreement from the bride and her parents. This gave the groom's side time to prepare to show their homestead, to straighten up the hut and the courtyard, to do small repairs, and the like. It was not uncommon for the groom and his parents, who desired to make a good impression on the bride's parents, to borrow quality agricultural equipment, carts, sledges from neighbors or friends, to exchange horses and to drive others' livestock into their yard, to place grain from one or another of the villagers into their barn, and to ask permission of neighbors to pass off their buildings, timber, ricks of grain and the like as their own. The bride's parents … and her close relatives took part in the inspection of the groom's household. They inspected the outbuildings, grain barns, equipment, livestock, and so on. During the inspection of the hut they looked into all the corners and the storerooms.

At the conclusion of the *osmotr*, the groom's family hosted a meal for the bride and her relatives (Balashov et al. 1985, 30).

The *osmotr* was designed to allow the bride's family to see the groom's family home before making a final commitment to the marriage. If they decided favorably, they arranged a reciprocal viewing of their own goods, called *smotriny*. Unlike the *osmotr*, which focused entirely on material wealth, the *smotriny* was designed to show off the quality of the bride's work, namely her skills at sewing, knitting, weaving, embroidery, and cooking. Makashina (2003, 478) notes that the bride was obliged "to appear in all her dresses … and it was not uncommon, in addition to the demonstration of the bride's physical appearance, to set up tests of her work skills—they made her weave, sew, and do other types of work." In addition, as Zorin (2001, 56) discusses, they assessed the bride's character:

> the bride walked around the hut and fulfilled the guests' requests (she served them drinks, brought food). Sometimes the matchmaker, supposedly accidentally, dropped a needle, pin or some other small object on the floor and asked the bride to find it and pick it up … she demonstrated her ability to set up a samovar and the like.

Firsov and Kiseleva (1993, 242) conclude that "in a bride the ability to work, health and chastity are valued most, and in a groom sobriety and *rodstvo* (a

---

[7] Zorin (2001, 55) notes that in the central region by the late nineteenth century, the *osmotr/smotriny* were generally performed by only about 30 percent of the population.

synonym for wealth)." If both families were satisfied after the inspections, then the parents established a date for the formal betrothal of the couple, usually two or three days later (Makashina 478; Kargin 2000, 1: 94; Kolpakova 1973, 243).

On the day of the betrothal, the groom's father, the groom, and other relatives came to the bride's home. The bridal couple left, while the two fathers bargained on the dowry (and bride price, if there was one) and gifts between the families (Kargin 2000, 1: 114; Kuznetsova and Loginov 2001, 16; Firsov and Kiseleva 1993, 247–48). Zorin (2001, 59) observes that the most important issue was finances:

> At the betrothal the two sides that were about to become relatives most importantly resolved the financial questions of the marriage. The bride's parents announced the contents of the dowry and requested a bride price from the groom that correlated to the level of his economic status and the cost of the dowry. The groom's parents, in turn, asked for linens for the bride, clothing for the groom, and sometimes food to feed the "young girl" until the next harvest as well.... At the betrothal they agreed what presents the groom and bride should give to whom and when. They discussed how many people from each side would take part in the wedding, whether there would be "help" from them, etc.... It was essential to resolve the question of the timing of the wedding and its various elements: when the groom would bring presents, when the bride's friends would go get the shirt, besom (here, a bundle of twigs used to stimulate circulation during steaming) and soap from the groom, when the *devichnik* (girl's party to mark the end of her girlhood) would be, and the like.

Maslova (1984, 12) describes the dowry in this period:

> [it] usually consisted of underclothing, dresses, bed linens, some equipment: scythes, sickles, rakes, looms, spinning wheels, reels ... the dowry included a blanket ... tablecloths, bed-curtains, coverlets for chests, towels, *nakvashniki (nablinniki)*—covers for buttermilk, pancake coverings—sheets, canvas, cotton fabric, from which the future mother would clothe her family.

Her gifts included clothing for the groom, belts for his male relatives and towels, scarves, and kerchiefs for female relatives (Maslova 23–25). Maslova (19) also emphasizes the fact that the bride produced these linens and clothing herself, "the dowry ... was prepared by degrees, beginning when the girl was a child, but she had to sew some objects for the wedding (the groom's shirt and pants, the presents for her mother and father-in-law, etc." The bride price included money and clothing, shoes, fabrics and other goods for the bride and her family, including the gifts for the bride's parents (Maslova 21). Chizhikova (1989, 177) states that "the betrothed girl was freed from house-work, she occupied herself with the preparation of the dowry and gifts with her friends' help." She generally was isolated during this period from the out-side world (Kolpakova 1973, 243). Zorin (2001, 65) observes that this isolation lasted from one week to a month, during which period she was already no longer part of her own family:

> The bride-to-be during this period was completely removed from all familial household duties, she became a "guest in her own house." She went almost nowhere. Her only obligations during this period were getting her dowry in order and preparing the gifts for the groom, his relatives, and his retinue. Her young female relatives and friends of the same age helped her with this.

As we saw in the birth ritual, isolation not only aided in transition to a new social status (and, in this case, to finish up the required preparations for the wedding), but also was designed to protect the couple. Baiburin (1993, 66) notes that they were generally at risk for evil sorcery in the pre-wedding period:

> The taboo on independent movement is motivated within the tradi-tion usually by the fact that in this period the bride (and, incidentally, the groom) is especially susceptible to spoiling. I will cite only one of the many descriptions of the pre-wedding period: "In the Rybinsk *uezd* the bride, 'to prevent the evil eye,' ... does not leave the house, plus both the groom and the bride are warned that while walking they should not touch, should not step on the threshold, and should not touch door jambs, or else they might be cursed by an evil person."

On the evening before the ceremony, the bride's retinue went to the groom's home to collect the soap, birch branches, and wood for the bride's ritual bath on the eve of the wedding as well as presents and accessories for the wedding; in some cases the groom and/or his retinue brought these items to the bride (Baiburin 1993, 75; Ananicheva and Samodelova 1997, 120). The groom gave the bride's retinue candy, nuts, and fruits (Zorin 2001, 71–72). The groom often returned to the bride's home for the *devichnik* or the party that marked the end of her girlhood and loss of will (*volia*) and maidenly beauty (*krasota*).[8] Baiburin (1993, 68) notes that the beauty or will was gener-ally represented by a physical object: "the use of a small tree, ribbons, or a

---

[8] While *mal'chishniki* 'boy parties' to say farewell did exist, they were much rarer (Gvozdikova and Shapovalova 1982, 275). The wedding was, as Baiburin (1993, 66ff.) discusses, primarily a ritual directed at the woman's transition and not the man's.

tow (flax fibers ready for spinning) in this role was characteristic for the Central and Northern regions of Russia." The *devichnik* generally involved the unbraiding of the bride's hair, a ritual bath (and possible rebraiding into the single braid of girlhood one last time) and the destruction or transfer of the bride's "will" (Baiburin 1992, 68; Kolpakova 244; Kabakova 165; Ananicheva and Samodelova 90–92, 115, 133–34, 165–66). Zorin (2001, 72) provides a description of the ritual bath at the *devichnik*:

> A series of ritual actions accompanied the transfer of the bride to the bathhouse. As a rule, her friends carried along a decorated burdock, besom, or wreath…. In the bathhouse the bride and her friends bathed with the groom's soap and steamed themselves with the groom's besom. "The washing away of the maidenly beauty" was accompanied by the singing of songs by her friends and the bride's "wailing"…. In the bathhouse the bride's best friend or younger sister braided her hair for the last time, and she asked her, using a special lament, to braid it so that the matchmaker could not unbraid it…. After the braiding of the hair, the bride gave her friends ribbons.

The ribbons represent her maidenly beauty or will, which she is leaving behind to her unmarried friends. The groom, accompanied by his own retinue, arrived and brought gifts for the bride and wine for the party (Kargin 1: 64, 75, 95; Zorin 2001, 74). The bride's family offered food to the guests, who were seated when the bride entered to receive her gifts from the groom and to give him his wedding clothing (Maslova 26; Zorin 1981, 96). The bride's retinue sang songs, and the guests paid them for the music. Ananicheva and Samodelova describe this process from an 1852 wedding in the Moscow region: "then songs of praise for the groom, bride and guests follow. At the end of the song, each person to whom the song was dedicated gives money to the girls by placing it in a glass that is placed on the table before that guest by the girl." This party also featured laments by the bride about her impending loss of will (which continued on the morning of the wedding as well, until the groom arrived) (Zorin 1981, 97–98). The dowry was either delivered that night or in the morning before the wedding; in either case, it was put on display in the groom's home for the reception (Maslova 20).

On the day of the wedding, the groom and his friends decorated the wedding vehicles with ribbons and bells. Kargin (2000, 1: 65) cites a description of a wedding train in the Vladimir region:

> [T]he horses with bells hung on the harness. There can be up to ten horses in harness. If it is winter, everyone has sleighs, not woodsledges. But those in the rear also harness horses to wood-sledges, there are a ton of wood-sledges. In the summertime, some have a carriage, some a cart. The groom went with his *druzhko* and with his

friends. The groom's parents did not participate in the *siden'e* (*devich-nik*) or in the wedding ceremony, that's not done.

The groom's retinue included his best man, *druzhko*, the *tychiatskii* 'godfather', the matchmaker, and *druzhki, poezhane* 'friends and relatives' (including the *starshii* 'senior friend'). Mahler (1960, 110) notes that the *druzhko* "plays a very important and serious role before and during the wedding celebration: he is the master of ceremonies and at the same time the intimate friend of the engaged couple." The bride's retinue included the *podgolosnitsa* 'a woman who lamented in place of the bride', her matchmaker, *podruzhki* 'female unmarried friends' (including the *pravoplechnitsa* 'senior friend'), and godparents as well as a *starosta* 'elder', who negotiated with the groom's representatives (Kuznetsova and Loginov 2001, 17).[9] The elder also brought some beer or wine to toast the bride and her retinue upon arrival (Balashov et al. 1985, 107).

The bride's family would often set up a series of roadblocks to prevent the wedding train from passing, which they removed only if they were paid (Balashov et al. 1985, 119; Mahler 1960, 206). In addition, when the wedding train finally arrived, the bride's retinue blocked the groom and best man from entering the home until they received beer and candy or money (Kargin 2000, 1: 58, 88, 118; Zabylin 1990, 141–42). Makashina (2003, 483) notes that the groom was not always welcomed when he arrived:

> The company was faced with locked gates. The matchmakers knocked on the gate with a truncheon, But the bride's relatives would not let them in. Negotiations would begin. The *druzhko* approached the window and asked to spend the night. As a rule the negotiations took on an allegorical form. In response to the demand for a *vykup* (buying of the bride, ransoming) the *druzhko* gave a pie, wine, or money. In some locations the groom answered riddles.

Once he entered, the groom bid for various items associated with the bride, including the place next to her at the table, the table itself, the farm gate, the stove door, her braid, the couple's bed or the floral wreath she had worn (and removed) at the *devichnik* as a symbol of her girlhood (Zabylin 1990, 145; Makashina 486; Zhekulina 1982, 244; Baiburin 1993, 75; Kabakova 2001, 165). Zorin (2001, 82) notes that "the average number of ransomings in several villages reached eight to ten. However, in most cases the wedding rituals of individual localities included from three to five ransomings." If the bride had not been bathed as part of the *devichnik* ritual, she was bathed on the morning of the wedding, before being dressed by relatives or friends. Zorin (2001, 77)

---

[9] The titles for these various figures vary from region to region, as do the participants themselves, e.g., not every wedding had a lamenter who took the bride's place. For a complete list of the titles and participants region by region, see Kargin (2000, 1: 26–32).

notes that it was important to protect her from "spoiling": "in order to protect the bride from spoiling, while she was being dressed, it was not uncommon to wrap a fishing net (open work), a specially woven belt or thread with many knots around her waist, to stick needles and pins in her clothing, and to sprinkle millet, rowan leaves, or money in her shoes." Afterwards, she joined the party in her family's home. In some cases (either on the wedding day or at the betrothal), she and two other young women dressed as brides were veiled, and the groom had to pick out which bride was his (Makashina 484; Zorin 2001, 75). Kargin (1: 67–68) includes a story by a Vladimir informant about this practice:

> She is under a shawl, she can't see, is standing there.... The bride lamented when they came to take her to the wedding. They cover the bride with a shawl.... She is already in her wedding dress. Yes, they used to bury in the wedding dress too. The wedding dress used to be not white, but another color: green too, my mom had a magenta one.... Oh, I'll tell you about one time... They put the bride in a cabinet, put a chair there and put her in a big box. And she is sitting there. And here, they substituted for her, they covered an old, old woman with a shawl.

The bride then gave her final round of presents (and most elaborate) to the groom's wedding party as an unmarried woman (Balashov et al. 1985, 118), and the bride's family served a meal to the wedding party, in which the bride and groom did not participate (Zorin 1981, 106). During the feast before departing for the ceremony, the bride sang a final farewell to her family and home, because she was joining the groom's family and leaving her own (Firsov and Kiseleva 1993, 253; Zorin 2001, 78). When the train was ready to depart, after singing this song, she kissed the stove; thereafter, she was veiled and carried out of the house to the cart or sleigh. Those following behind swept the path as she left the house, to remove any possibility of the evil eye (Balashov et al. 289–91; Moyle 1996, 229). They were led to the vehicles and departed the house. On their way to the church, their retinues took measures to protect them from the evil eye and to ensure that they would have a prosperous marriage, including setting straw on fire before the bride's house (Kabakova 2001, 168); sprinkling (by the bride's mother) grain on the path behind them (Chizhikova 1989, 187); clearing the path of all who meet the wedding train to prevent them cursing the couple (Makashina 2003, 487); saying charms against sorcery before leaving (Zabylin 1880/1990, 150); and throwing coins to children (Kuznetsova and Loginov 2001, 234) to name but a few. An informant from Riazan' recounts the departure for the ceremony (Kargin 2000, 1: 77):

The groom and bride were blessed together for the departure to go "under the crown"[10] by her parents, also on their knees on an inside-out fur coat, the bride is no longer lamenting now. Accompanied by a song ... the couple sets off for the church separately, the groom in one sleigh, the bride in another. The parents were not present at the ceremony.

The tracks of the wedding train were swept away as they left, to protect the couple and also to remove all traces of the bride from the path away from her home, so that she would not return (Moyle 229). A sorcerer was often invited to protect the couple with incantations during the wedding procession and reception (Lobanov 2004, 26; Zelenin 1927/1991, 341; Balashov et al. 289–90).

After the church ceremony, the couple proceeded to the groom's home for the reception. The groom's parents welcomed them with an icon and bread and salt. They kissed the icon and bread (or took a bite of it) and were showered with candy, seeds, nuts, grain, hops and/or money (Kuznetsova and Loginov 2001, 237; Chizhikova 1989, 187; Zorin 2001, 87–88; Zabylin 1880/1990, 152), Ananicheva and Samodelova (1997, 134) cite an 1852 wedding from the Bronnitsk region in which

> [u]pon the completion of the ceremony the wedding train sets off for the groom's home. In the entry way the groom's parents meet the couple with an icon and bread and salt. The couple bows to the ground before his parents, kisses the icon, then the bread and enters the hut and sits at the table. As they are entering the hut, the matchmaker (male or female) sprinkles the couple with oats as a sign of future happiness.

In the Kaluga region, a similar ritual was observed, but in this case, the couple visited both sets of parents, first hers and then his, where the wedding feast was held (Kargin 2000, 1: 84):

> The bride's father and mother, neighbors meet them. The groom is the first to enter the house, then the bride and her godmother.... The bride's hair is loose over her shoulders. When she was getting married, she was covered, but to braid her hair, they take off the cover.... The bride used to have one braid and now it is braided into two, she is "in two" already. The godmother braids one braid and the groom the other....

---

[10] The wedding ceremony was often referred to as being under the or taking the crowns, since the Orthodox ceremony involves placing crowns on the couple's head to marry them.

After this ritual, the couple sets out for the groom's house:

> The parents meet them with bread and salt, with an icon on towels.
> They throw a fur coat with the furry side up underneath the cou-
> ple.... This fur coat is placed there, so that the couple, they say, will
> have abundance so that they get rich. The bride bows to her father-in-
> law, mother-in-law (but the groom doesn't), kisses the bread and salt,
> the icon, her father-in-law and mother-in-law ... and (the *druzhko*)
> leads the couple into the house.

Only the groom's relatives were present for the beginning of the feast. Often a member of the groom's family went to invite the bride's relatives to the celebration after the ceremony. When the bride's family arrived, the meal began anew (Zorin 2001, 89; Makashina 2003, 488). The wedding feast was a typical one, distinguished only by the *karavai*, a yeast-raised wedding bread baked in a special ritual a day or two before the wedding (in some cases there was a *karavai* in both the bride's and the groom's home) (Chizhikova 1989, 179; Kabakova 2001, 172; Makashina 485). The baking of the *karavai* was sur-rounded by great ceremony, as Baiburin (1993, 79–80) describes: "the ingredi-ents for its preparation (flour, salt, eggs, oil) are brought by '*korovaishchitsy*'—young married women" who sang special ritual songs as they prepared the bread. Baiburin (1993, 81) notes that the bread was decorated with elements made from dough, twigs, ribbons, and flowers and served as another symbol of maidenly beauty. The breaking of the wedding bread served as the culmi-nation of the ritual feast (Baiburin 1993, 82). As noted above, after the wed-ding ceremony, the bride's hair was rebraided into the dual braids charac-teristic of a married woman (Kuznetsova and Loginov 2001, 239; Worobec 1995, 167; Makashina 488; Zorin 2001, 87). The bride gave presents to her new relatives in the last of the gift-giving rituals associated with the wedding (Maslova 1984, 24). She also received presents from the assembled guests, of-ten in exchange for the *karavai* or for some other baked good, such as *bliny* (crepes, pancakes) she had made (Kabakova 172; Chizhikova 190). Makashina (491) describes a similar ritual, in which the couple's relatives accept "hospitality from the couple—vodka and appetizers—and give them something 'for the cheeses.' The collection from the cheeses was given to the newlyweds, but most often for the bride to use. At the end of the feast there was a mutual gift giving to the newlyweds and the guests...."

The reception typically lasted for two to three days and included meals for the entire village and the bride's family, who often lived in another village since Russian marriage was typically exogamous. As a result, weddings were often planned for the fall, after the harvest, to ensure that food was available for all the guests and that agricultural demands did not interfere with the celebration. There were also religious reasons for this timing, since there were no major fasts or holy days in the fall that would prevent a full ritual meal

(Worobec 1995, 151). The bride underwent various tests of her ability to work either on the day of the wedding or on the second day of the celebration; her mother-in-law often required her to sweep the floor or bring water from the well (as well as cook *bliny* and/or light the stove). Guests generally tried to interfere with this process by scattering trash or spilling the water, which meant that she had to perform the tasks again (Chizhikova 1989, 188; Baiburin 1993, 87; Kabakova 2001, 189; Worobec 1995, 172; Kuznetsova and Loginov 2001, 248; Zorin 2001, 96, 99). One woman (cited in Kargin 2000, 1: 85) from Kaluga recalls her own wedding:

> And now, when they bring the mother-in-law (her mother), they lead the couple to the well to get water. They test, so to speak, the bride's ability to work. They used to carry water on yokes in wooden barrels, called a tub.... I was sixteen years old. We went to get water. The well was deep, so deep, that well had no bottom. And you had to fill a wooden tub, maybe six buckets would fit into there. And while I am carrying each bucket, as young as they come! And I pour it into the tub.... But you know, the wells weren't always close. You have to carry it into the yard, where the livestock are.... They threw a bast shoe in the first tub. They brought up the water from the well and all over the groom, all over me!

Another common tradition, on the second or third day, was the *poiski iarki* 'search for the ewe' and mumming. Makashina (2003, 491) provides details about these practices:

> The bride's relatives came to her husband's home and announced that a girl had been lost. Searches began. They led the new bride out to them. They acknowledged that she was their own, but after an inspection found many changes and refused their rights to her.... Mumming was a common amusement everywhere on the second day. The mummers dressed in inside-out pelts, men often dressed in women's clothes and women in men's. They dressed as various wild animals, gypsies, soldiers, etc.

The wedding celebration featured several contests between the bride and groom or between their families to predict the couple's future, including who would dominate the relationship and the number and sex of their children (Kabakova 2001, 181, 185). The simplest predictor was that the first to step on the stair outside the church or the carpet in the church aisle would dominate; in some cases the first to step on the ritual cloth at home would be in control (Ananicheva and Samodelova 1997, 162; Kargin 2000, 1: 63; Kuznetsova and Loginov 2001, 237). There was also a ritual attested in which the matchmakers from each side broke a *karavai* and the one of the couple whose representative had the larger piece would be the head of the household (Ananicheva and Samodelova 134). In addition, there were rituals to ensure the couple's fertility, from showering them with hops to placing a boy on the bride's lap, so that she would have sons (Worobec 1995, 168). Makashina (2003, 487–88) describes the rebraiding of the bride's hair into two braids as a means to predict the sex of the first child: "during which the matchmakers raced to braid her hair, while saying: 'bear girls' (the bride's matchmaker said), 'bear boys' (the groom's matchmaker said), because there was a superstition that whoever matchmaker finished her braid would determine the sex of the first child." Kabakova (185) notes that often a clay pot was broken and "read" to determine the number and sex of the children the couple would have.

The first day's festivities culminated in the consummation of the marriage, typically in a barn or outbuilding, while the guests would make an abundance of noise to ward off evil spirits, by banging on pots or firing shotguns (Zorin 2001, 90; Makashina 2003, 488–89). The bed was often occupied by an elderly, happily married couple or by the godparents or relatives who *greiut postel'* 'warm the bed'. The groom or bride had to buy the bed from them, so that the couple could occupy it. Often, at this stage, the bride took off the groom's shoe to show her submission. She kept the money he had placed inside the boot for herself (Zorin 2001, 90; Worobec 1995, 169; Kuznetsova and Loginov 2001, 245; Chizhikova 1989, 188). Ananicheva and Samodelova (1997, 117) cite a description of this ritual from an 1851 wedding in the Zvenigorod region:

> The matchmaker approaches the couple and breaks their pie over their heads. After which the couple walk around the table in a circle bowing to the guests and go to bed. Once they have entered the hay loft, the groom has to buy the bed, since it has been occupied by one of his female relatives. The bed is bought in exchange for wine. The bride undresses the groom and removes his shoes. At which point the groom puts money in a boot as a present to his wife.

This practice helped to ensure that the couple would have good fortune in their lives together.[11] After the marriage was consummated, the bride's shift and/or linens from the wedding bed were displayed to prove that she had been a virgin (Zorin 2001, 93). Kargin (2000, 1: 85) describes this practice in the Kaluga region:

> [T]hey would demand that they show the shirt to see if the bride was chaste or not. And they broke dishes. Not because she wasn't chaste,

---

[11] Baiburin (1993, 83) notes that life-cycle rituals are particularly associated with *dolia* 'lot in life, both good and bad', such that many ritual acts are performed that can establish the nature of the participants' future.

just the opposite, because she was. They broke dishes, they stuck money in the attic, they forced the bride to sweep it up, to get it, so that it would be more fun. The bride sweeps up the money and they scattered it again. They also broke a clay pot with poppy seeds, threw it all over the hut, so that it would be dirty. You just try and wash that!

In some areas, the bride's mother served a meal to the groom (often *bliny* or eggs), which he ate only if her daughter had been a virgin (Zabylin 1880/1990, 158; Zorin 2001, 100; Makashina 493) He may also have given his mother-in-law an object to indicate that her daughter was not chaste, as one of Kargin's informants (1: 85) notes: "And so, they say, the groom then gave his mother-in-law, if she wasn't chaste, a wooden spoon with a hole burned through it and a crepe with a hole as well: 'here you go, mother-in-law, for your daughter.'" The couple underwent a ritual bathing by the groom's relatives on the morning after the wedding was consummated (Zorin 2001, 93; Makashina 490). They often took part in rituals with the unmarried members of the village for the first year of their married lives. The couple was generally still in transition until the birth of their first child, when they officially became adults (Baiburin 1993, 87, 89).

Funerals in the Nineteenth-Century Central Russian Village[12]

Funerals were of four types in the village: for a man (the most elaborate); for a married woman (the least elaborate); for an unmarried woman (essentially a wedding ceremony); and for children (Mahler 1935). Below we will discuss a married adult's funeral, as it provides the full range of ritual acts that will be essential to an understanding of the Russian funeral in the contemporary period. Elderly people generally prepared their burial clothing before they died (Sedakova 2004, 242). Kremleva (2003, 520–21) describes the practice and the burial clothing:

> It was a widely known tradition to prepare one's funeral clothing. They laid aside "the death bundle" or "death clothing" ahead of time. Clothing for burial was distinguished by the way it was sewn, cut, material and color. They did not dress the dead like the living. The shirt worn "for death" was not fastened with buttons or studs, but was tied with a ribbon or raw threads. They did not make knots in threads while sewing burial clothing ... fabric was not cut with scis-

---

[12] Portions of the material on funerals in this chapter and in chapter 6 previously appeared in article form in *Folklorica*. They are reprinted here by gracious permission of the editor.

sors, but torn. Funerary clothing retained its ancient cut and traditional forms that were already out of style.

The woman's funerary costume was a white shirt with long sleeves and a
white or colored *sarafan* 'jumper' and white kerchief. Men wore a white shirt
and dark pants. Both sexes wore funerary *lapti* 'bast shoes' (woven differently
from the *lapti* worn on a daily basis) and belts (Kremleva 2003, 521; Zelenin
1927/1991, 346–47). It was important that the clothing be new and unworn or
freshly washed (if not new), although Zelenin (346) notes that burial clothing
may have been worn on holidays: "many old people sew their own *funerary
clothing* [italics original] themselves and wear it before big holidays."

When a person died, all the mirrors in the house were covered, and all
water was thrown out, since it was believed that water and mirrors (symbolically similar to water due to their reflective nature) might trap the soul on
this earth, which might result in unquiet or restless dead or in another death
(Kabakova 2001, 261; Zelenin 1927/1991, 349; Firsov and Kiseleva 1993, 288).
Typically married women (not relatives) washed and dressed the body and
wrapped it in a white shroud,[13] leaving only the head and hands uncovered;
they were paid with cloth or with items of clothing that belonged to the
deceased (Kremleva 1993, 13; Firsov and Kiseleva 288). Ananicheva and
Samodelova describe this process from an 1856 funeral in the Zaraisk region:
"While the body is still warm, and sometimes even half an hour before death,
they wash the dying person, put a clean shirt on him and put him under the
saints … they put him headfirst toward the icons and, having covered him
with cloth, light a wax candle before the icons." As part of the process of
preparing the body, they closed the deceased's eyes and covered them with
coins and tied the feet and hands (Baiburin 1993, 106, 108; Sedakova 2004,
248). The materials used to wash the body were thrown away; the water was
poured where no one would walk (Sedakova 249; Kremleva 1993, 14). Zelenin
(346) remarks on this tradition: "Everything that is used for the final
washing—the basin, the washcloth, and also the straw[14] on which the person
died, sometimes even the boards on which they washed him—all this the
Russians carry out to the fields or beyond the outskirts of town, in fact the
basin in most cases is smashed."

The deceased remained in the house for three days,[15] lying on the table
under the icon corner, with the feet facing the door and head beneath the

---

[13] Trice (1998, 26) notes that the shroud "signified his or her membership in the
broader Orthodox community. It marked the dead person's lifelong adherence to the
'promise' made at his or her christening, symbolically reinforcing the ongoing cycle of
birth and death."

[14] Typically the dying person was placed on straw to "soften" death.

[15] This tradition was influenced by a decree of Peter 1, who established three days as
the requirement (Sedakova 2004, 71).

icons (Zelenin 1927/1991, 347; Kremleva 2003, 521; Baiburin 1993, 110). While the deceased was in the house, it was the custom to bring him/her gifts. Ana-nicheva and Samodelova (1997, 189) note that the most common gift was a candle: "Everyone takes pains to bring a gift of a wax candle to him: the constant flame in front of the icon at the head of the deceased is maintained by these candles they had brought." Firsov and Kiseleva (1993, 287) cite a similar tradition of bringing gifts to the dying: "If it became known that someone was dying in the village, then any housewife would hurry to visit and say farewell to him, leaving behind a gift for him. The women whose gift the dying person liked are pleased and remember this: 'My bread and salt went with him to that world!'" During the vigil, no cleaning was performed (Zelenin 349). A glass of water or vodka and some bread or a *blin* were placed near the icons (Kremleva 2003, 521; Sedakova 2004, 244; Firsov and Kiseleva 288). The reasons for this vary, as Zelenin (345) notes:

> For the *washing of the soul* [italics original] they always place a vessel with water near the dying person, in fact many claim that they have seen how the water in the vessel shook as though as a result of bathing as soon as the soul has departed. This vessel with water stands on the table or on the windowsill for forty days after death. It is thought that for that time the soul has not yet reached the otherworld. There is also a notion that the soul drinks this water.

During this period (and also after burial on various anniversaries of the death), a *panikhida* 'requiem mass' was performed (Trice 1998, 29).

The deceased's female relatives (or invited "sitters") maintained a vigil over the body and ensured that the lamp at the head of the deceased remained lit during the entire vigil; no one was allowed to sleep with a corpse in the house (Sedakova 2004, 243). The coffin was not made by family members. Typically they asked a priest or deacon to come and bless the coffin with holy water and incense before they placed the deceased into it on the day of burial (Kremleva 2003, 522). They placed items in the coffin as well (Kremleva 2003, 522; Firsov and Kiseleva 1993, 287). These items related to the person's life on earth, as Kremleva (1993, 17) notes: "For a tailor they put in pieces of fabric, a needle, threads; for a coachman they put in a whip, reins, and a bunch of hair taken from a horse's mane and tail. For a farmer they put in various seeds. They also put a pipe and a bag of tobacco in the coffin, a besom, so that he would have something to steam himself in the bathhouse in the otherworld." Baiburin (1993, 111) notes that coins were put in the coffin as well "'for payment for a place in the cemetery' or 'for payment for transport across the river.'" Kabakova (2001, 256) argues that the Russians of this period perceived the land of the dead to be just like life on earth, so that the deceased was provided with items (s)he would need that he had needed on earth.

During the vigil, older female relatives would sing laments and read prayers (Kremleva 2003, 521, 522; Baiburin 1993, 110). Families also hired "readers" and professional lamenters (Kremleva 1993, 12; Zelenin 1927/1991, 355; Trice 1998, 28–33). According to Listova (1993, 57) the sitters were there because of a taboo on leaving the corpse alone: "It was not acceptable to leave the deceased alone. One of the older people sat nearby and read from the Psalter or religious verses." Ananicheva and Samodeleva (1997, 189) include a description of the vigil:

> The widow, mother, and the closest female relatives of the deceased begin to wail, that is together with cries and tears to speak in a sing-song voice about their loss, about their bitter fate, about the spiritual and physical qualities of the deceased; during this they remember various events from his life, his hospitality, his leisure time, they remember his last days and hours ... the whole time the deceased is lying in the hut under the icons, and until he is carried out, they continue to lament him in this way a few times a day.

The lamenters, generally widows, guided the ritual and led the singing, since they were familiar with the ritual songs required to ensure that the soul made the proper passage to the land of the dead. In fact, older women generally fulfilled many roles in the funeral, from sitters to lamenters to those who prepared the body (Sedakova 2004, 108). Laments typically included information, as we saw in the description of the funeral above, about the man's life and death, an attack for leaving his family and a laudatory section about his qualities as a father, son, husband, worker, etc. (Kremleva 1993, 13).

Men were prohibited from touching the body, just as they were isolated from the birth process, since it was dangerous for them to have contact with the spirit world. Women were more protected in dealings with the spirit world, and married women in particular served as intermediaries between this world and the next (Adon'eva 1998, 27; Moyle 1996, 230; Rouhier-Willoughby 2003a, 21–22). This attitude may have originated in the wedding, which was a major transition for the woman and perceived as a type of "death,"[16] or in her ability to bear children, which naturally brought her into contact with the otherworld, such that she was polluted (Worobec 1991, 21). Whatever the reason(s), women were the primary ritual figures in the funeral (with the exception of the priest, of course, who performed the religious services). However, pregnant women were not allowed to come in contact with the corpse or attend a funeral, since the child's health might have been adversely affected (Zelenin 1927/1991, 348; Sedakova 2004, 109). Listova (2003, 503) states that a pregnant woman "should not kiss the deceased while saying

---

[16] See Baiburin 1993, Levinton 1990, and Rouhier-Willoughby 2003a for a discussion of this issue.

farewell to him and even should not accompany the coffin to the cemetery." Men (not relatives of the deceased) did, however, carry the coffin out of the house and placed it on the cart or sleigh (Kabakova 2001, 264).

When the corpse was removed from the house on the third day for burial, they first carried out the lid, then the priest exited, followed by the coffin itself (the corpse faced feet first). They often removed the coffin (like the bride) via the back door or a window (Moyle 1996, 229–30; Zelenin 1927/1991, 348–49). This practice not only helped to prevent the threshold from being tainted by the corpse, but also helped to prevent the corpse (like a bride) from returning to the house. As with a wedding procession, the tracks of the funeral train were swept away, again to help prevent the deceased's return.[17] The neighbors gathered to say farewell to the deceased, especially if they were not going to the funeral mass and burial (Firsov and Kiseleva 1993, 288). To this gathering, Kremleva (1993, 18) states, people brought along "a candle, two kopecks or a bag of rye flour. All these supplies were donated to the church." Generally a few neighbors (older, married women) stayed behind to clean and remove the "traces of death" from the house. They swept and washed the floor, and the table and benches where the deceased had been placed; all the materials used for this purpose were destroyed or thrown away (Sedakova 2004, 244, 250; Kremleva 2003, 524; Kabakova 2001, 260). Ananicheva and Samodelova cite an interesting tradition that combines the washing of the dead with the purification of the house:

> First of all they rush to sweep and wipe the floor in the hut; they wash off the table and benches and the rags and broom used for this purpose as well as the straw on which the deceased laid, the pot from which they took water to wash the body, the comb used to comb his hair after death, are all gathered together and taken to the outskirts of town and thrown onto the crossroads.... (1997, 190)

The cleaners typically inverted the tables and benches before washing them, so that the death would enter the soil (Tolstoi 1990, 120). The priest also said a prayer of purification after the deceased had been carried out (Ananicheva and Samodelova 190). These same women prepared for the funeral feast that took place after the burial.

The women lamented as the funeral procession proceeded to the church for the *otpevanie* 'funeral mass' (Kremleva 1993, 18). Trice (1998, 31) describes

---

[17] Note that the Russians feared the return of the corpse, in the form of the walking dead, but not of the soul. There were yearly cycle rituals, including *Maslenitsa* 'Butter Week, Shrovetide' and Christmas, during which the souls of the dead were invited back, then "fed and bathed" by setting an empty place and heating the bathhouse for them. In addition, dreams about the dead were expected and interpreted as a return of the soul.

the procession as follows: "Typically, an icon bearer led the way, followed by choristers, then the clergy. Pallbearers, a hearse, or horse-drawn cart followed with the coffin. Close relatives, then friends, and finally acquaintances or by-standers usually brought up the rear." The procession stopped several times along the way to allow the corpse to say farewell to the living world and also to give a pie and piece of cloth to the first person met along the way in the deceased's name; they also took a roundabout way to the cemetery and did not return by the same road (Baiburin and Levinton 1990, 113; Kremleva 2003, 522; Firsov and Kiseleva 1993, 288). In some regions the path was strewn with some type of organic matter, such as fir branches or straw (Surkhasko 1985, 93; Nosova 1993, 60). At the church, the priest sang the funeral mass; the priest may or may not have been at the graveside itself (Kabakova 2001, 264; Kremleva 1993, 19; 2003, 523). According to Trice (33–34), the *otpevanie* was

> a ceremony of psalms, scripture readings, short sermons, and hymns.... Among the poor it was a communal service, observed over many corpses at a time, although rich and poor alike seemed to prefer an individual *otpevanie*. By the nineteenth century eulogies had become common as well. At the close of the service a priest placed a long paper streamer inscribed with a special prayer of absolution (*razreshitel'naia molitva*) in the deceased's hands, an indication that the dead person enjoyed the church's favor and ritual attentions. The singing of the hymn *Vechnaia pamiat'* (Eternal Remembrance) marked the final stage of the service when the mourners filed past the coffin to give the corpse a farewell kiss.

At the graveside, the coffin was nailed shut, but not until after the deceased's hands and feet had been untied, either at the cemetery or in the house (Baiburin 1993, 111). Funerals usually occurred around noon, when the sun was high in the sky (Kremleva 2003, 522). As was the case with preparing the body for burial and making the coffin, non-family members dug the grave (Sedakova 2004, 244, 250). Limitations also existed on who lowered the body into the grave. Zelenin (1927/1991, 350) notes that "it was considered a sin if parents lowered their children into the grave or children, their parents." The coffin was lowered on towels or ropes; the towels were sometimes distributed to pallbearers and gravediggers (Kremleva 2003, 523). Those present typically threw coins in the grave (to buy a space for the deceased in the graveyard or in the otherworld) and each threw some dirt onto the coffin as the grave was being filled (Baiburin 1993, 114; Kabakova 265; Kremleva 2003, 523). Everyone waited until the grave mound was formed before departing, and they may have had a commemorative meal at the graveside (Kremleva, 1993, 20). Some-times this meal (with food left for the deceased) occurred on the second day after burial (Sedakova 244).

After the burial, the *pominki* 'wake' for all those present at the funeral (and often for the entire village) was held at the deceased's home, often in shifts to accommodate all the attendees (Baiburin 1993, 117; Kabakova 2001, 266; Firsov and Kiseleva 1993, 288; Trice 1998, 34). Kremleva (1993, 23) provides details of the typical funeral meal: "The obligatory foods for a funeral meal included *kut'ia* (grain and raisins with honey), honey and oaten (in some places cranberry) *kisel'* (fruit drink), and in some regions fish pie and *bliny*. Everyone who had participated in the funeral was invited to the meal on that day." Zelenin (356) notes that people also served cooked grains and fried eggs at these meals and that they "put a separate place setting for the deceased either on the general table or on a special table in the corner under the icons. Onto the corner of the table they pour out the first spoonful of some type of food and the first cup of water for him." Typically people did not eat with forks at the wake, since sharp objects "pricked" the soul and discouraged its presence at the feast (Kabakova 266). Baiburin (1993, 118) concludes that "if the basic efforts in funerals are directed at distancing the deceased and along with him, death itself, from the living ... then in wake rituals the dead are invited to come to the living; the gates to the cemetery and the doors to the house are opened; they are met and given food and the like." Mourners began the funeral meal by taking a piece of a *blin* and, after filling it with *kut'ia*, wishing *tsarstviia nebesnogo* (lit. 'heavenly realm') 'may (s)he be in heaven' to the deceased (Ananicheva and Samodelova 1997, 190). The meal usually ended with *kisel'* (Kremleva 1993, 24). In some areas, the bathhouse was heated for the deceased to bathe (Chistiakov 1982, 112). There was a tradition of giving food and items to the poor (both openly and secretly) in honor of the deceased for 40 days (Kremleva 1993, 20–21; Nosova 1999, 127).

The most important events after the burial included additional *pominki* on the ninth, twentieth, and fortieth days after death and again at six and nine months and after one year and for every year thereafter (Kabakova 2001, 268; Sedakova 2004, 244; Kremleva 1993, 24-25; Firsov and Kiseleva 1993, 287). The degree of complexity of these additional commemorative rituals varied, as Ananicheva and Samodelova (1997, 190) show in their description of the practice:

> For the repose of the soul of the newly buried they order several masses from the priest ... these *pominki* occur on the third, ninth and twentieth day, and also after six weeks or on the fortieth day and in a year. At all these services and *pominki*, especially if they fall on a holiday, when there are lots of people at mass, then on the porch at the main entrance to the church, near the wall, in full view, they spread out a towel or a scarf and place *bliny* and pieces of cut wheat bread on a wooden or a stone saucer ... everyone who exits the church is invited to remember the deceased by a woman, almost always elderly or old, dressed from head to toe in white (this is peasant mourning

clothes) ... the woman who has commemorated the dead, while carrying the remnants of the bread and *bliny* back home from the church
suggests that everyone she meets remember the deceased.... On the
third day they bring the parish clergy *bliny* and bread to the church,
on the ninth and twentieth day only *bliny*, and on the fortieth day a
mass and a requiem are ordered in the home.... After the requiem the
hostess serves a meal, during which the priest and all the clergy must
be served. They try to make the wake as abundant and good as they
can so that everyone present, while eating the delicious items, will
truly commemorate the deceased.

As this passage suggests, the most important and largest of the commemorations were on the fortieth day and then again in one year, when once again
the entire community gathered to commemorate the deceased at another
meal. On the other days, only the family joined in the *pominki*. The fortieth
day was particularly important since on that day the soul left the earth
(Zelenin 1927/1991, 356); Yelena Minyonok (personal communication) also
observes that the meal on the ninth day is generally attended by the entire
community. The Orthodox Church holds that, on the fortieth day, God judges
the soul's fate and determines where it will reside, in heaven or hell. From the
ninth to the fortieth days, its guardian angel travels with the soul to heaven
and hell. As a result, the living performed various accts to ease the passage
out of this world to heaven during these forty days. Kabakova (267, 268) notes
that "for forty days they do not put out the light in the house, 'so that the soul
would find the road to the otherworld'" and that "bread and vodka (or
water)—the deceased's share—stands in the house on the windowsill or
under the icons for twelve or forty days." Over the course of these forty days
people often visited the grave daily with food and vodka for the dead
(Kabakova 268).[18] Kremleva (1993, 21) cites the tradition of giving away the
deceased's belongings on the fortieth day as well. As part of these additional
pominki, they visited the grave and left food and drink as well as grain for the
birds[19] (Zelenin 357). Yearly commemorations for the dead also occurred on
Parents' Days, on Saturdays during *Maslenitsa* (the carnival period before
Lent begins), during Lent itself, during Passion Week, on the Tuesday of St.
Thomas's Week (called *Radonitsa* 'Resurrection Day', the second week after
Easter), the Saturday before Pentecost (called *Sviataia Troitsa* 'Holy Trinity',
seven weeks after Easter), and on Saint Dmitry's Day (first Saturday in
November) (Zelenin 356–57).[20]

---

[18] Sedakova (2004, 113) associates this behavior with the Slavic ancestor cult.

[19] Birds represented the souls of the dead in Russian lore (Gura 1997, 20; Afanas'ev
1994, 3: 215ff.).

[20] People did welcome the return of the dead, both in dreams and for *pominki*, particularly when they gave advice to the living, and at yearly cycle rituals (Nosova 1999,

Early Soviet Period

While not all of these ritual practices were performed in the life-cycle rituals in Russian cities by the time of the revolution, many of those that did occur survived well into the 1930s and even beyond. Birth was perhaps the most radically altered, even before the Bolshevik revolution. As Ransel (2000) has documented, medicalization of childbirth had already begun in the pre-revolutionary period. The medical establishment had attempted to eliminate traditional village midwives or *povitukhi* and replace them with village women who had undergone medical training. However, it was only in the upper classes or in cities that a doctor or a professionally trained midwife, an *akusherka*, would be called in to attend labor (Ramer 1992, 109; Listova 2003, 502). In villages these women were perceived to be outsiders and were not often asked to assist at a delivery; the villagers preferred to use the services of a local woman, who would keep intact the childbirth traditions deemed necessary for the child and mother to thrive (Listova 1989, 144). As a result, the medicalization of birth only came to fruition in both urban and rural areas between the 1930s and 1950s (Listova 2003, 502). Ransel (2000, 44) asserts:

> The breakthrough in medical care for women and children in the villages came only after the upheavals of the early 1930s.... Even so, it took many more years for regular obstetrical and child-care services to arrive in much of the country, because the personnel for such services had to first be lifted mainly from the village population itself and trained. Not until after World War II did services reach a majority of rural districts. Still more time passed before the government could break the chain of intergenerational, female child-rearing knowledge....[21]

The religious components of birth, such as the baptism and christening party, also survived openly in cities until the 1930s and were common among some families even into the 1960s and beyond (Rudnev 1979, 119; Ugrinovich 1975, 104). Only when the Soviet government began a serious attack on religious ceremonies and attempted to create new birth rituals did these traditions

---

139–40; Baiburin 1993, 119; Chistiakov 1982, 112; Kremleva 1993, 24–25; Kabakova 2001, 272). However, there was always a danger that the dead were unhappy if they returned, because the burial had not been done properly (Sedakova 2004, 245; Razumova 2001, 108). If this were the case, then the living could try to appease the dead either by digging a hole at the grave and putting objects the deceased had requested in a dream or by putting objects into another person's coffin. Similarly, the living also asked the deceased to take messages to other dead souls (Kremleva 1993, 18–19).

[21] Folk material, however, did not entirely disappear among medical professionals, as Belousova (1998, 1999, 2003) and Rouhier-Willoughby (2003b) have shown. Survivals from the folk system will be discussed in more detail in chapter 3.

begin to fall by the wayside. The *oktiabriny* celebrations introduced in the 1920s for the birth of a child, according to Lane (1981, 68), "failed to gain acceptance beyond a small band of political enthusiasts and proved to be a short-lived experiment." As time went on the Soviet government recognized the fact that religious rituals persisted and there was nothing with which to replace them, since their own early attempts enjoyed little success (Rudnev 16–17). As a result, they were missing a chance to indoctrinate people into Soviet values and they took action to create new Soviet substitutes. In 1944 the Presidium of the Supreme Soviet accepted a resolution on motherhood. Article 30 of that resolution addressed the issue of "introduction of ceremonial order of conduct of the registration of newborn children and of marriages" (Zhirnova 1980, 82). However, as Zhirnova notes, World War II interfered with progress on ritual creation. We can also surmise that the abandonment of older (religious) rituals may have been the result of generational change; as older generations who remembered pre-revolutionary rituals died off, there was no one to insist on the ceremony. In addition, the rituals went underground. I had informants, for example, who said that during the Soviet period they christened their children secretly. The secrecy (and fear of reprisals) prevented a public christening party, but core aspects of the ritual were nevertheless retained to some extent.

According to Zhirnova (1980, 35ff.) city wedding rituals during the pre-revolutionary period retained many traditional elements, including the matchmaking process, the occurrence of *smotriny*, gift-giving by the bride, and customary roles for the couple's attendants found in villages. The cities were not all uniform though, as one would expect. Zhirnova (65–66) shows that the practices such as the *devichnik*, mumming, and breaking of pots "that played such an important role in traditional peasant weddings were seen primarily among the population of satellite cities and residents of city suburbs that maintained familial ties with rural relatives," By the twentieth century, however, many traditions had been lost, including the ritual bathing of the bride, rebraiding of her hair and concealing and unveiling the correct bride by the groom (Zhirnova 67; Makashina 2003, 495). Urban residents did not sing traditional ritual songs, nor did the bride lament (Zhirnova 59). Since the bride and groom traveled separately to the church, there were no rituals related to the groom's arrival, such as buying the bride's braid or the place next to her (Zhirnova 51).

Makashina (2003, 495) discusses the nature of the wedding in the early years of Soviet rule: "[T]hey celebrated the wedding everywhere with all the old traditions, the exception being, as a rule, members of the party, Komsomol and forward-thinking young workers.... By the 1930s church marriages had become a rare phenomenon, civil weddings, registered in a ZAGS and accompanied by new rituals and often by a simple party had become widespread." The wedding itself, like the other two life-cycle rituals, resisted change, according to Guseva (1989, 221). As Makashina mentions, one significant difference, of course, was the institution in 1917 of the ZAGS, an abbreviation for (*otdel*) *zapisi aktov grazhdanskogo sostoianiia*, the state registry office, which kept records of all births, deaths, marriages and divorces in the country. Zhirnova (1980, 79) notes that the Soviet government passed a law on civil marriage in 1917: "The force of law was recognized primarily for a civil marriage registered in a ZAGS.... The church ceremony of marriage was not forbidden, but all legal significance was removed from it: church marriage now no longer created legal marital relations in and of itself." Despite attempts to institute some Soviet rituals, such as the *krasnaia svad'ba* 'red wedding' and birth rituals such as *oktiabriny* in the 1920s, older traditions won out (Sukhanov 1976, 184–85; Rudnev 1979, 16–17). As with birth, it was not until the first decade after the war that any progress was made in instituting a Soviet wedding ritual. Until then, the society was firmly divided, with some revolutionary enthusiasts embracing the new rituals, but most rejecting them. From the 1950s on, interaction between state ideals and traditional folk practices became more prevalent in all three rituals (Makashina 495; Ugrinovich 1975, 127; Rudnev 26). This process came to fruition in the 1960s, when more formal weddings with an established official ceremony were held in *doma kul'tury* 'houses of culture' and *dvortsy brakosochetaniia* 'wedding palaces' and had an established formal ceremony (Makashina 496; Ugrinovich 127–29; Mar'ianov 1976, 4; Rudnev 132; Lane 1981, 75).

Funerals followed much the same path as the previous two life-cycle rituals. In the early years after the revolution, much of the ritual as described above was practiced in Russian cities. Trice (1998, 217–18) notes that the Soviet authorities tried to eliminate, as with the wedding and birth, vestiges of religious belief in the funerary rite:

[W]ith the promulgation of the "Decree on Cemeteries and Funerals" in December 1918, Lenin and the other members of the Soviet of People's Commissars (Sovnarkom) launched the most ambitious plan to refashion burial ever attempted by a Russian government. The decree called for the nationalization of all cemeteries, morgues, and funeral parlors, and authorized the introduction into Russia of cremation. It also required that citizens register every death with the local Bureau of Civic Registration (ZAGS). More importantly, this new law mandated the abolition of the Nikolaevan rank system for funerals and cemetery plots in favor of a new, more egalitarian system based on unranked plots and an "identical (*odinakovyi*) funeral" for every Soviet citizen. Under new social insurance and pension programs, the state intended to pay a prescribed amount for the burial of all toilers (*trudiashchiesia*), pensioners, and residents of orphanages, almshouses, and invalid homes. Local soviets were to assume responsibility for the burial of the destitute and homeless ineligible for the new programs, as well as the setting of funeral fees for all other "citizens."

Anyone wishing religious funeral services was free to choose them, but according to the new law the socialist state would not pay for them, regardless of the social status of the persons involved.

Despite this decree, the Soviet authorities did not establish a system of funeral homes, at least not to bury the average person. As Aasamaa (1974, 178) notes in her Soviet-era etiquette book, *Kak sebia vesti* (How to Conduct Oneself), in the case of a famous person "they create a funerary commission that directs the memorial ceremony." Famous personages, such as military and revolutionary heroes, were thus honored with a "red funeral." Trice (262) describes the red funeral:

> [O]stensibly a civil rite, the Russian red funeral actually combined sacred and secular elements to effect a spectacle of the first order. Participants in red funerals frequently carried icons along with red-ribboned wreaths, sang Orthodox hymns and revolutionary songs, or listened to the ritual chanting of a priest in addition to the revolutionary rhetoric of radical orators.

However, with the exception of these public events for the most famous members of Soviet society, most funerary rites were private celebrations within the family home, which enabled people to retain many traditional practices. Nevertheless, graveside rituals changed as time passed; by the 1930s religious figures could no longer be invited to say the funeral mass, and funerals were civil celebrations (at least publicly) (Kremleva 2003, 530). One significant change that had already occurred in cities by the time of the Revolution was the loss of lamenting. That is not to say that lamenting did not occur, but that it did not have the structured, poetic form that it did in the village funeral (Nosova 1999, 163, 185; Kremleva 1993, 34). Listova (1993, 49) argues that the funeral also kept its "folk" character longer precisely because it was focused on the "irrational" and spiritual, on life after death, not on the secular and "rational" aspects of life on earth. Precisely because of these characteristics, the Soviet authorities faced a dilemma. In their atheistic society they could not openly or easily deal with the concept of the afterlife, and therefore they left the funeral relatively untouched longer than they did the other two life-cycle rituals (for a discussion of attempts to deal with these issues by Soviet ritual theorists, see Ugrinovich 136ff.).

One attempt to resolve this conflict was the introduction into Russia of cremation. The Orthodox church had held that cremation was antithetical to its faith. Trice (1998, 340) argues that those within the Soviet government who espoused it thought that cremation "functioned as a psychological tool for replacing the religious beliefs and superstitions of Russia's 'backward elements' with the values and ideas of a more egalitarian, technologically advanced age." In addition, it would help address problems of public health (e.g., by protecting the public from infected corpses) and also lack of space in urban cemeteries. While cremation itself was supposed to solve many of the problems facing the Soviet authorities in the creation of a new society, it actually illustrates the dilemma they faced regarding the funeral more broadly. Trice (344–45) summarizes this problem in his discussion of cremation:

> [O]n the one hand they had to compete with Mother Earth, the "cheapest" medium for burial once the Bolsheviks nationalized all cemeteries, while on the other hand, they felt compelled to combat earth burial in accordance with the new regime's anti-religious policies. In place of older, secular and sacred ideas about the integral relationship between the human body and identity, both in this world and the next, cremationists offered people medical, scientific definitions that failed to resonate with their daily experiences and long-term expectations.… Like the cemetery reformers they criticized, they labored to put the loathsome, natural body out of sight, and if possible, out of mind. Yet at the same time … also insisted on monumental crematoria-cathedrals and spectacular rituals for the disposal of the dead.

This conundrum, in fact, was to be at the heart of the Soviet government's desire to reform all the life-cycle rituals. The models for Soviet theorists derived from a grandiose, religious tradition exemplified in Russia by the Orthodox Church and the tsars. Nor could they easily adopt ritual models from Western countries, given their rejection of the capitalist, bourgeois lifestyle. Native folk material was likewise off limits, since they viewed it as a symbol of backwardness and religious faith. Nevertheless, as we will see in our discussion of the life-cycle rituals in the following chapters, it was precisely these three sources that formed the basis for the Soviet ritual complex. Despite their revolutionary idealism, the Soviet authorities (depending on one's point of view) either inevitably succumbed to the models of their past in the creation of rituals, or cleverly adapted their past to suit the government's changing needs over time.

Even though they had attempted to build Soviet rituals earlier, it was not until the 1950s that the Soviet ritual complex began to thrive. This attitudinal shift toward life-cycle rituals resulted from several factors, among them: generational change; a shift in Soviet domestic policy; a recognition that the government could use these rituals to its advantage (as it already used public rituals tied to the yearly cycle, e.g., May Day, Victory Day, etc.); an ongoing desire to eliminate religious faith (and its rituals); a generally positive shift in the official stance on folklore; and a recovery (or a perception thereof) from the devastation of the Second World War. These social trends interacted in an intricate way to create a new environment for ritual development and for the celebration of the life cycle, as we will see in the next three chapters in our discussion of Soviet Russian birth, wedding and funeral rituals from the 1950s to the 1990s.

Chapter 3

The Soviet Russian Childbirth Ritual (1950–90)

Soviet-era childbirth practices were derived from three distinct sources: the folk tradition, established (Western) medical practice, and Soviet ideals. Beginning in the nineteenth century, the medical establishment was already attempting to change village traditions related to birth (Ramer 1992). The Soviet medical system continued this trend of modernizing treatment of pregnant women, and labor and delivery by introducing a Western medical model that would be applied throughout the country. As Ransel (2000) has discussed, by the 1950s, they had essentially achieved this goal. Childbirth itself, of course, is not limited to the actual delivery. The Soviet government was also concerned with eliminating religious practices such as baptism. These changes were based on the Soviet desire to remove Russia from the scientific and cultural "backwardness" that had characterized the pre-revolutionary period. They also were designed to show how the state was providing for its citizens; free, quality medical services were one way to convey that the state cared for its people more than the tsarist government had. They also ensured that future generations of workers, whom the Soviet Union would rely upon, would enter the world properly. Children would not only thrive physically, but would receive socialist messages about the nature of the family and the relationship between the citizen and the state from birth. In this sense, Soviet Russia's medical system correlated to those across Europe from the eighteenth century on. Foucault (1984, 280–82) argues that, as a result, the family became a unit designed to meet the goals of the state through the creation of healthy children. The family then shifted from "just a system of relations inscribed in a social status, a kinship system, a mechanism for the transmission of property. It is to become a dense, saturated, permanent, continuous physical environment which envelops, maintains, and develops the child's body." Soviet-era literature describing the development and goals of gynecological and obstetric medicine certainly supports his view. The authors of a standard book for gynecological-obstetric professionals, Shening-Parshina and Shibaeva (1967, 14) assert: "The Party thinks that one of the most important duties of Soviet medical science and public health is the raising, beginning from the earliest age, of a healthy generation with harmonious development of physical and spiritual forces." They continue by discussing the need for medical personnel to improve the "hygienic culture" of women from all walks of life through their medical practice and education. Given that the doctors were state representatives in the USSR, these attitudes illustrate the importance of the state in family life, particularly in the area of pregnancy and child rearing.

None of the women interviewed, who gave birth in the period from 1954 to 2003, gave birth at home.[1] Similarly, they were all treated by medical professionals during their pregnancies and deliveries, which was a major goal of Soviet medical reform. Shening-Parshina and Shibaeva (1967, 143, 148) strongly oppose both home birth and home remedies of any kind; they repeatedly talk of the dangers of delivering a child without proper medical supervision and of the potential harmful effects of non-medical treatment. They also are adamant about the threat posed by relatives in overruling medical advice: "They [mothers] often fall under the influence of older women (mothers, mothers-in-law, aunts, and so on), who do not always give proper advice." As a result, it is surprising that anything at all from nineteenth-century village traditions survived, given the attacks by Russian medical professionals on the practices of *povitukhi* 'village midwives' (Ramer 1992). However, as Belousova (1998, 1999) and I (2003) have shown in previous research, doctors and medical personnel were products of the same folk belief system as their patients. When a traditional belief did not directly contradict medical practice, it was often adopted into the birth process, generally with a "rational" medical explanation for its existence.

While the state might have espoused a scientific view of birth, people also relied on their own experiences and belief systems, as the warnings to medical personnel in the literature (cited above) indicate. It was not a simple task, as doctors and ritual specialists discovered, to eliminate centuries of belief about how to behave while pregnant or while delivering a child, or even what it meant to be part of a family. The patients brought with them, as Humphrey and Laidlaw (1994, 192–193) discuss within the context of the Jain *puja* ritual, their own interpretations of ritual acts and the cultural messages behind them. When agents perform a ritual, they do not simply follow a pattern of rote acts, but actually negotiate their position in the social structure and establish a state of affairs in the world on the basis of *habitus*. Bourdieu (1977, 72) defines *habitus* as: "systems of durable, transposable *dispositions* [italics original], structured structures predisposed to function as structuring systems, that is, as principles of the generation and structuring of practices and representations...." Not surprisingly, then, people continued to hold onto folk material, one essential form of *habitus*, particularly given its central position in the definition of the family and gender roles. Therefore, familial (e.g., traditional and/or religious) knowledge was often perceived to be much more

---

[1] This practice is being revived among some urban Russian women, as Belousova (2002) has shown.

powerful than the messages the Soviet authorities sent about the institution and the society and the family's position therein through the life-cycle rituals they had devised.

In their ritual practice, Soviet Russian citizens demonstrated their resistance to certain aspects of state ideology that contradicted their own conceptions of family life. In this way, they behaved much like the Malay in Scott's *Weapons of the Weak*. Scott argues that

> it is in the immediate interest of most poor villagers to uphold the official realities in nearly all power-laden contexts…. But we would commit the error of not realizing that mystification and impression management are as much a pose of the powerless as ideological domination by the rich…. The realm of behavior—particularly in power-laden situations—is precisely where dominated classes are most constrained. And it is at the level of beliefs and interpretations—where they can safely be ventured—that subordinate classes are least trammeled. The rich in Sedaka can usually insist on conforming public behavior and get it; they can neither insist on private ideological conformity, nor do they need it.

The urban Soviet Russians in this study also conformed in public, "power-laden structures." We cannot, however, simply assume that they did not accept official ideology in some cases. Not every act could be characterized as one of resistance to the state and its norms. As Yurchak (2006, 8) has shown,

> many of the fundamental values, ideals, and realities of socialist life (such as equality, community, selflessness, altruism, friendship, ethical relations, safety, education, work, creativity, and concern for the future) were of genuine importance, despite the fact that many of their everyday practices routinely transgressed, reinterpreted, or refused certain norms and rules represented in the official ideology of the socialist state.

This chapter will address these issues, first by describing the medical process of pregnancy, labor, and delivery. We will then examine the three sources for childbirth practices and, most importantly, how Soviet Russians interpreted them and created social and familial identity through this lens. In the description below, we will see a complex series of behaviors that derive from these three sources, i.e., science and medicine taken from the West; beliefs about the nature of the family in Soviet society and how state institutions related to citizens; and folk ideas about behavior during pregnancy and in childcare. None of these are isolated entities; they intertwine and complement (or conflict) with each other within the rituals to form the Soviet life-cycle complex.

Description of Soviet Childbirth Practices[2]

As is the case with all personal narratives, my informants' stories are not identical. Some had easy childbirth experiences, others remarkably difficult. Some were full of praises for their doctors and *akusherki* 'nurse-midwives', while others had nothing but complaints about them. However, I found that each woman I interviewed, regardless of her attitude toward the pregnancy and delivery, underwent the same essential process. Once a woman suspected she was pregnant, she went to the *zhenskaia konsul'tatsiia* 'women's depart-ment' of her local clinic. She was placed *na uchet pod nabliudenie* 'on the regis-try for treatment'. Women did not choose their doctors, but had one assigned based on the region of the city and the on-call doctor on duty the day she had her appointment.[3] Once she had completed this step, an expectant mother, so long as she did not have a difficult pregnancy, saw her doctor once a month for the first five months of pregnancy. For the next three months, they met twice monthly. For the last month, she was examined weekly. At each visit, she was weighed, her stomach was measured, and blood and urine were taken for analysis. If a woman had complications during her pregnancy, then she was generally admitted to the *rodil'nyi dom* or *roddom* 'maternity hospital' for observation and treatment. These periods ranged from a few weeks to nearly the entirely pregnancy in one serious case. The *rodil'nyi dom* is gener-ally a free-standing building separate from other hospitals or treatment cen-ters. Each region of a city had its own *roddom*, although in smaller cities there may have only been one *roddom*.

Doctors recommended a regimen for each mother during pregnancy to ensure delivery of a healthy child. They strictly controlled both diet and liquid intake, particularly the latter, because the strain on the kidneys during pregnancy was of general concern. Women were advised not to eat too much and to eat properly. The recommended diet consisted of vegetables and fruits, dairy products and good protein sources; salty and spicy foods, coffee and alcohol were to be avoided. For example, Klara K., who gave birth in 1967, said that she was limited in her salt intake: "I was on a no-salt diet. Usually cereals, soups, milk.... I ate fruit." Tatiana K. gave a similar answer about her pregnancies (1970, 1974, 1984): "You have to search out food rich in calcium. That means farmer's cheese ... and generally food should be very varied, butter, vitamin A.... Now meat, eggs, farmer's cheese, cheese are a must ... and of course fruit." As in Klara's case, there were general limitations on salty

---

[2] Portions of this chapter previously appeared in print in *Slavic and East European Journal*. They appear here with the kind permission of the editor.

[3] Similarly, this doctor did not deliver the child. A different set of doctors and mid-wives worked in the maternity hospital; thus the doctor on-call had probably not seen this patient before she arrived at the hospital. In addition, yet another group of doctors supervised the postpartum wards.

and spicy foods; plus, as Olga V. noted, certain foods, including chocolate, honey, and citrus, caused allergies in children and thus were not allowed. If a woman gained too much weight, she was put on a strict diet or even admitted to the *statsionar* 'inpatient clinic' in the maternity hospital. Nadezhda B. described her own run-in with these controls during her first pregnancy in 1971 as follows:

> You have to watch that a woman doesn't gain too much weight ... if it is too much, then the woman is put on a diet. Or they also put her in the hospital under observation, on diet food.... Once I gained too much weight and I had to go on a fruit diet, only apples, without water, without bread for a day and I lost a little weight.

All the mothers agreed that alcohol and coffee were off limits; some mentioned carbonated drinks as well. The most common theme, though, was a limitation in the amount of liquid consumed, as Lidia C. describes, "I was limited to one and a half liters of liquid every 24 hours." While Lidia had some complications with her kidneys that resulted in water retention, many other mothers restricted liquid intake simply as a means to control weight gain. Lena L., for example, said that "they controlled my weight, so that I didn't drink too much." In their book on sanitary enlightenment for obstetricians and gynecologists, Shening-Parshina and Shibaeva (1967, 123) recommend that pregnant women limit water intake from one to one and half liters a day, particularly in the second half of the pregnancy to avoid edema in the legs. The medical personnel I interviewed echoed these ideas about diet. Tamara B. stated: "They recommend, for example, not eating food that will bring about allergies in the fetus.... During pregnancy, of course, both milk products and farmer's cheese are required, sour cream, meat is a must.... They recommend a healthy way of life, such that they don't drink alcohol or smoke." Other limitations on behavior include: non-binding clothing, especially at the waist and low-heeled shoes; wearing a bandage to support the stomach both during pregnancy (and after delivery, so that the stomach does not sag, e.g., make the woman less attractive); well-ventilated rooms without heavy drapery or aromatic flowers; changing underwear twice weekly during pregnancy and daily after delivery; ironing bras after washing them while breastfeeding (presumably to reduce the likelihood of infection); getting six to eight hours of sleep; avoid baths in favor of showers or sponge baths; abstinence from sexual activity for the last two months before delivery and for six weeks after; and preparation of the breasts for nursing throughout the pregnancy to avoid mastitis (Shening-Parshina and Shibaeva 121–22, 137–38, 143–44).

Doctors also advised daily walks to maintain general health, but warned that a woman should also not overexert herself during pregnancy, by lifting heavy weights, doing too much intense housework, or sewing on an automated sewing machine (Shening-Parshina and Shibaeva 1967, 120, 142). This is not to say that a pregnant woman was to do no housework, but that she needed to abstain from the heavier work (family members are told to take on such chores). Shening-Parshina and Shibaeva (142) recommend that she should rest first when arriving home from work and only then begin housework. This advice certainly encapsulates a woman's double burden within Soviet Russian society, i.e., she was both a working professional and yet was largely responsible for the housework. Prenatal exercises were rare, despite Shening-Parshina and Shibaeva's (120, 138) recommendations for them (only two mothers who gave birth before the nineties said that they did any special exercises).

Because a woman's mental state could affect the child's well-being, they were told to avoid stress and disharmony as well. Tamara B. also noted the importance of these factors; expectant mothers "should be outside more … should get enough rest." Several mothers mentioned that their children's problems were connected to their own stress during pregnancy. Liuba S. did not have a place to live early in her first pregnancy, having just moved from Chita to Novosibirsk. She reported, "I cried a lot … maybe that is why my older girl is a little high strung." Elena B. expressed a similar opinion; her son was ill during her second pregnancy, and one doctor was convinced the fetus would get infected and be born disabled. As she says,

> I had lots of worries with my daughter…. Because it turned out that in the middle of the pregnancy I went to Leningrad to have my blood checked to see whether there was any infection and my husband's son from his first marriage died at about that time…. Now I think that the complications that my daughter has with her development were basically brought about by that.

The concern for the mother's peace of mind and its effect on the child continues into the delivery, as the doctor Evgenia Z. explains:

> When a woman goes into labor, I always say to her, that she should go into labor with joy…. One should not give a child life if the mother is crying or upset, because from the beginning there is a kind of feeling that when the woman has the proper attitude the delivery will end well both for the child and for the mother.

Shening-Parshina and Shibaeva (1967, 39) make similar recommendations to ease the pain of delivery: "It has long been known that from 7 to 14 percent of women in labor feel absolutely no pain during delivery. A great portion of these are women with a healthy, stable nervous system, and most importantly, these are women who await the birth of the child joyously and without fear." Fear and negative emotions may result not only in more pain during labor, but can also harm the child, so that positive feelings should be the goal for both the mother and those around her (Shening-Parshina and Shibaeva 43).

All gynecological clinics and *roddoms*, according to Shening-Parshina and Shibaeva (22), should establish pre- and post-natal classes, which were to be used to improve the "cultural hygiene" of pregnant women and new mothers. Cultural hygiene was based on proper scientific knowledge about the woman's body, behavior during pregnancy and delivery and care for the child. Some women who had children during this period did attend prenatal classes (eleven women did not have access to classes; three had classes on labor and delivery and two had classes on childcare). If there were no other serious health issues to consider, mothers had a four-month maternity leave (two months before birth and two months after). However, many mothers also used their vacation time or took unpaid leave after the maternity leave to be with their children. For example, Liuba P., who had her children in 1970 and 1978, explained how she managed her situation: "At work I had a two-month maternity leave before delivery, paid, two months paid after the delivery, for the third month I took my vacation also and I could be home until a year. Back then they didn't pay, now they pay. But you could stay home up to a year, your position was held, but without pay."

Once labor began, the family typically called an ambulance for transportation to the *roddom*. Both the mother and father traveled to the hospital in the ambulance.[4] Upon arrival, the woman was admitted by a nurse, who took her medical history and prepared her for delivery. The mother was asked to remove her clothes and any jewelry (which were given to her waiting husband, who then left). She then took a shower, was shaved and given an enema and a hospital gown and slippers. Many women described these admissions procedures as the worst part of the birth process. For example, Nadezhda P. said, "And there the terrible procedure when they did the enema before the birth itself is fixed in my mind most of all. Either it was at the wrong time, or it was during a contraction, but it was so painful, so difficult and I had never felt so bad." Lidia C. described her arrival at the *roddom* in similar terms:

> I gave birth two weeks early. So that I couldn't prepare anything. And I paid for that, I have to say. Because the worst recollection about labor was not how you give birth, but how they prepared you for delivery. When they shave you below with cold water and a rusty razor, that was torturous. That was the most nightmarish moment.

Once they learned of these requirements, women often prepared themselves before they got to the hospital, to spare the embarrassment of the admitting

---

[4] Only one mother in my informant pool was unmarried. Some other mothers did not go to the hospital with their husbands, but that was because the husband was not home at the time.

procedures, as Liuba P. did: "Yes, that time [the second birth] I was already wiser. I already sensed that my delivery was close. I did everything myself. At home. I arrived and everything was fine. I arrived, having prepped myself [shaved], they did an enema and I washed."

The *roddom* is divided into three *palaty* 'wards': *predrodovaia, rodovaia,* and *poslerodovaia* 'pre-birth, delivery, and post-birth'. There was also a separate children's ward, where the babies were kept after birth. Once admitted, a patient went into the *predrodovaia palata*. Present here were not only women in the early stages of labor, but those who had been admitted because of various complications with their pregnancies. The pre-birth ward was generally on the first floor of the three-story *roddom*, while delivery was on the top floor and post-birth on the second.[5] When a woman was in active labor, an obstetrician or nurse-midwife periodically checked her status and cervix dilation. My informants reported that they were free to walk during labor in the pre-birth ward as well as to consume food and water, if desired. These wards each had a separate role to play in the institution of proper "cultural hygiene" in women, according to Shening-Parshina and Shibaeva (1967, 47–48). It was essential for medical personnel to use both one-on-one consultations with their patients and the radio system in each *roddom* to present proper information on both pre- and post-natal behavior and childcare.

Once she was ready to deliver, a woman walked to the delivery area and got onto a delivery chair. While in the pre-birth wards the mother was free to move about (except during examinations), during delivery she was forced into one position in a Rachman bed, a type of delivery chair. The chair is configured so that her shoulders were slightly elevated and she was in sitting position with her feet in stirrups. Thus women did not give birth in an absolute reclining position as in the West, but the chair was still designed to maximize the medical personnel's comfort, and not the mother's. The doctor stood at the patient's shoulder,[6] while a nurse-midwife sat at the foot to receive the child. These positions also allowed for communication between the two medical specialists, because they could see each other. There were often a nurse and another nurse-midwife present, as well as a neonatalogist (beginning in the 1970s). In most cases, the delivery wards had from two to six chairs, so that several women could be in labor in the same space, which would necessarily entail more personnel in the room. The doctor on call might attend several deliveries at the same time, while a nurse-midwife was assigned to each birth. Unless there were complications, it was generally the nurse-midwife's

---

[5] All the *roddoma* I visited were three-story buildings, but some women described a different configuration, such that delivery was on the same floor as the pre-birth ward, while the post-birth ward was on another floor.

[6] If the doctor was present. In some cases the doctor had several patients in labor at the same time or would just stop by to check on the patient. If there were no complications, the midwives would attend the birth alone.

job to control the birth process. Tatiana K. described her midwife as, "extremely experienced, she controlled everything very carefully, how to behave oneself, what one should do, at what point." Nadezhda B. mentioned: "She helps, mainly with advice, how to behave properly, how to breathe properly, when you should inhale, when you should hold your breath, that is, she regulates all the woman's work during labor. She watches how the fetus is coming out, helps the woman." Natalia I., an obstetrician, concurs with these mothers' descriptions of the midwife's duties:

> The doctor examines the mother, if everything is normal, then only observation follows.... The nurse-midwife used to listen to the heartbeat [now performed by a fetal monitor], timed the contractions ... she must also examine, control ... she is directly instrumental in the birth of the head, the rest of the fetus's body, she ties off the umbilical cord.

Shening-Parshina and Shibaeva (1967, 124–25) echo these sentiments. In their advice to laboring mothers, they emphasize the naturalness of birth for women, the use of proper breathing techniques and pressure points to reduce pain, remaining calm and confident, and, above all, following each instruction given by the doctor and the midwife to the letter.

Intravenous drips, if given at all, usually were administered after the patient's arrival in the delivery room. In general, pain medication was only very rarely administered to women who delivered vaginally. Liuba P. noted: "We don't think it's acceptable to have medication for pain, the women themselves [do everything]."[7] Most of the women I interviewed (unless they had a cesarean section) delivered by means of what could be termed natural childbirth. The labor and delivery processes they described are consistent with those of the Lamaze method, including the breathing instructions from the midwife and the absence of analgesics or anesthesia.

After the child was born, the midwife would announce its gender[8] and show it to the mother. A nurse or neonatologist would take the baby, wash and swaddle it, weigh it, and perform any necessary treatments. The baby was then removed to the children's ward, while the mother stayed in the delivery room until she delivered the afterbirth and was stitched up, if neces-

---

[7] Of the informants' thirty-four births during this period, only seven women had pain medication. In at least three of the cases, it was administered because of an extended, difficult delivery. Pain medication was often given after delivery, however, while any tears were stitched up.

[8] A minority of women reported that they had to identify the sex of their child when (s)he was held up. They could not account for why this was the case, but Olga V. said it was "a very important moment."

sary (usually about an hour). Unlike before the delivery, she did not walk to the post-birth ward, but was transferred there on a gurney.

The woman was allowed to sleep for at least eight hours after giving birth (sometimes sleep was extended by the pain medication given after delivery). Generally within the first twenty-four hours, the nurses would bring the child, swaddled, for the mother to see (in cases of difficult births, mothers may have only seen their children after two or three days, either because the child needed treatment or because the mother was deemed to be too weak to feed it). Typically, as Shening-Parshina and Shibaeva note (1967, 125), the first feeding was twelve hours after delivery. They (126) reassure mothers who cannot see their children or feed them, due to medical complications, that the medical personnel will feed and care for them properly.

The regime in the post-birth ward was the same across the country. In the morning, the nurses brought the children for their first feedings of the day (they generally fed them every three to four hours, with the last feeding between ten p.m. and twelve a.m.). Shening-Parshina and Shibaeva describe the schedule as follows: "It is necessary to take into consideration that after delivery a woman needs a special schedule that takes account of her feelings and that her day has a fairly heavy load: it begins at 5:30 a.m. and ends at 12 midnight." At night the nurses would feed the babies from bottles using breast milk women had previously expressed. After the first feeding they had breakfast, and the doctors made daily rounds. There was a *tikhii chas* 'quiet hour' in the afternoon for naps.

Women were encouraged to get up as soon as possible after delivery (sometimes unavoidable because there was only one toilet per floor, and it was located down the hall) and to take regular walks around the ward during their stay in the hospital. Liudmila K. noted: "There is one toilet or one bath on the floor and many women stand in line to wash." Visitors were not allowed, but they might have had access to a telephone, so that they could talk with relatives. Most commonly, though, they communicated through open windows, so that the family's first view of the newborn was through a third-floor window. As Taisia V. said of her experience: "The birth ward here is a forbidden zone. No one was allowed in. It's strict. Only under the window. They'll come up to the window and take a look."

In the post-birth ward inexperienced mothers were given instructions in feeding the baby, expressing breast milk, and swaddling and diapering the child. Shening-Parshina and Shibaeva (1967, 45) place special emphasis on thorough training for the first feeding, because the child's health depends on proper breastfeeding techniques. They also state (47) that new mothers should have lessons on bathing, dressing, and swaddling a baby, but they practiced on a doll, not on the baby itself. First-time mothers who delivered vaginally stayed in the hospital from seven to ten days, while mothers who had children already stayed for five to seven days. Those who had had caesarean sections remained for at least ten days. Once the mother and child were released from the hospital, friends and family gathered to greet them in a ritual called the *vstrecha* 'meeting'. They brought clothes for both, because everything had been removed when the mother was admitted to the hospital. While the nurse dressed and swaddled the child, the mother got herself ready. She exited first, without the baby, and received flowers and congratulations from those assembled. The nurse brought out the child (wrapped with a pink ribbon for a girl and a blue ribbon for a boy) and gave it to the father for the first time. The father brought gifts for the medical personnel which he gave to the nurse, including flowers, chocolates, cakes, champagne, and even cash (some informants reported that it was customary to give more money for a boy than for a girl). The family left, in a hired car if they did not own one, and returned home for a brief celebration. While there may have been friends and colleagues from work at the *vstrecha*, they generally did not return to the house at this point. The family would get the child settled and then share a simple meal, with toasts to the child and to its parents. The child was generally isolated from additional contacts for the first month after being released from the hospital (discussed in more detail below) and then officially welcomed into society with a party for friends and family at the end of this period.

While it is perhaps odd to view a medical process as a ritual, in this book we will consider the prenatal periods and the delivery to be an inherent part of the rite. As such, we are going beyond what might normally be termed birth ritual, which often focuses only on christening rites or similar celebrations. However, this approach is consonant with the assumptions of practice theory with regard to ritual analysis. Bell (1997, 76) observes that "in contrast to the static view of structuralism, which tends to see human activity as a matter of enacting cultural rules, practice theory claims to take seriously the ways in which *human activities, as formal as a religious ritual or as casual as a midday stroll* [italics mine], are creative strategies by which human beings continually reproduce and reshape their social and cultural environments." On the basis of this theoretical approach, the entire birth process, from pregnancy through delivery to the post-natal period, is a candidate for study as ritual. In addition, Davis-Floyd (1992) has shown that medical birth displays ritual features, both symbolically and structurally. Structurally, as we would expect for a rite of passage, the ritual is divided into three parts: separation (entry into the *roddom*); transition, including the period in the maternity hospital and the month-long isolation period thereafter; and finally incorporation, when the child is welcomed by a formal celebration. Symbolically, it conveys messages about social roles, particularly parenthood, within the family and society and "completes" the child by making it human.

One important fact about birth is that the ritual acts are designed for both the parents and the child, who are undergoing two completely different transitions. That is, the child enters into life and must make that transition successfully; (s)he must be protected while in the vulnerable liminal phase and also must be properly welcomed to the community. In addition, the parents are entering a new phase of their lives. They needed to recognize the awesome responsibility they will face as they raise their child. This process begins not with the delivery or with baptism, but with the pregnancy itself. Thus these events indeed merit consideration as ritual acts that convey different messages about the social belief system to the parents and the community (and indeed to the child, even if (s)he does not yet register them). The participants use the ritual to create a new identity and to establish their family's role within the hierarchy of the social system. In the case of the rituals under consideration here, we must consider not only information from folk tradition, but Western and Soviet material as well.

Folk Material in the Soviet Birth Ritual

Much of the Soviet-era labor and delivery process was derived from Western medical practice, as we will discuss in more detail later in this chapter. Certainly many of the folk practices, such as birth alone in a non-sterile bathhouse, were lost, because they were in direct conflict with medical standards. However, some important behaviors have been inherited from the folk tradition. They include: the primacy of female professionals involved in obstetrics and gynecology; secrecy and the concern about the evil eye during pregnancy and delivery, with remnants of protective magic; isolation of the mother and child after birth; and community involvement. While professionals and parents may give medical reasons for their behavior, they reflect the common practice of groups to give "rational" reasons for folk beliefs. The medical personnel who devised the system, after all, were also products of folk tradition. If folk material does not contradict medical practice, then it can easily be adapted into medical birth, especially when it supports current scientific theory about hygiene.

Birth: The Province of Women

All told, an average of three doctors and three midwives supervised the pregnancy, delivery, and postpartum period in the Soviet Russian medical system. Therefore, roughly 210 doctors and midwives presided over the thirty-four births in this study that took place from 1954 to 1989. Of that group only five male obstetricians (2.3 percent) delivered a baby and only one male obstetrician (.47 percent) monitored a pregnancy. There were no male midwives, no male neonatologists, and no male doctors involved in postpartum checkups or house calls. All the doctors and midwives I interviewed were women. The doctors and midwives themselves noted that they were trained in overwhelmingly female groups as well; one obstetrician, Natalia R., said that she had primarily a male group, for which all the other groups envied her, because this was so unusual.

Most of my interviewees, whether medical professionals or mothers, expressed opinions that correlated to the traditional view that only women should be obstetrician-gynecologists or nurse-midwives. Regarding male gynecologists, Liuba P. stated:

> Yes, I somehow don't like male gynecologists, that's somehow unpleasant to me. I like men generally, but, you know, I wouldn't want gynecologists.... I understand that doctors are doctors, you don't need to care that this is a man, well, somehow I can't do it. Of course, they say that the best gynecological doctors are men, but I don't like it.... I trust women more.

While not every woman agreed (Olga V., for example, said that she felt no difference between the female and the male doctors who supervised her pregnancies), the general attitude among the mothers was that women were better suited for the field.

The medical personnel I interviewed disagreed on this point. On the one hand, Marina S., an obstetrician, argued,

> How can a person in general who has not given birth, not been pregnant ... even a woman sometimes has trouble imagining it if she hasn't given birth. Everything changed for me after my own deliveries.... How can a man, who hasn't given birth, not carried a child, make sense of anything?

On the other hand, some medical professionals expressed the opinion that men were better doctors. One midwife, Larisa S., thought that this perceived difference might exist precisely because men cannot give birth and thus have no preconceived ideas or experiences to interfere with their jobs. Two obstetricians, Natalia R. and Natalia I., said that men might be better doctors precisely because they are not limited professionally by giving birth to children and related family concerns.

Despite these minor disagreements, the folk belief that only women should attend births had played a major role in the development of the Soviet Russian medical system. Not only were most of the medical personnel involved in the process women, but the mothers preferred to be treated by women. The opinion that gynecology was "women's work" as expressed by the young male intern I interviewed, seems to have been influenced by folk attitudes about the suitability of women to serve in this capacity. This village belief survived and was adopted into the nascent Soviet medical system. The history of this development merits some comment, however. In her study of Russian women doctors in the late nineteenth century and the early Soviet period, Tuve (1984, 60) states that in 1869 a law was passed in Russia that allowed women to obtain training as medical midwives. This law was designed to reduce mortality rates for both mothers and children in Russian villages, where traditional midwives (*povitukhi*) still generally delivered children, even if doctors were available. By 1876 Russian women were studying all types of medicine (with the exception of "legal medicine and animal diseases" in St. Petersburg (Tuve 65). Tuve (107, 109) notes that medical courses for women were closed in 1887, despite their success, but that the trend for women of all walks of life to become doctors had been established by that time.

When the Bolsheviks assumed power, they sought to eliminate much of the "backwardness" associated with the tsarist period through social change (see chapter 1 for discussion). One of the primary problem areas they faced was public health. Solomon and Hutchinson (1990, xi) describe this process as follows:

> As early as June 1918 the outlines of Soviet public health policy began to emerge. In his report to the First All-Russian Congress of Soviet Medical-Sanitary Sections, N. A. Semashko, soon to become the RSFSR's first commissar of public health, declared that henceforth health care was to be free, accessible to all, and universal.... As part of the revolution, the Bolsheviks introduced a variety of progressive social programs that gave evidence of the high priority which the new regime placed on the prevention of disease. In July of the same year, the new approach to public health was given organizational form: the RSFSR Commissariat of Public Health (Narkomzdrav) was created for the express purpose of integrating, coordinating, and centralizing the delivery of health care.

However, they inherited from the tsarist regime an extreme shortage of doctors (Weissman 1990, 106). Davis (1990, 162–63) states that the number of doctors increased substantially in the period following the civil war; "much of the increment in medical staff was generated by the recruitment of women. The female share of health sector employment rose from 64.6 percent in 1929 to 70.2 percent in 1932." Ramer (1990, 137) remarks, like Tuve, that feminization of medicine had begun already in the pre-Soviet period, and that "the reason that young men in particular were not attracted to medical school was that they could attain a 'more decent existence' by going to technical schools."

This trend continued throughout the Soviet period as well. Despite the Soviet government's espousal of gender equality, certain work had been designated as feminine or masculine by 1930 (Goldman 2002, 163). As a result, Goldman (269, 283) cites statistics which demonstrate that women predominated in certain areas of industry (primarily light industry), agriculture, enlightenment (i.e., propaganda work), and health care and the service sector by 1935. This gendered attitude toward jobs did not disappear after Stalin's rule. Tuve (1984, 127) cites a study of Leningrad high school graduates in 1970 in which girls rate being a physician as the top profession, while boys only rank it as tenth. Ryan (1990) makes reference to research (quoting from El'shtein 1986) in the Rostov-on-Don Medical Institute in which "women are distinguished from men students 'by great application to work and by higher success rates.' Moreover, women scored higher in respect to those personality traits appropriate to a career in medicine: 'compassion, sympathy, consideration, responsiveness etc.' (The single exception is 'reticence')." Therefore, the feminization of the medical profession in (Soviet) Russia was based on several factors: 1) women were "naturally suited" for medicine in both the folk worldview of women as healers and in the Soviet worldview of women as "caring and nurturing"; 2) the Soviet commitment to gender equality opened the door for women to work in all fields, but certain jobs were established as more suitable for women, and official propaganda and even some laws pushed women into these professions; 3) medical professionals (and other service sector jobs) were paid less, so that men were reluctant to enter these professions. While the medical authorities did not limit the number of males who applied to the field, there were simply fewer men that wanted to enter this profession, despite the fact that the Soviet authorities tried to reverse the feminizing trend by allowing men to enter medical institutes with lower scores on entrance examinations (Ryan 1990, 42).

The predominance of women in this role is consonant with the traditional belief that women are best suited to deal with the transfer from one state to another, from one world to another. Adon'ieva (1998, 27) discusses how women served as mediators between the worlds of life and death in Russian culture. My own research on nineteenth-century Russian life-cycle rituals (2003, 22) shows that married women in particular, who had undergone initiation themselves when they married, were instrumental to successful transition in all three rites. While the people in this study may not express their attitudes in the same terms as those in pre-revolutionary villages, it is clear that they believed that women can conduct the ritual acts of childbirth more effectively. These professional women not only share common experiences with their patients, but also are perceived to be better suited emotionally to perform transitions for the mother and child. This attitude is also connected to the patriarchal system itself, which has had a profound influence on Russian family structure. Even today, mothers are generally most closely involved with child rearing (as the doctors themselves observed in their interviews). They also dominate in professions related to children, such as elementary and pre-school teachers, pediatricians, childcare workers, and the like. Certainly women in the West have traditionally occupied many of these positions as well. However, women in Russia were not limited to professions in education and childcare, but occupied a central position in village and urban medical practice. As Glickman observes, most village healers of all types were women, and although some men did serve as folk healers (albeit in the minority), they never acted as midwives (Glickman 1991,

149, 156). In the West medicine has traditionally been male-dominated in all areas of specialty, but in Russia the opposite was true. One could argue that Soviet ideals of equality between the sexes played a role in prompting women to become doctors. However, while the Soviet authorities did profess gender equality, it was rarely achieved. There were still "male" and "female" professions, even in the medical field itself. For example, more men were surgeons, the most prestigious of medical specialties. Thus we can conclude that traditional views about women as healers played an important role in the professions that women chose (or had chosen for them) during the Soviet period.

Secrecy and the Evil Eye

In the nineteenth-century village, pregnancy was a taboo subject, not only because of its connection to sexual behavior, but because discussing the pregnancy might result in harm to the mother or child through *sglaz*, the 'evil eye'. Clearly, close family members would know about the mother's state, but it was not openly discussed among themselves or with outsiders. As Tian-Shanskaia (1993, 9) notes, there were many euphemisms, such as "putting on weight," used to avoid direct reference to the topic. Similarly, in contemporary Russian, my informants mentioned that the word pregnant, *beremennaia*, was not typically used to refer to women but to animals. Russians continued to use euphemisms, such as *v polozhenii* 'in a condition', to discuss pregnancy. Indeed Katia K. replied that she did not talk about her pregnancy in 1970 openly before she had to go on maternity leave because

> in Soviet times it was considered to be a very intimate issue, it wasn't widely advertised, widely paraded, there was even a prejudice of a sort to try to let fewer people in on it. Because of superstitious notions that everything would be fine if fewer people knew. So that they wouldn't attract the evil eye.

Katia's response is typical of many of the women in my study. However, women's opinions range along a continuum. Not every woman has the same attitudes about the degree of secrecy required to ensure that a child would be born healthy. All eighteen mothers who gave birth during this period, except for one, immediately told their husbands and mothers (and in most cases their siblings) that they were expecting. Anna I. told neither her mother nor her husband. Her husband only discovered she was pregnant from a mutual acquaintance who was a doctor. Her mother was in another city, so that she did not trouble her until the child was born. Within the first three months pregnant women generally told close friends as well; some told right away, but others like Olga R. delayed:

I told gradually, not right away. There is a sort of omen so as not to attract the evil eye, maybe we don't recognize it, but it is somewhere deep inside.... Who knows how a pregnancy is going to go? I didn't feel like telling before time ... roughly speaking there was no desire to attract the evil eye.

Most informants concealed the pregnancy at work for as long as possible (although some had medical complications that made the pregnancy obvious). Two women, Katia K. and Elena S., concealed it until the seventh month, when it was time to go on maternity leave. They both said that the fashions of the time (billowy, loose dresses) effectively hid the pregnancy for that long. Others did not actively conceal it at work or school, but they did not talk about it directly either; Lidia C., for example, replied that "I didn't say anything until the fifth or sixth month, when it was already more or less obvious, but everyone knew." One woman, Nadezhda P., said that she never concealed her pregnancies and that she thought women who did so were foolish, because their condition was apparent due to physical changes.

In addition to some level of secrecy about the pregnancy, women took other protective measures similar to the magical protections used in the nineteenth-century village. For example, Krugliakova (2001, 225; 241ff.) notes that her informants reported that being frightened or knitting might perhaps harm the child in some way, a belief also recorded in previous centuries in villages. I also found that women tried to protect the child by not buying too much before birth. Only four women bought a significant number of things for the child before birth. Three of them did not share the superstition that buying things might potentially harm the child. The fourth gave birth in 1986, when most things had to be purchased with ration cards. In other words, the economic situation forced her to override any superstitions she may have had about purchasing goods for the baby before birth.

Those who did not buy items clearly connected it to protection for the child. Lena L. described the attitude as follows:

It is thought that one should not buy anything early, before birth. Children may not come to term or be stillborn. I bought, probably, a minimal set of swaddling cloths, a blanket, shirts, caps ... diapers. The tradition is to buy nothing big, you can buy everything in the first ten days, when the children are alive and healthy. But another thing exists also. Children should feel as though they are expected and prepared for. You have to prepare a little bit.

Lena L.'s comments might be seen as a practical approach to the situation, because she did not want to spend money unless the child was born healthy. However, other mothers made it clear that this practice was designed to protect the child. For example, Olga V. was even more strict than Lena L. in her interpretation of this practice:

> QUESTION: What did you buy before birth?
> ANSWER: Nothing.
> QUESTION: Absolutely?
> ANSWER: Absolutely.
> QUESTION: Why?
> ANSWER: It's a bad omen.
> QUESTION: What kind?
> ANSWER: I don't know if you have this omen or not, but it is thought to be bad if you buy things early for a child, the child may get sick or may even be stillborn. It is best not to do that.

Liuba S., who had recently become a grandmother, said that she bought things during her daughter's pregnancy, but hid them from the family, so that she would not curse the child.

As a result of this attitude, the concept of a baby shower was shocking to these women. When I asked Anna I., a woman who did actually buy everything she needed for the child before birth, about whether she had a shower like we do in the United States, she replied: "One cannot buy presents before birth, because the woman might not give birth, or might have a stillborn, or might have a miscarriage. You do it wrong [*Nepravil'no u vas*]." While presents for a child are expected, they only are given after the child is born healthy. As I have argued elsewhere (2003, 237–41), this practice could be connected to the desire for secrecy. That is, by buying goods for an unborn child, people learn about the pregnancy, which might result in harm to the baby. However, there is also another issue to consider. This practice may also be related to the traditional Russian fear that by doing or saying something positive about the future, one may cause bad things to happen. The typical response to such transgressions is to spit three times over the shoulder or to knock on wood. In the case of a pregnancy, the risk is so great that people do not tempt fate.[9]

Medical professionals also participate in these folk traditions for protection. One central aspect of the midwife's power, according to Belousova (1998, 25), is her ability to establish the fate of a child, both physically and

---

[9] I witnessed a good example of this attitude in the summer of 2004. There is a Russian superstition that it is bad luck to return to a place after one has left it. If forced to, one should look in the mirror before departing again. My pregnant friend had left a significant sum of her firm's money in the office by mistake and refused to return to the office, despite the risk of burglary. While she generally prefers not to return, I had seen her do so in the past (and look in the mirror). However, while she was pregnant, she would not take the risk at all, not even by letting me go in for her.

psychologically, like *povitukhi* in the Russian village before them. Both village and medical midwives had the duty of ensuring that the birth went well. The village midwife used a series of magical means to ensure that the child was born physically and emotionally healthy. Nurse-midwives and doctors relied on scientific knowledge, not on charms. Nevertheless, their medical judgments establish the "fate" of the child even today. Belousova argues that their descriptions of how a child reacted during and after delivery, e.g., "he cried right away," "he nurses well," "he is weak," or "sluggish," endure throughout a person's life, i.e., become part of the child's *dolia* 'lot.' As a child develops, parents and other adults attribute later complications or success to the same characteristics the medical personnel commented upon at birth.

Despite the fact that they are trained in modern approaches to health care, medical personnel have also adopted some traditional protective magic in labor and delivery. When a woman arrives at the *roddom*, she must remove all her clothing and jewelry. This requirement helps to maintain sterility, doctors argue. One might see the value of this practice in the case of cloth, which might indeed carry disease-bearing organisms. However, metal items are unlikely to cause infection. Rather, it appears that, as in the nineteenth century, there is a belief that women should not have anything tied or wrapped around them. Nor should they wear things that might kink. One mother told me that she happened to have a long braid when she arrived at the *roddom* to deliver her daughter. The intake nurse told her to unbraid it or the delivery would be harder. Similarly, the nurse-midwives I interviewed say that they have seen complications in delivery when a woman did not comply with these rules. Lidia S. reported, for example: "And somehow one woman had three rings on one hand and the umbilical cord had wrapped around three times." Her colleague Evgenia Z., an obstetrician, said that one woman wore a chain during birth that had been repaired and that the umbilical cord had a knot in it as well.

Belousova states (1998, 24) that medical professionals who know both the medical practice and folk traditions are the most highly respected. They have at their disposal a wider array of knowledge to protect the mother and child. While clearly these medical professionals would not rely only on folk knowledge, they will use it (if it does no harm) or even rely on it in the case of an emergency. For example, Lena L., the mother of twins, was having a difficult time delivering. Her sister, a general practitioner, had been allowed to stand in the doorway and watch the delivery. She told the doctor she would not allow her to remove the child with forceps for fear of trauma. Thus the doctor decided the use an old folk method:

Then two nurses came and using an old method, from our grandmothers, took a large sheet … pressed on my stomach, on its entire surface. And at that moment the doctor says, "you rest for a second now, we'll press now and you push at that moment" … and they

pushed on me with the sheets, and at that moment I pushed hard....
They pushed one more time, and my boy was born.

Thus both lay people and medical personnel used any means at their disposal, both scientific approaches and folk traditions, during pregnancy and
delivery. As we will see in our discussion below of the practice of isolating
the mother and child, those traditions that do not harm the child or directly
contravene established medical practice were not only embraced, but given
scientific, "rational" interpretations. In the case of the evil eye, the mothers,
even those in the intelligentsia (professors, for example), recognized the
superstition for what it was. Nevertheless, they also refrained from buying
things for a child, because it might pose a threat to the pregnancy, but also
perhaps because it was not a rational use of limited funds. Similarly, medical
personnel were aware of folk beliefs and made use of them. Their job, as they
saw it, was to ensure that the child was born healthy, and they used any
means at their disposal to achieve this goal. Thus, removing one's rings was
said to preserve sterility (a medical reason), but also to prevent choking of the
child with the umbilical cord (a folk reason). Ultimately, it did not matter
which reason was "true," only that mothers needed to observe the restrictions
that might threaten a safe delivery for themselves and their children.

Isolation of the Mother and Child

After a village birth in the nineteenth century, both the mother and child were
kept isolated for forty days. For the first few days, they generally remained in
the bathhouse where the mother had delivered. They then returned to the
home, but were not allowed interaction with those outside the family. After
that period had passed, the woman resumed her duties within the household,
and the family arranged for the christening party, during which the child was
presented to the community by the midwife.

Isolation was also the norm during the Soviet period within the urban
context. While medical personnel and mothers might first have said that it
was to protect the child from infection, not from the evil eye, both belief systems coexisted and, in fact, complemented each other. As in the village in the
previous century, urban Russian women in the twentieth century were isolated from everyone in their family and the community from a period of four
to ten days after birth (the average hospital stay for my informants was a
week). Even after some maternity hospitals established visitor rooms in the
1980s, women only had access to them before birth; that is, after they had
been admitted, but were not yet in active labor. During labor or after they had
delivered, they were not allowed to have visitors in the wards or to see them
in the visitor room.

After their release from the hospital, isolation continued until the child
was a month old. There were rarely visitors to the house during this period;

nor did many women want anyone outside the closest family to see the child. For example, Klara K. said: "At first we don't really let people see children. Either we cover them or we say that he is sleeping." Elena B. expressed a similar opinion: "We think that during the first month it isn't good to look at the child. When the child reaches a month, then acquaintances begin to visit." Even mothers who did not actively hide their children from others noted that they worried. Olga R. said that she if people came up to the carriage while she was out walking, then she thought to herself "only don't let them give him the evil eye." Some women also stated that they put pins in children's clothing when taking them out of the house to help ward off the evil eye. One exception to this rule was doctors and nurses or nurse-midwives, who generally visited once a week for the first month or so. While the child was not openly shown to people for the first month, daily walks with the child bundled up in a carriage were the norm.[10] Natalia T., for example, said:

> We have a superstition. It is thought that you should not praise a baby, that is, he is lying in the carriage, let him be. Because you are afraid to give him the evil eye. And these things really happen, that is black-eyed, dark women can look at the child and then the child cries for a long time. That happened to me, yes.[11]

Not every mother was concerned about showing the child after birth. Nadezhda P., for example, neither hid her pregnancy nor was afraid of showing her children to people after birth. However, most mothers and the medical personnel recognize that the first month is a vulnerable period for the child and try to protect it by limiting its access to the outside world. For this reason, doctors and nurses visit the home for the first month, and it is not until after that that a mother takes the child to the local clinic for regular checkups or treatment. Both the period of isolation and the fear of buying items before birth contribute to a great deal of community involvement in the post-partum period, because the mother stays with the baby, while others in the family mobilize to provide for them.

---

[10] Some women who delivered during particularly cold times of the year did not take the children out for walks until the temperature moderated. But they would wrap the child well and open the windows for a brief period every day, so that (s)he could have fresh air.

[11] There was disagreement about the physical characteristics of those who might cause the evil eye; some said dark-eyed people, others said those with light blue eyes were the most likely to cause the evil eye. It seemed to depend on what characteristics the informant herself did not have, i.e., light-eyed people blamed those with dark eyes and vice versa.

Community Involvement

The community involvement that is characteristic of the birth process also stems from multiple sources. The Soviet state was interested in the development of a collective society, one in which people relied on each other and shared burdens to achieve governmental and social goals for the common good. Bronfenbrenner (1970) discusses the issue of collective child rearing in the Soviet Union. He (8) states that this is the "distinctive feature of Russian upbringing, the readiness of other persons besides the child's own mother to step into a maternal role. This is true not only for relatives, but for complete strangers." However, such "collective" notions were also inherited from family patterns in pre-Soviet village life. The community (*mir*) was responsible for its members. Because mothers were often busy with farming chores outside the home in the nineteenth century, children were raised in extended families. In her study of urban families in the 1970s and 1980s, Shmelova (1989, 65) notes the retention of family unity and other traditional rural values related to finances, culture, and morality. For both reasons, it is not surprising that community involvement during pregnancy and after a child was born was a significant feature of the entire process.

The first indication of the importance of community involvement occurs during pregnancy itself, because families (and friends) often sacrificed to ensure that the pregnant woman had the proper nutrition and care needed to bear a healthy child. Particularly in times of shortages, others would give up their own food as well as stand in long lines and/or pull strings, so that a mother could have what she needed, as Tatiana K. reported:

> They try of course, when she is pregnant, then they try to go beyond the norm somehow, so that, well, they can create certain conditions for her, distinct from the conditions for other members of the family, they try then to buy her ... to limit yourself then in something, but then to buy her farmer's cheese, then to buy cheese, to buy fruits, which are very expensive for us, very with our salaries, well, they try, try to provide the woman with some kind of nutrition that is more or less valuable.

Other mothers also reported that their relatives went out of their way to get food that they thought was essential for them during pregnancy, particularly during times of shortages. They also brought food to their daughters in the *roddom*. Anna V., for example, remembers that her mother came to the window after her delivery and yelled: "Anechka [diminutive form], what kind of caviar do you want, black or red?" At the time, Anna reports, caviar was extremely difficult to obtain, so that her mother's question indicated how much she wanted to provide the best for her daughter, but also to celebrate the newborn in a fitting way. While not everyone received such luxurious food, families did make a concerted effort to provide good food for the new mothers, even when they were under the care of the state directly, because Soviet hospital food was not only unappetizing, but was nutritionally inadequate.

After the child was born, and before the mother and child were even released from the hospital, new mothers took on responsibility for each other's children as well. Women in the maternity wards were all required to express breast milk, which was used to feed other children whose mothers did not have enough milk. Marina L, describes this situation: "Other moms express milk, they disinfect it and feed the children." Other informants described making trips to the *roddom* after they were released to get milk for their children (as well as to the *molochnaia kukhnia* 'milk kitchen', which provided farmer's cheese, *kefir* 'a sort of buttermilk', and other dairy products for children during the Soviet period). Thus, each mother and the state itself were potentially responsible for children's care and well-being.

Community involvement continued when the mother and child were released. Belousova (1998, 25) argues that the presentation of the child by the nurse at the *vstrecha* parallels that of the village midwife at the christening party:

> In the modern maternity hospital there is also a custom of "buying" the infant; the father gives the children's nurse, who is carrying out the child, money, flowers, candy....This nurse is only a symbol of the maternity hospital.... The "buying" is a component of the birth ritual; it symbolizes thanks ... to the mediator, to the initiator for the performance of the ritual.

According to Belousova, the social contract between the *roddom* and the family is established during this ritual. Both mothers and doctors reported that they have formed lifelong connections with the children they deliver and with their parents. For example, Klara K. noted that she had wonderful relationships with her doctors and nurse-midwives. While the doctors are now mostly deceased (she had her children in 1966 and 1970), she still sees the nurses: "And the nurses who were young then, they remember my children and when I meet them on the street they always ask all about them." A neonatologist and two of her colleagues, nurse-midwives, remarked that they have excellent relationships with the women, and as a result, women try to walk with their children near the hospital, to see the people who helped them deliver. According to Vera S.: "Yesterday a woman came by, we went down to the cafeteria, she called the nurse-midwife only to show her the child. And recently a woman was being released, went up to the nurse-midwife with flowers, and said that the child was wonderful and that she would be back in four years." Just as the *povitukha* blessed the child at the christening, the midwives and doctors drink a toast to the child at the *vstrecha*. Lidia S. said that "it is customary to raise a glass to the newborn, they [the family] bring a bottle, and we drink it with all the relatives." The relationships these women describe are remarkably similar to those in the village; the bond between the midwife and family lasted as long as they lived.[12] Children she had delivered brought her presents yearly on *babin den'* (midwife day) and they were considered to be kin.

Rivkin-Fish (1997, 351–52) observes that doctors and midwives were glad to receive and share the gifts they got for delivering babies with their colleagues. Nevertheless, they were also insulted when people tried to give them gifts before the child was born. One could argue that this anger stemmed from a belief in the evil eye, and they may have feared that if they received gifts before the birth, the child might be harmed. Rather, it seems more likely that these doctors were insulted by the taint of bribery, as though without the gifts they would not perform at their best in the delivery room. The doctors, like the *povitukhi* before them, did not have the right to refuse to help and were honor-bound to fulfill their obligation to the community as a whole. These gift-giving rituals in the *roddoms* paralleled those in the village. The family and community at large publicly acknowledged the role the medical personnel played in the delivery of a healthy child and honored them for their contribution to society.[13] The obstetricians and midwives themselves recognize this responsibility. One midwife, Tatiana V., replied: "The birth of a child is the most responsible moment in our lives and we would like for the woman to remember the midwife and doctor her whole life." Vera S. emphasized the feeling of responsibility as well,

> And for us there is also a feeling of responsibility, this huge feeling of responsibility, after all the midwife answers for the life of both the mother and the child. And then there is also a feeling of agitation. And then the woman should retain a memory such that she would like to come to us in particular.

In the nineteenth century, the midwife may have lived with the family for anywhere from three days to a week and continued to visit until the child's

---

[12] I am not suggesting that each midwife and mother became the best of friends nor that there were not women who were disappointed with the quality of care as we will see below. However, if the birth experience was positive, the bonds formed between midwife (and indeed the *roddom*) and family paralleled those of the nineteenth-century village.

[13] Certainly an additional factor in the degree of responsibility is that family sizes were (and continue to be) small, typically one or two children, in the (former) Soviet Union, so that each child was much more precious. Due to the demographic crisis, obstetricians often tried to dissuade women from having abortions or were pleased, as my informants reported, when they told the doctor they intended to carry the child to term.

christening. While contemporary nurse-midwives did not live with the parents, they often made daily visits for the first week after the mother and baby were released from the hospital. They visited once weekly thereafter for the first month. These visits not only illustrate the desire to protect the infant in this early state of life, but also the role of the midwife as a representative of the community at large. She was an outsider who was nevertheless trusted during this dangerous period to ensure that the mother and child were thriving. Thus, *akusherki* 'midwives' and *medsestry* 'nurses' were not seen as threats, unlike other outsiders. Rather, they served as enforcers of proper childcare (within the Soviet model, of course, as representatives of the state) and as a source of support for the new mother.

One of the most important aspects of communal involvement with and responsibility for the child results from the superstition that one should not buy anything before the birth. While the mother and child were in the *roddom*, the family bought everything the child would need. As Olga V. described: "And while I was in the maternity hospital, then all my relatives snapped to and were stocking up urgently, they made the rounds, everything that's necessary." Tatiana K. stated that this system also helps the mother, because she is allowed to relax, while the husband is shopping: "So on the second day he wakes up and has to go to the store to buy up all the beds, carriages there ... that is to say, she has given birth, everything is fine, he goes and buys everything right away, diapers (or swaddling cloths), shirts there." She emphasized that the birth is the most important event in a family, next to a wedding, and it affects everyone:

> In a family this is a big event, so that everyone prepares. Well, and before the delivery usually lots of people or husbands take a vacation during the time when you take care of the child after the hospital, or grandmothers or some other close relatives ... whoever can ... take a vacation to help out there.

In general, the whole family became involved at this stage by providing items for the child. This practice shows the close connection between family members and the child, such that the entire group, and not just parents, was responsible for providing for and raising the child.[14] Childcare in general shows

---

[14] Community involvement in upbringing stretches beyond the immediate family. In point of fact, there is a general tendency in Russia for outsiders to tell a parent how to raise a child. Elvira S. noted how an American of her acquaintance was shocked by this behavior from a stranger, but how it seemed acceptable to her. In fact, this behavior is encouraged from the earliest age, so that at a gathering in July 2002, I heard the Russian mother of a three-year-old boy telling an unrelated six-year-old girl about how she was responsible for instructing her son. His mother explained, "After all you should teach him. You are bigger and know better. Tell him 'no, no' if he misbehaves."

the importance of community involvement not only in providing for the child after birth, but in raising and caring for it. Most of my informants either lived with their mother after birth or had their mother visit them for the first few months.[15] In addition, they often had an older family member care for the child when they returned to work after their maternity leave ended. Some women took advantage of the longer, unpaid leave after birth precisely because their mothers were not available to care for the child (either because they were not yet retired or due to the grandmothers' poor health).

The contemporary urban system of birth, like that of the village in the nineteenth century, was designed to foster communal responsibility for every child. Whether people were related to the child by blood or only by the accident of proximity, other adults (and, in fact, even children) must shoulder the burden of its upbringing. The *vstrecha*, shopping spree for baby goods and childcare arrangements publicly acknowledged the family's communal role from the beginning of the child's life. The participation of the midwife, friends and colleagues in these birth practices similarly represented the dedication of the larger community to the child's well-being.

Orthodox Tradition Preserved

While most of my informants were not active participants in the church during the Soviet period, baptism did occur in a minority of cases. Some people were (and remain) atheists or were either Muslim or Jewish, so that they would not have baptized their children in any case.[16] Of those that were believers, two admitted to baptizing their children secretly.[17] Taisia V., a Suzdal resident, said that she baptized her sons

> immediately after birth. Maybe a month had gone by or about three weeks. Well, how can you have a child that is not baptized? God save us, what might happen? You can't. I baptized my granddaughter Irina right away, even though it was forbidden. So we went to the Ivanovsky region to baptize them. Here everywhere they know, it is frightening, you can't. To the Ivanovsky region to some village. We

---

[15] Shlapentokh (1983, 193) notes that 41 percent of families had help from grandmothers in childcare and housework.

[16] The folklorist Larisa Fialkova (personal communication) and one of my Jewish informants both confirm that circumcision of male children was rarely practiced among the Jewish population during the Soviet period. Irina V. reported that it was in theory possible, but that the official stance made it difficult to perform the ritual. Elvira P. told me that it was still practiced among the Muslim population.

[17] Some women did not risk baptism at that point due to the official atheistic stance of the USSR and the risks associated with participating in a religious ritual. Many of them had their children (and themselves) baptized after the fall of the Soviet Union.

got stuck. The church was not functioning. We went to the F
house, we asked him. And we baptized them.

Similarly, Tatiana K. of Sergeev Posad reported that she also had secret
christenings:

> So we christened Serezha and kept it secret from everyone. Why? Be-
> cause everyone knows that in the country that was monitored, so we,
> you had to baptize secretly, because my grandmother wanted it, she
> was taking care of the baby, she was always a believer, and she
> thought that it was necessary. And now, now it's the reverse, it is
> spreading, absolutely everyone baptizes … it is all very formal, it is
> all in the church … as it should be. But for us in 1970, in 1974, and
> again in 1984, when Marina was born in 1974, either they tried to do it
> farther from home, so we baptized her in Moscow, it never produced
> any complications for us, no one would have to say anything to any-
> one there, didn't find out anything, so it all went off well, they are all
> baptized.

It might be significant that these informants are from smaller Russian
cities with a long-standing connection to the Orthodox church through their
local monasteries. As a result, they may have held onto the religious tradition
more closely than those in larger cities. However, Tatiana K. was not native to
Sergeev Posad, but moved there for work. In addition, it is noteworthy that
both mothers left the immediate area to baptize the children and did not rely
on local priests. In fact, Tatiana K. went to Moscow, not to some remote village, which shows that even in the heart of the Soviet state, its capital, religious tradition remained active for those that desired to participate. The ritual
specialists of the period used this fact as an argument for the creation of Soviet rituals to replace Orthodox ones. They recognized that baptism was still
fairly widespread even in urban areas, even if it was restricted to only two of
my informants (Rudnev 1979, 119; Ugrinovich 1975, 108). The Orthodox tradition and the folk traditions both survived (albeit in a limited and, in some
cases, reconstructed way) well into the twentieth century. They were often
combined in people's perceptions as well; folk behaviors that were unconnected to the church, at least in origin, were interpreted as part of the Russian
Orthodox heritage. While this attitude is less clear in birth, it will be obvious
in both the wedding and funeral rituals. For example, one Jewish informant
rejected certain wedding practices because they were "Orthodox," when in
fact they were Russian village traditions unconnected to the church in any
way.

Western and Soviet Elements in the Birth Ritual

We have seen that many Soviet-era medical practices were consonant with those in the village. Those that conformed to modern standards in particular were actually encouraged and incorporated into the medical model of pregnancy, labor and delivery. It was clear that the practical reasons for preventing infection and maintaining sterility were overlaid with traditional symbolic beliefs about the evil eye and isolation of the mother and child. Medical professionals themselves called on traditional as well as medical sources of knowledge during treatment. The model of health care adopted by the Soviet medical institutions, of course, was developed out of Western medical practice (see Carson Banks 1999 for a discussion of the development of birth practices in Europe and the United States). In her discussion of American birth practices during the period under consideration, Davis-Floyd (1992) argues that the medical model of birth conveyed the idea that institutions and technology are more important and powerful than families. The child is the result not of a natural process, but a product (in the industrial sense) of medical technology. The mother's body is not her own; she is a tool doctors use to obtain the product. Barney (2000, 83) discusses one example of this shift in the attitude toward birth as a community event to a medical one and concludes that, in the process, "women were convinced that subordination to a scientifically educated physician was the only way to protect the health of their families and communities." This attitude toward the body emerges from the longstanding philosophical debates on the opposition between humans and nature. Lakoff and Johnson (1999, 248–49) argue that the mind (and, I would contend, the body that houses it as well) is viewed metaphorically in the European (and American) intellectual tradition as a machine. Foucault (1984, 268) discusses this issue in his *History of Sexuality*, when he states that the "hysterization of women, which involved a thorough medicalization of their bodies and their sex, was carried out in the name of the responsibility they owed to the health of their children, the solidity of the family institution, and the safeguarding of society." Thus the body became a tool for the state and its institutions to produce a child to serve its interests.

While this conceptualization of the body and mind emerged from Western philosophy and practice, Soviet theorists built upon this model and strengthened it. Stites (1989, 151) discusses the "cult of the machine" in the Soviet Union. In an effort to create the ideal worker, humans (and their bodies) were conceived of as machinery. Natural human inclinations prompted by emotions and by physical needs had to be eliminated (Stites 1989, 153). Not surprisingly, the same attitudes surfaced in pregnancy and labor. Soviet medical professionals instituted a set of strict controls on the pregnant woman designed to produce a healthy child in the most efficient manner, such that a woman's body became most closely tied to the machine metaphor. Hyer (1996, 113) argues that the pregnancy was considered to be "productive or unproductive, depending on whether it ended in a miscarriage, abortion, or if the baby died during birth or while still being nursed. Mothers were described as producers (*proizvoditel'nitsy*). Producers came in two types—productive and unproductive." Issoupova (2000, 34) concurs in her study of maternity:

> As well as being concerned with the number of children women produced, the state was also interested in the quality of future generations. This implied that the state had an interest in the "protection" of women's bodies ... promoting healthy living ... active control of women's bodies. Such control was justified on the grounds that women's bodies were the incubators of the new generation of communists.

Note that I am not suggesting that European and American doctors do not also have their own models of the body as a machine as well as try to advise (and control) their patients. However, Soviet revolutionaries based their society on a fundamental belief in the power of science and on materialist explanations of the world (Stites 1989, 108; Timasheff 1946, 225). In addition, they were able to espouse this model from within the confines of a system that did not allow for patient choice. Women (if they had no contacts in the medical field) were treated by doctors assigned to their region. In comparable Western cities, if a patient is displeased, (s)he can find another doctor. In Soviet Russia, this was not an easy task. Mothers could not even pick the person who attended their labor. It was all determined by the luck of the draw, i.e., by whose shift it was when the woman actually delivered. Thus, while the Soviet process shared many surface features with Western medical practice,[18] they were overlaid on a different traditional system and were designed to foster the Soviet worldview. As a result, we cannot presume that the messages intended were either identical to those in Western Europe and the United States or that they were received in the same way. In fact, instead of fostering a reliance on the state and its institutions, in many cases they resulted in the opposite reaction from families, who relied on friends and family to survive and escape from the system itself.

---

[18] These include: shaving and administration of an enema, separation from one's spouse, replacing one's clothes with hospital gowns, amniotomy, fasting and control of liquid intake, examinations to determine the degree of cervical dilation, administration of labor stimulants, control over when and how to push, transfer to a delivery room for the actual birth, maintenance of sterility in the delivery room, and separation from the child, who is kept in a nursery while in the hospital. Episiotomy was rarer, as was administration of analgesics. Women were also required to walk to various places in the hospital, even in the final stages of labor, rather than be transported in a wheelchair.

The Manufacturing System

Not surprisingly, because Soviet ideology viewed the body as a machine and also glorified industrial processes devised by Americans such as Ford and Taylor (see Stites 1989, 146ff. for a discussion), medical procedures were also subject to the metaphor of the manufacturing process. There was a type of assembly-line control over the process of childbirth; each woman's body was seen as an object that must be controlled (by a representative of state institutions) to result in a healthy product. In order for this system to work, the Soviet medical establishment had to convince women, through "sanitary enlightenment," that the medical system was the only possible way to have a child safely. Shening-Parshina and Shibaeva devote a considerable amount of their work on obstetrics and gynecology to this end. For example, they (1967, 117) assert that the state's goals will be met only if a woman goes to the doctor regularly, so that she can receive the proper information about how to behave, e.g., internalize the message about her body as an object of state control. This message was first conveyed by the obstetrician who monitors the pregnancy. Doctors instituted stringent controls on the mothers' behavior during pregnancy, limiting weight gain to ten kilograms. While, as noted, European and American doctors also had (and have) norms for weight gain, diet, etc., the Soviet system was completely standardized. There was no consideration of variables. If a woman exceeded the ten-kilogram limit, she was put on a diet, regardless of the health of the fetus or her own physical status.

Doctors, as Rivkin-Fish (2005, 21–22) argues, were governmental representatives, and thus patients questioned the rationale of doctors' advice, given that they had some concerns about the state's aims for their citizens as a whole. However, the doctors themselves, while they may have resented the system, constantly strove to control their patients to ensure that the child would be born healthy. Rivkin-Fish (2005, 60) records doctors' assertions that Soviet Russian women were used to being told what to do and that doctors gave them orders as a result. Belousova (1999) reports that the physicians monitoring the pregnancy used threats, orders, and invective to control their patients' food intake, sexual behavior, exercise regimen, and hygiene practices. She claims that doctors and nurse-midwives functioned as a bridge between nature and culture. As a result, they controlled the natural processes as much as possible and imposed normative cultural meanings upon birth and the child that resulted from it. One of the primary messages was that the state itself "owned" its citizens and could control all aspects of their lives, as the birth procedures described above suggest. People, of course, did not completely accept this message, and both openly and subversively resisted it by ignoring doctors' advice, by using whatever pull they had to undermine the system, and by relying on the family more than on the state.

The manufacturing analogy becomes even more obvious if several women were in labor together in the pre-birth wards. Doctors or midwives could check the patients on a regulated schedule of rounds, moving from bed to bed as if in a mass production system. The transfer to the delivery room was similar to the next stage in the product's preparation, like a car moving along an assembly line. In fact, two women actually used this analogy when discussing their experiences in the *roddom*. Liudmila K., who gave birth in 1986 and 1988, said: "You understood that it was like a conveyor belt. You, a second person, a third, it's as though it is an impersonal condition, I always felt that." Lidia C., who had her children in 1976 and 1985, conveyed her sentiments using the same expression: "We felt like we were on a conveyor belt." Davis-Floyd contends (1992, 81) that medical procedures designed to regularize labor and delivery convey the idea that the institution is more powerful than the individual or the family. This message was particularly relevant in the Soviet Union. The children being born in these hospitals represented the future of the socialist state. As Rivkin-Fish (2005, 14) notes, the medical system was "put ... to work for the goal of strengthening traditional families." It was not a neutral system subject only to science, it was also subject to socialist ideology. Babies and their parents had to be indoctrinated into the idea that children did not belong primarily to the family, but to the state and its representatives. For this reason, the woman and child were separated from their families and became, in effect, the property of the state while in the maternity hospital. Similarly, for this reason medical personnel visited the home after birth, to ensure that the family was maintaining proper standards according to Soviet medical norms of childcare. Thus, Soviet ideology combined with the folk tradition of community involvement in this practice. The complexity of the rituals under consideration is that in many cases there are potentially multiple sources for the behavior that intertwine and in some cases, conflict. Visits by medical personnel may be a comfort for a new mother, but also may be an intrusion by state representatives into private familial space. In fact, it may be interpreted by the family in both ways, depending on the medical professional's behavior during the visit.

Because Soviet doctors viewed birth as a manufacturing process that could be controlled and timed, if it was not convenient for the doctors to have a patient deliver at a particular time they could actually change the "production" schedule, e.g., interfere in the delivery to speed it up or to retard it. For example, Lena L.'s labor was not progressing according to the doctors' wishes, so that they took action: "They weren't pleased with the intensity of the contractions ... parallel with when I woke up, they introduced a stimulant. Because my contractions weren't getting stronger ... and apparently they began to stimulate me. I only found that out later." Then an entire contingent of medical personnel came to give her a cervical exam. As she described it:

> The head of the medical division really examined me intensively, it seemed to me that she did that on purpose, and the waters broke.... Once again they started measuring my contractions, the contractions

were maybe a little stronger. I can't say that I felt like going and giving birth … the obstetrician said to me, "Lena, go into the delivery room, it is time to start."

Not unexpectedly, because it appears that Lena had not been ready to deliver, she had a tough time giving birth to her twins. They had to use yet another artificial means to deliver them, wrapping her in a sheet and pushing them out (described above). Her sister, a doctor, said that by breaking the waters, they were forced into a situation where they had to deliver the children, no matter the circumstances. A similar situation occurred with Olga V. after the birth of her first child:

The first time, because it was the middle of the night, they did not feel like taking care of them [the tears she had suffered as a result of delivery] and they left me lying on that gurney in the hallway until morning and only when a new doctor came in the morning did they take me into the operating room and give me anesthesia and sew up all those rips, the tears that had happened.

In these cases, a natural process was converted into a technological production that could be performed at a time that was convenient to the institution according to its schedule, regardless of the patient's actual physical condition.

A similar scenario occurred after delivery; the baby was removed to the children's ward and the mother to the post-birth wards with their regimented schedules. Mothers were at the mercy of medical personnel, who only brought the children to feed every three hours, regardless of whether the child was awake or was even hungry at that point. One mother said that she was not able to feed her son for days, because he was always asleep when they brought him, which caused her a great deal of anxiety, as one would expect. The strict regimen was to continue after release from the hospital. Shening-Parshina and Shibaeva (1967, 128) describe this schedule: "at home feed the child seven times every day, every three hours from six a.m. to twelve midnight." If the child oversleeps a feeding, it is the mother's duty to wake it up, so that the child not only keeps to the schedule, but also so that the mother is free to do essential household chores and rest herself at regular intervals. It is of utmost importance that the mother not feed the child after midnight, so that she (and the child) get the requisite six hours of sleep, necessary for the child's development and for the mother herself, as exhaustion and stress lead to a loss of breast milk. Other recommendations include feeding out of only one breast at each feeding; giving the child boiled water out of a spoon, if (s)he does wake at night, and not a bottle or pacifier; having the child sleep in its own bed; and expressing milk not only to keep an adequate milk supply, but also to make sure that any "old" milk is removed from the breast before the child's next feeding.[19]

Women who had difficult deliveries or caesarean sections often did not see their children for two or three days.[20] In Natalia Z.'s case, she had been in labor for twenty-four hours when the doctor decided that she needed to stimulate labor; nurses began to give her shots (she counted up to twenty and then lost count) to no avail. Then the doctor decided to break her waters, but that also did not intensify labor as expected. By this time, that doctor had gone off duty, and no one recalled that her waters had been broken until fourteen hours later. They then rushed her in for an emergency caesarean section. Afterward, they did not change her bandages, and the wound became infected, so that for three weeks she only saw her son through a window, because the doctors were afraid her infection would spread to the child. This situation, admittedly the worst of all the accounts I gathered, was the direct result of the manufacturing attitude toward birth. The doctors tried to force the body to conform to their rational schedules, with disastrous consequences, as it turned out. In post-birth wards, the medical personnel and the institution had ultimate control. They could withhold the child, if desired, rather like a superior can withhold employee rewards. For this reason, none of these women fed their children at night, because the nurses only brought the children for a final feeding between ten p.m. and midnight. Thereafter, i.e., between midnight and breakfast, the child was perceived to be the "property" of the hospital. By these means, they could control the mother and keep her (and her child) on their "production" schedule.

Once again, I reiterate that I am not arguing that women who delivered in Western hospitals during this period would not have similar complaints (and many do, as Davis-Floyd's research shows). The difference, as I see it, is the lack of options for most women and the fact that every doctor was part of the socialist system.[21] The physicians thus were not viewed as impartial figures trying to help (even if in fact they were) the mother and child, but instead carried with them the baggage of Soviet ideology about families. As state repre-

---

[19] This description is markedly similar to the breastfeeding policies of the medical system under Mussolini's pro-natal Fascist regime, policies which persist to this day in Italy; see Whitaker (2000). The author ties these behaviors not only to the attempt to reduce infant mortality, but also the government's desire to control citizens and to support traditional family values, all goals that Soviet Russia espoused as well. Ironically, the schedule actually results in a reduction in breast milk.

[20] Certainly in some cases there were medical reasons for the delay, e.g., the child or mother had to be treated. However, many mothers said that they could not see the child even if both were fine.

[21] Rivkin-Fish (2005, 9) also discusses this issue and the conflict in the doctors themselves, who saw themselves as outside (and at odds with) the system and were hurt when patients did not trust them.

sentatives, they were associated with the difficulties of dealing with Soviet institutions and bureaucracy in daily life. One of the most common responses to the stories about labor and delivery among Russians is that "they were just more of the *khamstvo* 'boorishness' we had to undergo in the Soviet system." Shlapentokh (1984, 2) observes that such treatment by representatives of the system ultimately promoted the focus on the individual and one's private life even more, such that personal interests could predominate over state ideology and institutions. While the Soviet government wanted to strengthen the family for a variety of social purposes, it also ironically could not prevent the family from becoming a refuge against state institutions in reaction to the institutional conditions patients and their families experienced. Shening-Parshina and Shibaeva recognize this dilemma, just as the ritual specialists cited in chapter 1 did. They (1967, 50) lament that, while they can dominate and influence the mother, medical professionals have little real control over the family itself. Nevertheless, they should attempt at all possible opportunities during pregnancy and after delivery to convey proper medical values to them via posters, exhibits, one-on-one conversations, lectures, and brochures/letters addressed to the father and to other relatives.

Science versus Nature

As noted above, the view of labor and delivery as a manufacturing process stems from the inherent conflict between science and nature in the philosophical tradition. From its inception, the Soviet Union and its leaders held science in the highest possible esteem. Scientific advancement was a significant measure of the USSR's ability to match up to the West (and to distance itself from its backward past). Although the birth procedure described above is actually less technological than in the West (less sophisticated equipment being available), it nonetheless mimics much of the Western desire for control of nature by technology. In theory, the underlying Soviet assumption (one also experienced by women in the American context (see Davis-Floyd 1992 or Michaelson 1998 for a discussion of these issues) was that any anomalous process including birth can be predicted and controlled through scientific knowledge. Accordingly, Russian doctors used techniques identical to American ones— precise measurement of the cervix to indicate when it was time to deliver, maintaining sterility to protect from infection, and the same preparatory procedures. Beyond that, they even instituted some scientific norms not found in the West, including additional guidelines on nutrition and weight gain during the pregnancy and total isolation of the mother and child after birth.

Throughout, however, the medical personnel, not the mothers, were the prime movers in the process. For example, in Lena L.'s case, the doctors did not consult with her about whether she was ready to deliver. While it is certainly possible that her twins were in distress, these complications seemingly arose from the doctor's own actions in breaking the waters. Most mothers characterized the midwife as the controller of the delivery process. She told the mothers when they could move, how to breathe, what to do at every stage, and her authority was not to be challenged. As Tatiana K. put it: "She regulates all the work of the woman during labor completely." Nadezhda B. expressed a similar sentiment: "She helps, mainly with advice, how to behave oneself, how to breath properly, when it is better to inhale, when it is better to hold one's breath, that is, she regulated all the woman's work in labor."

Medical personnel also conveyed the message that the woman's body, a natural entity, was defective and weak and potentially at odds with scientific rationality and order, too capricious and unpredictable. Taisia V. reported that her midwife was disappointed in her efforts: "And then they put me on the table, but the baby just wouldn't come out. And then someone, either the nurse or the doctor said, 'oh, how weak she is.' I still remember that." One woman reported that her friend, who gave birth in Moscow in the 1950s, was furious when the *akusherka*, who was displeased that she could not push hard enough, screamed: "You are a freak, not a woman." In response, she got angry and furiously pushed out the child. She was then amused when the same midwife walked to the woman in the next bed and said: "See how well she delivered, and you just can't, you are a freak, not a woman." However, there is also a great deal of material that sends a different message about the body's strength and level of endurance. Women were expected to walk from place to place in the hospital, not to be transported in wheelchairs (except after birth, when they were transferred to the post-birth ward on a gurney). All the women said that when it was time to deliver, they walked from the pre-birth ward to the delivery room, which could require going upstairs. Medical personnel wanted them to be active and walking soon after birth, typically within eight hours (except in the case of caesarean sections). They were expected to be able to endure the pain of childbirth without screaming (if they screamed, they were scolded, because it could have had an adverse effect on the baby, both physically and mentally, according to midwives). In other words, they were seen simultaneously as capable, powerful beings and as weak and fragile.

This image of the female body, I argue, stems from folk belief and is one piece of evidence of the conflict between an attitude developed from the upper-class Western European view and the Russian peasant one. Women in the village were expected to perform physical labor in the fields; they were chosen as brides due to their robust body type, which could withstand famine and also endure pregnancy. This attitude toward women survives today in Russia. As the popular Russian films *Adam's Rib* (1990) and *Moscow Does Not Believe in Tears* (1980) show, Russian women are perceived as a people able to overcome severe hardships, to experience both physical and emotional pain and to survive, even to thrive, under these conditions. However, Western ideals of woman as "fragile creatures" also entered into the equation. Thus, mothers were expected to be powerful in the "Russian" way (some doctors even refer to how much stronger women were in the past). Nevertheless, it is not surprising that they also "broke" under the pressure, at which point they were subject to scolding by the midwives, essentially for being too weak, a conception derived from the Western scientific and cultural models of the woman's body.

On the other hand, if they were not able to cope with the pain or did not follow orders (e.g., if nature overcame their "rational" scientific side), medical personnel scolded them for their failures. Nadezhda P. reported that her son was delayed in the birth canal for several hours, because the doctors would not allow her to push, fearing damage to her heart. They finally decided to perform a caesarean section, but the child had suffered from his arduous birth, with the result that he was high-strung and cried a lot, and it was difficult to settle him for feedings. When other mothers complained about his persistent crying, Nadezhda P. was shifted to another ward. Then a pediatrician came to see her to discuss the child's problems: "The pediatrician came to me and said that if my child were more peaceful—what's more in such a tone—that he would long ago have gained weight. What does that have to do with me, am I really to blame that he is like this? I haven't yet had a chance to train him." Belousova (2003, 345) reports similar attacks on women for their bodies' failure to respond "properly." These attitudes emerge not only from the idea that birth is a manufacturing process, but also from the notion that science and reason should be able to control natural processes. Indeed, the medical personnel also emphasize that one's body needs to be controlled after birth. Lidia S., a midwife, discussed limitations on sexual intercourse, not getting overstressed, walking a lot, not smoking, eating well, in general "to lead a healthy life." These, of course, are eminently reasonable steps to take after birth and while nursing. However, women who did not follow the instructions were seen to have somehow "failed," to have put the child (the future of the Soviet state) at risk, and are scolded accordingly. Shening-Parshina and Shibaeva (1967, 26, 28) argue that it was essential to appeal to the mother's natural instinct to protect her child by citing scientific evidence and giving examples of women who did not behave properly and how they (or their children) suffered as a result.

Doctors and midwives then had at their disposal two sets of beliefs, one that emerged from the folk tradition and one from the medical tradition. They could use either to their advantage to ensure their control over the process. This "dual" belief system began to operate during the pregnancy, as Belousova (1999) has shown, and continued throughout the delivery and postpartum period, as my data illustrate. Control and power were recurring themes throughout the birth process in Soviet Russia. The fact that the women were essentially kept powerless corresponds to Turner and van Gennep's observation that in many societies around the world rites of passage involve ritual and institutionalized humiliation for those involved in the process. However, the source of the need for power was also related to the phenomenon of egalitarianism characteristic of Soviet society.

Egalitarianism and Power

Turner (1969, 193) notes that strict hierarchies in rituals often occur when the society itself is characterized by egalitarianism. All of the doctors described in this study were trained within a Soviet worldview that encouraged leveling of social differences. Rivkin-Fish (1997, 271) concludes that the doctors and midwives themselves felt powerless within the medical institutions where they worked and resented the lack of respect directed at them in everyday situations both from superiors and from patients. Thus, whenever possible, they asserted their control over the process and as a consequence denigrated their patients. The medical personnel were faced with a situation in which they did not feel validated for their efforts and were themselves victims of what they called "the system," which they could not really change (Rivkin-Fish 2005, 22, 28). They also were reacting to the fact that their patients ignored their advice, in some cases to the mothers' detriment (Rivkin-Fish 2005, 131). Therefore, they tried as much as possible to dominate patients, both by trying to convince the mothers that their doctors and midwives were outside of the system and by taking advantage of the status the state accorded them.

As discussed above, doctors were not viewed as objective figures within the Soviet Russian system, but were in fact figures representing state and institutional authority (Rivkin-Fish 1997, 241). Rivkin-Fish notes (1997, 243) that "medical discourse became intertwined with moral reprimands … doctors' communication with patients aims to construct a world of rigid hierarchy and overt subordination." The linguistic forms the physicians used varied between a hostile, highly formal register of rapid-fire, medical questions and highly informal discourse including diminutives and endearments. These linguistic techniques showed that the doctor was in a position higher than the patient. This behavior was one indication that the process was designed to assert the patient's lack of agency and result in ritual abasement. Both Rivkin-Fish's and my informants discussed such feelings. Liuba S. reported that:

> The fact is that it turns out there that you transfer to other doctors. Before that [the delivery] you go to your gynecologist and she treats you like an individual, as a woman. And then you constantly go to the doctor who treats the child, a pediatrician takes care of them…. You rarely go to the first doctor, and then the gynecologist is interested in you for a while, you are pregnant. And later on you go, when you have to get an abortion, to have something checked out, to get something treated, you have fulfilled your function as a woman [by

having a baby] and they already look at you there without any special interest.

While Liuba is describing the attitude of doctors during and after pregnancy, other informants cited problems with relations between medical personnel and patients in the *roddom*. Liudmila K., for example, said that:

> I didn't have any desire to give birth, because I was already falling asleep. I lay down on that table, everything was cold, terrible, you lie unclothed, it's very uncomfortable. No one said any tender words, no one comforts you. There is a feeling that everything is bad, that something awful is happening. At one point they understood that there were no contractions, my birth process had completely subsided. They said that they had to push the baby out. And I remember that a male doctor came, he, they tied a towel around my stomach and began to simply push him out of me. And the baby had a trauma to his skull, he was suffocated, that is he had asphyxia, a hematoma, thanks to my weak labor. True, they tried to give me an IV, so that I would get some vitamins, but I didn't care. I felt bad, as though you have fallen under a train, but no way are you expecting a child. And a lot was riding on my attitude, I needed some support, help and comfort then. I could cope now. Back then it was the first time from inexperience, and there was this feeling that everyone was somehow behaving badly and you were really alone.

This description is also striking for her assertion that her body had failed somehow; the doctors told her that the child's problems were her fault, not theirs, and she accepted this diagnosis.

Anna V. gave birth in 1982 in Krasnodar, under the care of an experienced midwife, whom the family had paid before the delivery to attend the labor. Because the midwife was not on duty the night Anna went into labor, Anna's father went and fetched her. However, even this arrangement was no guarantee that she would not be subject to the same humiliation as women who did not have such influence, as she discovered. Another doctor, who came to stitch her up after the delivery, told her: "I can give you [informal pronoun] some anesthesia, but I won't." This situation is a clear illustration of the way power could be abused by medical personnel, who in this case not only used language designed to show the patient's inferior status (the informal pronoun), but who also refused to ease the patient's pain to show dominance. Natalia T. expressed similar negative feelings about the medical personnel in the *roddom*:

> It's [the delivery room] nearby, you don't have to be wheeled anywhere, there right next door is the room, I myself somehow walked

there, because I got up onto that high table in a very clumsy fashion. The midwife also yelled at me. I didn't climb up there the right way, she said to me that I am not climbing onto a stove. I didn't understand anymore, because I had such pains and it was all the same to me how I climbed up.

She went on to describe the ward in the hospital in Nizhnii Novgorod where she gave birth to her first child:

And then in the ward there were about ten people, if not more. It was a huge room and there were either ten or sixteen mothers there. It was not very pleasant, especially because I had problems with my milk.… You had to do the correct motions, and a doctor or a midwife or a specialist should have done it. But no one helped me at all.… When they released me, people always came to help here, acquaintances, relatives, friends of friends, they were giving me advice from folk medicine, folk methods, because mastitis was starting, I put all kinds of leaves on, I remember that I steamed plantain.

Shening-Parshina and Shibaeva recognize that such behavior was an issue within their profession and institutions. They (1967, 43, 45, 49) admonish medical personnel, from intake nurses to doctors, to recognize that women need to be treated sensitively and given clear and specific information in order for the process to end in a healthy child and a happy mother. The training for breastfeeding was particularly important, because the child's health depends upon its success. Clearly, however, medical professionals did not always take official recommendations to heart. In general, Natalia T. said that what was missing for her in the *roddom* was medical personnel who were *druzheliubnye i dobrye* 'friendly and kind'. Liuba S. said that those who treated her "are not sympathetic to women. Those people that dealt with me, they somehow do not have much sympathy, because with a little more attention on their side, a person would come out healthy" (she had multiple tears that she attributed to their inattention). In these cases, the mothers were either scolded for their failures or simply ignored, despite complications. The doctors were asserting their power over them, to treat or not to treat them, to admonish or not to admonish them, to pass blame to them or not take responsibility for problems themselves, as the whim struck them.

That is not to say that every woman in my informant pool had a bad experience with Soviet obstetrics. Some were lucky in their doctors or in their physical reactions; for example, women like Lidia C., who said she bore pain well and thus did not scream and upset the midwives, or Elena B., who said that she followed their orders, because she is *poslushnaia* 'obedient', so that they were not ill-disposed to her. Better relations could also be established through frequent visits to the *roddom* (because of complications, as Klara K.

reported), thereby establishing a personal relationship, or through *blat*, that is
connections to the doctor outside of the hospital. Olga R. was fortunate to
have an acquaintance who worked in the *roddom* where she delivered; she
needed to pull strings to deliver there, because it was outside of her region:

> I would say that they [relations between doctors and patients] were in
> some way colorless, very ordinary. Not like in the women's clinic
> [where pregnancies are monitored].... Only this acquaintance was
> better disposed and there were warm relations with her, although
> maybe this is a trait of all midwives, mothers complain about them
> that they are rude. What's more, during delivery. They yell. But
> maybe that is how it should be done, because you have to force the
> woman to work, because every second is precious and maybe here
> even you also have to force her to mobilize somehow and maybe it's
> not rudeness, but commands. Maybe that is good even, I don't know.
> This midwife was better disposed toward me only because we are ac-
> quainted. But once they said that she screams at poor women. But
> that didn't happen to me.

Women without such connections were at the mercy of the system, a system
that seems designed to impress upon them their inferiority in the relationship.

In admittance interviews to the *roddom*, a woman was treated alternately
as an abstract medical case, with the doctor distant and cold, and then as a
child, spoken to in language associated with those either subordinate or dear-
est to the speakers. Patients became disconcerted, because they did not know
what to expect from one moment to the next. Rivkin-Fish (1997, 245ff.) notes
that one woman was referred to as *moia khoroshaia* 'my pretty one' in one sen-
tence and then was subjected to a series of questions designed to show her
woeful state of preparedness for pregnancy and motherhood, which resulted
in a verbal attack by the doctor. A similar situation came up in one of my
informants' retelling of her conversation with the doctor about her physical
situation. Natasha M., a nineteen-year-old first-time mother, had thought she
was in labor the night before; they told her she was not, to go to sleep. When
she woke up, she felt that her waters seemed to have broken, but she was
frightened to approach the doctors then, after being scolded before. When the
doctors came for daily rounds, they asked about her condition. First, the doctor referred to her by her last name, an impersonal technique designed to
show her authority: "Where is Medvedeva?"[22] Then, when Natasha admitted
that she had concealed some developments, the doctor switched to the informal register: "What is wrong with you [*ty*-informal pronoun]? Quickly, to my
office!" These linguistic forms may indicate affection, but also superiority, as
though the doctor were speaking to a child. In fact, the semantic content of

---

[22] Medvedeva is a pseudonym.

the phrases containing the informal pronoun indeed suggests that the doctor believes the woman has behaved foolishly. While some women were able to overcome this imbalance in power and foster warmer, more equitable relations (typically after difficult pregnancies and deliveries, which allowed for more prolonged interaction with doctors), most women felt the distance between them and the medical personnel. Olga R. reported that when a doctor came to visit her home after she was released, she was the first medical professional to actually say anything nice: "The next day the doctor herself came, a children's doctor, a pediatrician who was supposed to treat him. She came the very next day. She liked him. Those were the first nice words that I heard from the people who delivered my child. She looked and said that he was a *bogatyr* [epic hero]." It is significant that these words came outside of the hospital itself; that is, in the mother's home the doctor was free to create a social bond that had not been not possible in the official institution, where power relations were maintained much more strictly to preserve social and ritual hierarchies.

In one case Rivkin-Fish (1997, 250) describes how after one doctor berated a woman for not preparing properly for the pregnancy; the two doctors present at the interview proceeded to discuss her ignorance of her condition as though she was not even in the room. Not surprisingly, the woman was abashed as a result of this treatment and could or would not answer the doctors' questions, which resulted in more denigration. Women, it seems, could not win. If they found out too much about their pregnancies from books or other sources, the doctors attacked them for acting "superior" and trying to usurp medical power. Nevertheless, if they appeared ignorant, they were admonished for that as well. Thus, in the case of this patient, one doctor asked:

"Have you read any books?"
 "No."
 "Good going (sarcastically)."
 The other doctor interceded.
 "There is stuff all over the place, as much as you want, just go and find it. You do not even have a desire. You got pregnant, what are you thinking? How are you preparing for the birth? You need to know how the pregnancy progresses… It is your pregnancy, and this should interest every woman."

When the woman then volunteered information about the pregnancy, showing some measure of knowledge, her doctor responded that she did not understand the process properly:

"Last week there was a lot of movement, now it is stopped and I got scared…"

"At twenty weeks you cannot hear anything, you cannot hear the fetus's heart…"

"I myself can feel the movements…"

"No, your aorta is so strong, the beat goes through your whole body."

The interviews cited by Rivkin-Fish (1997, 2005) to illustrate the power structure between the patients and doctors are but one indication of the ritual debasement that these women underwent. The interactions with medical personnel resulted in the message that mothers were part of a process that was controlled by the state institution and medical science. This message was also evident in the treatment women experienced in the hospitals, from the difficult admittance procedures to the post-birth wards, as Liudmila K. explained:

Where I delivered, it is a very old building, there is one toilet or one bathroom per floor, and many women stand in line to wash. They stand right there in the corridor and wait. Plus they didn't give us underwear, there wasn't any, it was thought to be unhygienic, and there were these diapers, and you are holding a diaper. Now it is just terrible to think about it. It is uncomfortable without underwear, why? Everything has to be gloomy there for some reason. And a woman can only feel like she is not a person there.

Such opinions were also reflected in the interviews I did with medical personnel. They are of course not monsters, but conscientious professionals who tried to use their power judiciously to meet both the goals of the state and the needs of their patients and their families. Nevertheless, their patients reported that they used this power in ways that patients found difficult to bear. Tatiana V., a midwife, said that they are directors of the process: "There are all kinds of women, those who can stand pain, there are those that cannot withstand pain, therefore even during contractions, and during labor, it happens that they do not listen to what you tell them, therefore the role of a director also exists." Nadezhda B., one of the women who did have prenatal classes, said that the goal was to teach mothers that the midwife was in control: "They get women disposed to the idea that during labor you have to completely trust the midwife. You have to listen to what she says, that is, to perform all her commands. It's only in your best interest."

If women did not fulfill this charge and behave properly, however, midwives were not above scolding their patients, as Elena E. reported: "The process is in principle one and the same, everyone works at a delivery, they try to help the women, to pet her, to talk with her, and if necessary, to reprimand her." Belousova (2003, 342) also describes how doctors and midwives used invective to humiliate patients and maintain their own position in the hierarchy. As Turner (1969) has shown, life-cycle rituals themselves require those passing through them to be torn asunder from the old way of life and be ritually humiliated to enter into the new stage. It seems that the Soviet Russian childbirth process conforms well to his theory. As one mother put it, "Their number one goal is to humiliate you. The thing is, you are totally under their control. When they have the power, they can decide at any moment not to answer your questions, not to listen to you" (Rivkin-Fish 1997, 361). However, the ritual process was not just directed at the patients. The doctors were able to exercise their own power within the confines of the ritual. They were able to espouse state values and scientific knowledge with their patients or to reject them in favor of "folk" material, without any apparent conflict, in order to recover some of their own status in the face of an institutional system that had degraded them as well.

The Family and the State

As discussed in chapter 1, the attitude toward the family was a complex one in the Soviet period. The family was both a necessity within Soviet society and a potential threat to it. Thus, rituals were designed to foster the family, to strengthen it as a fundamental basis of social organization. Nevertheless, by creating such rituals, Soviet theorists risked losing control of the family. Therefore, they embedded within the rituals a series of messages about the preeminence of the state over the family. I should note that my claim that the state wanted to maintain control of the family does not suggest that the state had as much power over the family as it did during the Stalinist repression. At that point, the concern was for controlling the individual's very thoughts. During the period under consideration here, as Shlapentokh (1989, 31) concludes,

> Soviet public ideology is as aggressive about control over human mentality as it was in the first decades after the Revolution, and it still insists that the average Soviet individual should perceive the world through its glasses … after 1953 the leadership … softened its requirements regarding human emotions and thoughts.

Thus, deeds (e.g., behaving as a Soviet citizen or family member publicly) outweighed actual beliefs. Shlapentokh (1984, 248) describes precisely this situation in the Soviet Union:

> [T]he majority of Soviet people do routinely observe most of the norms imposed from above. Yet these norms are generally not internalized, but are perceived merely as external roles, the observance of which depends largely on the efficiency of the mechanisms of external social control.

Yurchak considers this issue during the time frame under consideration here. He argues that in the Stalinist period there was a significant shift in the reading of government messages, such that people no longer examined the constative (e.g., semantic) content of the messages in a literal way. What became more important was the performative process, which allowed for people to engage in "pragmatic" interpretation of the content. By "pragmatic" he means that interpretations were variable, based on context and not on the "dictionary" meaning of the words themselves. As we have discussed, people did not reject all the values espoused by the Soviet Union out of hand, but were selective in how they interpreted them and brought to bear a plethora of meanings based on other factors. He (25) concludes:

> They therefore emphasized the centrality of the performative dimension of this discourse in the reproduction of social norms, positions, relations, and institutions.... It became increasingly more important to participate in the reproduction of the *form* [italics original] of these ritualized acts of authoritative discourse than to engage with their constative meanings. It is crucial to point out, however, that this does not mean either that these ritualized acts become meaningless and empty or that other meanings in public life were diminishing or becoming totally constrained. On the contrary, the performative reproduction of the form of rituals and speech acts actually *enabled* [italics original] the emergence of diverse, multiple, and unpredictable meanings in everyday life, including those that did not correspond to the constative meanings of authoritative discourse.

Life-cycle rituals were one mechanism for the "emergence of diverse, multiple, and unpredictable meanings." Socialist ideology was intertwined with folk notions of family identity along with the Soviet-era concept that the family was a refuge against state institutions. For example, people did not buy things for their children before birth to avoid cursing the pregnancy (a folk notion). As a result, while the woman was in the hospital, her family bought all the things a child would need. Due to the constant shortages of the Soviet period, the family thus became a provider for the child in a much more essential sense than the state did. However, the state was successful in its goals in framing itself as "parent" to its citizens to some extent. For example, it provided free access to medical care, which enabled the authorities to medicalize birth, to change perceptions about the woman's body, and to establish the predominance of science over nature, as we have seen. They also effectively reinforced the primacy of the mother in the family circle, as Ashwin, Lyon, Kukhterin, and Gal and Kligman have all discussed, a phenomenon which this ritual clearly illustrates. They also were somewhat effective in conveying the message that the state was a type of surrogate "breadwinner" for the family, through maternity leave policies and stipends for women who had children. However, the state and its representatives were less successful in assuming this role as effectively as they had medicalized birth. The state did not consistently provide adequate goods in stores, wages or even living space for children. It also did not pay an adequate child-support stipend for a family to survive on one income for very long. These issues were noted by some of my informants in discussing why they returned to work as quickly as possible and are also discussed by the characters in the *Women's Decameron* (13, 82, 121, 218). As a result, the family succeeded in assuming a large portion of the status the Soviet state desired for itself. In sum, while many of the norms espoused by the Soviet state were internalized by mothers and families, not all of them were.

Through the birth practices described above the state also attempted to show that it ultimately had control over the family as a core institution in Soviet life. However, because of the isolation period, the *vstrecha* 'meeting' at the hospital upon release became more important than the institution itself. Indeed, the *roddom* arranged the release from the hospital in such a way that a state representative could formally bestow the child on the family, as though the state had created it. However, when the entire family gathered to welcome the child, for which they had shopped and prepared, the state lost much of its primacy. State institutions, in fact, fostered a situation that made the family that much more valuable to the mother and child after what was frequently a difficult time in the maternity hospital. In one sense, the Soviet authorities wanted to engender just such a reaction, because they recognized that the family was a font of social stability. However, institutional practices also posed a threat to state supremacy in family life. The triumph of the family over state institutions becomes most evident in the party the family held after the isolation period ended. This party to introduce the child to the larger world was not held at a public place associated with institutional power, but rather at home in the family circle. This fact may also explain why Soviet naming ceremonies never gained much ground. The child should (and many would argue must) be welcomed by those who are responsible for its upbringing, who want to teach it the values associated with the "real" society, one potentially separate from Soviet ideals. While the Soviet Union tried to assert that it was a "parent" to its citizens, it was actually never able to fulfill this role (either by design, because it recognized that the family was too important to its goals to reconstruct it, or by accident, because it could not adequately provide for its citizens or their children).

The bond between mother and child was ultimately strengthened by *roddom* practices, a bond which the Soviet authorities desired, because it would ensure that the mother dedicated herself to raising the next generation. Because the medical procedures worked to remove all sense of individual control from the mother, the only firm tie she had was to her child. The mothers I interviewed discussed this bond. They were willing to undergo both physical and institutional ordeals and to sacrifice themselves to bear and raise a child within the Soviet system. When I told Nadezhda B. that there had once been a tradition for complete anesthesia in American hospitals, she responded that the lack of pain killers produces an entirely different relationship between mothers and children in Russia than in the United States: "Therefore we have a different relationship to children. Because you endure specifically pain, suffering during labor." Mothers conformed to institutional ideals about science over nature, their bodies and manufacturing processes, because they believed that their child's health depended upon these sacrifices. This belief system fostered a connection between the mother and child that belied the state's goals for assuming primacy in the child's life. As Klara K. said: "I thought that it [labor] would be really painful, but I … thought I would withstand all the pains, it was necessary for me that the child be born normal and that everything would be normal with me. And I bore it with dignity."

Nevertheless, because the institution did not give women much opportunity to really interact with their children, new mothers were often nervous about caring for their children after their release (as are all new mothers, of course, but these women had little or no exposure to their children in the *roddom*, which intensified their fears). Recall that the lessons about childcare in the maternity hospital were performed on a doll, not on the baby itself. The hospital maintained control over the children, sending the message that it was more important than the mother and knew best how to care for the child. Lidia S. put it succinctly: "They didn't trust us with our own children." Nadezhda P., for example, described the first day after her release from the hospital as follows: "Of course I was afraid to approach the child. I didn't know what to do with him. I was scared of him, how to swaddle him, how to do anything. It was hard. But gradually it seemed not to be so scary." Lena L., who had twins, expressed similar concerns: "I put the children in their beds in the other room and went to sit with everyone [relatives who had met her at the hospital], but I was so weak that I could only think one thing: the problem is that when children are in the maternity hospital, a nurse takes care of them.… I am over here, they are over there."

As a result, they relied even more on family, particularly on their mothers, in the early days of the child's life, a situation that the Soviet medical authorities actually were most concerned about, as discussed above. Most of the women in my study either lived with their mothers after they gave birth or had their mothers visit them for some time after the birth, which also promoted a sense of family unity and community child rearing.[23] Olga R., for example, reported that she went to live with her mother:

---

[23] Certainly this practice is not uncommon in other societies, but it does not change the fact that within the Soviet context, it played a role in the primacy of the family over state institutions.

We went home with my mom, and it seemed that she was really experienced, but it took time for us to get used to our child and to learn
how to deal with him. The nurse dressed and swaddled him there [in
the hospital], when we brought him home and put him on the table
and we had to unswaddle him and then reswaddle him, we were confused at first. We didn't know which side to start from.

It should be noted that the Soviet government established an earlier retirement age for women, who then generally assumed responsibility for their
grandchildren's after-school care. The state could not provide enough quality
childcare, despite its claims to the contrary. Thus it enacted a policy that
prompted a (female) family member to demonstrate that she was more valuable to the family than the state was.

The immediate family retained its powerful, communal role in child
rearing throughout the Soviet period and into the post-Soviet period, even
when women were working outside the home. Interestingly, at the same time,
this sense of community child rearing went beyond the immediate family,
extending to neighbors in apartment buildings, who all embraced local
children and helped to raise them by instructing them in proper behavior and
keeping watch on their actions outside in the yard. Katia K. described such a
situation and how she relied on her neighbor, a pediatrician: "A pediatrician
lived right in our building. Therefore it was easy for us. With any problems or
difficulties we simply ran to her."[24] In fact, Russian children call all adults
"aunt" and "uncle," which promotes a claim of kinship between all members
of the community. This communal responsibility toward children, I believe,
results from a combination of factors. The Soviet Union effectively
encouraged a communal ethos, with the idea the children did not belong to
the family, but to the society as a whole (see Bronfenbrenner 1970 for a
discussion). However, traditional folk beliefs also promoted this sort of
communal child rearing, because the extended family has always been
involved in providing for and raising the child. One's friends and neighbors
formed the essential bonds that allowed the family to thrive and fostered
individual social identity. Grandmothers and other intimates were part of *svoi*
'one's own' and were "normal people" who forged a collective on the model
of Russian village tradition and not only on the basis of Soviet ideology. As a

---

[24] This relationship with a medical professional on a personal level parallels the situation when the pediatrician makes house calls. Doctors are then outside of the
established power structure. They may become part of the community and may be removed from their roles as representatives of the system. As noted above, this conclusion also depends on their behavior. The pediatrician making a house call who praised
the child was willing to step outside the system; others may not have behaved so
warmly and may have used this opportunity to assert their power over the family to
try to advance official behavioral norms.

result, grandmotherly care (and family involvement more broadly) simultaneously supported the state's goals for social unity and also threatened them, by making relatives and its folk traditions more central to family identity than state institutions and representatives. This paradox illustrates the complexity and flexibility of the ritual system in establishing family identity. Therefore, as Yurchak (2006, 283) argues: "For great numbers of Soviet citizens, many of the fundamental values, ideals, and realities of socialism were of genuine importance, despite the fact that many of their everyday practices routinely reinterpreted the announced norms and rules of the socialist state." While the state's ideology was seemingly univocal, participants in the rituals created their own interpretations not only of the ideology, but of their own notions of family identity. The roles women negotiated within this rite correspond exactly to Yurchak's description of the Soviet citizens' relationship to governmental ideology and the opportunity to reinterpret it through their own lens in daily life from the 1950s to *perestroika*.

Negotiating Identity in the Birth Ritual

In his discussion of the rites of passage, Bourdieu (1991, 115) makes the following argument:

> One has to ask the questions ... regarding the *social* [italics original] function of ritual and the social significance of the boundaries of limits which the ritual allows one to pass over or transgress in a lawful way. One can ask oneself whether, by stressing the temporal transition—e.g., from childhood to adulthood—this theory does not conceal one of the essential effects of rites, namely that of separating those who have undergone it, not from those who have not yet undergone it, but from those who will not undergo it in any sense, and thereby instituting a lasting difference between those to whom the rite pertains and those to whom it does not pertain."

In the Soviet Russian birth system, then, we must establish what it meant to be a mother, because only she was defined by the children she bore within this society. The father was essentially excluded from the process. Therefore, his shift into this familial role was much less significant within the Soviet system (fairly or unfairly), because his identity was based on his professional and public roles above all else. We will consider the following questions: by joining the ranks of mothers, what identity did the woman create for herself? What role within the social hierarchy did she assume, and how did she negotiate the various conceptions of motherhood within this context?

At first glance, it would seem that the system described above conveyed a set of conflicting messages to the participants. At the outset, the scientific medical practices represented a Western worldview. While Soviet medical authorities adopted the Western system, they also reinterpreted it through their own attitudes toward social structure. Some ideals happened to correspond to Western notions, namely the power of science over nature, birth as a manufacturing process, and the preeminence of institutions over the family and the individual. Nevertheless, while these messages might have been similar to those in Western countries, the values that underlay them were radically different. They were based on Soviet-era ideology that viewed the family as a socialist construct dedicated to the state's goals and centered around communal child rearing and the development of socialist values of egalitarianism, altruism, a strong work ethic, and self-discipline. In addition, folk material, some of which directly conflicted with socialist values, as we have seen, continued to thrive within Soviet society. However, as Yurchak (2006, 162) asserts, "within this discursive formation of late socialism, diverse public statements that might seem contradictory in fact coexisted as logically linked and mutually productive." In our terms, they formed a coherent whole as part of the Soviet ritual complex. Ritual participants negotiated these various systems and performed rituals that established their social roles through their actions, e.g., were creative agents of their own identity. The Soviet ritual specialists, like Ugrinovich (1975, 39), basically adopted a structuralist view of ritual as a means to convey a unitary set of symbols and messages. They did not take into account the fact that actors in a ritual bring their own expectations into the performance, which may radically differ from the messages intended, and thus may negate or resist them. Humphrey and Laidlaw (1994, 101) lay out the intricate nature of ritual as follows:

> The actor feels there to be some reason for the act, that the ritual has its own point, or to speak metaphorically, that the act has its own ritual "intention." ... Because ritualized acts present themselves as it were "objectively" to experience, they may be felt to have their own character, to be there for some purpose, to "be meaningful." The actor might apprehend such "objects" in a number of ways.

Thus what the establishment intends or "means" by ritual acts may well not coincide with the interpretations drawn from the ritual by the participants, who may take a variety of contradictory symbols and merge them into a coherent vision for their social role.

While Yurchak (2006, 27, 286) argues that it is not appropriate to speak exclusively of resistance to state norms in the late Soviet period, my data show that there was certainly evidence of resistance strategies within these rituals. For example, mothers such as Natalia T. turned away from the state's medical institutions to folk remedies, because the doctors had not provided her with adequate information or effective treatment. Many of the women I interviewed discussed in detail, as we have seen, how the state failed to pro-

vide what they needed medically or financially, so that they relied on themselves and their personal networks to support and rear their children. It is
significant, I believe, that Yurchak focuses on youth culture, not on the life-
changing events described here, where one's social status was significantly
altered by ritual events over which the state had substantive power. In matters of life and death, it is not nearly so easy to negotiate alternatives as in
one's work place or at a university. Although Yurchak correctly concludes
that people did not resist the state's norms in every instance, even in these
serious matters as we have seen, it is clear that resistance to the state's institutions and ideology was a factor in ritual performance. Abu-Lughod (1986,
102–04) discusses how in a strictly hierarchical social system, people "can negate the hierarchy through resistance strategies," such as refusing to comply
or by complying outwardly, in public, but resisting in other venues, e.g., in
our case, within the ritual itself, as these women clearly did.

Negotiation of identity through a ritual then involves both resistance and
acceptance, an essential tenet of the practice theory of ritual. Bell (1997, 76)
characterizes this approach as an investigation of "the political dimensions of
social relationships, especially with regard to how positions of dominance
and subordination are variously constituted, manipulated, or resisted." This
view of ritual encapsulates the situation participants faced in the Soviet
Russian birth rite given the role of state institutions and ideology in family
life. Ritual agents, in this case primarily mothers, had to create an identity for
themselves by negotiating the variety of societal and cultural elements and
strict hierarchies described above. In sum, ritual participants used the rites to
establish a state of affairs in the world and to make a statement about their
positions in society.

Let us turn then to the question of how women established these roles as
mothers through the rite of childbirth. Child rearing in Soviet Russian society
was, simply put, women's work. Shening-Parshina and Shibaeva (1967, 146–
47) assert baldly that a woman bore sole responsibility for caring for and feeding a child, but that fathers should help out around the house, a message that
most men seemed not to accept. In most Soviet Russian families, women did
most, if not all, of the domestic labor. This was the result both of the traditional family structure inherited from tsarist times and of Soviet conservatism
about gender roles, despite claims of gender equality within the society.
Women were indeed ultimately responsible for rearing the children who were
the future of the Soviet state. The humiliation and control inherent in the
treatment at the Soviet *roddoms* led mothers to conclude that they needed to
sacrifice both their bodies and their identities for their children. The most important job they would do was raise their children, and the bond between

them became the primary one in their lives.[25] The state thereby tried to ensure that their future representatives would be well cared for and also be indoctrinated into the Soviet system from birth. Mothers recognized that they were subject to the state's power, which the *roddom* system effectively conveyed by instilling in these women a sense of inadequacy. However, while they clearly did accept the primacy of Soviet medical science (for the most part) in giving birth and in their child's health as (s)he grew, they also rejected some state ideals. The Soviet birth ritual sent the message that the state should be the primary and indeed the main provider for the family, but people did not entirely accept this view. They turned instead to their families for financial and emotional support and advice. This situation ultimately undermined Soviet goals about the state's primacy over the family itself and yet also created social stability by fostering middle-class family identity.

The Soviet medical authorities and ritual specialists were particularly concerned about the retention of folk practices. The former tried to abolish traditional childcare and pregnancy beliefs conveyed by older women. While they were successful to the extent that mothers primarily relied on medical treatment for pregnancy and delivery, and for their children after birth, medical authorities could not eliminate the relationship between new mothers and their female relatives. These older women effectively passed on traditional beliefs about how to feed and care for children and indeed for how pregnant women and nursing mothers should behave, some of which were in direct conflict with scientific norms. To take one example, the women in my study repeatedly told me that the key to ample breast milk was drinking lots of liquid and/or eating certain foods, such as black currants. Shening-Parshina and Shibaeva (1967, 137) state that such "overdrinking" will not help at all. And yet, women of all ages continue to espouse this belief. Ritual specialists were also worried, rightly so it would appear, that these older women also passed on religious ideas and insisted on baptism for their grandchildren (as discussed previously). These "folk" practices, despite attacks by the authorities, came to represent an essential core definition of motherhood and indeed family relations. In the face of the Soviet authorities' attempts to control the family, the stubborn reliance on the wisdom and experience of older women served to connect new mothers to "Russianness" through the folk tradition. It also functioned as a means to resist total control of the family by the state.

Not all folk traditions were a form of resistance. As we have seen, many folk practices were also reinterpreted from the point of view of the Soviet and medical systems. Evil eye beliefs were retained fairly intact, especially after the child was born. Isolation also served to protect the child from infection (a medical reason) and to show the dominance of the state over its citizens (a

---

[25] Note that I am not arguing that mothers who give birth in other cultures do not forge bonds with their children, but that the Soviet system resulted in an especially strong bond because of the difficulty of giving birth under these conditions.

Soviet reason). Community involvement in child rearing was also a folk behavior that survived into the Soviet period. It supported the Soviet state's
goal of making the nuclear family less powerful than the state. However, it
also had the opposite effect in elevating the family and community, not the
state, to central figures in child rearing.

To create their identities as mothers within the Soviet childbirth system,
women relied on a series of images of motherhood. To a great extent, they
adopted the socialist state's ideology about themselves as central figures in
the family, one that was supported by folk belief as well. They also viewed
their bodies as tools for the state in the production of the next generation and
largely acquiesced to the demands of medical science for treatment during
pregnancy and delivery. Finally, they espoused many of the socialist values of
character in a child, such as responsibility, altruism, and a good work ethic.
However, there was a limit on the degree of compliance. Being a mother
meant establishing one's own identity separate from the state and its demands. In particular, they rejected the state's preeminence over the family
unit and placed their own relatives at its center. This rejection, as noted
above, was often due to the failure of state institutions to live up to their
promises of financial support or considerate, professional treatment. For example, while it might seem medically reasonable to have specialists in pregnancy, delivery, and post-partum care treat a woman during pregnancy, the
result of this practice in the Soviet context was that the patients felt as though
they were faceless individuals being shuttled from doctor to doctor. Soviet-
era medical institutions fostered a situation that prevented women from
forming bonds with medical personnel. Indeed, the medical personnel themselves felt trapped by the state system, as Rivkin-Fish (1997, 2005) discusses in
detail. When medical professionals tried to regain a modicum of power, in
doing so they fulfilled their roles that the Soviet government had designed for
them and conveyed the message that the state was more powerful than its
members. Nevertheless, this system actually encouraged people to subvert it,
which also ironically corresponded to state ideals about families, so as to ensure that the society would remain stable.

Bonds between citizens (whether relatives or friends) both fostered Soviet
ideals and potentially threatened them, because, as we have seen, the family
could potentially be a place to espouse anti-state values. In some cases, medical personnel, particularly those that treated women who had difficult pregnancies, did forge individual relationships with patients. As Klara K.
reported, her doctors "carried me in their arms." Because she experienced
serious complications, without their assiduous, constant care she would never
have had her two children. Doctors who did not conform to the model of
Soviet power relations could become part of the community and thereby
undermine the state's goals. They stepped outside the system and became exceptions to the norm of impersonal medical professionals associated with the
state, what Yurchak (2006, 109) calls a "normal person (*normal'nyi chelovek*)."

Such examples illustrate the fallibility of the state medical system and support the claim for the essential nature of personal connections, particularly the family, within this society. In these situations, folk belief stood out as resistance to the rigid Soviet Russian social hierarchy. These beliefs established the familial sphere as distinct from the state's goals, as an entity that had its own traditions, as a space wherein mothers exhibited their independence and own ideas about their social role.

While the mother was the central figure of the childbirth ritual, other family members also had to negotiate their roles through this ritual. The medical personnel in the *roddom* ensured that a newborn child received its first introduction into Soviet society.[26] The child was subject to the same regimented schedule that the mother was, so that from birth the institution tried to control it. Belousova (2003, 362) emphasizes that the *roddom* serves as the intermediary between the "otherworld" and the world of humans. It is the *roddom's* job, in the early isolation period, to "complete" the child and its transition into the human world. She notes that children, at first, do not have the trappings of human society. They are not called by their name, but only "the newborn" or "child." They do not wear normal clothes and they are protected from outside forces through isolation. Medical personnel also try to program the child into a set of scientific and cultural norms from pregnancy to birth; if the child does not conform, then it may be branded for life with some deficiency (Belousova 2003, 362).

The messages that a man received about his role were fairly simple to decode: you are a secondary figure in this process, excluded from your child's birth and from child rearing generally. While I did not interview men about their experience with birth, since they did not participate in the bulk of the ritual, other authors have considered this issue in some detail. Kukhterin (2000, 85) argues that "the position of Soviet men was highly contradictory. On the one hand, Soviet men and women tended to adhere to traditional ideas regarding natural sexual difference. On the other, the state was jealous of patriarchal prerogatives in the private sphere, and wanted men to direct their energy into their work." Therefore, as Khasbulatova (2005, 324) concludes, men were essentially excluded from the domestic sphere, both due to traditional

---

[26] It is not clear, of course, that the child absorbed these messages, but it is likely that the parents (and family) read the messages directed at the child. The fact that the child might not recognize the meaning behind the information did not stop adults from trying to instill social values. For example, in the program "The Immortal Genes," aired on the Discovery Health Channel in 1994 as part of Desmond Morris' *The Human Animal* series, a nurse at a Russian *roddom* is swaddling a child just after birth. When she is done, she holds the baby up to the camera and says, "Oh, what workers we are, we are workers. Look at us, oh how we want to work." This supposed expression of the child's desire to be a worker conformed to the official state attitude about a child's future goals and conveyed this ideology even if the child was not yet aware of it. His mother, who was lying nearby, certainly would be.

values about gender roles and also due to Soviet-era ideology about men's roles as public actors. In sum, this ritual was not directed at men, who negotiated their identity in society through their professional lives. That does not mean that men did not feel conflicted about this reality, as Kukhterin (88) has discussed, but that the ritual really did not provide the opportunity for them to identify what it meant to be a father in all but the most simple terms. Since fatherhood was not a man's primary role within Soviet Russian society, it is not surprising that the ritual as designed excluded him.

The birth ritual we have examined illustrates how Soviet Russian citizens were not oppressed, faceless automatons who lived in a divided world of public versus private. The two spheres intersected and influenced one another profoundly. Therefore, the birth rite demonstrates how, as Ortner (1989, 11–18) argues, the ritual agents both change and recreate social structures within society. People actively participated in the public realm and accepted some core values of Soviet ideology, particularly those related to gender roles in the family and the medicalization of birth and the body. At the same time they responded to the strictures of social organization the Soviet state had created. They adopted notions of "proper" birth within the *roddom*, but also created a family that did not entirely conform to Soviet ideology. Although the state wanted to serve as a "parent" that could control the family, it could not entirely achieve this goal, since it did not provide essential goods, services, or salaries to its citizens. Soviet Russians had to rely on their own connections for both emotional and financial support of their families.

Despite the state's intentions, as citizens performed the rituals, they were dynamic actors in the creation of social reality, particularly in the creation of familial identity. The state could not counter its citizens' independence as actors, since their understanding of ritual and its functions was limited by the view that a rite conveyed a unitary set of norms to its performers. Participants in childbirth rituals negotiated their roles within the family and society on the basis of a variety of sources. Soviet Russians relied on their understanding of folk material inherited from the nineteenth century, on Western scientific models reinterpreted through Soviet conceptions of materialism, and indeed upon state ideology about gender and the family more broadly. In some cases, folk material directly contradicted the authorities' ideals, but it also helped to foster a stronger, stable family unit. The stronger, stable family unit both supported and threatened the state's goals. It helped to maintain the government's power by creating an environment in which the status quo was valued, but it also provided an arena for dissent. Soviet theorists and medical personnel recognized this dilemma, but could only attempt to solve the problem by exerting more control over the family. However, ritual actors did not completely internalize the state's claim to total control, despite their acceptance of much official ideology, but instead relied on folk traditions to establish family identity. The definition of the family via folk practices also served to preserve core cultural notions of "Russianness" in the face of a state that had attacked folk beliefs since its inception. In some instances, however, folk practices were consistent with state ideology and were actually adopted into the medical birth system. The end result was a ritual that reflected the intricate coherence and dissonance of the Soviet family and the society that contained it from the 1950s through *perestroika*. This social opposition was not limited to the childbirth ritual, but also appeared in the wedding, a ritual in which family identity and conceptions of gender from a myriad of even more complex sources came to the fore.

Chapter 4

The Soviet Russian Wedding Ritual (1950–90)

In the early years of the Soviet Union, marriage and family were institutions that many believed should be eliminated entirely or would eventually disappear with the introduction of communist social policy (Junler 1980, 228; Goldman 1993, 3). Traditional family structures represented backward, patriarchal, and bourgeois society and were thus inimical to a truly revolutionary social policy. The Bolsheviks called for a policy that would institute governmental control of the traditional roles of the family unit (such as raising children) or of the housewife (such as cooking meals, doing laundry, etc.). The Soviet idea, according to Goldman (1993, 6), was not to promote equality between the sexes in marriage, but to simply eliminate the traditional "female" responsibilities. However, the Soviet Union quickly realized that it could not provide the services to eliminate women's work in the home. By the 1930s it also became clear that the family served important social functions that the Soviet theorists had neglected to consider. A rise in juvenile crime and a falling birthrate provoked a shift toward strengthening the family, albeit in a newly conceived Soviet form (Goldman 1993, 288, 296, 324, 333; Ashwin 2000b, 9). Goldman (1993, 336) concludes that the law enacted in 1936 to protect the family "offered women a tacit bargain. It broadened both state and male responsibility for the family, but in exchange it demanded that women assume the double burden of work and motherhood. The idea that the state would assume the functions of the family was abandoned." Because there was no push for the sharing of domestic tasks between couples, women both worked outside the home and continued to perform the bulk of domestic tasks, a problem that persists today.

The nineteenth-century wedding rite was essentially a folk ritual officially sanctioned by the church and designed to create a family unit. Revolutionary theorists believed that rituals themselves, particularly life-cycle rituals, were a danger to state ideology regarding atheism and socialist reconstruction of society and family identity. Therefore, the Bolsheviks originally adopted a policy to downplay them, so as to eliminate outmoded family and religious traditions. Wedding ceremonies were a particular concern in this regard. The revolutionary Brandenburgskii argued that an elaborate ceremony "would ultimately mislead the population, hinder the development of new views, and

retard the transition to a higher form of completely free marital union"
(Goldman 1993, 49, 208). As a result, the Soviet authorities instituted a simple,
bureaucratic ceremony in the registry office of the ZAGS. The wedding ritual
remained essentially unchanged until the late 1960s. The shift after this period
to a more formal ceremony and changing attitudes toward the family, however, complicate the study of the wedding rite over time.

Ritual theorists had to cope with "outmoded" folk content, religious faith,
and family identity as they devised a new Soviet wedding ritual. They
wanted to create a rite that ensured that the family would be bound to state
ideals. Thus, they had to recast folk (and religious) material in a new light and
also introduce values that promoted the socialist family they sought. We have
seen that some people resisted the elimination of the religious facets within
birth rites. We might therefore suspect that they would also resist elimination
of religious wedding ceremonies. However, the Soviet authorities were remarkably successful in shifting people toward a civil rite in lieu of a religious
ceremony. Goldman (1993, 104) notes that "by 1925 less than a third of the
civil marriages registered in Moscow were accompanied by a church ceremony."[1] This trend continued throughout the Soviet period, so that none of
my informants, for example, had a religious rite of any kind. The successful
shift from religious to secular ceremony was the result of two factors. Certainly the civil marriage laws enacted in December 1917 contributed to the
demise of the religious ceremony. In addition, even in the village, the central
focus of the celebration, the "real" wedding, was the reception after the
church rite. Therefore, it was fairly easy for the Bolsheviks to shift citizens' attention away from the church ceremony toward a secular replacement.

As Zhirnova (1980, 84) notes in her study on urban weddings in the Soviet Union, in 1975 the Central Project Planning and Technical Office of the
Ministry of Social Services began to develop a contemporary Soviet wedding
ritual; regional attempts at a more formal ritual had already been established
in Leningrad and in the Baltic states (Rudnev 1979, 131–32 discusses the Leningrad ritual in detail). Ritual specialists began to publish descriptions of the
proper way to conduct a wedding, which included reviving folk material as
well as Soviet-era innovations in how to celebrate the reception, including
music, food, and other elements.[2] When they began their quest for a Soviet
ritual, the state and its representatives did not limit themselves to East Slavic
tradition, but also returned to Western traditions already found in Russian

---

[1] Certainly Moscow was not all of Russia, but later data found in the work of ritual
specialists suggest that this trend was characteristic of the country as a whole by the
1970s, even as baptisms and religious funerals still occurred. For a discussion of these
issues, see Ugrinovich (1975).

[2] Some examples of these works include: E. Lisavtsev (1966); S. Zagradskaia (1980;
1981); Iu. Krasovskaia (1983); and I. Leitsadu (1982, 1983).

cities in the past (e.g., the formal white wedding gown, the exchange of wedding rings, and a special ritual space).

As secular rationalists, Soviet theorists could not rely on religious or emotional appeals to explain the shift in party policy. Thus, they turned to the notion of Soviet "spiritual values" and ritual as a means to inculcate the positive values of the ancestors (see Rudnev 1979, 7ff. for an excellent discussion of these issues from the point of view of a Soviet ritual specialist). The ideal marriage then was, as Goldman (1993, 6) notes, a "partnership of equals, a union of comrades founded on mutual affection and united by common interests." In addition, they relied on psychological studies that showed how people are better (for "better" read "more productive") members of society if they have happy home lives. Shlapentokh (1984, 93ff.) briefly describes the decision to base the arguments for marriage on rational, scientific approaches, namely social psychology and computer models of compatibility. Attwood (1990, 32–99) discusses many of these specialists and their arguments about marriage and gender roles in more detail. Based on her reading of the psychology and sociology of the period, she (122) concludes that the general consensus at the time was that "the socialist woman should still have a strong commitment to marriage and the family, but should also expect to play an important role in economic and social life and have a strongly developed sense of the greater social need." It is precisely this situation that led to much of the conflict about gender roles that arose in Soviet Russia. Indeed, the text of the wedding ritual itself reflects some of these conflicting messages.

Ritual specialists had to walk a fine line between the work of early revolutionaries and the more recent party line in order to justify their newly-created life-cycle ceremonies. As a result, the wedding ceremony they created was designed to foster particular values from various periods in the Soviet Union, some of which were at odds with each other on the surface. Certainly, the ceremony had to demonstrate that the couple were equal partners in the relationship to support Soviet gender equality ideology, so that no traditional male and female roles were mentioned in the ceremony itself. Rather, the text focused on the "moral demands" of marriage, particularly "the consciousness of responsibility for the life and happiness of a near one" (Lane 1981, 76). The ceremony also highlighted two other issues relevant to Soviet-era policies: child rearing and the Soviet state's dedication to the family. The latter is emphasized at the outset, when the celebrant stated that the family "is the most important cell of our state. Soviet law protects the family and facilitates its strengthening." The reference to the law brings to mind the constitution's declarations regarding gender equality, mutual property, and family structure in Soviet Russian society. However, marriage in the Soviet Union was also perceived to be a means to solve the demographic problem, such that the celebrant asks the couple if they are "prepared to create a harmonious, strong family, to care for each other and to provide a fitting education for your future children?" Children were the assumed result of marriage, as were love,

stability and harmony, despite the low birth and high divorce rates throughout the period. The text of this ceremony illustrates the various ideological
constructs that underlay the concept of the family within the Soviet Union.
There were others, of course, that were not overtly mentioned in the ceremony, namely materialism and traditional gender roles, both of which were
significant characteristics of the Soviet wedding as it was practiced.

Theorists such as Verdery (1996), Shlapentokh (1984; 1989), Bushnell
(1980) and Dunham (1976) have argued that the Soviet Union wanted to create a middle class that was concerned with material well-being and domesticity. The wedding was undoubtedly one key to this process. Shlapentokh
(1984, 25) notes that a stable family was vital to a totalitarian state, because it
"weakened people's inclination to opposition activity, made them seek material well-being, and so made them much more dependent on the state." The
wedding celebration (if not the ceremonial text), as ritual specialists developed it, was therefore tied to consumerism. Marriage, of course, has always
been an economic union to some extent, but it seems unusual at first glance
that a socialist state would promote this aspect of the wedding if not for political reasons, particularly in light of earlier attacks on bourgeois marriage.
However, given the desire for family stability, one way to ensure this was to
focus on material comforts in the domestic sphere.

In addition, while the text may have espoused gender equality in accord
with the Soviet constitution, the actual practices of the wedding did not.
Many of the acts in the ceremony itself and in celebrations afterward focus on
the Soviet (and indeed Russian) folk conceptions of the husband as a provider
(and a dominant figure) and the wife as a homemaker. The wedding emphasized another aspect of this disconnect between equality in gender roles and
traditional expectations for men and women as well. Women were valued for
their physical beauty and delicacy, characteristics emphasized by the introduction (in the late 1960s) of the elaborate white formal gown, elegant hair
styles and makeup they sported for the ceremony. In contrast, men's stoicism
and power were conveyed by their severe, dark formal suits. These subtexts
about materialism and traditional gender roles, which would seem at first
glance to contradict Soviet ideals about the family, and indeed about society
more broadly, will be examined in more detail below. Like the dissonances in
the birth practices we have already discussed, they actually form a coherent
whole within the Soviet wedding ritual and demonstrate how ritual functioned within this society.

Bourdieu (1990, 97) contends that

to understand ritual practice, to give it back both its reason and its
raison d'être, without converting it into a logical construction or a spiritual exercise, means more than simply reconstituting its internal
logic. It also means restoring its practical necessity by relating it to the

real conditions of its genesis, that is, the conditions in which both the functions it fulfils and the means it uses to achieve them are defined.

From the theoretical perspective of ritual as practice, we have concluded that Soviet Russian birth rites allowed for the creation of an independent conception of parenthood and the family. This conception emerged from a series of sources, but did not only depend on the unitary set of norms established by the government. Mothers took advantage of the ritual process to negotiate their identities, relying on various types of *habitus*, including folk ideas of motherhood and family as well as ideals of motherhood endorsed by official socialist ideology and consumerism designed to foster a stable and contented family. These women were not consistently resistant to state ideals, but applied them to their benefit when it suited them. However, they did not slavishly recreate any of these norms through the ritual, but created a new state of affairs in the world by combining elements from all these belief systems. This process transformed the social system, even as it simultaneously reinforced cultural norms and hierarchies. Couples who married during this period also had to negotiate these seemingly contradictory belief systems to establish their identities. Indeed, the wedding itself was a much more complicated ritual for several reasons. First, opinions about the family and marriage had changed rather significantly over the Soviet period, so that there existed a variety of "official" norms about married life. In addition, folk material was much more pervasive in determining familial roles, while consumerism and borrowed Western practices played as great, and possibly an even greater role, than in the childbirth ritual.

Humphrey and Laidlaw argue that rituals may not actually communicate symbolic meanings as theorists on ritual have long asserted. In essence, they object to the misconception which the Soviet ritual specialists themselves displayed in their theory of how life-cycle rituals functioned. Quoting Searle, they conclude: "one can intend to mean something, which is to represent an idea, without intending to communicate, which is to produce beliefs in an audience" (1994, 78). The Soviet life-cycle rituals, by contrast, were designed to produce beliefs in the audience. Ritual specialists mistakenly thought that these ceremonies could mold people, that the messages they sent would be received intact, but ritual actors did not conform as theorists had expected. Citizens relied instead on a wide range of conceptions about their roles within the family unit. Rudnev (1979, 4–5) begins his discussion of Soviet rituals with the following statement: "The development of a new ritualism allows for the establishment and reinforcement of the Soviet way of life to its utmost, for the perfection of people's mutual relations in production, in the family, and in daily life." Similarly, Ugrinovich (1975, 58, 60) contrasts capitalist and Soviet rituals by saying that in a capitalist country, rituals pass on bourgeois norms, while Soviet rituals convey socialist behaviors, values, and ideals. However, Humphrey and Laidlaw (34–36) show that the participants in a ritual take away a wide variety of meanings from a ritual, often not those intended, and in some cases take away nothing at all from the acts they perform, other than the sense of "I performed the ritual correctly and that is what is important." Within the context of official Soviet discourse from the 1950s on, the issue of performance and the reading of a plethora of meanings from acts in various contexts was not just a characteristic of ritual, but as Yurchak has shown, of life within the society more broadly. Ritual and other performances allowed people to reproduce the form of Soviet ideological norms, while simultaneously engaging with diverse ideas, some of which meshed with ideology, and some of which did not. Since the messages were not read for their literal semantic content, people interpreted them on the basis of contextual clues. As a result, the same behavior in two different situations could either support or undermine Soviet societal norms.

What is important in our discussion is not that the participants in these rituals did not read the messages "correctly," because they represented arcane behaviors whose original meanings had been lost. Indeed, my interviewees were most adept at reading the meanings intended by the Soviet government in the rituals it devised. Nevertheless, what the powers-that-be (and ritual specialists) failed to consider was that people could reject the information as sent (on occasion) and indeed, as Yurchak shows, bring to bear their own meanings that resulted in a great deal of diversity within Soviet society. In sum, the wedding (or other ritual) might not mold the citizens in the same way that the ritual creators had hoped. In fact, it might, as we saw with birth, have the opposite effect in some cases. The family could often be at odds with the Soviet ideals for it. Weddings, which establish a new family unit, are rife with discrepancies between the intent of the rituals as designed and the way they are interpreted. At the same time, there were certain values the Soviet government espoused that people accepted about the family wholeheartedly, as they did with childbirth. Thus, we are once again faced with a complex ritual, based upon a variety of social norms, which people used to negotiate their roles within the family and society. They were obviously constrained by Soviet values, given that it was the "only game in town" when it came to legal marriage. As a result they created family structures that both enabled the continuation of the society and its norms and yet potentially undermined them, sometimes actively through resistance to norms they found inimical to family identity, and sometimes unintentionally.

An additional complication in the study of weddings, as Matlin (2003, 371) states, is that there were also regional, ethnic, and class variations in the ritual as well as changes in the celebration that resulted from migration out of rural areas into cities. In this study I have eliminated the complications of class and ethnicity by focusing primarily on middle-class Russians. Regional differences are common more in the post-wedding activities than in the ceremony itself (e.g., in Akademgorodok near Novosibirsk, there is no World War II memorial or tomb of the unknown soldier; thus the practice of laying flowers at one or both of these places was often omitted by couples who married there, but not by those who married in Novosibirsk proper; in some regions people believe the bride should be carried across a bridge, while in Vladimir grooms carry brides through the Golden Gate in the center of town). Similarly, family tradition (possibly due to the influence of migration from the village and/or the regional practices Matlin notes) needs to be considered to some extent; those with strong ties to villages celebrated their weddings in more of a "folk" way than those who were exclusively urban. I would also add that the age, political stance, and religion of the participants played a definitive role in the way a wedding was performed. In order to describe the wedding and analyze how it functioned within Soviet Russian society, we must examine all these factors in turn. We will begin with the most significant issue for our purposes: the period during which the wedding occurred.

Weddings in the 1950s and 1960s

A minimalist attitude toward the marriage ceremony characterized the early post-revolutionary period and endured for over thirty years. This lack of ceremony in the official registration of couples who married between 1956 and 1966 was clearly the result of the Soviet distrust and scorn for wedding ritual. Another factor was that people were married in a small office, where such display would be inappropriate. However, as we saw with birth, once outside of the government's sphere of influence, people often resisted Soviet attempts to control the practice and reverted to a traditional celebration. People did have parties after their weddings, but they were much smaller than in Russian cities or villages of the pre-revolutionary period, generally as a result of the post-war economic situation. As Alevtina A. reported, "We got married in 1956. That's a time that was very difficult in the country. There wasn't the tradition of the white dress." People struggling to recover from the war did not have the luxury (or perhaps even the desire) to celebrate weddings lavishly. Therefore, the ceremony itself was not elaborate, given the Soviet disapproval of rituals in general (initially) as well as their desire to distance themselves from Orthodox wedding practices. The reception afterwards was similarly modest, but in this case not Soviet interference in the ritual, but poverty was the primary cause.

While my informants who married in this period were from different locations across the country (including western Russia, the Urals, and Siberia), there were some common practices among their weddings. Once they decided to marry, they went to the ZAGS with their passports to file an intent-to-marry document. The ZAGS workers then established a date for the wedding following a one- to three-month waiting period. The couple was not allowed to choose the day of their marriage, for the most part, and took the first available time. For all but one of these couples, parental permission (before the trip to the ZAGS) was imperative. After the wedding date had been decided, the families met to discuss the wedding reception (if the parents were in the same city).

None of the brides wore a formal, white wedding gown. Mee and Safronova (2003, 148–50) observe that this shift away from the gown occurred during the 1930s (in fashion magazines of the 1920s, ivory and cream wedding dresses had been common). Several factors, they argue, contributed to the "loss" of the wedding dress, including: the location of the ceremony in a stark registry office, where such a dress would be out of place; state disapproval of "ostentation" during difficult financial times (what Rudnev 1979, 26 calls *pokazukha* 'showiness'); a shift, during the constructivist era, to "simplicity, expedience, and functionality" in clothing; and the depressed economy (a factor that also played a role in the receptions during this period as noted above). The majority of the women wore work clothes, either suits or dresses, when they went to the ZAGS for the ceremony. One wore a borrowed dress. Only one bride actually wore a new dress especially for this occasion. The grooms wore suits, except for one student who could not buy one due to limited finances. They bought the suits for the wedding itself or wore suits they had already purchased for work or another important celebration, such as graduation.

In keeping with the lack of ceremony, there were generally no significant pre-wedding activities, such as a *vykup* (buying of the bride)[3] or formal arrival in a hired car. Most of them were married on a weekday, so that they left work or school and went to the ZAGS on public transportation, on foot, or in a friend's (undecorated) car. Nadezhda P., for example, said that before her marriage registration in 1964, "I had my defense that day, I defended, defended my diploma, then had the wedding." Her husband, Valentin P., noted that "[t]here was nothing like now. There was no ceremony, everything was workmanlike, businesslike."

Basically, the wedding ceremony consisted of presenting one's passport to the celebrant; she[4] gave a brief speech on marriage, asked if they were willing to be married, pronounced them married once they assented, and then congratulated them; then they and their two witnesses signed the official registry of marriage. Due to the tough economic times, only one couple purchased and exchanged rings at the ZAGS; some of them bought rings later, when their economic situation improved, or they received them as gifts from family members. After signing the registry, the couple received their new passports (with the names they had chosen on the first visit to the ZAGS) and then left. Few of these couples had guests at the ZAGS other than their wit-

---

[3] Only one couple reported that her neighbors arranged a *vykup* when the groom arrived to pick her up; he gave them candy and money to let him pass.

[4] ZAGS workers are overwhelmingly female. Only one couple of the twenty-three who married between 1956 and 1988 had a male celebrant.

nesses. Witnesses were exclusively school or college friends, not family.[5] However, the ZAGS officials still took the ceremony seriously, despite its simplicity, as Larisa T., who married in 1966, noted:

> For some reason or another it was funny to us, we laughed. And the lady even reprimanded us, "Have you come to a ZAGS or where?" Students had come and young teachers. We tried to be serious, but I didn't need that officiousness, and therefore we weren't serious.

After the couple left the ZAGS, they gathered with guests for the wedding reception. If they were students or far from home, then their fellow students or colleagues prepared a small reception, what my informants called a *komsomol'skaia svad'ba* 'Komsomol wedding'. Larisa T. described her wedding reception, as organized by her fellow teachers, in this way:

> We had lots of delicious salads, they made main dishes, there were fruit, vegetables.... My friends sang songs, thought up some kinds of poems, there were little performances, jokes.... And I am very thankful to my friends, who took the place of my parents and family for me at that time, who supported me.

In some cases, these couples also had a second reception at their family home later. As Nadezhda P. describes, after the ceremony she and her husband went "to the dorm. They [their friends] came to our room, set up the meal, they even took our picture." When they told her parents that they had married (they were the one couple that did not ask for formal permission to marry beforehand), her parents insisted on a formal reception at their home a month later: "They invited all their adult friends and our students that hadn't left yet. There were lots of presents, we had everything, even poems. Somebody presented some kind of comedy routine. They joked, there was a roast pig." Those who were not students went to their parents' apartment for a reception consisting of a full meal prepared by the family. Elvira A. noted that the families united for this purpose: "Not only mom, but his relatives and ours. The reception was at his parents' house. All the relatives got the meal ready, and then we all sat down."

There were generally no fixed traditional dishes beyond the wedding cake, which they typically ordered from a bakery. In some cases the wedding cake was not served until the second day. Two informants reported that they "sold" the wedding cake, that is, as the bride cut the cake the guests bid on the slices; the cash went to the couple. The number of guests at these family receptions ranged from thirty to fifty. The majority of these couples also did

---

[5] One couple brought no witnesses with them; as a result, their witnesses were two unknown people sitting in the corridor at the House of Soviets.

not perform many other traditional pre- and post-wedding activities, such as
having parents meeting them with bread and salt after the ceremony; requiring the bride to sweep the floor on the second day; breaking clay pots or
glassware; throwing coins, candy, or grain for future happiness and abundance; *riazhanie* (mumming games); *devichnik/mal'chishnik* (gathering of female
and male friends before the wedding); or carrying a bouquet brought by the
groom.

The receptions usually began in the early evening and lasted until at least
midnight (or longer). Reception activities, other than the meal, included
toasts, verses, or plays in honor of the couple (usually humorous) performed
by guests, cries of "*gor'ko*" 'bitter', so that the couple would kiss to make their
life "sweet," dancing and singing (both to recorded and live music), and the
presentation of gifts. A *tamada* 'master of ceremonies' controlled the order of
activities; for these couples, the *tamada* was a relative or friend of the family
with a lively wit who spoke well in public. Most couples received items they
would need for setting up their household; they cited items such as china services, linens, crystal, lamps, silverware, dishware, cash, and even books (the
latter especially popular with students). Only about half the couples organized a celebration on the second day of their wedding, mainly because they
lived far from their families. The celebration on the second day featured a
meal that began anytime from mid-morning to noon and lasted until evening.
Brides wore another dress for this event, which was typically a smaller celebration limited to family. In general, second-day activities were identical to
those at the wedding reception. None of these couples had a formal honeymoon, although some did take a trip soon after marriage to see parents who
could not be at the wedding.

Weddings in the 1970s and 1980s

The decision to create a Soviet ceremony dramatically changed the way weddings were performed. Not only were the registrations of marriages much
more ritualized and celebratory, but weddings were no longer held in a
generic registry office but either in a *dom kul'tury* 'House of Culture' or in a
dvorets brakosochetaniia 'Wedding Palace'. These spaces were designed for a
more formal procession and ceremony, as we will see below. But not everyone in the informant pool celebrated their weddings in the "Soviet" way.
Other factors also influenced decisions about the weddings—age at marriage,
and attitude toward both Russian culture and Soviet society and religious belief. We will begin with a discussion of those who married before the age of
thirty and who had no particular political or religious attitudes that influenced the wedding.

Unlike the couples who married before 1970, for those in this later period
parental permission was not essential to the wedding ritual. As Lidia C. remarked: "Usually parents are informed when they have decided to marry."

While some maintained the tradition, they usually had a formal "asking for the bride's hand" only after they had already decided between themselves and filed an intent-to-marry form at the ZAGS. None of these couples said that their parents were against the marriage; in fact, most of them expected it. As before, the ZAGS workers determined the date, after a waiting period of about a month (or even longer in some cases). The waiting period depended on the law as well as on the popularity of the ZAGS itself and the time of year, summers being preferred over other seasons.

The next step was for the families to meet to discuss plans for the wedding reception. As Galina T. described it: "We did everything by the book. We gathered both families, and decided where, how, how much money was necessary. Both families were of very modest means, we decided to have the reception at home." The established tradition by this time was for the families to split the costs of the wedding celebration, as Alexander M. explained: "Here in Russia it is the norm to share the expenses equally. All that goes into the general total we divide in half, and then nothing is acknowledged, because what kind of material relationships can there be between relatives?" However, some people stated that if one family were to have more guests (or was better off financially), they might take on more of the financial burden. Another informant noted that Alexander M. was rather idealistic, because families do in fact remember who paid for what in later years, and it may cause bitterness.

Alexander M. referred to the "general total," which primarily includes costs for the reception, photographer, and hired car. Expenses that are not included in the general total include the wedding couple's clothing, the rings, the bouquet, goods and cash for the *vykup*, the expenses of the *devichnik/ mal'chishnik*, and small meals at home before or after the wedding (but before the reception), The brides and grooms (or their families) paid for the wedding clothing. The groom (or his family) was responsible for buying the rings and the bride's bouquet as well as furnishing objects and cash for the "buying" of the bride. The families also provided the food and drink for any meals at their homes (outside of the reception).

Brides during this period began once again to wear formal, white wedding gowns, unlike women in the 1950s and 1960s. Mee and Safronova (2003, 148, 154) note that wedding dresses disappeared from fashion magazines in the 1930s and only returned in 1954, after Stalin's death. While the wedding dress was no longer "anti-Soviet," the economic situation (and the lack of an appropriate place to wear such a dress) certainly played a role in the fact that the brides who married in the 1950s and 1960s still did not wear white gowns. Once the wedding palace was opened and finances improved, the gown became much more common. In fact, I have both seen wedding photographs of a bride married in the first Leningrad wedding palace in the late 1960s (now deceased) and spoken to another woman who married there during this period; both wore formal, white dresses. By the 1970s the practice was once again well established across the country.

There was a great deal of variation about whether the groom should see the bride's gown before the wedding. Some reported that this was a bad omen, while others had never heard of this belief.[6] They either had the gown made (by a family member or professional seamstress) or bought it at stores such as Ruslan and Liudmila, the Soviet-era bridal outfitters. Two brides wore borrowed or rented dresses. Many women reported that they wore the dresses again, after shortening them, or unaltered, for formal events. Grooms wore dark suits, generally purchased for the wedding, typically with the bride or a female family member (mother or sister). During this period, when it was especially difficult to buy goods, couples received a set of coupons when they registered at the ZAGS to buy wedding clothing and rings as well as household items. Elena I., who married in 1984, describes the situation:

> Then we had to have a certificate from the ZAGS that we were marry-ing, so that they would sell us those rings.... Also at that time, when we were getting married, because there was also a problem with household goods, we could, also with a certificate from the ZAGS, go in and buy a blanket, linens, towels in a special store.... Everything that there was a shortage of at that time. In that store you could also buy clothing.

One interesting fact is that the 1970s saw the revival of the *devichnik/ mal'chishnik* tradition. None of the women who married before 1970 had a *devichnik*, and only one of the men had a *mal'chishnik*. By the 1970s nine of the eleven men in the informant pool had a bachelor party, typically on the eve of the wedding. Nevertheless, the *devichnik* remained less popular; only one woman in the informant pool (who married in 1975) took part in a *devichnik* before her wedding. Others were not sure if they had one or not; Lidia C. remarked: "My girlfriends probably came by." Clearly, the pre-wedding party had become much more important for the man, because these women either did not organize a party or did not recall any special events beyond a gathering of friends for tea and sweets.

At the same time that the ceremony was becoming more formal, the pre-wedding activities increased accordingly. Most of the brides spent the morn-ing before the ceremony at the hairdresser and doing their makeup. The

---

[6] This is not a traditional Russian belief and is not found among the Germanic people of Europe, but does exist in France and in Francophone Belgium as well as in the United States. Thus, I would suggest that it was borrowed from one of these sources, but did not become a core belief in the folk tradition.

groom was responsible for getting the bride's bouquet,[7] getting together the items required for the *vykup*, and picking up the bride in the hired, decorated car. The car was typically decorated with ribbons (usually red and white), rings, or swans.[8] In some cases, informants, particularly those who married in Vladimir, noted that they had two cars, in which the bride and groom rode separately to the ZAGS when they left her apartment. After the wedding, they rode in the same car. When the groom arrived, the bride's friends or neighbors blocked his path for the *vykup*.[9] In all cases, the bride lived in a multistory apartment building, so that he might have to pay not only at the entrance, but also along the way upstairs and at the bride's apartment door. Alexander M. described his experience as follows:

> They were already waiting for us near the entrance. Relatives and friends from my spouse's side. I had to buy her and then go to the ZAGS. I remember that I gave some money. There were all kinds of riddles, there were posters with "we wish you happiness," I had to give some kind of payment.... And then while I was walking to the second floor (she lived on the second floor), I gave something, said something, until I had bought her.

After the groom entered the apartment, he presented the bride with the bouquet (generally red or white flowers or a mix of the two) and the bridal couple and the witnesses left for the ZAGS. All of these couples had close friends from school or work as their witnesses. It was also during this period that witnesses began to wear red ribbons to indicate their special status. Some informants expressed the opinion that the witnesses should be unmarried, or the couple would have bad luck. For example, Liuba S. said that she was the witness at her best friend's wedding a few months after she herself got married. Liuba tried to dissuade her, but her friend insisted, and the couple divorced soon after they married. While in the previous two decades there were few, if any, guests at the ZAGS, a ceremony at the wedding palace

---

[7] Two brides received their bouquets not from the groom, but from their witness or their sister.

[8] One couple did not decorate their car; another walked to the ZAGS, which was close to the apartment.

[9] Four couples did not have a *vykup*; one stated, "I hate them"; two had such small weddings, that there was no one to arrange it. The fourth, Natasha S., asked her neighbors not to arrange a *vykup*. She stated, "I lived in a four-story building. Usually they tie a ribbon in the entryway and the most lively women usually demand a payment, or they won't let him in. I told them that we would give them everything later, only not to arrange one.... So that they would remember me well, they got refreshments later, my mom took it out to them, and then they celebrated for my happiness." One couple had the *vykup* later in the day when they returned home after the wedding ceremony.

allowed for more involvement. Typically, close friends and family attended the ceremony, while parents generally did not. Some reported that it was a bad omen if parents attended; others thought that it was simply a matter of necessity, because the reception was held at home, and the parents needed to prepare for the party.

When the couple arrived at the ZAGS, they went into a special room for the bride and groom to wait their turn; often they waited separately, each with a witness, until called into the central room for the procession into the ceremonial hall. Elena I. described her experience as follows:

> They invite you in according to the time, the groom and bride go in, the witnesses stand at the side, and the guests behind. The hall is big, there is a carpet spread out, a table. The woman-worker says congratulations, asks if we are willing, proposes an exchange of rings, and says that now we are husband and wife. She asks us to sign the book, we sign, then the witnesses sign. And then right there in the palace is a special room, where there is a table, benches, you can sit down. There you can open champagne, drink.... Then we went downstairs and got our picture taken.

Lidia C. noted some other important features of the ceremony during this period:

> The Mendelssohn March is a must. There was a woman there. Usually women work in the ZAGS, I have never once seen a man. She gave a serious speech, then asked if we were willing to take each other as husband/wife, we said "yes," she asked us to sign the book.... Then some parting words are said about the meaning of family. Then it was announced that the relatives can congratulate the newlyweds.

Typically, after the celebrant pronounced the couple married, they were also invited to "to congratulate each other," meaning to kiss each other. Guests generally brought flowers to give to the bride, and if she could not carry all the bouquets, her witness took some of them.

When the couples left the ZAGS, they often went on a tour of the city with their witnesses (and in some cases other friends). The couple visited important city sights, such as the central park overlooking the city of Vladimir or Lenin (Sparrow) Hills in Moscow. The majority also went to Soviet-era monuments, such as those to World War II veterans or the eternal flame, where they placed flowers. They then returned home to a small meal before the reception, because often the wedding occurred several hours before the reception began. Only two couples had a restaurant reception; the others held these events at the family home. Just as many pre-wedding activities were revived in this period, post-wedding activities, such as the parents meeting the couple with bread and salt or showering the couple with grain, coins, or candy, were reestablished. In addition, of the six couples that performed this *karavai* ritual, four said that they bit off a piece of the bread to determine who would be the head of the household; the person who bit more would dominate the relationship. Some also mentioned that people broke glasses or clay pots as well at the reception or on the second day of the wedding celebration.

Receptions during this period did not differ much from those described above for the previous decades. The meals were typical holiday meals, with no special foods other than the wedding cake. In some cases, the cake was served on the second day; two couples also reported that they sold pieces of the cake to guests. Activities remained largely the same: singing and dancing, giving presents, humorous performances and poems, and toasting. One change was that the *tamada* was often now a professional (or semi-professional), who worked for some official cultural organization. As a result, the reception was more scripted, even those parts that were supposed to be improvised, such as games and performances (Matlin 2003, 379). The number of guests was also roughly the same as during the previous two decades. Two couples, who married in 1970 and 1975 as students, had *komsomol'skie svad'by*.[10] Igor D. describes his wedding reception as follows: "We had a Komsomol wedding, when a group of young people, friends, gather together. They each throw in a small sum and do the wedding as a common effort. Therefore it was in the dormitory." Both of the couples who had this type of wedding went to their parents' home in another city for a second reception akin to those described above.

Most of the couples had a second-day celebration as well, albeit smaller, limited either to only friends or to only family. The brides had a different outfit for the second day, generally a dress made by a relative or purchased for the occasion. On the second day, some performed traditional activities such as

---

[10] The Komsomol wedding as devised by the Soviet Union was not intended to be simply a gathering of school friends. Rather it was an attempt to unify political values with familial ones. Zhirnova (1980, 83) states that governmental or social organizations with which one of the couple was affiliated were supposed to take on the expenses and have the wedding in their club. Aasamaa (1974, 174–75), in her Soviet-era etiquette book, notes that the couple should be escorted in by representatives of the organization that arranged the wedding, followed by a woman carrying a tray of champagne for an official toast by the organizers. These weddings were a propaganda tool designed to foster a Soviet, non-religious ceremony and preeminence of the state over the family. Despite these efforts, people preferred weddings with an emphasis on family and community, not on the state. In fact, the political understanding of the Komsomol wedding seems to have eluded (or been ignored) by those that had them, because they clearly understood them to be student-organized receptions. A popular depiction of a Komsomol wedding can be seen in the film *Moscow Does Not Believe in Tears*, where one of the heroines has her reception in the workers' dormitory.

breaking pots to ensure the couple's happiness (or that they have a large number of children) or requiring the bride to sweep up dirt and coins off the floor. One couple combined these two rituals. Tatiana U. described her experience as follows:

> In this pot they gathered money, and they broke this clay pot and forced the bride to sweep and watched to see what kind of housewife she was. If she swept well or not, how she gathered money.... They didn't make him do it. I remembered that I was sweeping, and they scattered it again, and he ran around and protected me, fought with those scattering it.

The second day also involved another meal, toasts, and the like. Only one informant, from Chita, mentioned that there was *riazhanie* on the second day. Two couples also reported a tradition called *bliny*, during which a guest is offered a glass of vodka (typically with either *bliny* or some other food) and then must pay to drink a toast to the couple. The money goes either to the couple or to neighbors who were not invited to the celebration to have their own meal in honor of the couple. As with previous informants, most of these people did not have a honeymoon; only one couple who married in 1975 (one of the couples who had a restaurant reception) had a honeymoon trip.

Age, Religion, Politics, and Weddings Don't Mix

One of the primary factors in how elaborate a wedding celebration the couple had during this period seemed to be age. Three couples married when they were already in their thirties. They all recognized that many of the rituals described above took place during the time that they were getting married (1971, 1980, 1983), but they did not perform most of them at their weddings. One informant, Nina S., replied, when asked why she did not have a *vykup*: "We're already grown-ups. Liuda [her friend who had a *vykup*] got married as a young girl, but I was already thirty-eight years old." Olga R. responded similarly: "For me it was not an early marriage, and it was Boris's second marriage, and therefore we didn't want to arrange a big celebration with a large number of guests." Elena B. expressed the same opinion: "We had a meal, but without all of the additional tricks. Young people like to do that."

An additional factor that played a role in the level of ceremony appears to be religion and political attitudes. Irina V., a Jewish Muscovite, reported that she wanted nothing to do with Orthodox traditions, even though she was marrying into a non-Jewish family. Despite the fact that she was married at twenty-one, she also rejected the idea of these rituals as childish: "No, there was no buying of the bride, no one stole me away.... We said we were not going to play little children's games." Later she went on to say that she rejected many of these traditions that were associated with Orthodoxy: "I categorically refused any hint of Orthodox traditions, therefore no grain, no shoe that you had to throw somewhere, there was nothing." Note that while Irina did not want any of these acts performed at her wedding, or even a large reception, her non-Jewish in-laws did arrange for some of them as part of the restaurant reception:

> We went to a restaurant, and there were some acts already ordered, there was already an organizer of cultural activities, an entertainer with an accordion who led everything. There was already bread and salt, they had to break a glass. I made terrible faces and turned up my nose on account of this.

We can conclude that people actively rejected some aspects of the wedding ritual because of their associations with youth or with another, competing tradition. Interestingly, the practices that were omitted were those associated with folk tradition. To Russian "Orthodox" people, these traditions were associated with marriage at a young age and with the transition into adulthood. These couples had already "entered" adulthood, and it was not necessary to perform these acts. In fact, it would have been foolish to do so, because such games were the province of the young.[11] Another complication, of course, was the association between these behaviors and the Orthodox wedding, as Irina's comments show. While they were part of the Orthodox wedding in the nineteenth century, they were not Orthodox in origin and did not actually relate to the Christian belief system. However, folk traditions like these were tied to Orthodoxy and, as a result, were taboo, either for those who were unbelievers or for those who were of another religious heritage. For this reason, ritual specialists, as discussed in chapter 1, strove to remove the religious connections to the folk material they espoused for the Soviet wedding. Irina also rejected Soviet-era elements, such as the visit to the tomb of the unknown soldier in Moscow, as a form of protest against the Soviet system itself.

The wedding, then, served as a battleground between various traditions in post-war Soviet Russia. It could be used to make a statement about religious belief or political opinion or about attitudes toward adulthood and marriage. While these statements may well have belied Soviet theorists' intentions for the ritual, it is not surprising. The attitudes toward and performance of Soviet Russian birth and wedding rites support Bell's (1997, 79) contention that ritual "is not primarily the communication of messages about the social order.... Ritual is a tool for social and cultural jockeying; it is a performative

---

[11] That is not to say, of course, that the couples had not already internalized the material about gender roles that these practices illustrated. They would have seen them at other weddings and they were certainly modeled in other aspects of daily life, e.g., from relatives and friends.

medium for the negotiation of power in relationships." In the end, ritual establishes a state of affairs in the world, as Bourdieu (1991) argues in his discussion of rites of passage. The people I interviewed created a reality that meshed with their own concepts of family, society, and adulthood, and relied on a plethora of sources, not only on those fixed meanings the ritual may have been designed to convey. As such, they exemplify the Soviet citizens Yurchak discusses, who reacted to the "meaninglessness" of official discourse by expressing divergent ideas rich in meaning as they performed rituals. Rituals opened the door to a variety of interpretations and new types of "realities," which the actors themselves created.

These different types of celebrations show the complexity of describing the wedding, because it was not only dependent on family and regional traditions, but also on individual preference. Officialdom controlled the birth ritual much more effectively, because it took place within state institutions. Most of the wedding acts were performed in private, in the family circle. While the Soviet authorities attempted to standardize the reception as well, e.g., through the Komsomol wedding, people rebelled and family traditions won out (except, of course, in the ZAGS itself, where the ritual was predetermined). As Zhirnova (1980, 83) reports, the Soviet Union ultimately succeeded in getting the wedding palace ritual established only through concerted informational campaigns and ideological efforts to institute it. However, they were not as effective as they might have hoped once the couple emerged from the wedding palace.

Folk Tradition in the Soviet Wedding Ritual

At first glance it would seem that folk material did not retain as much of its life in urban weddings as it did in birth. That may well be because many changes in the wedding had already been instituted by the time the Soviet Union was founded. The roles of changing attitudes toward marriage and of general Soviet attacks on formal ceremonies cannot be discounted. Nevertheless, some material seems to have survived, although perhaps not continuously. Remnants of folk practice were indeed cited by informants, primarily those who married in the 1970s–80s, but their elders performed fewer acts associated with the village wedding. One might argue that the apparent break in tradition is the result of several factors. First, the Soviet authorities no longer disapproved of wedding celebrations, but in fact supported them, so that folk material was given the opportunity to flourish. There were certainly still older people who remembered folk traditions at this point, so that the material had not yet totally died out. Second, the ritual specialists, some of whom were trained ethnographers, included folk tradition as part of their descriptions of the Soviet wedding, so that some people took these practices from written sources. Third, it is possible that village in-migration had an effect, that those who actively retained folk tradition from rural areas came in ever larger numbers to cities, bringing their traditions with them.

All three factors certainly had an effect on weddings during the 1970s–80s, but the first is the most important. After all, some people who married in the 1950s and 1960s kept some of these traditions, which indicates that there was some awareness of them. Others, of course, tried (or were forced) to conform to the lack of ceremony the Soviet government had instituted. Those that were less bound by Soviet ideals celebrated a wedding that included folk practices. For example, Alevtina A., who married in 1956 in Vladimir, reported that she sold her wedding cake to the guests, and her mother met the couple after the ceremony with bread and salt, which she and her husband bit to see who would dominate in the marriage. Thus, I would suggest that, once freed from social and institutional constraints, the natural reaction was to reinstitute folk behaviors. This was also occurring at a time when the Soviet Union in general was emphasizing ethnic heritage, as Makashina (2003, 498) observes, which encouraged the revival of folk tradition.

The literature on the Russian wedding ritual is typically divided into three periods: pre-wedding, wedding day, and post-wedding. In keeping with this tradition, we will examine which, if any, folk traditions were preserved in each of these time frames. In our discussion below, we will primarily focus on the more elaborate celebrations from the period of the 1970s–80s, because they exemplify the Soviet wedding at the height of its development.

Pre-Wedding Folk Traditions

As discussed in chapter 2, pre-revolutionary urban wedding rituals retained the following folk elements: the matchmaking process, the occurrence of *smotriny* 'inspection of property/handicrafts', gift-giving by the bride, and the wedding procession to the church as well as the traditional roles of participants, such as the couple's attendants. In addition, in some smaller, regional cities, the *devichnik* and *riazhanie* were common, along with negotiations about the bride price and dowry (Zhirnova 1980, 65–67). While the Soviet wedding did not include formal matchmaking or dowry negotiations, it did retain a similar meeting of parents to discuss wedding finances. In many cases, this meeting was often the first one between the parents, so that they were getting acquainted over a meal (generally at the bride's home) and discussing wedding plans. By this time, of course, negotiations were fairly simple, because the tradition was to split expenses evenly. However, they still had to decide issues such as where the reception would take place, how lavish it would be, how many guests would be invited, who had family connections or informal connections (*blat*) that might help with the wedding details,[12] and also where

---

[12] For example, one informant reported that they had lots of fresh fish at the reception, because her uncle lived on the coast; another said they had meat, because the hus-

the couple would live.[13] This joint negotiation contrasts strongly to the Western tradition, which specifies a fixed set of expenses for both families. In the Soviet Russian tradition, the wedding was a much more communal affair, like that of the nineteenth-century village.

In fact, community involvement extended throughout the festivities. Only two of twenty-three couples had a reception outside the home, which meant that the family had to prepare for the reception as well as for the celebrations on the second day. These preparations involved not only cooking for roughly thirty to fifty guests (the average wedding size), but also purchasing the food and drink. During times of shortages, buying goods for the wedding could be extremely complicated. Several Vladimir residents reported that they had to make trips to Moscow for both food and clothing, because nothing was available in the local stores. In addition, female relatives often sewed either the wedding dress or the bride's outfit for the second day. The involvement of the family in the wedding is not only similar to the nineteenth-century village tradition but parallels Soviet-era childbirth ritual as well. The mother and child relied on the family to provide the essential goods needed for the baby while they were confined to the hospital. Wedding couples were certainly not isolated in the same way as a mother was, but they were limited by their financial resources, because most were young (often still students).

Friends also played an important role, making the Soviet Russian wedding truly a community event, similar to the village wedding. While the large number of traditional attendants had been lost, they were replaced by witnesses who took on some of the tasks associated with the groom's and bride's attendants in the folk wedding (as well as the Soviet-era function of signing the registry book). For example, in the folk wedding the groom's *druzhko* 'best man' or the *tychiatskii* 'godfather' managed the *vykup*. They negotiated for his place at the table and also paid the amounts required of the groom as a result of these negotiations. I observed similar functions by the groom's witness in a contemporary wedding; he paid the women blocking the groom's path and helped him complete the tasks set for him. In addition, the bride's witness performed functions traditionally done by *podruzhki* 'bride's attendants', such as *vykup* negotiations and helping the bride dress. Friends not only served as witnesses, but also took the place of parents for some couples in the wedding. Four couples reported that their friends arranged for their wedding reception, because their families were living elsewhere. While they typically had a second reception later on at their parents' home, it is significant that the friends took the responsibility of providing for the couple seriously, so that despite their own limited financial means, they banded together to give them a

---

band's family lived in the country. Connections were important not only for food, but for other wedding necessities, such as clothing; one bride got her wedding dress made at the best Moscow tailor shop, because she knew someone who worked there.

[13] A majority of these couples lived with their parents after they were first married.

"proper" reception. Thus, community involvement in the wedding included both friends and family, and would seem to derive from the folk tradition.[14]

Another pre-wedding activity that seems to have its roots in the folk tradition is the asking for parental permission before the marriage. While not every couple performed this ritual (thirteen of twenty-three did), it parallels the village ritual in which the groom's family comes to visit the bride's family to ask for her hand in marriage. There were various reasons why a couple omitted this ritual; the most common was distance. Couples who married in their thirties also did not see the need to ask for permission to marry. As we have seen, they rejected most wedding practices associated with youth. The remaining group felt that, although they were young, they knew what was best for themselves. As a result, they omitted this step. Nevertheless, I would argue that the fact that nearly fifty-seven percent of the couples performed this ritual implies that this folk tradition is a persistent one.

The *devichnik/mal'chishnik* parties may also have their precedent in the village. In the nineteenth century the more important of these parties was the *devichnik*, the bride's final farewell to her girlhood and to her family on the eve of the wedding. The *mal'chishnik* was not so widely celebrated, although it did exist (Makashina 2003, 483). While couples organized and participated in these parties in the twentieth century, these celebrations had changed their character remarkably. To begin with, the *mal'chishnik* had become much more widespread than its female counterpart. Most of the men had these parties, while few of the women did (before the 1990s). The *mal'chishnik* took on much of the character of the Western bachelor party. In fact, it may have been borrowed from this tradition, given the limited range of the *mal'chishnik* in the nineteenth century.

The groom and his friends gathered on the eve of the wedding to drink and toast his departure from the bachelor ranks. The tenor of this party suggests that traditional attitudes toward who gained and lost by marriage had shifted by the twentieth century. In the village, the party to say farewell to the single life, to lament one's loss, was for the bride; the groom only gained status by marrying, while the bride lost it. Thus the party was designed to vent some of her fears and anger about the situation. In the twentieth century, the practice would seem to be parallel to the European / American idea that a bride gains status when she marries, while a man loses status. I would suggest that while the tradition seems to be related to nineteenth-century village practices, it has been reinterpreted within the modern worldview of marriage. Support for this claim would seem to be the lack of interest among the brides in the informant pool in celebrating a *devichnik* for themselves. If they had one, and most did not, it was basically a tea party for friends, not designed to mourn a loss, but to celebrate her entry into a "higher" status as a married

---

[14] As with childbirth, the Soviet social system also contributed to community involvement, as will be discussed below.

woman. Thus it was more akin to a Western bridal shower (albeit without the presents).

Presents, in fact, were limited to the day of the wedding or after the wedding. As with childbirth, it was not deemed proper to give presents before the event. While people did not use the same term (*sglazit'* 'to give the evil eye'), it was clear that pre-ceremony gift-giving was not consonant with the Russian worldview. Gift-giving before the fact seems to tempt fate. No one received any presents before the wedding day, either at a party such as a shower or from guests who could not attend the wedding.

In the twenty years after World War II, people did not have a formal wedding procession to the ZAGS. However, with the renewed emphasis on a formal ceremony, the Soviet ritual specialists called for the restoration of the wedding train, which had been characteristic not only of the village, but of pre-revolutionary urban weddings as well. People once again began to decorate the automobiles in which the bride and groom traveled to the wedding palace. In some cases, particularly in the Vladimir region, the bride and groom traveled in separate vehicles before the ceremony, as they had in the late nineteenth and early twentieth centuries. The cars themselves were special, typically high-end Volga sedans, often provided by the employer of someone in the family. While the decorations themselves were not traditional (interlocked rings, inflatable swans and dolls, red ribbons), they were a revival of an established folk tradition. The rejuvenation of this tradition is also significant in that it illustrates the fundamental shift in Soviet attitudes toward the wedding ceremony. Couples had gone from arrival at the ZAGS on the trolleybus, as Klara K. had done in the early 1960s, to transportation in a visibly marked luxury sedan by the 1970s. The wedding procession was also tied to the elements of conspicuous consumption that were introduced as part of the Soviet urban wedding during this period, which will be discussed in more detail below.

The pre-wedding traditions show a much more uneven distribution of folk elements inherited from either the nineteenth-century village or city than we found in birth practices. Certainly the urbanization of the wedding before the revolution had an effect on folk tradition. Soviet interference in the wedding also played its role, in both the elimination of some folk behaviors and the restoration of others, such as the economic elements (dowry negotiations and gift-giving by the bride to the groom's relatives) and the wedding procession respectively. The changing nature of the wedding relationship, from an economic to an emotional one (another aspect that arose in the twentieth century in Europe generally), and the reinterpretation of who gained by marriage produced a shift in the symbolism of some behaviors, like the bachelor party and the financial negotiations. An additional issue is the influence of Western popular culture and the decision by Soviet ritual specialists to (re)adopt some features associated with European/American weddings. All of these factors complicate an assessment of the folk inheritance in the wedding. Nevertheless, they are essential to an illustration of the Soviet wedding complex as a whole, with its myriad of sometimes contradictory sources.

Folk Traditions in the Wedding Proper

The day of the wedding brought with it more folk traditions than the pre-wedding period, including the *vykup*, the meeting with bread and salt, throwing of grain (or coins and candy), and the restrictions on the parents' attendance at the wedding ceremony. One could also cite the performance of *chastushki* at the reception as well as accordion music and some Russian folk dances. It is not surprising that there were more traditional practices on the wedding day, given that it was the focus of the ritual, and as such would tend to be more conservative. Significantly, these portions of the ritual were held in a private setting, at home, and were not as influenced by Soviet norms and ZAGS institutional requirements. They also conformed to the "new" attitude toward marriage as an emotional bond between the couple and their families and established gender roles in the family, as we will discuss.

The *vykup* is perhaps the most widespread of the nineteenth-century traditions that was retained. While my informants assured me that the bride was purchased "*chisto simvolicheski*" (purely symbolically), this portion of the ritual was considered to be an important one for most people. This practice served several functions within the Russian system in the twentieth century. First, it was an act of ritual humiliation for the groom. He was a healthy, powerful young man being told how to behave by a group of women. They, of course, could not actually have stopped him physically from entering, but he accepted their role as more powerful as part of the rite of passage. The ritual imbalance of power was a significant factor in this transitional rite. In order to assume his new, more responsible role in society, the groom must first be abased. In addition, this practice shows what role the groom was expected to have in the marriage relationship; he must provide money and food to his family. If he could not perform this duty at the *vykup*, then he was not ready for marriage. It was a trial, albeit a humorous one, that symbolized his new responsibilities. The bride's family and friends, as in the nineteenth century, also demanded payment to show that they possessed an object of great value that they were "losing" to the groom. In turn, he was obliged to recognize her worth and compensate them for their loss. While the two families were joining, there existed a natural amount of competition and antagonism between them. When either family got the upper hand, it illustrated their superiority in the newly-founded relationship. For all these reasons, the *vykup* was a persistent tradition that conveyed important messages about the organization of the Russian family and gender roles within it. Soviet ritual specialists disapproved of the *vykup*, saying that it was not consonant with equality between the sexes (see Ugrinovich 1975, 153).

However, they made few inroads in stopping the traditional practice, not only because it was enjoyable, but also because it was meaningful to the participants.

While family involvement was crucial to a successful wedding celebration, as I have noted, there was one area in which it was not welcome: parents generally did not attend the ceremony itself at the ZAGS. Makashina (2003, 486) notes that they did not usually go to the church ceremony in the nineteenth-century village either. In fact, there was a law against it established by Peter I in 1724 (Zhirnova 1980, 52). In the nineteenth-century wedding, the couple made the transition under the protection of the *druzhko* 'best man' and *svakha* 'matchmaker', not their parents. They were in transition during this period and belonged neither to one family nor to the other. Thus they were physically separated from both sets of parents to indicate their liminal status. Once they passed through the ceremony, they returned to the groom's home and were officially welcomed into the family by the groom's parents with a *karavai* (a ritual bread held by the mother) and an icon (held by the father). Later in the day, the bride's parents also joined the celebration, but it was clear that she was now a member of the groom's family, because she had to call his parents "mother" and "father" and would live within their household. Simply put, in the Russian tradition, it was a bad omen for the couple if the parents were present at the church ceremony. Even in the Soviet era some people agreed with this idea, as Liudmila B. reported: "Although there is this superstition that it isn't good for parents to go to the ZAGS."

In the nineteenth-century village, the bread and salt ritual described above was a ritual that welcomed the bride into the family and helped to determine the couple's future. The icon ensured that the new union would be blessed, while the bread and salt symbolized future prosperity and abundance. In the twentieth century, where this ritual still existed, it continued to show the family's hopes for the couple's good fortune. Note that in keeping with the shift in social structure (the bride no longer automatically joined the groom's family), either mother (or even a grandmother) could present the bread and salt to the couple. Although some people reported that it should be the groom's mother who performed this ritual, they were in the minority. This ritual was often combined with the throwing of grain, coins, or candy (or a combination thereof) to ensure that the couple's life together would be fruitful, abundant, and sweet. The icon was typically omitted from the rite as one would expect, given the official atheism of the state.[15]

This practice also had an additional component that was first recorded in my data in 1956, but became fairly widespread only in the 1970s. When the

---

[15] One couple, who was married in Vladimir in the 1970s, stated that her mother did meet them with an icon, which had been passed down in her family. It is possible that such blessings had been preserved in other families as well, like secret baptism, but they were not mentioned by any other informants.

couple was presented the bread (after receiving the parents' blessing), they were to bite off a piece; the person who bit more would be the head of the family. The nineteenth-century wedding featured various practices which were designed to show who would be dominant in the relationship. Ananicheva and Samodelova mention one wedding in which the bride's and groom's matchmakers broke a loaf in half to see who was dominant.[16] Nevertheless, there is no mention of biting bread. Thus it would seem that the divination practices shifted from rebraiding the hair or crossing the threshold to the bread ritual, which was not recorded in the nineteenth-century ethnographic material.[17] While the means of divination shifted, the fact that awareness of the practice still existed in the twentieth century leads me to conclude that this ritual is a reinterpretation of folk practices inherited from the village.

One interesting fact about this bread ritual is that it is designed to favor the man. The nineteenth-century divinations did not give an advantage to either partner; they were essentially based on chance. However, physically men simply have a better chance of biting off a larger piece than women do and were seemingly not afraid to try to win. Most of the women interviewed with their husbands denied trying to bite off a larger piece of bread. One woman said it would look offensive for a bride, with her face made up and wearing a formal, white dress, to cram food into her mouth in this way. In contrast, the men all said that they had bitten off a larger piece and as a result were dominant in the relationship. Women interviewed alone often said they bit off more. This ritual (and indeed my informants' answers to the question about it), like the *vykup*, sends a message about gender roles in marriage. The man is expected to be the head of the household within the Russian family system. By devising a ritual that all but ensures his success (either because of a physical advantage or because women are more concerned with appearances), they reinforce his social and familial power. Nevertheless, men were not always successful in their attempts. Natalia S. said that her husband tried to bite off more, but did not; as a result: "There are five men in my family, one woman. But it is a matriarchy. Everything is through me." Natalia was indeed interviewed without her husband, who was not willing to be recorded. These discrepancies between opinions illustrate an interesting fact about gender roles in the Russian family. Publicly the women and their husbands often send the message that men are dominant, but privately the women, at least, often have a different attitude. This ritual gets at the heart of gender conflict in the Soviet Russian marital system (discussed in more detail below).

---

[16] This ritual might also have indicated what sex the couple's first child would be, according to Makashina (2003, 487).

[17] I should note that some informants who married in the 1990s reported that they knew this omen: the first to cross the ZAGS threshold and step on the carpet would be the dominant partner. However, none of the people who married in the previous four decades mentioned it.

Receptions during the Soviet period also featured several traditional practices. While *chastushki* were not part of the village wedding celebration, they
had become part of the urban tradition by the end of the nineteenth century.
These humorous songs conveyed a sense of folk tradition in the urban setting,
and also dealt with erotic or subversive topics (not only political comments,
but also issues of relationships between families and the bridal couple) in a
socially acceptable way. People could express these sentiments under the
cover of humor. They became an essential part of the ritual humiliation of the
couple (and their families), because they were public acknowledgements of
sensitive familial issues and sexuality.[18] They were often performed to an accordion, which many informants said was played at their weddings. Some
people also danced traditional dances of some kind to the accordion. While
they may not have known the village songs or dances (in all of their complexity), these practices connected them to folk traditions of the past and to the
village. Olson (2004, 106ff.) has shown that such material, whether truly
inherited from the folk tradition or not, bound both urban and rural people to
a mythical sense of the "Russian folk," a situation similar to the desire to
maintain "Russianness" through traditional birth practices. People reacted to
these acts, even in a revised form, as continuity in the village tradition, as they
did with the bread and salt ritual described above.

Folklore, after all, is not static, and people adapt it to their changing circumstances. The urban situation did not call for the same type of ritual songs
as the village wedding in the nineteenth century, but it demanded songs
nevertheless. Thus the songs could be the urban folk genre of *chastushki*, as
well as popular songs from World War II about love and marriage or *zhestokie
romansy* 'cruel romances' (Matlin 2003, 381; Zhirnova 1980, 114). These forms
may not be considered by some folklorists to be "authentic" folk genres, but
they served the same function for ritual participants: to express social conflicts inherent in the society, to teach about the couple's roles in marriage, and
to relive their own ritual experiences from the past. The songs allowed those
already married not only to ensure that the couple was properly inducted into
their new status (through humor and humiliation), but also to express their
own feelings, both negative and positive. Similarly, popular romantic songs
enabled them to reconnect with their past and their own initiation into the
married state.

The reception itself as a whole was inherited from folk practice. The meal
to signify the unity of the couple and their families was a centerpiece of both
earlier urban and rural weddings.[19] This unification necessarily involved an
elaborate meal with frequent and intricate toasting rites, the heart of any Rus-

---

[18] For more on the subversive nature of *chastushki* in another context, see Olson (2004, 230–31).

[19] I am not claiming that this practice is unique to Russia, but that it was part of an older tradition in this culture.

sian celebration.[20] The formal exchange of gifts, during which people often offered toasts or read poems they had prepared, reinforced the level of community involvement in this ritual. People's good wishes and gifts were meant to support the young couple in the future, not only monetarily or physically, but with their kind words. Within the Russian tradition, putting something into words ensures that it will come to pass, be it good or bad. If bad, the omen can be converted by 'spitting' three times over the shoulder or by knocking on wood three times. In this case, the toasts were a ritual that could bring about a bright future for the young couple. Each guest's words and gifts then symbolized the tie between the people at the wedding and their ability to influence the couple's future or *dolia* 'lot.' The weddings were necessarily fairly small by American standards, because they were held in apartments. Thus each guest already had a special connection to the couple (close friend or family member) and hi(s)her participation in this event strengthened the ties between them.

We saw in our discussion of birth that the folk tradition was strongest within the family circle, outside of the auspices of officialdom. This pattern repeats itself in the wedding as well, as we can see. In the family home, at the reception after the ZAGS ceremony, the family was much freer to maintain folk practices. As noted above, there were more folk traditions present during this portion of the wedding celebration due to the historical changes in the country overall (improved financial situation, greater acceptance of folk tradition, and approval of a more elaborate ceremony by the authorities). They were also an essential component in defining marital and family roles in this society. What was maintained was relevant to the bride and groom's future, not only as a means to ensure their happiness, but as a signal of the newly formed relationship between their families and between the couple. The *vykup* and the greeting with the *karavai* provided a message about the couple's roles within the marriage. They also illustrated the families' bond and their sense of competition in this new relationship. Many of the events, including the *karavai* ritual and the activities at the reception (toasting, gift-giving) conveyed the importance of the new union to the community of friends and family. They also functioned as a type of charm, designed to influence the couple's future together.[21] Finally, participation in the dances, games, songs, and toasts

---

[20] Students in my Novosibirsk State University American Folklore course were shocked to learn that American receptions last only a few hours, often do not involve a full meal, may not provide alcohol, and have no second day. They asked me why people bother to attend at all.

[21] Some other forms of charms that have been preserved from the folk tradition do not belong to a particular portion of the tripartite wedding system described above. They generally involve superstitions designed to protect the couple or to ensure their future happiness. Three of these (the absence of the parents at the ceremony, the groom seeing the bride's dress, and the risk of married witnesses) have already been discussed.

serves to express possible conflicts within the social structure as well as to re-
new bonds between members of the community and between other married
couples. The traditional post-wedding activities also reflected these concerns,
in particular expectations about gender roles in marriage, charms to influence
the future, and the centrality of community involvement in the couple's life.

Folk Traditions in the Post-Wedding Period

The post-wedding period in the Soviet Union consisted mainly of the second-
day celebration. In the village, weddings often lasted at least three days.
Given people's work schedules, such an extended celebration was generally
not possible in the contemporary period. Most people tried to have their weddings on Friday or Saturday, so that they could maintain the tradition of the
second day. There were fewer guests on the second day, so that only those
closest to the couple were invited, which again emphasized social bonds. As
one would expect, it entailed yet another meal for the guests and more work
for the family. The second day in the village wedding was characterized by
another meal, *riazhanie*,[22] games and divinations about the newlyweds' future,
and the bride's tests to see whether she would make a good wife.

One folk practice that many people mentioned when describing the
second day was the breaking of goblets or clay pots. Traditionally dishes were
smashed and read to discover the number of children the couple would have.
This act has been retained as a divination, but with two possible interpretations: either as a (humorous) means to ascertain the number of children the
couple will have; or as a means to ensure happiness (the couple would have
as many happy years together as their were broken pieces). As Tatiana U.
noted, this ritual could be combined with the sweeping ritual designed to test
the bride's talent as a housekeeper.

Just as the *vykup* evaluated how well the groom could fulfill his expectations as a provider for his family, the bride had to sweep up coins (sometimes
with trash thrown in) to show that she would be a good housewife. This task
not only demonstrated that she knew how to keep house, but also that she
would be able to use money wisely. Interestingly, the groom's primary humiliation in these weddings came before the wedding ceremony, i.e., before he
"lost" status by marrying, while the bride's comes after she has "gained" status by marrying. The practice is particularly evocative of the dilemma faced

---

Two others that my informants mentioned that were inherited from the nineteenth
century (Makashina 487) include: if it rained on the wedding day, the couple would be
happy; if they dropped a wedding ring during the ceremony, it was bad luck. Another
belief some mentioned is that if there were a fistfight at the reception, the couple
would be happy.

[22] Only one informant, from Chita, said that people participated in mumming on the
second day.

by women in Soviet Russian society. They had to marry in order to fulfill their duty to the state as well as to their family (to bear children). Unmarried, older women, of course, were less socially acceptable to both institutions. Nevertheless, once they did so, they assumed a subservient role in the marriage, at least in the public eye, as discussed above. Because the woman swept the coins with a *vennik*, a short Russian broom which required her to bend down lower than the guests, this act was physically symbolic of the social role she assumed by marrying. Her husband did not help her sweep, but he fulfilled his role as protector by trying to prevent people from scattering the coins again.

The final folk element of the second day related to the wedding cake. The wedding cake did not exist in the Russian village, but was borrowed from the Western tradition into the urban Russian wedding. Neither was there a tradition for the bride to "sell" items at the wedding meals. However, both the cake and the selling of it are characteristic of the gathering on the second day in the twentieth century. Zorin (2001, 97) does describe a nineteenth-century village ritual during which the bride had to "buy" access to the well with small cakes. Zelenin (1991, 342) refers to a practice from this period in which the bride's relatives sell the ritual bread. In addition, the bride's *podruzhki* did sell their songs and/or sweets to the groom's party (Ananicheva and Samodelova 1997, 121, 133). Any of these practices might be the source of this contemporary ritual act. Cake-selling could also be a reinterpretation of the *vykup*, which involved not only buying access to the bride, but also the place next to her, her maiden's headdress and her braid, typically by the bride's retinue, but the act of selling may have shifted to the bride herself in the twentieth century. It is also possible that selling the cake is a modern version of the trials a bride underwent in the nineteenth century. Just as she had to demonstrate her talents as a housewife by sweeping, carrying water, and lighting the stove a hundred years ago, she must show her ability to be a good financial manager in the twentieth.

As we have seen, the folk practices, while they may have lasted until the twentieth century (or may have been revived after a break in the tradition), cannot all be equated with the same elements in the nineteenth century. The events not only take place within a radically different socio-cultural context, but also reflect another view of marriage itself. That is not to say that there are not some commonalities, such as some aspects of gender roles in the marriage and the community's desire to support the couple and ensure their happiness. However, the folk elements also intertwined with Soviet ideals for marriage and the family and the consumerist wedding traditions characteristic of the capitalist countries of Europe and America. It is to these issues we turn now.

Western and Soviet Elements in the Wedding Ritual

The Soviet state conceived of the family as a rational unit that would benefit society by creating contented citizens who would produce the next generation of workers. In order to achieve this goal, as we have discussed, it introduced a thinly-veiled consumer ideology to support the middle class. They believed that the promise of material goods and the desire to support one's family would keep people in check. However, the Soviet Union could not (or would not) deliver on all the promises it made to its people. Verdery (1996, 26) examines production during socialism and notes that light industry was never as fully developed as heavy industry, which meant that people did not have access to all the consumer goods they needed. As a result, the black market (and dissatisfaction with the state) grew. One might argue that the black market actually served the Soviet government's purposes by providing goods and keeping people's attention directed away from politics. While this assertion has some merit, Verdery (29) convincingly argues that

> consumption goods and objects conferred an identity that set you off from socialism, enabled you to differentiate yourself as an individual in the face of relentless pressure to homogenize everyone's capacities and tastes into an undifferentiated collectivity. Acquiring objects became a way of constituting your selfhood against a deeply unpopular regime.

However, Yurchak (2006, 162) argues that this situation was more complicated than Verdery suggests. Rather than simply being a form of resistance, goods and indeed ideas from the West were interpreted in various ways: "Western cultural influences were both criticized for bourgeois values and celebrated for internationalism, circulated through unauthorized networks and official state channels, transported from abroad and invented locally." With reference to Western goods in particular, Yurchak (200–02) concludes that while these objects may have been desirable, they did not necessarily indicate rejection of Soviet values. Many of those who had or wanted jeans, for example, were dismayed by the greed displayed by black marketeers and found it distasteful to interact with them. In sum, the jeans themselves were not contrary to Soviet ideals, although people obsessed by materialism were. The buyers did not see in themselves the images of negative propaganda about youth who had rejected Soviet morality. That is not to say, of course, that some people did not react to their Western goods as Verdery suggests. However, this fact only reemphasizes Yurchak's contention that there was a wide array of responses to Soviet-era ideology, a society in which seemingly contradictory messages were at once resolved and also interpreted variously. This issue is particularly important within the wedding ceremony, because it also introduced "bourgeois" practices that would seem to contradict Soviet values about consumerism.

When the ritual specialists began to devise a formal Soviet wedding ceremony, they not only revived some folk practices, but also resurrected or introduced elements from the bourgeois wedding they professed to despise. In fact, they had little choice, because there were few models but those weddings if one wanted to establish a formal ceremony. Certainly a complete return to folk practices, with a dowry, a bride price, and a religious ceremony (to name but a few elements) would be incompatible not only with Soviet ideology, but with the modern world as well. In addition, some allowance for luxury fit into the policy decision to emphasize consumer comforts among the middle class. However, these practices brought with them values about male/female relationships and conspicuous consumption that could not be controlled. The ritual specialists also make reference to this problem. They assert that weddings should not focus on elaborate fashion and entertainment or on excessive drinking, all of which they had observed in contemporary weddings (Sukhanov 1976, 205; Ugrinovich 1975, 150). While Soviet ritual specialists were sending a message they had carefully crafted, they could not guarantee it would be received intact. Ritual participants could reinterpret the message to their own ends or reject it outright. Unlike in birth practices, where it is reasonably easy to tease out the three strands of the ritual (folk behaviors, Soviet policy, and Western medical practice), the individual strands are less clear for the wedding, because many of the behaviors overlap. Thus, the Soviet and Western (consumerist) elements will be discussed together, with reference to the folk tradition as needed.

Women in the Ritual Tradition

It is of note from the point of view of both the folk inheritance and Soviet ideology that ZAGS workers are overwhelmingly female. Women were particularly well-suited to play an integral role in all three village life-cycle rituals (Adon'ieva 1998, 27; Moyle 1996, 230; Rouhier-Willoughby 2003a, 21–22). While women did not, of course, perform the wedding mass in the Orthodox church in the nineteenth century, they were instrumental in other aspects of the rite of passage, including matchmaking, singing ritual songs, arranging the ritual bath for the bride, rebraiding the bride's hair, preparing the dowry and the like. Without their participation, the couple could not have made a successful transition into their new state. Therefore, it seems that the role of women as celebrants is also connected to the folk tradition as well as to other traditional ideas about women's talents. ZAGS workers I interviewed emphasized their ability to be creative. They were in fact not lawyers, but were generally trained in the humanities.[23] Galina V. described her love for her work as follows: "Therefore I really like talking to a large number of people, I like being useful to them, I like helping in different situations. And plus also creating a celebratory atmosphere. I like that a lot, to come up with something, to think up something." Lilia T. remarked that it was not only their duty to perform the ceremonies, but to take on the role of a sort of surrogate mother and counselor, both typically female roles, to their clients:

> Because you respect yourself, you converse with the people when they submit an application, how deep is this, how serious are they. To speak with the young couple, after all we, one can say, have lived life and young people might not listen much to relatives, but we are people from the outside. When people from the outside speak, they take it a little differently than when their mom talks: it is early for you to get married, study some more, he isn't going to make anything of himself.... You have to talk things over with people, and this is a seriously responsible thing and you have to relate to people with respect. In any case to their choice. Anything can happen here. He has already left his family and kids and is going to marry another woman and his first wife and children meet him here. With them you have to calm down both one and the other.

The role of ritual coordinator, advisor to youth, and holiday organizer is especially suited for women in the traditional Russian worldview. Not surprisingly, throughout the Soviet period these attitudes did not change and were in fact reinforced (as the introduction of the gender role course and the typical "female" and "male" jobs during the Soviet era illustrate; see chapters 1 and 3 for a discussion). The stereotypical view was that women were creative souls who could be sensitive to family problems and were suited to working with those in transition, in both amateur and professional capacities.

Like female medical doctors, women in these positions also served Soviet ideological and social purposes. As Lilia highlights in her comments, these women represented the state, as outsiders who could advise couples about proper behavior from the point of view of Soviet and traditional norms. The ZAGS staff was made up of essentially clerical workers. Like other service jobs, including medicine, it was a job without much social status. As we have seen, in the Soviet period, such jobs were typically filled by women (see Buckley 1996, 215–18 for a discussion of women in lower paid, less skilled jobs; see also Marody 1993, 856; Molyneux and Posadskaia 1991, 135; Attwood 1990, 131). More importantly, female celebrants also further distanced the Soviet ceremony from the Orthodox one, because women, not

---

[23] The requirement for legal training for ZAGS workers was instituted in 1997 in the post-Soviet period.

male priests, performed the wedding. Therefore, there was less of a risk that people would "confuse" these ceremonies with religious ones. They were thereby participating in a new world order as devised by Soviet society. These female professionals thus represented the Soviet Union's rejection of outmoded bourgeois and religious values and its espousal of equality between the sexes, but simultaneously conformed to traditional gender stereotypes within society about women's roles in rites of transition.

Ritual Space: The Soviet "Church"

In order to have a formal ceremony, the Soviet authorities had to create a suitable space, namely the wedding palace. The Soviet Union, in this regard, behaved like other European societies that had undergone significant social shifts (see Hobsbawm 1983b, 271–76). They created buildings and monuments that reflected the new social order and devised ceremonies that conveyed its ideals. Stites (1989, 238) also discusses the Soviet impulse toward "monumentalism" from the 1930s on in an effort "restore the old respect for hugeness, order, symmetry—all associated with solemn and unchallenged authority." The wedding palace exemplifies this trend. The buildings are typically large, white structures with vaulted ceilings. Interiors are usually white stone with red carpets and contain furniture with sumptuous red upholstery. There is a waiting room on the ground floor, where the wedding couple and their guests go before the ceremony. In some cases, the bride and groom were separated into two rooms to wait and then joined together for the procession. There is generally a long, curving staircase upon which the couple can process to the chamber where ceremonies are performed. The chamber itself is accessed by large double doors that open onto a red carpet runner along which the couple walks, accompanied by Mendelssohn's Wedding March (played while entering and exiting) into a room of vast proportions, so that they (and their guests) are dwarfed by the space. The celebrant stands at a table at the head of the carpet. On the table are the official marriage registry book, the marriage certificate, and a plate for the rings. Behind the celebrant, on a large wall flanked by windows, is a huge Soviet coat of arms, often bas relief (in the same location a cross would hang in a church).[24] Built-in benches along the walls allow the guests to sit during the ceremony. After the ceremony and the congratulations, the couple left and went to a separate room for toasts and pictures.

The design of these palaces united Soviet ideals (the state crest; the use of the revolutionary color red; the official registry book; marriage by a state representative; the grandiosity of the space itself) with those of both the Ortho-

---

[24] Because they are part of the wall itself, it is nearly impossible to remove them. As a result, they remain in place in all the palaces I visited more than ten years after the fall of the Soviet Union.

dox and other religious traditions (elaborate spaces akin to churches in form; the formal procession; the choice of music; the wedding rings). When the ceremonies were little more than brief formalities at a registry office, there was little or no symbolic content in either the events or the location. In these later ceremonies, the physical space itself is symbolic of the rite of passage and its renewed importance in Soviet life. Restricted movement through the physically impressive space that is specially demarcated parallels the couple's transition into their new state. These practices also highlight the couple's specialness during the ritual, a practice that was in sharp contrast to earlier Soviet practices.

Certainly, if the ritual specialists are to be believed (Sukhanov 1976, 54), the Soviet government did not want to suggest anything religious in its ceremonies and would not willingly have introduced church-like elements if it could have avoided them. However, it had little choice in the design of the buildings. As with many of the other marriage traditions (the rings, the white dress), there were no other precedents for them to rely upon in the creation of a formal wedding ceremony. Thus, they created a space that is strikingly reminiscent in form to a church, but that also highlighted both the consumerist and monumentalist ideals they emphasized in the post-war period. They used fine materials in the construction and in the building's appointments. They provided an official ZAGS photographer and a place to drink champagne afterward. The physical space, like other aspects of the ceremony we have discussed, represents an amalgam of religious, revolutionary, and consumerist ideas and illustrates the complexity of the wedding ceremony in the Soviet period. Just as the medical system was reenvisioned through the lens of Soviet materialism, both Western and religious elements were reinterpreted through the cosmopolitan internationalism espoused by Soviet ideology. Despite their surface appearance, they did not directly contradict state goals. However, they did leave room for multiple interpretations, as we will discover from my informants' comments about the ceremony itself. As a result, participants in the wedding, like those in birth, were negotiating identity and creating social reality through the ceremony, in some cases consonant with Soviet ideology, and in some cases directly contradictory to it.

Institutional Power: Egalitarianism, Institutions, and the Individual

Birth was typified, as we have seen, by the strict hierarchy characteristic of egalitarian societies like the Soviet Union. Not surprisingly, the Soviet wedding also contained messages about the preeminence of the state and its institutions over the individual and the family.[25] In fact, it is even described that

---

[25] Recall that I am not suggesting that the state controlled every aspect of family life as it tried to do in the Stalinist period. Rather, it attempted to foster a message that the state was a provider for the family's needs as well as the arbiter of family values.

way, both in Aasamaa (1974, 171), who writes that a marriage is legal from the moment of its registration at the ZAGS (emphasizing the state's role in the process), and in the ZAGS director Lilia T.'s description of marriage: "the wedding is state registration with ritualistic elements." Some might claim that this approach to marriage is not unusual; that is, every civil society has rules about marriage, e.g., blood tests, licenses, and restrictions on relatives' marrying. However, the situation in the socialist state was complicated by what Verdery (1999, 47) describes as the state's "claim to special knowledge of how society should be managed." According to Verdery (46), particularly emblematic of such control of the individual and hi(s)her time was the prevalence of lines—lines for food, fuel, and other items—which illustrated the government's power over resources, both physical (consumer goods) and abstract (the citizens' time). This argument is supported by Shlapentokh's (1984, 190; 1989, 66) data on the problems of daily life in the Soviet Union, the two most common complaints being "lack of time" and "lack of consumer goods." Control of how people spent their time maximized the state's power over the individual. A similar situation existed in the ZAGS. Couples were not able to pick their wedding date, but had to take the first available time (or wait). Therefore, the ZAGS structured the couple's time, regardless of their individual wishes.

There were, of course, those who managed to subvert the process. For example, Natalia T. wanted to marry during Passion Week, a time when the Nizhnii Novgorod (then Gorky) wedding palace did not perform weddings, in keeping with the old Russian tradition of not having weddings during a fast.[26] However, she was graduating and was going to be assigned to a teaching post in another city the following week and wanted to marry before she left. The ZAGS, however, refused to grant the couple's wish. Thus, as Natalia T. relates:

> We went by indirect means using our connections. The director of that wedding palace was a relative of my husband's friend. And he went to her with flowers and perfume and she opened the wedding palace for our sake and registered us. We were the only couple.

Once again, we see that while the system could be a block to achieving individual desires, personal connections (as in the *roddom*) led to exceptions that subverted the system.

Another way that the ZAGS co-opted its citizens' time was by the institution of a waiting period, which fluctuated by law during the 1950s–80s from a month to three months. In an effort to reduce the divorce rate, the state did

---

[26] This limitation is quite surprising given the official atheistic position of the Soviet state, but it is yet one more piece of evidence that Orthodox (and other religious) practices were maintained not only by individuals, but by governmental institutions.

not want couples to marry without considering the consequences. Thus, they forced people to delay, regardless of their social status or degree of maturity. By determining the scheduling of the ceremony as well as establishing a waiting period, the state was indicating that it was wiser and more powerful than its citizens. They, in turn, could only comply, pull strings, or else not marry at all. Most cities had only one wedding palace or a wedding palace determined by place of residence, and thus couples had no alternative.

At the same time, like medical personnel, ZAGS officials were not above capitalizing on the power accorded them. In this way, they were able to regain some sense of their own influence in the face of a constrictive social system to which they too were subjected. They served not only as creative advisors to the wedding couple, but also as bureaucratic functionaries, a group that represented the *khamstvo* 'boorishness' Soviet citizens recognized in all aspects of daily life—from shops to medical institutions and in government offices as well. Lilia T. noted: "A month-long waiting period is required. But in exceptional circumstances one can reduce the time. We, the directors of the department, are given the right to reduce the time of registration. It is established by law." However, it is likely that the "law" was only invoked in cases like the one Natalia T. described above, through the couple's personal connections. Those without such access were at the mercy of the system in their wedding planning.

Certainly, the ceremony itself was not designed according to a couple's wishes. While a wide palette of options has only been possible in the West from the 1970s on, the Western ceremony was, even when fixed, often tied to meaningful institutions such as family tradition and religious faith.[27] The words classically spoken in vows (e.g., "to love and to cherish, in sickness and in health, until death do us part") were cultural icons that represented not only the institution, but the bond between the couple. The Soviet ceremony was not characterized in this way by my informants. Rather, they viewed the event as another example of officialdom that was not really memorable. If they did remember it, it was because the ceremony was the same at every wedding. However, the sameness did not produce the same feeling of affectionate recognition as the vows cited above might. Rather they were treated as more evidence of the Soviet institution's disregard for the individual. Natalia T. expressed this opinion in her description of her wedding ceremony: "The registrar woman read a pre-set text in a heartfelt tone, the usual words. When I hear your text in American or British films, it is prettier.... But ours at

---

[27] This trend began in the 1960s, but came to fruition in mainstream churches in the next decade. Certainly more left-leaning churches like the Quakers and Unitarians either had always allowed people to write their own vows or had alternative versions of ceremonies, but this phenomenon spread throughout Protestantism and even into Catholicism, which began to accept variations in the marriage ceremony after Vatican II in 1965.

that time was some kind of formal thing, I don't remember it exactly, but it didn't leave an impression."

Olga R. remarked: "I must say that there was such an attitude to those formalities, to the bureaucracy. It was however a bureaucratic part of our life." Liudmila K. expressed her opinion in similar terms: "It was all so formal, we understood that, therefore we didn't react to it with any emotion, we just signed our names, observed the formalities." Irina V. called the words "stupid." Alexander U. said: "It was an official speech, it was bureaucratese, it was written. They said the same thing to everybody." Liudmila N. emphasized that the speech was done in the name of the state: "First she says, that in the name of the Russian Federation she asks first if we are willing to marry … and then in the name of the Russian Federation, she announces that we have married."

These attitudes certainly are not those of people who remembered their wedding ceremony fondly. Rather, they recognized that in order to really celebrate their wedding properly, outside the state's control, in the family home, it was a hoop they must jump through (regardless of the lovely surroundings, music, and special clothing). Natasha R. summarized the situation succinctly as follows: "The most important part happens after the ZAGS." These opinions support Lane's (1981, 203) opinion that Soviet "rituals and ceremonies are overloaded with non-symbolic verbal ballast, which deadens rather than sensitizes the emotional response of ritual participants." In addition, it conforms to Hobsbawm's contention (1983a, 3) that bureaucratization is a flaw in the invented tradition, because it forces the ritual to become routine, incapable of dealing with "unforeseen or inhabitual contingencies."

That is not to say that the ceremony was entirely meaningless, an idea which Yurchak (2006, 25) also supports. After all, it was the key to the joining of two families, of the marital union, and of having children, all values that both the Soviet Union and the folk traditions supported. While participants condemned the bureaucratic and ideological content, as we have seen, they clearly accepted certain values about marriage that the ceremony espoused. The event itself may have been less than ideal, but the performance of the ritual allowed them to create a social role that they found to be necessary and important. It offered them entry into full social membership within Soviet Russian society, as adults, as family members, and as parents. While, as we have seen, their notions of family identity could directly conflict with Soviet ideology, there were some aspects that were consonant with their views. Without the performance of the ceremony, no form of resistance or acceptance could be played out, and the citizen would remain on the outside of established social norms, regardless of the antecedents of these norms in folk material, Western consumerism, or Soviet ideology. Therefore, the citizens took the necessary steps toward legal marriage, despite their dissatisfaction with the process, because it enabled them to get to "the most important part," the celebration with their loved ones, through which they could finally create their identity within the social sphere.

After the ceremony at the wedding palace, the couple generally took a tour of the city, including stops at major Soviet-era monuments, particularly the eternal flame or World War II memorials, before going on to the family home. This practice of a city tour after the wedding was a tradition in nineteenth-century urban weddings as well (Zhirnova 1980, 53). I would argue that ritual theorists adapted it to conform to their desire of highlighting the role of the state over the individual. This tradition is one area where the Soviet government would seem to have succeeded to some extent. Most couples felt that it was important to perform this ritual.[28] However, I would argue that while the Soviet authorities wanted this act to be a ritual dedication to the state, rather it was a ritual dedication to the nation itself. Those memorialized were remembered not for their "Sovietness," but for their sacrifice to the country, as ancestors who deserved respect. Similarly, nineteenth-century village couples might have gone to the cemetery before a wedding, particularly in the case of orphans, to receive a parental blessing. In the royal Russian wedding, the tsar would go to the church where his ancestors were buried before the ceremony. Lobanov (2004, 22) notes that he would order prayers for the dead and ask for forgiveness at the graves of his forebears. While the Soviet tradition was probably not directly inherited from these earlier practices, there is no doubt that there was a long-standing Russian connection between the souls of the dead and the living in the wedding ritual. Thus it would seem that the visit to the graves or memorials may have been intended to focus on state power, but in the end these visits were reinterpreted to show love of the homeland, political considerations aside, and respect for the dead who sacrificed for it. This interpretation of the practice might explain why, even fifteen years after the fall of the Soviet Union, many couples still perform this ritual on their wedding day. This is one area where the Soviet ritual specialists were able to foster authentic emotion within the ceremony, as they had hoped to do.

Ritual specialists such as Sukhanov (1976, 185) and Rudnev (1979, 115–16) criticize the *krasnye svad'by* 'red weddings' of the post-Revolutionary period for not appealing to the emotional concerns of the couple. They contend that the new Soviet ritual had overcome these limitations and no longer had the feeling of a political meeting. While I agree that these ceremonies could certainly not be characterized as political meetings, they did have a particular ideological slant and a faceless character. These traits are particularly evident from the fact that the most important moment in the ceremony was not a set of vows between the bride and groom, but signing one's name in the registry book. In fact the only "vow" is to the state, an implicit promise to create a pro-

---

[28] As noted above, some couples who were anti-government or who did not have a monument nearby omitted this step.

ductive family and raise good socialist children. The bureaucratic nature of the ceremony (and primacy of the state's role) was also emphasized in the culmination of the ceremony. As the couple left, they received the all-important and omnipresent (in Soviet life) government certificate (*svidetel'stvo o brake* 'certificate of marriage') as well as their new passports. In point of fact, the Soviet celebrants really could not do otherwise (as will be discussed below), because to truly access the emotional core of the ritual, they would have to turn either to religious faith or to the family itself. They would thereby reduce the state's role in the proceedings, something they were reluctant to do. In sum, there was an emotionless character to these ceremonies, one that was reinforced by a trait that affected the birth ritual as well: the manufacturing process.

Weddings as a Manufacturing Process

The ceremonies, which took an average of ten to fifteen minutes according to my informants (both married couples and ZAGS workers), resembled an assembly line. The wedding palaces, like any production facility, had a strict order of business. The elaborate restrictions emphasized not only state control, but also the concept that this process was timed to be maximally efficient. Lilia T. described the routine of the wedding palace she directs as follows:

> When there are no ceremonies going on, we don't have ceremonies practically only on Tuesday. We accept intent to marry forms, they bring us documents ... certificates about one's maiden name and all kinds of certificates on marriage.... People that register on Friday, they bring their passports on Tuesday or Wednesday already. They check them again, because someone could have lost a passport during that time, anything could have happened.... And on Wednesday there will be non-ceremonial registration, the older generation, pregnant people, those who are not up to a ceremony. And on Thursday, Friday, and Saturday the ceremonial registrations happen. Newlyweds come, and we give them their documents.[29]

Her description is indicative both of the assembly-line feel and of the bureaucratic control of the process. Various activities are scheduled for certain days, and cannot be performed out of order, or the production schedule will be disturbed.

Both the ZAGS workers and the couples I interviewed stated that the ceremonies were no longer than fifteen minutes. Their brevity also contributed to the sense that this was a faceless manufacturing process and not a significant ritual performance. On the days designated for "ceremonial regis-

---

[29] Wedding palaces and ZAGS offices are typically closed on Sunday and Monday.

tration," especially in the summer, there was an endless stream of couples arriving at and departing from the wedding palace. On one particular Saturday in June 2003 at the Vladimir ZAGS, I watched as five couples married within an hour.[30] The first floor was crammed full of brides, grooms, and their guests, who had to wait in the large foyer until the ZAGS photographer called them for a group picture. They were then sent upstairs into the wedding chamber for the ten-minute ceremony, then down the back stairs, so that the next couple could process up the stairs. The entire process was controlled by two older women who told the couples where to go and when to go there.

This hurried and impersonal system promotes the idea that the ceremony itself is not truly special for the couple or their guests. The state and its representatives are thus not only the controllers of the individual, but also run a type of wedding processing plant.[31] The wedding palace and the ceremony itself are designed to get the couples in and out efficiently within the allotted time. The weddings I witnessed as well as those described by my informants parallel the goals of modern manufacturing systems. It perhaps explains why most guests do not attend the ZAGS ceremony, because it truly is not the focus of the wedding rite. It also illuminates the couples' responses cited above that they felt no actual emotional connection to the ceremonies, because they were overlaid both with Soviet bureaucracy and the feel of an assembly line.

Thus, while Soviet ritual specialists tried to create a more formal ceremony that would ritualize the wedding, they did not succeed in convincing Soviet citizens that this rite was truly memorable or indeed even the core of the ritual. They could not escape the bureaucratic, impersonal nature of their creation, which people viewed as a pro forma obligation that must be performed before beginning the celebration with family and friends, the "real" wedding. In essence, as with birth, there was a conflict between two ideals. In the childbirth system science and nature represented the two dichotomous ideologies that underlay the process. A similar conflict is at the heart of the wedding, an emotional bond, but one which Soviet authorities justified by relying on science and rationality (Shlapentokh 1984, 93ff.). While the arguments about the "rational basis" for marriage may have been effective in convincing the powers that be that it was a valuable institution that should be celebrated formally, they did not have much resonance with the average per-

---

[30] While this observation took place after the fall of the Soviet Union, the essential system has not changed much and is still subject to the tradition of Soviet bureaucracy. The post-Soviet system will be discussed in more detail in chapter 6.

[31] Contrast this schedule to the typical American church. Reverend Mark Pitton, the minister of Bethany United Church of Christ in Montpelier, VT, says that the policy at all the churches where he has worked over the last twenty years is, for example, two weddings on a Saturday. They allow at least two hours between the end of the first ceremony and the beginning of the second, so as not to "hurry people along, which nobody wants to do."

son. If we combine these various aspects of the state's role in the wedding (including bureaucratic control of the individual and rationally organized schedules) then we can see why they did not react positively to the ceremony itself. It also was not a significant factor in reducing the divorce rate, as the government had hoped it would be. In short, ritual specialists, even with their inclusion of a section in the wedding on the meaning of the family, could not access the spiritual, emotional nature of the wedding from their position as secular rationalists.

Reason versus Emotion

In our discussion of the birth ritual, we considered the inherent conflict between science and nature. The state tried as much as possible to control the birth process, through rigid medicalization, and to eliminate both the natural, unpredictable aspects of birth as well as the folk content. In the wedding, of course, science, at least medical science, plays no role. However, there is a similar conflict, referred to above, between reason and emotion. While Soviet theorists made references to love in their discussions of marriage, the argument in favor of weddings and indeed the ceremony itself was based on "reason," not on emotion. Despite these limitations, a ceremony at the palace became *de rigeur* from the 1970s on. One wonders why, if the ceremony was not viewed positively, it became so popular.

One factor, of course, was that while the actual ceremony might not be particularly significant to the participants, the wedding itself was, so that being able to celebrate it in a formal way appealed to people. Tatiana K. summed up the attitude toward weddings and birth as follows: "The birth of a child in a family, this is also a big event, and we think that after the wedding, the birth of a child, that's the second event in a family, that is, the wedding and then the birth of a child." The formal ceremony offered couples a valuable opportunity to announce their marriage to the world publicly and to negotiate their new status within society through ritual practice. In fact, the performance of the ceremony seemed to be key in taking up one's social role as an adult. If it were not, then most people could have just lived together without the benefit of marriage, something that was not common within Soviet Russia. The "informational campaign" Zhirnova (1980, 83) refers to capitalized on this desire by making the formal, relatively luxurious public wedding ceremony a mark of social status that apparently also met psychological and social needs.

I would hypothesize that tradition and peer pressure also played a role. These weddings became expected, and challenging the system required a particular strength of character and political stance. Yurchak (2006, 118–19) argues for the importance in the Soviet Union of the collective performance of ritual acts, such as the wedding ceremony, to allow for a "life with meaning, the 'normal life,' which went beyond the constative reading of ideological

messages and was not determined by the dictatorship of the party." My informants expressed just this view of their ceremonies. They did not actively attend to the messages the ZAGS celebrant conveyed about family life, but not
because they did not care about marriage itself. Whether they agreed or disagreed with the sentiments she expressed in the ceremony, ritual participants
basically ignored them as more of the largely meaningless ballast that characterized official discourse. However, they did not reject the concept of marriage itself nor indeed all of the Soviet ideology about marriage out of hand.

Rather, they took advantage of the official ceremony to enter into significant and valuable social and family relationships. Within such frameworks,
the semantic content of messages, regardless of their original source, was indeed read more assiduously, was respected and, therefore, applied in the
negotiation of social roles. In this way, what linguists term "illocutionary
force based on pragmatic context" became central to discourse in the post-war
Soviet Union, not just for ease of communication, as it does in all languages,
but in order to truly understand semantic content itself. Average Soviet Russian citizens generally did not publicly dissent against ideology and the official acts required of them, and not only out of fear of reprisals, but because
they worked within the system to create identity and meaning. Yurchak
(2006, 93) describes how this process functioned for Andrei, a Komsomol
(Communist Youth League) secretary he interviewed. These secretaries

> learned that in order to conduct work with meaning, one needed to
> perform the pro forma rituals and activities—making formulaic
> speeches, compiling formulaic reports, conducting formulaic rituals,
> and so on. In other words, performing the pro forma enabled Andrei
> to engage with other types of work and meanings including those
> that coincided with ideological plans of the Komsomol organization
> and those that did not. Andrei also learned how to minimize the pro
> forma so that it enabled meaningful work by not taking too much
> time or energy. This meant that he reinterpreted for himself much of
> what the Komsomol stood for in everyday life. However, such active
> displacement of "ideological" work did not mean that Andrei was
> acting in opposition to broader ideological goals or resisted broader
> communist ideals. On the contrary, for him, ignoring the constative
> meanings of the Komsomol pro forma while engaging wholeheart-
> edly in the Komsomol work with meaning were all part and parcel of
> how he understood communist identity, goals, and ethics.

From the point of view of many people, the bureaucratic routine may not
have fulfilled an emotional need, but was required in order to open the door
to a larger, more meaningful world.

There was, however, a significant difference between the birth and wedding rites in Soviet Russia. Birth was still connected to a religious ritual, bap-

tism, while weddings were not. None of my informants (even those that had their children secretly baptized) had a religious ceremony.[32] This behavior could, of course, be connected to the fact that even in pre-Soviet Russia, weddings were not primarily religious rites, but social community events. Worobec (1995, 162) provides evidence that in some cases the religious ceremony in the nineteenth-century village actually occurred after the reception and even after the consummation of the marriage. As a result both of this perception and the legal requirement for civil marriage, the Soviet Union made greater inroads, as we have seen, in secularizing this ritual. Another factor, of course, could have been the public nature of weddings, so that the risk of a religious rite was greater than for baptism, which could be performed in secret more easily than a wedding. Certainly, the couple had to have been christened themselves in the church in order to have an Orthodox ceremony. Baptism, while still practiced in the Soviet period, was the exception at least among the urban population. Most people, even if they had wanted a religious ceremony, did not meet the essential church requirements. However, it seems most likely that religion was not a factor in the wedding, either from the point of view of folk tradition or from the point of view of Soviet life. Rather, a formal ceremony of any kind, be it simple in a registry office or elaborate in a wedding palace, was the key to entry into marriage and into the emotional bonds that the marriage represented between the couple and among the families.

As we saw in the birth ritual, the inherent dissonance that existed between two (or more) worldviews did not necessarily negate the importance of the rite itself. In both cases, ritual participants took advantage of the official institutions to make their entry into a new phase in their lives. They also adopted many Soviet-era notions about the family as the core of the socialist state that enabled them to further strengthen the family unit and their identity within it. Participation in these rites both reinforced Soviet norms for social roles and also allowed people to create identities that may not have conformed to those norms, often through folk practices, as we will see in the following section.

---

[32] Alexander U. said that if anyone told me (s)he had had a religious ceremony, it was a lie designed to impress me, because it was just not done. However, Voznesenskaia (1986, 268) does mention one couple in the *Women's Decameron* who had a church ceremony. Admittedly this is a work of fiction, but it does address issues related to the daily life of the period under consideration. The tone of the description in the novel does suggest, as my informants and data presented by ritual specialists confirm, that this would be a significant exception to the norm.

The Family and the State

In the discussion of the childbirth ritual, we examined the complexity of the attitudes toward the family within Soviet Russia. Ritual specialists designed life-cycle rites to establish a strong, stable family that would help to maintain the status quo and serve as the basic unit of socialist society. Ashwin (2000b, 9) argues that, throughout the Soviet period, the authorities never abandoned the idea that the family must be restructured within socialist society. However, the vision for the socialist family was modified over time. The Bolsheviks initially sought to remake the family entirely. In the post-war period, during Stalin's rule and thereafter, this vision was forsaken, and the family was officially endorsed as the fundamental socialist cell. In order to effect all these transformations in family identity, from the elimination of the patriarchy to the remade socialist family, the state appealed to women. The end result was that women became the center of family life, while men were supposed to find their realization in their public lives at work. Within the context of the post-war Soviet Union the wedding ceremony itself became, over time, particularly important in defining familial roles. However, as with the childbirth ritual, the wedding produced a family that not only supported Soviet values, but also potentially undermined them. For this reason, the celebrants did include material on the nature of the Soviet family to convey the proper (socialist) messages about married life. Several informants noted that the celebrants included commentary on the young family and its importance to Soviet society. Irina V. described this portion of the ceremony as follows: "With an inspired face and a heartfelt tone she told us that we are beginning a new life, that this is such an event for us, the first document of our young family, et cetera.... The fact is that they said parting words to us, that we have to love and value each other."[33] In fact, the words about family life that the celebrant spoke were essentially the implicit vow to the Soviet state noted earlier, a promise to create a family in keeping with Soviet norms.

Nevertheless, the participants certainly knew that the Soviet social structure was in many ways inimical to the family itself and that they could only rely on their family (or other close connections) in order to survive within the system. When the state attempted to instruct them on the nature of family, portions of the message were therefore rejected. Citizens simply did not value certain aspects of Soviet beliefs about marriage and the family. However, to a great extent, Soviet Russians adopted state ideals about love and support between the couple, the importance of the family and its child rearing functions to society as a whole, and indeed notions about gender roles within the family. For these reasons, people chose to participate in a ritual that they

---

[33] One should also note that even when trying to create some emotional significance in the ceremony, the celebrant referred to a government document, the primary focus of the ceremony.

may have found to be less emotionally satisfying than the private aspects of the celebration with family and friends. They did not reject marriage as the Soviet society defined it, but used the ceremony as an entry point for the creation of social status within the public and private arenas.

Based on the decision for the family to be the center of socialist society, Stalin fostered the creation of a middle class to maintain the social stability he desired (see chapter 1 for discussion). As he saw it, revolutionary ideals were well and good, but they could easily threaten the government's power. This new emphasis on family values was designed to create a socialist family based on communist morality, as we have seen, but this policy required financial support of the familial unit to succeed. In the post-war period the Soviet government began a push for a consumerist ideology that would promote the family. After Stalin's death, these policies were further enhanced in order to solve the demographic crisis. The Soviet Union under Khrushchev and Brezhnev emphasized women's roles as mothers over that as workers. It was during this period that the *torzhestvennaia tseremoniia* 'formal ceremony' at the wedding palace began to gain popularity, at the same time as the economic problems that resulted from World War II improved as well.

At first glance, the emphasis on bourgeois conspicuous consumption characteristic of the weddings of the Western world would seem to contradict core socialist ideology. The clothing, special cars, bouquets, and wedding palaces all seemed to send the message that expense and display were important factors in the wedding ceremony. However, they were in fact consonant with the goals for the family outlined above. As Yurchak (2006) has shown, Western symbols, like the medical science adopted for the birth ritual, were not in and of themselves negative from the Soviet point of view. They could represent the internationalism and cosmopolitanism that the Soviet Union wanted to foster in its citizens. An additional benefit was that the state also was able to demonstrate that it was supporting the family financially, serving in the role of "surrogate father." One could argue that the Soviet government belied this message by not providing the goods in the stores to truly have such a wedding or indeed to truly support the family. However, they did give couples special certificates that allowed them access to goods that others did not have. In short, the government conveyed the idea that the wedding should focus on material goods that it would furnish for the young couple.

Nevertheless, there was a risk in this policy. Rather than be content with the modicum of luxury goods the wedding allowed, participants might have longed that much more for the extravagant, consumerist weddings characteristic of the West that they saw in movies.[34] Marina K., for example, said

---

[34] Another risk was that the wedding would be turned from a "union of people warmly loving each other," as the Soviet wedding ceremony calls it, to an economic one. Shlapentokh (1984, 84) discusses the economic considerations that played a role in people's decisions to marry. In this case, marriage was not based on the emotional

that while her wedding dress was fine, it was not nearly as nice as those in the West or in the post-Soviet period. People faced with the promise of consumer comforts that the government could not supply became more and more disheartened with a system that could not provide for them in their daily lives, let alone on special occasions. This is not to say that the state did not make available some goods for the couple's needs, as noted, but that ultimately economic realities, more than political ideology, led to conflicts (Shlapentokh 1989, 97). These attitudes were also reflected in popular culture. For example, the characters in the *Women's Decameron* (1986, 218, 269–70) discuss their disappointment with regard to the lack of consumer goods and the government's provision for their daily existence. Similar problems are described by the characters in Baranskaia's *Nedelia kak nedelia (Just Another Week*, 1989). Because the Soviet Union never lived up to its promises, citizens were even more likely to reject messages from the ceremony about how the state supported the family.

The family not only could serve as a refuge from state interference, but also sustained its members better than the state, both on a daily basis and in the wedding itself, as we have seen. It became a predominant force that both conformed to the Soviet desire for stability and also destabilized society, because it could (and did) lead to individual beliefs inimical to established values. Families, not the state or its officials, represented the emotional and spiritual core of the marital union, as they had within the folk tradition. Thus messages about the Soviet family from its representatives did not take root unequivocally. People recognized that some information did not conform to their daily reality. Shlapentokh (1989, 13) asserts that "since the late 1950s the Soviet people have gradually, but unswervingly diverted their interests from the state to their primary groups (family, friends, and lovers) and to semilegal and illegal civil society...." Disappointment in the state arose because it could not sustain the family unit as it promised to do.

Humphrey and Laidlaw (1994, 95) argue that participants often interpret ritual actions in ways other than celebrants or creators may have intended. As we have discussed, Soviet citizens were adept at reading the messages the establishment was sending their way, but also, Yurchak (2006, 27) contends, at applying a plethora of interpretations based on context. They might have known what the government and its representatives were trying to say, but my informants made it clear that they did not always accept the content wholeheartedly. People did not read the isolation in the *roddom* as parallel to a mother protecting her children, but as interference in their personal lives by a state institution. Similarly, they did not accept the wisdom of ZAGS officials with regard to waiting periods before marriage and advice about family life in the ceremony, but rather resented or simply ignored these institutional at-

---

bonds that the authorities hoped, but on financial gain, certainly a notion that ran counter to socialist ideology.

tempts to interfere in personal decisions. On the other hand, they clearly valued some aspects of Soviet ideology about the family. They did not choose,
for example, to forego marriage entirely, but thought that it was worth
participating in the civil ceremony, even if it may have been unpleasant. They
also accepted the idea that the state should support the family, even though it
fell short in its promises. Certainly, they endorsed the idea that the marital
union was designed to produce children and be at the core of their
upbringing. They believed in the concept of two people supporting each other
in the marital union, emotionally and financially, and certain notions of
equality between the partners and women's right to work. Most importantly,
they agreed that the family was the core of socialist society.

Scott (1985, 282–307) describes, within the context of a Malay village, how
the mutuality of values shared by both the powerful and powerless members
of a society reinforces social norms and also allows for resistance to them.
Soviet Russian citizens were faced with a similar situation and indeed, reacted in much the same way as the Malay peasants did. They parlayed their
participation in the official wedding ceremony that the state so strongly endorsed into distinct social (and material) advantages. However, by complying
with the state's wishes, they were free to take advantage of the opportunity to
negotiate individual and familial identities that may or may not have complied with socialist ideology. As a result, they prized and emphasized the
independent role their families, particularly female relatives, played in the
reception in the creation of this identity. The reception celebrated the couple's
new union separate from the state, at home, and yet was sanctioned by it.
This portion of the wedding rite was the core of the celebration, an event
designed to highlight family tradition and public recognition of the newly-
wed's status within the personal social sphere. Not only did this party reinforce the emotional ties between the couple and their social circle, but also
illustrated where actual financial provision for the newly-formed young
family was to be found. This, I would suggest, is precisely the relationship
between the Soviet wedding ceremony, characterized by my informants as
bureaucratic and "officialese," and the reception that followed it, during
which the family and emotional content came to the fore. In this way, the
ZAGS ceremony and the reception parallel the childbirth ritual with its contrast between the official space of the *roddom* and the party for family and
friends afterwards in the home.

Kiblitskaia (2000, 55), in her study of female breadwinners in the Soviet
Union, discusses how the attitude toward work and family shifted in the
post-war years:

These women also saw work as important, but their motivation was
somewhat different. Ideology was less a part of their lives: they did
see work as a duty, but not necessarily one which they conceptualised

in relation to the state. They were also driven by their sense of responsibility for the comfort of the family.

With the family at the center of social identity, providing for it was also a core
value, one that the state had seemingly abandoned, but which friends and
family had not. While the ceremony was necessary to sanctify the union in the
eyes of the state and the larger public, its recognition within one's social circle
came during the two days of celebration in the family home. Certainly, the
reception also highlighted the emotional and financial support the couple
could expect from relatives, since without them providing and paying for a
proper celebration would not have been possible. While families did view the
entire wedding as a seminal event in their lives, it is clear that the core of the
celebration was not the ceremony itself, but the reception afterwards in the
private space of the home with loved ones. The family relied on its own
resources and ingenuity to obtain and create the items required for a proper
celebration; they sewed, cooked, made special trips to urban centers for food,
and pulled strings to ensure that their children's celebration was worthy of
the significance of this event, despite the lack of goods provided by the state.
While most people said that their receptions were *skromnye* 'modest', they
recognized the sacrifices their family made to ensure that the marriage was
celebrated properly. Liuba S. reported, for example, that her mother did
everything she could to arrange a wedding for her daughter: "Mom went into
debt, so that the wedding would be done as it should be: both the dress and a
new coat they sewed for me, a hat, a pretty fox fur collar, everyone did their
best." Thus the Soviet wedding of the 1970s and 1980s can be characterized as
a multifaceted event, one that was based on three distinct worldviews: the
folk tradition, consumerism, and Soviet ideology. Participants clearly
negotiated their way through these various meanings, choosing what was
relevant for them, despite the state's intentions to convey a unitary message
about family life.

Negotiating Identity in the Wedding Ritual

In our discussion of childbirth rites, we argued, based on Bourdieu's (1991)
analysis of the function of life-cycle rituals, that the rite separates and defines
those who have undergone the ritual from those who cannot do so. We focused primarily on the definition of motherhood as displayed by the Soviet
Russian ritual performance, given that men were largely excluded from the
process. Bourdieu (1991, 118) argues that

> one can see in passing that, as the process of institution consists of
> assigning properties of a *social* [italics original] nature in a way that
> makes them seem like properties of natural nature, the rite of
> institution tends logically … to integrate specifically social

oppositions, such as masculine/feminine, into a series of cosmological oppositions—with relations like: man is to woman as the sun is to the moon—which represents a very effective way of naturalizing them. Thus sexually differentiated rites consecrate the difference between the sexes: they constitute a simple difference of fact as a legitimate distinction, as an institution.

Therefore, based on Bourdieu's argument, we must broaden our scope from just the woman's role to the expectations for the husband and the wife within the context of the Soviet Russian wedding ritual. As we have seen, identity in this context was derived from multiple sources, including folk tradition, Soviet ideology, and indeed Western views of men and women. Despite the state's aims to convey a single image of proper family life, the couple (and their families) actually defined their roles based on these divergent messages. The wedding, like all rituals, was a creative event that allowed participants to form new identities, identities that adopted, manipulated, and resisted cultural norms to establish social reality. Bell (1997, 79) argues that ritual "molds consciousness in terms of underlying structures and patterns, while current realities simultaneously instigate transformations of those very structures and patterns as well." In the case of the Soviet Russian wedding ritual, the participants, as we have seen, used the official institution of a new family not only to reinforce cultural norms, be they Soviet ideals or folk notions, but also to undercut them, by manipulating the Soviet Russian notion of a "stable" family to suit their own needs. Let us turn then to the ways in which couples both accommodated and resisted notions of gender derived from three distinct and sometimes contradictory sources.

The nineteenth-century village wedding emphasized the work roles of the couple within the marriage; each were providers for the family in their own way. Women were expected to clothe and feed the family (not only cook, but also tend chickens, milk cows, maintain vegetable gardens, and gather wild foods, like berries and mushrooms), while men fed and supported it via cultivation of grain crops and rearing of livestock. The bride and groom in the Russian folk tradition were certainly not entering into an equal relationship, one the Soviet constitution would have espoused. Nevertheless, the village wedding illustrated that the husband and wife each had a role to play and that both had to work for the family to survive (even if the male's role was more prestigious within the society at large). The traditional inspections of the groom's household and of the bride's home and handiwork were designed to ascertain not only the financial stability of the parents, but also the quality of the bride's and the groom's work as expected within the culture. Similarly, the trials of the bride during the wedding celebration (detailed in chapter 2) emphasized not only her ability to work, but also her willingness to be obedient and respect the social order.

The folk material that survived into the twentieth century also focused on the work roles of the couple in the marriage. From this point of view, the man was expected to be a provider and to be the public face of the family, while the woman had control of the domestic sphere and children. The rituals taken from the folk tradition that focus on work roles and the responsibilities of the couple include: the buying of the bride; the man asking for the bride's hand and buying wedding rings;[35] the bride sweeping up trash and money thrown by the guests, while shielded by her husband; brides and their female relatives cooking for the reception and sewing the wedding clothing. In games focusing on work roles, the woman is not viewed as being a beautiful, fragile thing, but an important contributor to the family circle. Certainly, Russian women of the nineteenth century performed traditional feminine duties, but the duties involve not the weakness conveyed by other facets of the wedding (discussed below), but the strength, dedication, and endurance required for the family to be successful. Similarly, the bride was required to illustrate her ability to be a good homemaker by sewing and cooking for the wedding (if she had a wedding reception at home and married when wedding dresses were not as easy to obtain). The man had to show that he was a good provider in these rituals, by buying goods and giving food to prove that he was worthy of and prepared for his role in the marriage.

Soviet ideology about gender roles had three distinct components, all of which were reflected in wedding practices. The first held that the couple were equal partners, who married for love and respected each other's life goals. The second image was one largely consonant with folk material and which the Soviet theorists took advantage of in their attempts to stabilize the family. Women were the heart of the family unit, defined by their success as homemakers, wives, and mothers. In contrast, husbands attained social status less by their familial role, but by their public, professional status. However, they still had to demonstrate their ability to provide for the family and assume the public role as "patriarch," as revised through the Soviet construct of gender equality in the public and familial spheres. The third conception had been adopted from the Western chivalric and class-based view of husbands and wives. Women were recognized for their fragility, delicacy, and physical beauty (as well as their *kul'turnost'* 'culturedness'), while men were strong, reliable, and stoic providers and protectors. It is not surprising that these widely varied conceptions of familial roles resulted in a great deal of family and social conflict.

As in the birth ritual, folk material was adopted into Soviet norms, but also served as a means to resist them. Soviet Russian women were essentially forced to work outside the home to support the family and to demonstrate

---

[35] In the nineteenth century men were required to buy rings. As noted earlier, in the post-war period, rings were not the norm, given the economic situation. When the practice revived as the economy got stronger, men once again bought rings.

Soviet gender equality. However, official propaganda pushed for them to embrace domesticity and maternity from the 1930s on, while continuing to participate in the professional labor force. Thus, the folk view of women's and men's roles was not that different, on the surface, from daily life in Soviet Russia. However, what was lacking was balance in the expectations. In the nineteenth-century village, each member of the couple had a defined set of expectations to meet. However, Soviet husbands did not become "feminists" in the sense that they took over half of the required household duties. Wives were expected to perform both their traditional duties and non-traditional "masculine" ones. Men may have eventually acquiesced and even embraced the notion of women having a career, although there is evidence that they (and their wives) idealized the notion of a full-time homemaker (Rands Lyon 2007, 32; Zdravomyslova and Temkina 2005, 108). Thus, to a large extent, the superficial similarity between actual village life and Soviet reconceptualization of these traditional gender roles is misleading and resulted in the discontent most people, especially women, felt in their daily lives.

In certain cases, folk material clearly contradicted and resisted Soviet ideology. For example, unlike the Soviet wedding ceremony, which tried as much as possible to eliminate difference and competition between partners, the folk material emphasized it. One repeated concern was who would be dominant in the relationship. Given that, as we have seen, the Soviet constitution specified gender equality by law, the persistence of the *vykup* was also worrisome to ritual theorists, because, along with highlighting consumer ideals, it also suggested that women were "objects" to be purchased. Another common practice that resisted socialist norms was the humorous certificates, diplomas, and passports that friends and family created for the couple. Both my informants and Matlin (2003, 380) described this practice. These documents highlighted the couple's roles in the family, relying on an established Soviet practice to parody official views on gender equality and reinforce roles derived from the folk tradition, e.g., by discussing how the woman's duty was to be subservient to her husband. They also dealt with erotic topics (using double entrendres and puns) at a time when such issues were not publicly discussed. Recall that even in the wedding ceremony the celebrant did not openly admit the couple could kiss, but said that they should "congratulate" each other (some of my informants were so confused about this statement, that they turned to their new spouse and said "congratulations"). These acts also subverted the seriousness of the documents Soviet officials bestowed at the wedding (as well as at other ceremonies) by poking fun at them and using them to convey material subversive to official ideology.

Official ideology (and the ceremony itself), of course, also espoused equality, love, and respect between the partners and took the stance that the Soviet wedding had freed people from the outmoded patriarchal system (Rudnev 1979, 12; Ugrinovich 1975, 20). It is difficult, if one observes only the folk material about gender roles in marriage, to conclude that people took this conception of marriage to heart. However, people I interviewed certainly supported the ideal, even if it did not mesh with their personal experience. Certainly, despite these ideals, a serious divide existed between men's and women's roles in their married lives. However, they married for love and expected their partners to support them in their professional and personal goals and to respect their needs and opinions. To a great extent, husbands and wives endorsed the Soviet-era idea that women should pursue an education and work outside the home. Most Russian men I spoke to did not object to their wives' employment or desire for a professional life. Either they have internalized Soviet messages in this regard or are realistic about the economic necessities of the modern world.[36] Interviews conducted by Rands Lyon (2007, 31–32) and Kay (2002, 66–68) support this claim as well. Both men and women advocated women's participation in the labor force, although some did express a wish to conform to the ideal of the wife as a full-time homemaker at the same time.

While the Soviet ritual specialists may have paid lip service to the ideal of gender equality, the wedding celebration they created in the 1960s fostered an entirely different view of marital roles. They based this portion of the ritual on the third component of Soviet Russian gender identity, namely on Western ideals for femininity and masculinity. To a certain extent, this third vision conformed to norms derived from folk material and from calls for women's return to domesticity in the Khrushchev and Brezhnev eras. In all these systems, women were obliged to bear children and create a cozy domestic life for their families, regardless of professional or public responsibilities, while men were required to provide for and protect them (see Attwood 1990, 127, 138–48 for a discussion). However, this perception also incorporated Western, class-based, chivalric views of men and women. From this point of view, the bride was perceived as a fragile, beautiful creature, while the groom was a powerful provider. These images would seem inimical to Soviet ideology and yet were also consonant with it. Like the Western medical system that had been reinterpreted through the socialist lens, these images too were revised from the point of view of state ideology about demography and stable families.

These differences first become apparent with the changes in the bride's appearance. Brides who married in the 1950s and 1960s wore nice clothes to the ZAGS, but they were work clothes, suits and dresses they already owned (or borrowed). In fact, many of them came to the ZAGS directly from work. Thus their clothes, either at the ZAGS or at the reception that followed, did not much distinguish them from the guests, who were also dressed for a party. Over the next two decades, the bride was transformed from a nicely-

---

[36] However, as other sources have shown, many women do feel conflicted about this requirement. See, for example, Kay (2002), Zdravomyslova and Temkina (2005), Rands Lyon (2007), Du Plessix Gray (1990), and Marsh (1996), particularly Sargeant's chapter "The 'Women Question' and Problems of Maternity."

dressed professional to a princess for a day. These brides not only had formal white gowns for the wedding, but spent the morning before the ZAGS ceremony doing their hair and makeup. I am not implying that brides in the earlier period did not want to look presentable for their weddings and may not have spent any extra time fixing their hair. However, the 1970s brought about a shift that was exclusively on the bride's appearance, an approach that seems "bourgeois," but in fact conformed to the new Soviet norms for women in the society as a whole.

The white gown, of course, was common in pre-revolutionary Russia and had already been borrowed from Western fashion by the upper and middle classes, as Mee and Safronova (2003, 142–43) discuss. Thus it is unclear if we can say that this is a true borrowing from the Western tradition, because the ritual specialists would have researched the history of their own weddings and known that the tradition predated the Soviet period. What we can conclude is that these dresses both convey a very different attitude toward the bride herself and support materialism and luxury as part of the wedding, both of which are significant shifts from the previous two decades. In addition, this bridal costume was not necessarily a contradiction to Soviet values, because the dress could represent "progressiveness." Yurchak (2006, 164) notes that Western goods and ideas could represent "bad cosmopolitanism or good internationalism; the former was a bourgeois product of imperialism, but the latter was a product of progressive people's culture...." Importantly, interpretation depended on the situation, that is, was a factor in the ritual performance and people's attitude toward that performance.

The groom, of course, had to support this delicate, fragile wife. His role was not much different in the Western worldview, as refracted through Soviet ideology, than in native Russian folk conceptions of the husband. However, the Soviet ritual specialists instituted several practices that further emphasized the imbalance between the partners, rather than each person's contribution to the marriage.[37] Men were now responsible for buying the wedding rings as well as a bouquet for their brides. The rings, like the nineteenth-century luxury goods the groom provided to the bride's family, emphasized his role as a provider; if he could afford the rings, he could afford to marry. The bouquet, another luxury item, also reinforced the romantic ideal of the bride as a delicate princess for whom the groom provided. Similarly, the groom now arrived in a decorated rented (or borrowed) car. No longer did these brides go on their own to the ZAGS independently. They

---

[37] We can conclude then that imbalance between the partners was only problematic to theorists when it highlighted unofficial and "subversive" folk material, e.g., overt expression of dominance in the relationship or women as objects to be purchased that challenged officially-espoused marital equality. It was acceptable, however, when it was consonant with socially-endorsed, genteel, and authorized conceptions of men as breadwinners who support their wives.

were driven in special cars after being fetched by the groom. Of course, the groom also traveled in these vehicles, which indicated the separation from the norm and entry into the ritual event. However, the bride never went to get the groom in a hired car, i.e., he was the pursuer, while the bride waited patiently to be collected.

This tradition would seem to be a result of the folk inheritance, where the groom came for the bride on the day of the wedding and endured the *vykup*, combined with the consumerist ideal of the bridal limousine. While Soviet Russians did not hire limousines, they often obtained cars that were synonymous with luxury, such as the Volga. The decorations on the car enhanced its specialness and helped to set the couple apart. Interestingly, the decorations on the car combined Soviet and Western practices; generally the cars had a red ribbon, the color of the Soviet flag, but they also sported swans, interlocked rings, or dolls dressed as a wedding couple, all symbols of romantic love from the Western tradition.[38] These aspects of the wedding, of course, also illustrate the delight in material goods that the Soviet Union was trying to foster in the middle class. Thus the Soviet wedding ceremony during this period led to a very different set of conclusions about family life than the weddings of the previous decades did. While Soviet ideology officially espoused equality, wedding acts fostered the idea that the couple was not equal, but rather consisted of an idealized strong male who was marrying a stereotypical delicate beauty. Femininity, then, became to be defined by appearance and grace, masculinity by power and wealth.

Recall that, at the same time that the "new" wedding had come to fruition in the 1970s, the Soviet Union simultaneously introduced a high school course entitled 'The Ethics and Psychology of Family Life' to instill "proper" gender roles in children. The curriculum for this course was derived from the complex array of gender symbolism we have described. The class taught that boys should "'protect and preserve the virtue and honour of the girl.' He should be honest, responsible, intelligent, brave, decisive, noble; he should possess self-control, a love of work, a readiness to defend the weak and take on himself the most difficult and demanding jobs" (Attwood 1990, 186). Girls are characterized by "kindness, concern for others, softness, tenderness, thoughtfulness, and their willingness to give in.... [They should be] kind,

---

[38] Again it is not clear that these practices were perceived as Western, because they were also consonant with traditions from the early twentieth-century Russian wedding and the culture of the period, e.g., Tchaikovsky's *Swan Lake* and the fairly common knowledge that swans mate for life; the occurrence of wedding rings in the nineteenth century (and earlier). The traditional use of dolls in Russian ritual, as in the *Ivan Kupalo* and *Maslenitsa* rituals, may also have played a role in the introduction of dolls in the form of the bridal couple to decorate the cars. Whether they are truly Western or not, they serve to highlight a new attitude toward romance as well as the shift toward excess in the wedding ritual.

affable, able to understand other people, tender, sincere, natural, trusting, modest, sensitive, loyal, intelligent: she should possess a high level of morality, the ability to love, and the ability to be a housekeeper" (Attwood 1990, 187). Teachers also emphasized the importance of multiple-child families for proper socialization, in an effort to promote a woman's role as mother to solve the demographic crisis. Attwood (1990, 165ff.) also makes reference to a simultaneous shift in the popular press of the period toward a discussion of the "proper" role of men and women in marriage and society. These changes in the official ideology stemmed from concern about the rising divorce and falling birthrates. It was assumed that women had become too "masculine" (and men too "feminine"), that this phenomenon threatened the stability of the Soviet state. The emphasis on women's traditional duties, particularly on motherhood, would help to solve these social ills (Attwood, 1990, 166).[39] Theorists failed to see (or purposefully ignored) that while these ideals about husbandly and wifely behavior might have meshed on the surface, they actually promoted widely divergent views of identity. This situation produced an even more acute gender "crisis" for both sexes.

The end result of these various views of gender was a complex range of interconnected definitions husbands and wives had to navigate. The folk message was that marriage would be successful if each partner worked at prescribed roles (woman in the domestic sphere and man in the public world). The official Soviet message was that both spouses were equal in society and should view their marriage as a partnership. The Western (capitalist and class-based) message (as adapted through Soviet socialism, to be sure) was that the husband was the bearer of burdens (financial and physical), who supported a delicate, beautiful wife. Layered upon this was the image of the wife as a homemaker and emotional nurturer designed to bear children, while her husband was a professional who defined himself via his public identity, not his familial role. These ideals emerged from a complicated Soviet reinterpretation of village tradition, revolutionary ideology and upper-class (Western and Russian) ideas about male and female roles.

Russian husbands during this period seemingly received fewer contradictory messages than their spouses, although they were in some ways divergent one from another. The Soviet message of equality between partners quickly got subsumed by the Western and folk messages the wedding conveyed so clearly. Every one of the divergent sources for a husband's role conveyed the image of a strong provider for the family. If he accomplished this task, he had fulfilled his obligations. However, as Olson (2004, 167), Kukhterin (2000, 85),

---

[39] These attempts did strike a chord with men and women, because they were the heart of the conflicts they faced in their daily lives. As a result, feminist ideals about gender equality were roundly rejected in the 1990s, because they were associated with socialist ideology as well as the difficulties of the "double burden." For more discussion of this issue and of post-Soviet gender roles, see chapter 6.

and Attwood (1990, 166) have discussed, there was a general concern that men had become emasculated by the Soviet system and could not live up to this fairly straightforward and unitary expectation. Simply put, the Soviet system did not actually allow a man to provide for his family as he had in the nineteenth-century peasant village, although he was still expected to. While men (and their wives) may have idealized the wife as a full-time homemaker, they could not organize their lives to conform to this vision within the socialist economic system in which they lived. Both husbands and wives typically had to work for a family to make ends meet, which produced dissent between spouses. Not only did women challenge male primacy in public life and indeed within the family itself, but women also complained that men did not bear their share of domestic tasks. Thus, the majority of men failed both as breadwinners and as domestic partners, because they did not earn enough and did not help around the house.

While male roles had some inherent conflict, female gender roles were even more rife with dissonance. Women had to live up to diametrically opposed standards: domestic goddess, productive professional, and beauty queen. Not surprisingly, divorces were primarily initiated by women, despite possible financial hardships, because they were seeking "to satisfy their needs better" (Shlapentokh, 1984, 208–09, citing Goldberg et al. 1982, 67). Reasons for divorces were many, from alcoholism to abuse, from irreconcilable differences to infidelity. Sargeant (1996, 271) also notes that financial trouble related to the "difficulty in creating the normal conditions for family life is the main reason for divorce." Without a doubt, however, conflicts related to gender and assumptions about roles in the family played a significant role in the divorce rate. It would seem then, despite its hopes that the family would grow stronger, the Soviet Union created an economic and social situation which actually led to greater instability between the couple.

Women repeatedly told me that they were stronger than their husbands; that because they have to meet a wide range of obligations, they are better able to handle adversity. Women thereby coped with the fact that they must fulfill three conflicting roles by inverting the original intent of the messages about their social position. They see men, who claim to be stronger and who have more social prestige, as the weaker vessel, dependent on women to survive. Men are variously affected by this perception. If they believe themselves to be in a position of dominance, whether factual or not, they do not seem to suffer adversely. If, however, their masculine power is effectively challenged, then they may suffer from the emasculation (and the resulting crisis) Olson, Kukhterin, and Attwood refer to in their studies. In all social situations women have been forced to cope with the fact that they are perceived as weaker, despite the strength, perseverance, and flexibility required to function in three varied social roles. Inversion of the message allows women to express their resentment toward a society that does not value their contribution. As a result, they were able to feel more powerful than the men around them and have retained a sense of self-worth.

As we have seen, both birth and weddings have elements that stem from the tripartite inheritance from the Russian folk tradition, the capitalist systems of Europe and the United States, and Soviet socialist ideology. Despite the inherent differences between birth as a medical process and weddings as a legal, social contract, similar themes are conveyed in both rituals. Soviet celebrants viewed these rituals as a type of manufacturing process controlled by the state. In addition, the rituals themselves advocated Soviet ideals about rationality and science over emotion and nature, and the state as provider of goods and services for the family. In some cases, the state was remarkably successful in convincing its citizens to accept its views of the relationship between the family and the state, but in others it failed. The marriage ceremony did become an essential step for both men and women to be full members of society.[40] Similarly, people accepted that the state was indeed able to provide them with the best setting for a wedding and, to some extent, a portion of the goods that a young family would need either for daily life or for a proper wedding celebration. This ritual also managed to convey some essential notions about what it meant to be a husband and wife in Soviet Russia. However, as is clear from the high divorce and low birthrates throughout this period, ritual specialists were not able to foster stable families through the wedding rite. In the end, it would seem, contradictory messages about the husband's and wife's (and indeed the state's) roles in marriage and family life led to dissonance and weaker marriages.

However, as in the birth rite, Soviet Russian citizens actively negotiated their roles as husband and wife based on their experiences. They relied not only on official socialist ideology, but also on the Russian folk tradition and consumerism, both of which in some cases directly contradicted state goals. The state could not subsume the family by means of the ritual process, but in fact enabled it to become the primary focus of these ritual celebrations, both financially and emotionally. While my informants recognized that transition from one status to another was formally controlled by the government and was necessary to them for full social membership, they viewed the state ceremony as bureaucratic and officious. In the face of this dissatisfaction, the pre- and post-wedding events held within the family home became all the more significant. They demonstrated the "true" source of financial and emotional support for the wedding celebration and ultimately in the couple's lives together as well as provided a venue to illustrate their conception of "folk" beliefs about spousal roles. In sum, both birth and wedding rites illustrate the intricate nature of the Soviet ritual complex and how participants negotiated identity through them. Through ritual practice citizens effectively resisted *and* enhanced Soviet ideology and social norms. As we will see, funerals were no

---

[40] Women, of course, truly became "full" members of society when they had children.

exception in this regard, but were in fact the most conservative and resistant of the three life-cycle rituals.

Chapter 5

The Soviet Russian Funeral Ritual (1950–90)

For the redesign of childbirth and wedding rites, Soviet theoreticians could rely on conceptions of the family built upon communist morality and on the *dukhovnye* 'spiritual' values of the individual. Expectations for these ritual acts had long been established in state ideology, which gave them license to create rites reflecting official policy. As we have seen, by the 1930s they had decided to reinforce the family unit because of its importance to social and governmental stability. Certainly, the view of the family may have shifted from the 1930s through the 1980s, but the aim of these two rituals remained essentially the same. However, the funeral ritual posed a problem for ritual specialists, because it is radically different from the other two rituals we have examined. Childbirth and wedding rites are designed to establish family identity. The funeral, in contrast, deals with the destruction of that identity as a result of the loss of one of its members. Because no obvious ideological vision existed for how to deal with the dissolution of the family, theorists were never able to realize the same kind of consistency in the funeral rite as they had in birth and weddings. In addition, they had no official institutions that allowed them to make much progress in remaking funerary practice, unlike the medical institutions and wedding palaces that played such a key role in the redesign of the other two life-cycle rites.

The funeral was the rite most closely tied to religious beliefs and was therefore the most threatening of the three to the official policy of atheism. The ritual specialists were acutely aware of this conundrum. They had to somehow create a rite that did not focus on the deceased's soul or the afterlife through redefining what the funeral was intended to do. Ugrinovich's discussion of the funeral demonstrates how he and his colleagues attempted, rather unconvincingly, to resolve this dilemma. He (1975, 136) remarks that Soviet funerals were not designed to commemorate a person's eternal soul or life after death. Rather, eternity for Soviet people signified their inheritance to those they leave behind. Thus the religious phrase *vechnaia pamiat'* 'eternal memory', a phrase from an Orthodox hymn still used in Soviet-era funerary rites, must be reinterpreted from its Orthodox meaning (a request for God and the saints to remember the dead in the afterlife) to a secular one (calling for people to remember). The focus of this legacy, according to Ugrinovich, is on the deceased's children and hi(s)her actions and involvement in material and spiritual values throughout life. It is imperative, he concludes, to create a funeral ritual that eliminates the associations with religion, while allowing people to share grief. If they achieved this end, Ugrinovich (143) argues, the Soviet ritual would allow for bonds to be formed to the collective and the society at large through mourning.

While ritual specialists agreed that the funeral should not be connected to faith, Ugrinovich does note that religious belief played a significant role in the rite as practiced in Soviet Russia. For example, formal remembrances of the dead often still occurred on Orthodox religious holidays, because the theorists had not yet created an alternative mourning ritual (at least for those who had died outside of war). Rudnev (1979, 179–80) concurs that the Soviet theorists had not been particularly successful in the development of funeral rituals for all these reasons. However, he remarks that some progress had been made in Leningrad from the late 1960s on, when the system of burial was regularized, a range of acceptable headstones was designed, funds for cemetery upkeep were increased, and a new civil ceremony for interment was established.

Despite their hope for a redesigned Soviet funeral ritual, many of the elements the Soviet ritual specialists incorporated were clearly associated with Orthodox belief. As we saw with the wedding, the models from which to choose were limited, but they had few options if they were to avoid religious content. It was nearly inevitable for them to base the Soviet civil funeral on a familiar prototype. As a result, Orthodox features were adopted into the funerary ritual and then subsequently were imposed even upon the non-Orthodox peoples of the USSR (Lane 1981, 232). Interment during the Soviet period remained largely unchanged from the nineteenth-century Orthodox ritual, except for the elimination of the priest who would celebrate a funeral mass.

However, it was especially difficult to divorce these remnants from Orthodox Christian symbolism, of which participants were clearly aware. Ritual specialists resorted to vain, and sometime contorted, attempts to redefine religious practices via socialist ideology. Ugrinovich (1975, 130), for example, discusses the throwing of dirt onto the coffin at the graveside. This act was not intended to bring to mind religious symbolism related to the return of the body to the earth, so as to free the soul. Rather, it served simply as a way to say farewell to the dead. We have already seen evidence of this conflict in our discussion of birth and wedding rites, but the dissonance between the acts and their reinterpretations via Soviet ideology was much more obvious in funerary ceremonies. It is telling, in fact, that most ritual specialists either omit funerals completely from their discussion of Soviet-era rituals, as do Sukhanov (1976) and Mar'ianov (1976a), or describe commemoration of the dead in other contexts. For example, Rudnev (1979, 178–79), who provides exhaustive descriptions of both the Soviet naming and wedding ceremonies, describes a Memorial Day celebration in detail, but gives only a few excerpts from a funeral service. We find the same situation in Ugrinovich (133–36), who elaborates on the former two rituals and speaks only generally about funerals, although he includes an extensive section on the remembrance of war dead. These theorists were clearly at a loss for establishing the change required by official atheism and also lacked an established ideology to cope with family dissolution. In the end, they decided to address the issue in only the most vague terms.[1]

This dilemma was not only limited to the 1960s and 1970s, when the ritual specialists were working in earnest to create new Soviet life-cycle rites. Karen Petrone (personal communication) observed that the Soviet Union had a difficult time dealing with death generally. Early Bolsheviks, particularly the revolutionary Alexander Bogdanov, held that Soviet science would actually be able to overcome death. He himself died after a blood transfusion during experiments designed to prolong life. Lenin's preservation in his Red Square tomb was partly the result of such early theories about defeating mortality. As we have seen, a faith in science and reason overwhelmingly characterized the Soviet worldview and thus, they held that their socialist society would eventually triumph over nature and emotion. In his study of Soviet and Russian funerals, Trice (1998, 243) argues that, in the work of medical professionals, "the human body became the physiological object of cultural progress, not the mortal casting of its spiritual analogue." This conception of the body clearly parallels the attitude toward the woman's body and natural processes in birth rites. Both had to be rationalized and indeed remade in accord with official ideology.

The Bolsheviks also desired to remold society more broadly by eliminating outmoded cultural norms. The official decree about funerals from 1918 illustrates this aim:

> The decree called for the nationalization of all cemeteries, morgues, and funeral parlors, and authorized the introduction into Russia of cremation. It also required that citizens register every death with the local Bureau of Civic Registration (ZAGS). More importantly, this new law mandated the abolition of the Nikolaevan rank system for funerals and cemetery plots in favor of a new, more egalitarian system based on unranked plots and an "identical [odinakovyi] funeral" for every Soviet citizen. (Trice 1998, 217)

---

[1] This omission is striking when contrasted to Serykh's *Voinskie ritualy* (1986, 198–222), which provides an elaborate description of the military funerals of Gagarin and Seregin, cosmonauts who died "for" Russia during a mission flight in 1968. Also included in this chapter is a discussion of memorials and commemorative rites to those who fell in World War II and their importance to Soviet national identity.

This law provides support for the claim that the government intended to usurp the functions of religious institutions as well. It hoped both to provide for and control its citizens in an elemental way, since the decree instituted for free, civil (not religious) funerals for the poor. Both of these issues, of course, were fundamental to the remaking of birth and weddings, as we have examined.

While the Soviet ritual specialists make specific reference to the commemoration of the war dead and their successes in this regard, the Soviet Union did not make immediate progress in this area either. The dead of the civil war and World War I were rarely commemorated or honored in the early years of the Soviet state. Theorists were much more effective at developing memorials and commemorative architecture for the war dead, particularly those of World War II, after Stalin's death (see Tumarkin 1994 for a consideration of the development of the World War II cult). As discussed in chapter 4, ritual specialists incorporated commemorations of the war dead into weddings through visits to the tomb of the unknown soldier or to World War II memorials. Although they had already established holidays that honored the fallen, such as Victory Day in May and Memorial Day in June, these celebrations became much more important during the 1960s and were accompanied by the construction of many monuments, including such iconic memorials as the Tomb of the Unknown Soldier in Moscow and the Volgograd World War II monument in 1967. Memorials became a major focus of the Brezhnev administration from the time he assumed the mantle of power into the 1980s (Tumarkin 127ff.). These structures were designed not only to remember the dead, but also to promote dedication to the Soviet Union in their name. In fact, the two major monuments built in 1967 were in honor of the fiftieth anniversary of the October Revolution, which suggests that the war dead were being used to cement faith in the Soviet system.

The funeral of an individual who did not die for the country, however, remained an unresolved dilemma for Soviet ritual specialists. They could refer neither to ideological sacrifice nor to religious beliefs. In her discussion of life-cycle rituals, Lane (1981, 192) concludes that the only symbols they had access to were those from Soviet history, which lacked the resonance of both religious and secular rituals from the past for the average person. The Soviet theorists recognized that their rituals did generally suffer from a lack of depth and thus turned to, as Lane (193) expresses it, concrete "symbols of ritual— badges, letters, diplomas, albums." However, such tokens are not especially appropriate for a funeral, even if they do serve some purpose within birth and wedding rituals. Merridale (2000, 264) notes that Soviet funerary rituals focused on the deceased's work life and party activities in keeping with the idea that a person's memory would live on in hi(s)her deeds on earth, not in the afterlife. Lane (84) describes the graveside service as follows: family and friends discussed "the merits of the deceased, putting particular emphasis on services rendered to society. A short speech by the official [conducting the service] on the same theme may conclude with words such as: 'Life continues, and everything that the deceased has managed to achieve will continue.'" Rudnev (1979, 181) also includes a summary statement of this sort: "The citizen of the Soviet Russian Federal Socialist Republic (gives the last name, first name, and patronymic)[2] has completed hi(s)her life's journey. The motherland bids farewell to her son (her daughter). Let fond memories of him (of her) be eternally preserved in your hearts."

As we have seen, the Soviet ritual specialists were able to develop more effective rituals related to the remembrance of the war dead not only because they died for the country (and thus fit with Soviet ideals of sacrifice for the nation), but also because the memorials were designed using a Soviet model. As discussed in chapter 4, the design and construction of monumental architecture characteristic of revolutionary societies was a particular forte of the Soviet Union. The cemetery, which was the locus of religious commemoration of the dead during yearly cycle rituals even during the socialist period, did not conform to Soviet ideals about monumental architecture. The gravestones themselves were anomalous, because they bore distinct ties to religious faith. In fact, Yelena Minyonok (2007) argues that the rural cemetery itself became a type of substitute for the Orthodox churches destroyed during the Soviet period. While Minyonok makes specific reference to rural graveyards, my informants' comments on the associations between burial sites and Orthodox commemorative rites make her observation relevant for the urban situation as well. This fact made the cemetery all the more problematic for theorists creating a new type of funeral devoid of religious content.

However, the Soviet authorities did try to redesign cemeteries to make them less "religious." They made few inroads in "rational" cemetery design. Merridale (2000, 279) notes that the new cemeteries were hybrids, which included both Orthodox symbols (tables for commemoration of the dead on Parents' Saturdays, "roofs" over gravestones) alongside Soviet ones (plastic red stars and gilded engraving). They were, she asserts, never preferred to older cemeteries, not only because of their poor design, but because they were far from the center of town (a location intended to reduce the frequency of

---

[2] While discussing birth, we noted the use of names as an indication of the doctor's attitude toward the patient. The last name alone is abrupt and illustrates the doctor's distance from and superiority to the patient. While the first name, particularly a diminutive, may be endearing, it also confirms the hierarchical relationship, because the patient cannot respond in kind, but must use the formal means of address, first name and patronymic, to the doctor. In this case, the use of the last name followed by the first name and patronymic (also found in the wedding ritual) is characteristic of bureaucratic language, a form that seems disdainful to the Russian ear. Thus, to have a celebrant in a ritual use this form (rather than a form of endearment, such as a diminutive form of the first name, or the first name and patronymic as a sign of respect) borders on the offensive and is certainly not conducive to creating a bond between the state representative performing the ceremony and the mourners.

religious commemoration of the dead). They particularly addressed the design of headstones, from which religious symbols were banned; epitaphs focused on the "earthly life of the deceased" (Lane 1981, 85).

One key to the rationalization and secularization of the funeral was cremation. Trice (1998, 319) states that it was "indeed a metaphor for far-reaching social, political, and cultural change—a hybrid that combined the civic values and ideas of ancient Greece, Rome, and enlightenment Europe with the technological wonders of the industrial age." Cremation appealed to the secular rationalism of socialist thinking, progressive faith in technology, and the desire to eliminate religious belief (Trice 339–42). It would also help to erase the remnants of Christian practices of commemoration of the dead at the cemetery. However, despite their best intentions, cremation never flourished. Certainly, cremation was unacceptable within the Orthodox tradition, which contributed to its limited spread. But we cannot conclude that Orthodox belief alone was the sole reason for the unpopularity of cremation. Another factor, one that cremationists did not consider, was the importance of the grave as the locus of the dead person's spirit, even for areligious citizens. Merridale (2000, 37, 264–65) stresses the long-standing association between the dead and the earth in Russian folk tradition, which was well-preserved throughout the Soviet period. Given the fact that there were no other meaningful ways to remember the (non-war) dead within the Soviet Russian context, it is clear that the gravesite itself became more important in the Soviet era. Therefore, Soviet reality, combined with religious and folk beliefs about the gravesite, all combined to predispose people to burial over cremation.

As a result of the Soviet inability to redefine these rites effectively, the funeral is the most conservative ritual of all three under consideration here and is remarkably close to the rite as practiced in the nineteenth century. As my informant Ekaterina Z. said: "It is more interesting to talk about funerals, because in the funerary ritual traditions have been preserved deepest of all. Because here, no matter how far people were from everything, whether educated, whether frightful preservationists, here everything has to be observed." Merridale (2000, 141) notes that the full Orthodox ritual was rare by the time World War II began, but that people preserved "the basic ideas behind their rituals." Similarly, Nosova (1993, 87) reports that the twentieth century Russian funerals she studied in the Voronezh region may be classified as one of three types: civil, civil-religious, or entirely religious, with the most common being the civil-religious one. The funeral then was the life-cycle ritual that was most ripe for resistance to Soviet ideology.

Nevertheless, before we can draw this conclusion definitively, we must return to our discussion of ritual theory. I have argued previously that ritual conveys not a single semantic message, but a variety of meanings based on context, what Humphrey and Laidlaw (1994, 91) call "illocutionary force" and what Yurchak (2006, 37) refers to as "performative." Both of these terms are derived from the study of speech acts in the field of linguistic pragmatics. For our purposes, these approaches to ritual illustrate how Soviet Russians were able to produce meaning from what seemed to be a "meaningless" rite. Certainly, the ceremonies themselves may have been pro forma. Nevertheless, ritual actors, as Humphrey and Laidlaw illustrate (34–36) in their discussion of the Jain *puja*, do assign meanings to their actions, albeit not unitary ones, even if those actions are not in and of themselves "meaningful." While the Soviet theorists might have intended for ritual content to be unitary, people did not always accept one single reading. Yurchak (50) contends that this attitude toward official language is the key to the understanding of daily life within the Soviet Union of this period. Official rhetoric was

> *hypernormalized* [italics original] — that is, the process of its normalization did not simply affect all levels of linguistic, textual, and narrative structure but also became an end in itself, resulting in fixed and cumbersome forms of language that were often neither interpreted nor easily interpretable at the level of constative meaning. This shift to the hypernormalized language in which the constative dimension was increasingly being unanchored is the key for our understanding of late socialism.

In the end, citizens did not even really attempt, according to Yurchak, to interpret the meanings in official discourse, because it had been disconnected from semantic content to a large extent. However, that does not mean that they did not, as I have shown, bring sense to the rites themselves. In fact, as Humphrey and Laidlaw predict, they brought to bear a plethora of meanings, some based on folk or religious practices and indeed some based on Soviet ideology or on Western tradition (as interpreted through the lens of the Soviet worldview). But they were not limited only to these three sources. Some politically aware or older brides, for example, rejected certain aspects of both "Sovietness" and "folkiness" in their rituals. Thus, while we can speak of trends in the way rituals were constructed and interpreted, we have to allow for radical individual variants as well, a fact that illustrates the argument we are attempting to make most clearly. People are not bound by particular intentionalities in ritual, but in fact, bring a wide range of experience to their performance, which enables them to create their own status via ritual.

Practice theorists support precisely this view of ritual performance. Ritual is designed to allow for identity negotiation within the hierarchy of a social system. Bourdieu (1990, 95) argues that the key to this process is an understanding of *habitus*:

> the generative principles constituting that *habitus* derive from the social structures (the structure of relations between the groups, the sexes or the generations, or between the social classes) of which they are the product and by which they tend to reproduce in a trans-

formed, misrecognizable form, by inserting them into the structure of
a system of symbolic relations.

Habitus, in our case the various sources for rituals we have discussed within
the Soviet Russian context, allows for people to reinforce social structure by
maintaining the status quo. However, the ritual performance itself necessarily
alters reality. It establishes a new state of affairs that takes into account the
personal experiences of the ritual participants. As such, their own individual
needs alter the ritual and the social situation it creates. I have shown that the
ritual practices in both wedding and birth allowed people to negotiate their
identities both within the Soviet societal norms and external to them. Bell
(1997, 99) (paraphrasing Sahlins 1976, 1981, 1985) makes a similar conclusion:
"In other words, ritual enables enduring patterns of social organization and
cultural symbolic systems to be brought to bear on real events; in the course
of this process, real situations are assessed and negotiated in ways that can
transform these traditional patterns or structures in turn." This chapter will
address this issue from the point of view of the funeral.

Of particular interest is whether this rite, like birth and weddings, resists
Soviet ideology with folk material. Because the funeral supported few Soviet
ideals, but rather fostered the creation of an identity that was largely separate
from the state and its norms, it would seem to be a clear form of resistance,
unlike the other two rituals, which exhibited some acceptance of official ideological norms. On the surface, it functioned most like the Bedouin poetry Abu
Lughod studied, which often directly contradicted the public statements of
those who recited it. She argues that poetry allows for resistance to social
norms that disadvantage particular citizens, especially women, but that it also
reinforces these same cultural ideals. Thus, she (1986, 295) concludes, the poems "are like secrets: secrets function to exclude those who do not share them
and to closely bind those who do. Thus, categories of equals gain cohesion
and divisions between non-equals are intensified, reinforcing the structure of
Bedouin society." We cannot, however, simply assume that each and every
act in the funeral was one of pure resistance to ideology, since the state itself
was ineffective in determining what the funeral should mean, as we have discussed. However, even if we will not be able to characterize these practices
only in this way, they are surely the most divergent from the socialist ideology that had been defined, particularly with regard to atheism and the preservation of folk beliefs. We will return to this question once we have examined
the funeral in more detail.

Both conservatism and divergence from official norms in funeral practice
are the result not only of the desire to ensure that a person was buried properly, as Ekaterina suggests, but also of the fact that this ritual is the most
private of the three under consideration. Birth, of course, was under the
control of medical institutions from the beginning of the pregnancy;
weddings were celebrated at a state office, and receptions might have also

been held in a public place. Funerals during this period, except for the burial itself, were centered on the family home. Thus the family could perform what ritual acts it deemed necessary within the private sphere without fear of governmental censure. Certainly the interment itself had changed, in that religious rituals common in the pre-revolutionary period were officially banned by the Soviet state (or difficult to perform, due to the lack of priests). However, given the official discomfort with the topic and the fact that funerals took place out of the public eye, it is not surprising that variation between ritual practices in different regions of Russia is most prevalent in this rite, when compared to the birth and wedding rituals we have examined. Despite these variants, however, funerals during the Soviet period were characterized by many of the same features we have seen already in birth and weddings, including the predominant role of women; conflicts between the values of the state institution and the family, and an intersection of folk tradition, Soviet ideology, and even consumerism, to some extent.

Description of Soviet Funeral Practices

Each life-cycle ritual introduces participants into their new roles within society. However, birth and funerals are quite distinct from the wedding in this regard. Weddings focus upon how the bridal couple and their families and friends react to the new marriage. In essence, while wedding guests are not marrying themselves, they are all aiming to establish the couple's identity within the social sphere. In birth, however, ritual participants undergo a single rite with two very different goals. The parents create their identity as mother and father, while the child essentially "learns" what it means to be human within the society into which (s)he was born. In that sense, funerals are much more similar to birth than to weddings. Mourners need to readjust their conception of the family (and society at large) without a particular member through the grieving process. The deceased (or hi(s)her spirit) needs to make the transition into the otherworld, in a shift parallel to that of a newborn into this world. However, the focus upon the deceased is much more elaborate than on the child in the birth rite. We have discussed how ritual celebrants attempt to "complete" the child and make it human, but those efforts are much less dominant than those for the parents themselves. However, in the funeral, nearly every act serves two constituencies: the deceased and the survivors. Thus in our discussion of the funerary rite, we will focus on how every practice affects both the living and the dead.

Most people died at home, and the corpse was kept there for two days, before being buried on the third day. There was some discrepancy about the timing of the funeral. Alexander M. said that people are never buried in the morning, "after twelve and before four. They don't bury people in the morning." In contrast, Marina K. and Natalia T. both said that a person should be buried by two p.m., without any mention of a limitation on the morning.

Informants in Shevchenko's study on urban funerals (2003, 397) reported that people should be buried before noon. If a person died outside of the home, either in an accident or in the hospital, then (s)he was generally brought home from the morgue for at least one night before the burial.[3]

The family would call a doctor, who would come to the house to sign the death certificate, so that the family could proceed with funeral arrangements. The family needed the certificate to organize transportation to and from the cemetery (often done through the deceased's workplace) as well as to obtain some goods required for the funeral. As Galina S. reported: "Once you had to buy tulle for the interior, a red fabric to cover the coffin from the outside. Then you had to order the headstone. Now it is easier, but then everyone used to be involved in this." Natasha R. elaborated, "Once, when you couldn't get these things, they issued funeral certificates, and with this certificate you could go to the store and buy something."

When a person died, those present covered all the shiny surfaces in the home (including mirrors, glass-fronted cabinets, and even televisions). If a person died at home, an older female acquaintance came to wash and dress the deceased, as Igor S. describes: "My mother-in-law lived with her second daughter, she died in her daughter's arms. She was ill for a long time, and then this sister said that these women came, who knew her well and who knew how it is done, they washed and dressed her." Most people reported that it was not a good idea if a close relative performed this ritual act. For example, Andrei M. said that "it is generally thought that a close relative should not wash the body, the very close ones." In some cases, despite the fact that they knew the taboo on family participation in the preparation of the deceased for burial, some people disregarded it. Although her mother had already asked someone to come prepare her body when she died, Natalia T. performed the rite herself:

> There is this strange superstition that relatives should not wash the deceased. Someone from outside should prepare and dress them. And when she said that when she dies, she had already made an agreement with some old woman and that she would wash and dress her, it really was painful for me, because I worshipped my mom. Therefore to think about the fact that some strange person, some woman would come and would touch her and wash her, and I would stand and watch, that was unbearable for me. And when my mother died, my sister and I washed and dressed her ourselves, we did everything ourselves.

---

[3] If the person died a violent death, (s)he was generally buried from the morgue, so that the final visitation and transport for burial occurred there.

Shevchenko (2003, 394) states his informants reported that all items used for washing the body were buried with the corpse; the water was poured down the toilet or where people would not walk on it, because it could be used to curse people.

Women typically had decided on their funeral clothing and had it prepared in a small bundle; wives or children usually chose the clothing for male relatives. The dress or suit could be old, that is, previously worn (although it had to have been laundered), but the underclothing and footwear had to be new and unworn. Once the body was prepared, it was placed in a coffin in the main room on a table or on stools with the head toward the window and the feet toward the door. A photograph of the deceased was placed at the head of the coffin, often with a candle next to it. The door remained unlocked, so that all who wished to enter and pay their respects could do so. People maintained a vigil over the deceased for the entire time (s)he was in the home; they often invited a *posidel'ka* 'sitter' who would come and read prayers or the psalter over the body, as Elvira A. reported, even during the Soviet period:

> Therefore when the deceased is in the home, we turn to the church, look for some woman to read prayers. She sits all night, reads prayers…. In 1984 they also came, we asked them to read. Mom died, a woman also came. We could sleep a little, but she sat all night and read prayers by candlelight.[4]

Merridale's (2000, 264) data on funerals support this claim. While official religious figures usually did not attend a funeral (due to the shortage of priests, not apparently because mourners did not want them to participate), people would rely on those who remembered prayers to read or recite them. In addition, Merridale (265) also found evidence of retention of the Orthodox practice of sprinkling earth (blessed by a priest) in the shape of a cross on the coffin or the deceased's chest. Visitors were welcome throughout the vigil, and on the day of the funeral, they generally brought with them an even number of flowers, which they placed in or near the coffin. While any flower was acceptable for funerals, the most common was red carnations. It was the norm for mourners to wear dark colors. Women usually covered their heads,

---

[4] My informants also included atheists, who performed no religious practices in funerals, as well as non-Orthodox people, who also did not observe these traditions. One Muslim informant said that because the family was mixed, that is, Russian and Tatar, and the traditions were different, they tried to have a neutral funeral, without any obvious religious practices from either tradition. Similarly, Jewish informants avoided Orthodox traditions, such as Irina V., who said that her grandmother, for example, was buried "in the Jewish way, that is without a funeral meal at home. That is not done among the Jews."

while men, in contrast, removed their hats out of respect. Some also wore mourning bands on their clothing.

The coffin was carried out by non-blood relatives, friends, or coworkers. Just as it was a bad omen for a relative to prepare the body, a relative should not carry the body out of the home. Thus friends, coworkers, or non-blood relatives took the coffin outside. As Liudmila B. stated: "Under no circumstances are relatives allowed to do this." Alexander U. expressed a similar opinion: "Outsiders should carry it out, not relatives." His wife Tatiana elaborated on this idea: "Usually they invite people from work." The procession out of the house followed a strict order, as Elvira A. reported: "First they carry out the wreaths from the apartment, then the coffin lid, and only then the coffin. And then come the relatives." The coffin was typically placed on stools in front of the house, so that mourners who were not attending the funeral could say farewell. In some cases it was also taken to the person's workplace for this purpose, as Nadezhda P. described for her father's funeral: "But then they took my dad to the institute where he worked, and there they held a civil memorial service, that is, they placed the coffin there and people on duty stood there." Mourners and the coffin were transported to the graveyard in buses obtained from work or through a worker's union.

The grave was dug either by graveyard workers or by the family and was ready when the funeral procession arrived. The procession was accompanied by a brass ensemble that played Chopin's *Funeral March* and the Soviet national anthem, as Elena I. discussed: "When they buried people in Soviet times, they could play the 'International,' communist songs. Usually when they bury people they play Chopin, the *Funeral March*, or some other classical works." If the person was a veteran, they also played military airs and there may have been a military component, as Tatiana D. describes: "And when they buried dad and set down the coffin, an orchestra first played a funeral march, and then the anthem ... and there was a salute. Soldiers went with us and they fired [their weapons]."

Most people made note of a brief speech at the graveside, but their opinions on who performed the eulogy varied. The majority also remarked that coworkers or union representatives performed this service. Others said that family and friends might also speak. Galina S. said that it depended on the nature of the funeral: "I was at a funeral while I was in school. A graduate of our school died in Afghanistan. At his funeral they gave a speech. When it is an official process, then they give a speech. But when it is within the family, then not always." Lidia C. concurred: "As a rule, if it is a funeral for a relative then they don't give speeches, but it is really the norm to give speeches over the coffin if they are political figures.... For them it is the norm, but for relatives it is somehow not done." Indeed while most people agreed that one might speak at any funeral, the funerals of those who were significant to some organization (such as an institution of higher education, factory, or trade union) or who were veterans received the most formal graveside speeches.

Aasamaa (1974, 178) concurs; she writes that if a famous person dies, then a funeral commission is established to direct the funeral ceremony; eulogies are delivered by "organizational representatives and coworkers."

Before the coffin was closed for the final time, relatives kissed the person goodbye, typically on the forehead. During the ceremony at the graveside (or in some cases before the coffin was taken out of the house), dirt in the shape of a cross was sprinkled on the chest of the deceased, as a symbol of the person's commission to the earth. It was a tradition to tie the hands and feet as part of the preparation of the body, and at this point, the bonds were untied. Tatiana U. mentioned that this had to be done, because "They also live there [in the afterlife], and [otherwise] they will have their hands and feet tied there." All flowers were removed from the coffin (although artificial ones might have been left inside). The grave may also have had fir branches lining it, and some informants described throwing coins into the grave as well. Cemetery workers lowered the coffin into the grave either on ropes or on long, waffle-weave towels. Each person, closest relatives first, threw a fistful of dirt into the grave. All mourners then waited until the gravediggers filled the grave and formed the burial mound. They arranged the wreaths and flowers on the grave, possibly around a photograph of the deceased. The first ritual partaking of food might have occurred at the gravesite after the burial, after which some food was generally left behind on the grave. If the deceased was a man, a shot glass of vodka was often placed on the grave as well. The food and drink were shared with those who dug the grave as well as with mourners. Some said that they did not eat or leave food on the first day, but only on the second day after the burial or at later memorial feasts or holidays.

For the funeral meal, the mourners returned to the family apartment, which had undergone a ritual purification. Generally a few female neighbors, friends, or distant relatives stayed behind to prepare for the funeral feast and also to perform this cleaning, as Elena P. describes:

> You ask a neighbor or a friend. As soon as the coffin is carried out of the house, the table on which it stood is turned upside down at once, the stools on which it stood are also turned over right away. Then whoever stays behind, they have turned the table over, stepped out, saw the coffin out, then they put the table back and start to wash the floors and the entryway also. We threw away all the rags, buckets, and basins we used for washing. And they uncover the mirrors.[5]

Katia K. notes that after the cleaning, they begin preparing for the funeral meal: "You had to prepare this [the funeral meal], therefore women stayed behind and made everything while people were at the cemetery." The funeral

---

[5] In Novosibirsk this ritual purification is performed with *polyn'* 'wormwood', which is dampened and used to clean the floors in the apartment and the entryway.

meal at the wake, *pominki*, included the following items: *bliny* 'crepes'; *kisel'* 'a drink from berries' or *kompot* 'dried fruit compote'; a grain, typically buckwheat; a main meat dish; and often a soup, most commonly *borshch* 'beet soup' or *shchi* 'cabbage soup'; and candies. Most drank vodka, although wine was also drunk at these feasts. Toasts to the deceased were proposed and stories about him/her were told, ending with the ritual words, *"pust' zemlia emu/ei budet pukhom"* 'may the earth be soft as down for him/her'. However, it was not acceptable to clink glasses before drinking, because that act indicates wishing people good health. Liudmila K. described this process as follows:

> Someone close begins, takes the initiative and says "let's remember, let the earth be like down for him." People pour a little vodka, drink, and everyone feels obliged to say something, to recall something, then simply share one's reminiscences about what kind of person he was, and they only recollect good things. That is, not hurriedly, but people recall something from their life.

Additional *pominki* with visitations to the grave (with similar meals) occurred on the ninth and fortieth days as well as on the one-year anniversary after death, and then for every year thereafter.[6] In some families, a plate and/or glass was placed on the table for the deceased and/or a chair was left empty. All my informants placed a shot glass with vodka (or more rarely water) covered with black bread next to the deceased's photograph for forty days.[7] The liquid generally evaporated in that time, while the bread was fed to the birds. When guests left, they were usually given candies or other food from the meal to take with them to share with others, especially with children.

One of the most striking factors in the funeral, as compared to the other two life-cycle rituals, are the distinct regional differences, particularly among western Siberian informants from Novosibirsk and those from European Russia, primarily Moscow and Vladimir. While informants in both areas overwhelmingly agreed that *kut'ia*, a traditional dish made of grain (usually rice), raisins, and honey, was an essential part of the funeral, they did not serve it at the same time. In Novosibirsk, for example, this dish was served at the funeral meal proper, while in Vladimir it was often eaten at the graveside and not served as part of the meal. For example, Elena B., a Novosibirsk resident, said that the *kut'ia* and *bliny* with honey come before any other dishes, while Alevtina A., a Vladimir resident, said that the first dish served at a funeral meal is *bliny* with honey, not *kut'ia*, because it is limited to the cemetery. Some Vladimir residents reported that *kut'ia* might be served at the

---

[6] One informant also mentioned a remembrance at twenty days and another informant at six months.

[7] Sometimes this glass was put next to the photograph immediately after death; in other cases only after the burial, at the funeral meal.

meal as well, but that it was not required. For example, according to Elena P., "They also make *kut'ia*. Before, when we buried my mom sixteen years ago, they made it without fail, even took it to the cemetery. And it also is on the table." Her husband Andrei elaborated, "It all depends on the age of the deceased and of those that are burying him. Because grandmother was old, she was eighty-eight … we took *kut'ia* to the cemetery, but we didn't order it at the cafeteria." Their decision was based on the idea that *kut'ia* is a tradition closely associated with Orthodoxy, so that when one buries an older person, who is more likely to be a believer, one should observe the requirement for *kut'ia* as part of the funeral meal at some point.

Two other distinctions connected to the meal relate to toasting and to the utensils used. Several Siberians said that it was mandatory to drink only three glasses of vodka at a funeral meal, so that one may drink the first and second completely, but the third was sipped, so that people did not get too intoxicated. Finally, all the Siberians agreed that one should not use any utensils but spoons at a funeral meal, but none of the European Russians knew this tradition. Lidia C. described this Novosibirsk tradition as follows: "It is not acceptable to provide forks at funeral meals, everything should be eaten with spoons, there should be nothing sharp, with a cutting edge, pointed.… They try to serve something for the main course that doesn't require forks."

Another significant difference between these regions occurs as the coffin was carried out of the house. In both areas, flowers were thrown before the coffin, but in Vladimir, there was the additional tradition of placing fir branches along the path, as Elvira A. described: "On the path along which they carry it [the coffin], they throw fir branches." The final variance between western Siberian and European funerals related to graveside practice. It was common to give out candies (or other food) after the burial in both regions. However, in Novosibirsk distribution of goods at the burial site was also the norm. In some cases, these included the long towels on which the coffin was lowered, which were then cut and given to those who had attended the funeral, as Katia K. noted: "It is lowered on towels. There are these long towels that are torn apart and they give them to those that took part, they give them out." Shevchenko's informants from Ulyanovsk also described this tradition (2003, 402), so that apparently it is not limited to Siberian Russia, but it was unknown among the Vladimir and Moscow residents I interviewed. Liuba S. and other Siberian natives also remarked that in addition to the towels, they may also give out kerchiefs or scarves: "Some kerchiefs had been prepared and they gave kerchiefs to everybody."[8] Galina S. also mentioned that she

---

[8] Shevchenko (2003, 400) does not mention limitations on utensils in Ulyanovsk funerals, but some of his informants did describe giving out kerchiefs and soap. A Samara resident, Marina L., confirmed that both limitations on utensils and giving of items at the grave are traditions in her region. Thus these practices have been attested in European Russia, even if they are not common among my informants there.

thought it was a tradition to give out spoons at the *pominki* on the ninth day, but no other informants mentioned this practice.

Folk Tradition in the Soviet Funeral Ritual

Recall that funerary practices aim to serve both the living and the dead. Within the Russian context both folk and religious aspects of the funeral allowed the living, first and foremost, to grieve over a long period of time. The duration of the mourning period in the Russian tradition was not fixed, but recurred at regular intervals over time. For the rest of hi(s)her life, each individual mourner had an opportunity to reflect upon and cope with the loss. An essential component in these mourning procedures was the ongoing connection between this world and the next. In addition, as a result of this enduring bond, certain ritual acts helped to protect the living from the dead, who could potentially be a threat to survivors. Sedakova (2004, 147–48) emphasizes that the folk conception of the funeral from the Russian worldview contained two major motifs. The first was the conception of death as a journey to one's ancestors. Chistiakov (1982, 114) notes that the dead were thought to live a life much like the one (s)he had led on earth. The second common funerary motif, according to Sedakova, was the concept of *dolia* 'fate, lot', which held that a peaceful afterlife was dependent on a "clean" death, that is a death at the proper time (in old age), without violence or excessive suffering. The funeral was designed to determine the dead's *dolia* after death by separating the living from the dead and, at the same time, preparing the way for ongoing and appropriate relations between them. As we will see, the urban funeral from the Soviet period not only served both the living and the dead, but also retained these two motifs from the past.

Not surprisingly, given that the funeral was so conservative, people preserved more folk traditions intact in this rite than in the other two life-cycle rituals. However, it did not remain totally unchanged. Certainly, the tradition of formal lamenting had already been lost in urban areas before the Soviet revolution. Lamenting was a core practice of the village funeral to ensure that the soul of the deceased made the transfer to the otherworld properly. It should be noted that some older women still remembered the tradition and attempted to lament at urban funerals, but this was by no means the norm. Tatiana S. described such a situation at her grandfather's funeral: "When my grandfather died in 1983, we felt so bad, because his death was totally unexpected, grandmother lamented, cried. And the other grandmothers, who were older, said that she did it all wrong, she lamented incorrectly, didn't do it as it should have been done, and that it doesn't count." As this statement shows, lamenting was not totally forgotten, but the forms of the laments, as these older women pointed out, were paramount to their success. If one did not follow the forms, then the laments did not serve their purpose. While this practice had been lost, there were other ritual acts that were seen as essential for the funeral to be successful, to help people grieve and also to ensure the passage of the soul out of this world peacefully. Even the atheists among my informants practiced some ritual acts that were inherited from the Orthodox tradition.

Orthodox Religious Tradition Preserved

Not all of these ritual acts performed in the traditional funeral that continued into the Soviet period were necessarily Orthodox in origin; some may have had pre-Christian roots. However, by the nineteenth century, most of these connections had been lost, and they were interpreted as Orthodox practice by the average believer and indeed by religious figures. The church, like medical authorities, had frequently endorsed or reinterpreted material that did not contradict "official" doctrine, whether that doctrine was scientific or spiritual. It is likely that the regular visits to the graves and celebration of *pominki* at certain intervals were inherited from pre-Christian ancestor worship. However, the church not only adopted these practices, but also made them mesh with Christian faith. One informant, Nina S., asked a priest about the significance of the ninth and fortieth day *pominki*. He explained to her that

> [t]he first three days, after they had committed him to the earth, angels take him to his favorite places, where he liked to be. Then after these three days and until the ninth day the angels introduce him to the places where he will be. But he has still not been assigned where he will be. And then from the ninth day to the fortieth day he undergoes torments. And only then it is determined where he will be.

People seemingly reinterpret remnants of pre-Christian tradition from the perspective of the Orthodox belief system. We will conform to this common understanding in our classification of these behaviors as Orthodox.

While the public celebration no longer contained an *otpevanie* 'requiem mass', many people did perform traditional religious acts in the funeral. Families continued to light candles (and even, in some cases, stand icons near the deceased) as part of the ritual throughout the Soviet period. In addition, as Elvira A. described above, women were also invited to say prayers as part of the vigil. These practices, contained as they were inside the family home, did not pose a threat to the Soviet push toward atheism. Even atheists described lighting candles as part of the process, although they did not have anyone read prayers. Nadezhda P. said that "They invite a priest. We didn't do that, because I don't believe in God, dad didn't believe either." However, all informants maintained a vigil while the body was in the home. The vigil, prayers, and the candles all traditionally helped the soul of the dead make the transfer to the afterlife. The candles lit hi(s)her way, while the prayers and vigil ensured that the body was protected from harm while the soul was still on the earth, before its transfer to the otherworld. As Tatiana U. stated, "When forty days is reached ... his soul leaves."

Many families did not, of course, have icons during the Soviet period, even if they were believers. Nevertheless, the tradition to position a visual image with a candle near the deceased was remembered and retained. It is not unusual for ritual acts to be conflated and reinterpreted, as we have seen in our discussion of the wedding rite. For example, the ritual to determine who would be dominant in the relationship was combined with the ritual greeting of the couple with bread and salt. In the funeral, it would seem that the placing of icons was replaced by the placing of a photograph of the deceased near the coffin. The picture remained there for forty days, often with a black ribbon attached, and next to the bread-covered glass of vodka. Thus, while not overtly a religious ritual, the placing of the photograph was, I believe, a reinterpretation of the older religious practice, also designed to help the soul make the transfer to the land of the dead successfully. The icon would protect the person on the journey, while the picture brings thoughts of the person among those looking at it that help the deceased along the way. In a similar vein, Merridale (2000, 279) suggests that the Soviet practice of putting a picture of the deceased on the headstone may also be derived from the tradition of placing icons on the grave.

The *pominki* were also retained according to Orthodox tradition. While there were fewer of them than in the nineteenth century (not everyone commemorated the dead on the twentieth-day or sixth-month anniversary, for example), they retained the essential character of the village tradition. The food practices at the cemetery and at home ensured that the soul would realize that it was remembered and be at peace. Marina K. remarked, "It is thought that the person who had already died, he is also being sated. Those who remember him are being sated, and that person is also sated. And there, where he is now, he will have a full, happy life." The timing of the funeral was extremely important as well, in keeping with the Orthodox tradition. People were buried on the third day after they died.[9] One informant noted that if it was summer, then the person might be buried on the second day, due to the threat of decomposition in the heat. The funeral schedule, both the time of burial and of the commemorations, derived from the Orthodox tradition. Without these strict guidelines in timing, the person's soul could not be assured of peace in the afterlife.

---

[9] Some Jewish informants attempted to maintain the tradition of burial within one day, but were not always successful. One noted that he could not arrange to return home until three days later, so that his grandmother was buried according to Orthodox tradition, as a result of circumstances beyond the family's control.

Feeding the Dead

Marina K.'s statement about ensuring that the deceased is satiated is interpreted not only in terms of the emotions generated at *pominki*, but also literally. The practice of providing food for the dead at the table on the day of burial (and at later *pominki*) is one of a series of traditions that may loosely be termed "feeding the dead." The empty place at the table symbolizes the presence of the dead at the funeral meal, and a glass of vodka with black bread next to the deceased's photograph is for him/her to consume while the soul is in transition. Tatiana D. describes this belief as follows:

> They say that on the fortieth day the soul of the person leaves his lodging, that is, his own home. And that during this forty days he drinks this glass completely, while he is here. I myself saw that the vodka evaporated within exactly forty days.

The bread, of course, does not disappear, but must be fed to the birds, a traditional Russian symbol of the souls of the dead (Afanas'ev 1994, 3: 215ff.; Gura 1997, 20). By feeding the birds this bread, one is also symbolically feeding the dead.[10]

Birds were also frequently mentioned with reference to the food left on the grave as part of the *pominki* ritual. Liuba S., for example, said that one must leave things for the birds on the grave: "It is a tradition to leave crumbs, candy, a shot glass on the grave. As though the birds would come and eat it, they are like God's creatures." Of course, the food may not be eaten by birds, but by other creatures (or humans) as well, but the concept of feeding the dead remains: by this provision of food, participants not only ensure that the deceased's soul is peacefully making the transition to the afterlife, but they are remembering him/her as well. Feeding the dead thus helps both the deceased and the living, who use this ritual to assuage their grief. It provides them a way to feel connected to the dead and also to mourn periodically in an open and socially acceptable manner.

The food itself is symbolic in this regard. A major component of the food is grain and honey. In the Russian folk imagination, burial paralleled the

---

[10] One might argue that the conception of the birds as dead souls is too far removed from the contemporary period. However, birds are omens of death in many *bylichki* 'memorates', including one I heard about a bird that flew into the window on a woman's porch and died. The woman who saw this event later died in a car crash, which her friends tied to the incident with the bird. Another informant said that a friend's husband had died a violent death and that on the day of his funeral, a pigeon with a wounded wing flew into the house and would not leave. When they returned from the funeral, the bird was gone, but it returned on the ninth day after death for that *pominki* and also would not leave until after the meal.

agricultural process of sowing grain for food, so that grain dishes were particularly important to the funeral meal. It was assumed that the dead in their
graves could likewise influence the prosperity of the surviving family. They
were connected to the crop cycle and ensured that the fields would be fertile.
They also watched over living relatives. If their souls were at peace, then they
could assure the well-being of living relatives more broadly (discussed in
more detail below). While the understanding of the connection between grain
and the dead has been lost in the modern world, the fact that these foods are
simple, everyday foods reinforces the bond between the living and the dead.
Grain dishes eaten in memory of the dead recall the many meals shared together and help in the mourning process. Similarly, honey is a food that is
traditionally associated with the afterlife, because it is the only food produced
on earth that is allowed on God's table, according to Russian tradition. The
bee (like birds and butterflies) was also viewed as the soul of the dead in Russia (Afanas'ev 1994, 3: 215). In the contemporary period, of course, these symbolic associations are no longer as prevalent. However, honey remains a special sweetener, one that is valued for its medicinal qualities as well as for its
flavor. Thus, while Russians want to serve everyday food at the funeral, there
must be something to mark it as a special meal. Honey used in this way, to
sweeten *kut'ia* and also with the *bliny* (which are normally eaten with jam, not
honey) distinguishes this as a funeral meal.

The consumption of sweet items within the rite is a practice designed to
help both the living and the dead, and is of particular interest not only in that
regard, but because sweet food is featured in the commemorations before all
others. While any leftovers from the *pominki* may be given away afterward,
there was a special emphasis on sweets, particularly candies and cookies.
These foods were not only shared with those who knew the deceased, but
with all and sundry that one met, either at the cemetery or in one's
neighborhood. Galina S. described this tradition as follows: "It is customary
to treat people. At the cemetery they give things even to strangers, when they
are remembering the dead." Tatiana U. said that it was important to give
sweets to those who had children: "Usually candies, cookies they give to
those who are leaving, especially those who have children. So that they can
give them to the children, so that they can remember the dead. And they give
them out in the yard, in the building to kids."[11] Nina S. said that when her
husband died, there were a lot of candies left over, so that she went out and
gave them away: "I was walking around and asking people to take the candy.
I walk up to these men, and they were drinking wine. I asked [one] whether
he would take the candy and cookies, he says that he had two children. And I
gave him all the candy." Eating candy in memory of the dead reinforced the

---

[11] This practice actually causes mothers some consternation, because most instruct
their children not to take candy from strangers, and yet strangers do offer them candy
and cookies as part of the ritual.

bond between the living and the deceased. It allowed people to remember and mourn in yet another public way, but consumption of sweet items also brought a small bit of pleasure along with it. One could thereby remember the deceased fondly. Such small commemorations brought with them an additional important benefit, but for the dead in this instance, namely peace for their souls. Sweets, then, were symbolically a means to influence the "sweetness" of the afterlife for the dead.

In traditional Russian village society of the nineteenth century, children themselves were perceived to have a connection to the otherworld. In this role, they had influence with the spirit realm and, as a result, were involved in rituals that ensured crop fertility during both the spring *Rusalia*, summer *Ivan Kupalo*, and winter Christmas rituals. One could theorize that this ancient association served as the source for contemporary commemorative rituals by children. In sum, by pleasing children, who were associated with the otherworld in many ritual events, one was also satisfying or helping the dead. However, given the fact that urban Russians are not agrarian people dependent on the land, this is an unlikely interpretation of the current rationale for this practice, even if it held true a hundred years ago. More likely, children's participation was motivated by a more psychological reason. Even among non-agrarian peoples. children are recognized to be the result of the life-cycle process which the funeral highlights. They are the most recent additions to the ancestral line. Feeding them funeral food reinforced the power of the life itself in a way that helped mourners themselves grieve and cope with death. An additional benefit was that this ritual act allowed children to be indoctrinated into the social belief system. They learned that commemoration of the dead with food, particularly sweets, was the norm. They could thereby continue the process in the future at other funerals as they matured. Rituals, after all, serve also as teaching tools, even if that is not their sole function. Thus, it served both functional and psychological purposes for children to share food with the dead and the living in the deceased's name. This ritual practice helped survivors adjust to a new reality after loss, and the deceased to make a proper transition to the afterlife.

Natalia T. also mentioned that one may give candy to elderly women after a funeral as well. In the Russian tradition, women are particularly associated with life-cycle transitions, as we have seen. Older women perform many of the ritual functions designed to ensure that the soul of the dead makes the transfer to the afterlife (including washing the body and reading prayers). They are "close" to the grave themselves, so they may have better access to the spirit world as a result. Finally, donations to the elderly reflect the desire for giving items related to the deceased to those in need, because those women have limited incomes. This practice echoes funeral practices in the nineteenth century, when the poor received alms after the funeral in the dead's name (Kremleva 2003, 523).

Sharing food undoubtedly also helps the mourners themselves, as we have examined. The Russian system allows for public grieving over a prolonged period. This system recognizes that reconciliation to loss and the process of remembrance are not simple, rapid events, dealt with in a few hours at the funeral. Sharing with others and the deceased results in an understanding of a broader community of souls, including both the living and the dead. Merridale (2000, 37) discusses the gravesite in particular as a place of communication between the living and the dead, one that lasted until the Soviet period, which was troubling to the state representatives. Recall that a central portion of the commemorative rites (and, I contend, the grieving process itself) was consuming a meal on the grave in a symbolic exchange between the living and dead. This practice served survivors, who could show respect to and mourn the dead through the partaking of food, an act that they had shared so often in life. It also ensured that the dead would remain at peace, since they were being so honored, and would continue to protect their families. In essence, sharing food with the dead is yet another illustration of the ongoing relationship between this world and the next. Merridale (278) concludes that the new design of cemeteries (often situated in an inconvenient location) was intended precisely to break these ties between the living and souls of the dead. Because it was much harder to go to the cemeteries for commemorative or communicative purposes, people might have stayed away, which promoted the policy of the government with regard to atheism. Kremleva (1993, 35) argues that there were other factors at work that threatened the living-dead bond. She enumerates the reasons as follows: cemeteries had been destroyed due to urbanization; people had moved from their rural homes to cities; and loved ones could not be buried together (as a result of Soviet bureaucracy, discussed more below). Thus, while she is no less sanguine about the results, she does not attribute the causes only to official state policy, but also to the result of urbanization more broadly, a factor that certainly has played a role in all contemporary industrial societies.

While the grave itself is a locus of communication, another common means to converse with the dead is in dreams. The majority of my informants agreed that dreams about the dead send messages to the living. The most common message cited by my informants is that the person wants to be remembered, as Liudmila K. described: "It is thought that the person's soul is not at peace, you have to remember him again. You have to make *bliny* and share them and say remember the one close to me, so that his soul will be at peace." Liuba S. had a similar interpretation of these dreams: "Somehow I dreamed about my grandmother, I made *bliny*. You take candies and give them to children. Whomever you see, you give them something. You treat them and tell them to remember grandmother." Communication between the living and the dead is not limited to dreams, especially if the person had died recently and the soul has still not made the transfer to the otherworld, as Tatiana S. recounts:

My friend is standing and making hot cereal, this is not in a dream, but in reality, and from behind she hears a voice "I want some cereal too." She dropped everything that she had in her hands and says that she heard the voice so clearly, it was not yet nine days since someone in her family had died. She put aside part of the cereal and placed it next to the picture [of the deceased].

The open lines of communication and the desire to appease the dead also allow mourners to provide for the dead in ways other than with food alone. In some dreams, the dead person might ask for something or seem to be unhappy for some reason beyond wanting to be remembered. In those cases, people take steps to give items to the dead, as Nadezhda P. described: "I know that people have buried someone close to them, and then they keep dreaming about him and he says that it is so cold here, bring me a sweater. They brought a sweater and put it [on the grave] and that's it, the dreams stopped." Tatiana S. concurred, but noted that the dead need not be the recipient of the objects; some living person could "stand in" for the deceased: "If you dream that the dead person is dressed poorly or badly or is hungry, then it is acceptable to give some item to relatives or friends."

The dead may also be unhappy with the state of their resting place, as Marina L, reported; she had recently visited her father's and grandmother's graves. Soon after, she had a dream that her grandmother was unhappy and was drinking alcohol (which she never did in life) and walked behind her crying. Marina decided that her grandmother was displeased with the state of her burial site. Because her grave was difficult to reach, it had become overgrown, and they needed to do something to solve this problem, so that her soul would be at peace. Liudmila B. expressed a similar opinion: "My daughter told me that she had dreamed about grandmother, and she was angry. I started to think why she might be angry, then I remembered that we had not painted her fence at the cemetery. My husband and I went and painted the grave." Olga R. summarized the attitude toward dreams of the dead as follows: "It seems to me that many of us believe that a connection between the dead and living, to people close to us, remains. And therefore we really pay close attention to these dreams. When we see the dead in a dream, then we absolutely have to share it with someone and to try to figure it out somehow." The dreams and the attitude toward them are evidence of the enduring folk religious conception of interaction between the living and the dead, the ongoing relationship after death that the living must honor in order for the soul to be at peace and for the living to grieve properly.

Another way of providing for the dead is to place items that the person loved or could not live without into the coffin. Shevchenko (2003, 396) noted that this practice was common in Ulyanovsk as well; he cited objects such as false teeth, glasses, or brushes. My informants noted similar items, such as hats, favorite toys, and teeth. While these are not gifts in the same manner as the objects given to others or left on the grave are, they also ensure that the person will live a complete life in the otherworld. Just as a person should not enter the afterlife with hands and feet tied, (s)he should also have all the things needed to live there as (s)he had on earth. A parallel means to provide for the dead is throwing coins into the grave, so that (s)he will have a "wealthy" life in the otherworld. Interestingly, the flowers placed in the coffin are all removed. Because placing flowers in or on the grave was not a nineteenth-century tradition, we can only theorize about the rationale for this practice. It is possible that nothing living should be in the coffin with the deceased, which may perhaps draw him/her back to this world and away from the afterlife. Another factor that might have played a role is that flowers were a luxury item, often expensive and difficult to find during the Soviet period. Thus, shutting them into the grave would not only hide the family's devotion to the loved one, but also would not allow people to illustrate their participation in the consumer economy that the Soviet Union encouraged in these rituals. Certainly, excess in the funeral was much more limited than in the other rituals, but it was not beyond the realm of possibility. An abundant funeral meal could always serve to assist the dead in their transition to the afterlife, but also to show off the family's resources. We can find evidence of this within Malay society, in which the poor held funeral meals that were way beyond their means to illustrate that they are "as good" as the richer members of society. Scott (1985, 237) relates these decisions to the need to

> define what full citizenship in that local society means. These mini-
> mal cultural decencies may include certain essential ritual obser-
> vances for marriages and funerals, the ability to reciprocate certain
> gifts and favors, minimal obligations to parents, children, relatives,
> and neighbors, and so on.... [They] assume a certain level of material
> resources necessary to underwrite them. To fall below this level is not
> merely to be that much poorer materially; it is to fall short of what is
> locally defined as a fully human existence.

In this way, the funeral flowers could serve a similar purpose to the elaborate wedding gown. They not only show respect for the importance of the ritual process itself, but also convey that this family is worthy of respect within a culture that valued material goods as a means to establish identity.

The most important gift to the dead was the headstone, which was usu-ally placed on the grave after a year. This event marked the end of the initial ritual grieving period, although periodic remembrances occurred over the years, either on the anniversary of a death or as a result of dreams, as we have discussed. According to many informants, headstones were placed not at the person's head, but at his or her feet. Galina S. described this tradition: "Where the headstone is placed on the grave is at the feet. I know that my grand-mother always said that you shouldn't put the remembrance food on the deceased's head.... You can't put it on the head, because the birds will peck at it and the dead person's head will hurt." Tatiana D. said that the person should be able to read the headstone, that it is placed at hi(s)her feet with the text facing toward the deceased: "The result is that the headstone is at the feet. He himself looks at his headstone." These decisions indicate, once again, the perception of the dead as animate beings, that is, beings who can have physical ailments and who want to be able to see their own headstone.

The grave then is akin to the deceased's residence.[12] It must be cared for and marked with a fence and professionally-done headstone, properly placed, for those who "live" inside to be at peace. It typically is "furnished" with benches alongside for occasional commemorative meals. My colleague, Daniel Rowland, describes how he and a friend, the Russian dissident artist Evgenii Rukhin, who could not meet at either's home out of the fear of official reprisals in 1972 St. Petersburg, met instead at a gravesite in the Smolensk Cemetery for a picnic. They were sitting on the benches which flanked the grave when a Soviet policeman approached them. They managed to avoid difficulties by telling him that they were remembering their uncle, whose name they got from the tombstone. The policeman took off his hat out of respect for the dead and left them alone. This interpretation of the grave as a dwelling for the dead is also associated with folk beliefs about the burial site as the locus of communication between the two worlds of the living and the dead. As noted above, this belief (in addition to church proscriptions on the practice) is one reason why cremation never became popular in Soviet Russia, despite attempts to foster it.

We can conclude then that the conception of the community of the living and the dead is one that had survived throughout the Soviet period and served important functions for both groups. The interactions described here served two main purposes. They provided an acceptable social means to mourn the dead. People could remember and honor the deceased's memory over the years without feeling uncomfortable or thinking that they should have already "dealt with the problem." Grief and remembrance are ongoing processes that may require many years for acceptance and not just a few days during the funeral itself. The funeral first and foremost ensured that the dead had made the successful transition into the afterlife. Later, as the living continued to commemorate their loved ones, their remembrances ensured that the souls of the dead remained content with their *dolia*. If the soul were at peace, then the relations between the two worlds were positive ones, as Elena I. described:

> Once I dreamed about granddad. When you see a dead person in a
> dream, it means that he doesn't like something, it's bad. I asked him if

---

[12] Anne Ingram (1998, 64–64, 181–82, 220–21) has noted a similar phenomenon among contemporary Ukrainians.

maybe he needed something, why did he come to me in my dream, he said that he came just because, to find out, to see how you are living. And after that I didn't dream about him any more.

However, interaction with the spirit world within the Russian folk tradition was fraught with danger. We have discussed how the threat of being "cursed" increases when one interacts with the unknown. If one says something negative (or good) about the future, one must knock wood (or spit three times) to reverse potential negative effects. If a pregnant mother openly buys too much for a child, she risks not delivering a healthy baby. If an unusual stranger praises a child, (s)he might give him/her the evil eye, and so on. Therefore, the relations between the living and the dead could potentially cause harm to the living as well. As a result, some people took steps to prevent any possible damage which might result from the ongoing interaction, even as they recognized that it was essential to maintain the relationship with their ancestors.

Evil Eye Avoidance

Because the connections between the living and the dead remain active, people take steps to ensure that the interactions are positive ones. The dead have the power, for example, to call people to the afterlife in dreams. As Olga R. reported: "If an older person dreams about their dead husband or wife, they say 'I have lived my life in this world. They are calling me already.'" Elvira A. recounted a similar situation:

> They say that you won't dream about those who love you.... But my friend died in 1992, and what is interesting, she also had a bad heart, she was in the hospital. She was lying there and she had a dream, he was a soldier, a colonel, the 23rd of February was Soviet Army Day, and he told her to come to him before the 23rd of February. She died the twentieth.... He was a real jerk, her husband, he had a severe character, and in that commanding tone he ordered her [to die] too. And that's that.

Thus not all dreams have a positive outcome and even those that end well, of course, point to the power of the dead over the living and their ongoing relationship. If the dead are unhappy, the living are responsible and must take steps to appease them.

While these interactions help both the living and the dead, they are also frightening. The resultant *pominki* are designed not only to assuage their grief, but to protect the living because the dead might harm them. One could prevent dreams about the dead by two means, according to Larisa S.:

They told me that in order not to dream about the dead, you have to go up and touch the socks of the deceased, I did that.[13] And I didn't dream about her. Then they say that you have to go to the cemetery and stay until the end. Because my colleague, Vitalii, we worked together, said that he did not go to the funeral at the cemetery and after that he dreamed about the deceased. But I didn't dream about my aunt. I dreamed about my father, I wasn't at his funeral, I couldn't go.

Not everyone performed these acts, but they knew of their existence. Thus we see abundant evidence of the ongoing relationship between the living and the dead in these various rites, from the recurring *pominki* to dreams of the dead and the charms for preventing them. The relationship was not a simple one. If they were unhappy, the dead could potentially hurt the living. In addition, people recognized that one should listen to the dead to avoid complications and also to ensure that they were content in the afterlife. These procedures also helped ease the pain of loss for the living, who were able to mourn and remember the dead throughout their own lives.

Relatives were particularly susceptible to the dead's influence, which is why close relatives should neither prepare the body nor carry the coffin out of the house, as noted above. While not everyone conformed to these traditions, they recognized that there was a threat from the dead to living relatives. They knew that it would be considered a bad omen for blood relatives to have too much to do with the body, because it might bind them together, and the living might suffer as a result. In addition, close contact between living relatives and the dead might also harm the deceased, who needed to make the transition to the afterlife. If the relatives were too involved in the preparation of the body, the soul might not make the transition, but rather might be drawn back to this world. People took steps to eliminate ties to the earth. These included: removing the flowers from the coffin, celebrating *pominki*, and distancing relatives from the corpse, all designed so that the soul could make a successful transfer to the otherworld.

Not only relatives, of course, were at risk from the dead. The objects that were in contact with the deceased might have been a threat to any living person, even those outside the family. For that reason, the water and cloths used to wash the body were removed to prevent further contact with humans. Similarly, the items used for the ritual cleaning of the home after the body were discarded. Shevchenko (2003, 395) notes that the bed where the person died was destroyed or thrown away. Items such as tables or stools that were in contact with the coffin might not be destroyed, but were inverted as if to pass all possible remnants of the "contagion" of death into the earth before they were cleaned (Tolstoi 1990, 120). All of these practices helped to protect

---

[13] Listova (1993, 54) says that the ritual of touching the socks is performed not to keep from dreaming about the dead, but to keep from fearing the dead.

the living from the dead by ensuring that the threat from their contact with the deceased was nullified by purification rituals.

Relatives also made a point of giving away the deceased's belongings within the first year after death. One informant reported that one should wait until a full year had passed, while a few said that one could distribute the deceased's belongings right away. However, most agreed that the optimal time to give things away was forty days after a person had died. The deceased's possessions also tied him/her to this world, and after the transition to the otherworld had been made on the fortieth day, it was necessary to pass those items on. While people did, of course, keep items of sentimental value or family heirlooms, they gave away most "soft" items, such as clothing. This practice paralleled the evil eye avoidance strategy found in childbirth rituals. One could curse children by buying things before birth, but one should buy enough so that the child knew that it was wanted. The dead also needed to know that they were honored, so that their things were kept while the soul was on the earth. Nevertheless, the living also needed to mark their shift to the afterlife to avoid cursing the dead (and themselves potentially) by drawing them back. As a result, they distributed these items in the deceased's name after the soul had left the earth.

There was some discrepancy about the best recipient for these items. Elvira A. said that one should give them to a charity directly:

> I gave everything of grandfather's to the invalid home, to the home for the aged.... They give away clothing, shirts, pants, coats. I took all that there. They have it bad. My mother left behind a lot that she sewed and hadn't finishing sewing, new things. I am not going to wear them, I don't have time to resew them, we gathered it all up and took it there.

Her daughter, Elena I., said that her friends took all the things and put them next to a garbage dumpster, so that people could go through them, a decision which dismayed her mother. However, others said that one should give these items to relatives and friends, as Marina K. reported: "They try to give out those things left by the deceased to relatives of the dead person. It is not customary to leave a single thing in the house.... But they do leave something valuable from him for themselves."

Marina's comment reinforces the idea that the objects tied the dead to a space, which was not good for the living. However, one should also remember the dead, as one did when giving out objects in hi(s)her name, be they food, towels at the graveside, or hi(s)her own belongings. Nadezhda P. commented on this practice: "When his brother's wife died, her children and their wives came to see us and brought me her black dress. I refused, because it was a little too tight for me, but they left it for me all the same. In her memory." These objects commemorated the dead and bound them to the living.

Like *pominki*, they served to help heal the living in their grief and promoted fond remembrances of the dead, which would ensure that they were at peace in the afterlife.

Funerals: The Province of Women

In the other two life-cycle rituals we found that women played an instrumental role in ensuring that the transition to the new status occurred properly, as they always have in the Russian folk tradition. Women also performed similar services in contemporary funerals. In the period before burial, women prepared the body, so that the soul could make the transition to the afterlife. In addition, typically it was women who maintained the vigil and read prayers over the body. They also helped to protect the living from the dead by performing the ritual cleaning after the corpse was removed from the home. These traditions were all inherited from Russian village lore, where women not only prepared the body and held the vigil, but also lamented to ensure that the soul would be at peace and get to the otherworld without complications.

In addition, my informants said that women prepared the funeral meals, as they also did for the other two rituals we have considered. The meals, with their emphasis on commemoration of the dead and fulfillment of the soul's needs, were the core of the Russian funeral rite. Without the ritual foods, the deceased would not be properly remembered and, as a result, would not rest as (s)he should. It should be emphasized that women were responsible for not just the funeral meal on the day of the burial. They also prepared later *pominki* throughout their lives. They maintained the grave as well. While men did take part in upkeep at the cemetery, it was usually at a female relative's request. In the Russian Orthodox tradition, female relatives visited the graves, bringing food with them, and cleaned them as needed, particularly during the period of *Troitsa* (literally Trinity; Pentecost or Whitsuntide in the Western Christian tradition). The responsibility for the soul's repose rested on them for their dedication to the proper remembrances and to cemetery upkeep. Thus they were not only instrumental in helping the souls of the dead make a proper transition, but also in keeping the living safe. Without their efforts, the potential threat from the dead would have increased.

Women, of course, also helped make the transition into death in their social roles as doctors or as ZAGS workers, because the ZAGS registered deaths, along with births, adoptions, marriages, and divorces. Women primarily held all the official positions that related to life-cycle rituals in urban Soviet Russia. I have argued that the prevalence of women was due, in part, precisely to the folk understanding of women's role in village rituals. Another issue that played a significant role in this phenomenon was the fact that the Soviet authorities established a range of "female" and "male" occupations. As we have discussed, female professions included those that featured typical

"female" personality traits, such as tending the sick, child rearing and nurturing, and sensitivity, e.g., doctors, ZAGS officials, childcare workers, humanities specialists, enlightenment workers, and teachers. Women's physical abil-
ities also were considered in these decisions. Jobs in light industry were
generally held by women. Similarly, women were concentrated in the service
sector. These were all professions which were often less well-paid than those
in heavy industry or science, both of which were seen to be "men's" work.
This gender-based distinction in work resulted, then, not only from traditional conceptions about gender, but also from official government policy that
relied on these perceptions. Just as the Soviet government had responded to
the folk notion that women were best suited to be healers, they also viewed
them as controllers of transitional rites, an attitude which stemmed from Russian cultural norms. Soviet Russians, even as they tried to remake society by
encouraging women to assume professional roles, responded to their native
folk knowledge that the rituals also conveyed.

Thus in all three life-cycle rituals women's traditional work was acknowledged to be an essential part of the transition between two different states. In
birth, female professionals controlled the process of indoctrinating the child
and its parents into their new social status. Similarly, women relied on female
family members as well as female professionals (teachers, pediatricians, and
childcare workers) for their help and experience in raising their child. In weddings, female ZAGS professionals performed the ceremonies, while female
relatives conducted the *vykup* and organized the reception. Finally, in funerals, female professionals provided the official documentation required for the
family to proceed with the funeral, and female friends and family controlled
the remembrances so essential to the deceased and the mourners. In addition,
one Moscow informant pointed out that at the larger cemeteries, there was often a female cemetery worker present at funerals who gave a brief eulogy.
The core of these rites was under the purview of women, just as it had been in
the nineteenth century. Note that I am not saying that men did not play any
role at all in these rituals (as we will discuss in the next section), but that the
main ritual acts which introduced participants to their new state were dominated by women.

Community Involvement

Soviet Russian citizens relied upon community involvement to ensure that
both weddings and birth rituals were properly celebrated (see chapters 3 and
4 for a discussion). Without their friends and family, those undergoing transition in a life-cycle rite could not have organized an adequate celebration,
given the paucity of consumer goods available during the Soviet period. But
support from family and friends went beyond just economic aid. Ritual participants relied upon them to create a proper ritual atmosphere for the transition into a new social identity. Parents, particularly mothers, relied on their

own female relatives as models as they negotiated their own roles within the family as well as in the broader society. Friends and family also functioned as ritual celebrants within all three phases of the wedding rite, during which the couple negotiated the wide array of gender roles to be found within urban Soviet Russian society. Community involvement in ritual not only served to strengthen family identity in Soviet Russia, as the authorities had hoped it would, but also created an ethos of independence from official ideology. In both rites, there is no doubt that the ritual actors relied on fellow participants to establish their new status within the social hierarchy. The community of intimates served both as the backdrop and as an enabling force for the creation of a new reality through life-cycle rituals themselves.

Funerals were no exception in this regard. The Soviet Russian funeral emphasized group interaction and mutual dependence, just as it had in the nineteenth-century village. Although women were essential to many aspects of the process, men also played a dominant role in certain ritual acts. In some ways, funerals were the most egalitarian of all three rituals. While men had little or no role to play in childbirth, and only a limited role in weddings (primarily financial), they did perform some important ritual acts in funerals, actions that emphasized the communal nature of Russian life-cycle rituals. Due to the taboos on the relatives' contact with the deceased, male coworkers and friends had to carry the coffin out of the residence. Male friends may also have dug the grave, if there were no workers available at the cemetery. At the graveside, every person present, both men and women, threw a clump of dirt into the grave and waited until cemetery workers filled the grave mound before departing. In doing so, they all participated in the burial and acknowledged their connection to the deceased. As at weddings and birth celebrations, both men and women gave toasts at funeral meals, the good wishes of the whole community being essential for the couple to be happy, the child to thrive and the deceased to be at peace. Indeed, in the funeral, saying farewell to the deceased was an essential component of the process and illustrates the significance of communal recognition of the dead. The coffin, as noted, was placed outside the home or taken to the workplace for all to pay their respects before departure for the cemetery.

However, the survivors also benefited greatly from communal involvement. The nature of the Russian funeral put tremendous stress on the family emotionally, physically, and economically. They depended on friends, family, and coworkers to perform many of the duties that they themselves were not able to do because of the emotional strain. Larisa S. said: "It is the norm for us to ask how we can help, what we can do. You have to cook, call, inform people, we have our traditions on the day of the funeral, maybe wash the floor, et cetera. And we ask at once how we can help, especially if these people are close to us." Galina S. said that this practice was the result of a feeling of community responsibility for the family: "When dad died, mom didn't even know who had ordered the coffin, where it was upholstered, how much it all cost. Sympathetic people took care of it, close friends, relatives."

Funeral expenses, of course, were a concern, and many informants mentioned that they helped neighbors financially. As Tatiana D. explained: "We have lived in our building for a long time and know each other well, the neighbors collected money and simply gave money. From the organization where the person worked they always gave money to help and a large wreath or flowers, and transportation." Due to difficulties with transportation, as Tatiana mentions, most people arranged for buses and a hearse through work or connections at work. During the Soviet period communal involvement extended beyond one's circle of intimates to the workplace. Katia K. described how her ex-husband, for example, was the designated funeral representative at his factory: "My first husband worked as the assistant director of a factory shop ... and he was responsible for funerals. He was always organizing cars.... My mom's funeral was organized by her hospital, for dad it was his geology administration, it was always the organization."

We have seen that people did resent the interference of the government into their personal lives through rituals. But in the case of the funeral, these acts were not perceived to be intrusions in the same way. Rather, this situation was analogous to the women who established a personal relationship with their midwives over time. The connections between coworkers and the deceased seemed to negate any hint of official control that might have been intended. Yurchak (2006, 109) attributes this attitude to the Soviet-era concept of the *normalnyi chelovek* 'normal person'. Such people, even if official representatives, maintained good relations to others even in the face of required bureaucratic and official acts. For example, he describes how Komsomol secretaries had to collect dues from the members, a duty that both they and the members dreaded and, to some extent, resented. To achieve this goal, the secretaries appealed to the concept of *svoi* 'one's own' through friendliness. In other words, the secretary asked the members to recognize that (s)he was not truly a representative of the state, but one of them, a 'normal' person, who was only doing what was required, so that no one got in trouble with Komsomol officials. As a result, Yurchak argues, "like other ritualized authoritative acts, this practice contributed to the production of something this ritual had not been designed to produce: not the collective of conscientious Komsomol members, but a sociality of *svoi* (us/ours), with a particular ethic of responsibility to others, which it implied."

In fact, people seemed to welcome the show of support from state institutions in funerals in a far more positive way than in other aspects of their ritual life, precisely because they viewed it as the functions of individuals acting like "normal people" by supporting each other in meaningful ways.[14] For ex-

---

[14] It is possible that a cemetery official who did not know the deceased and gave a eulogy such as the one cited from Rudnev above might well have induced such a

ample, Valentin P. said that his sister's funeral emphasized her professional life, but his attitude was that it was a positive thing: "My sister had lots of people, about 699–700 people, the whole street. For many years she was the director of kindergartens, first the parents walked by, then their children walked by." Liuba S. described a similar situation for her mother-in-law:

> Then we arrived there, the grave was already dug there. And usually they give a speech at the grave … coworkers, a representative from the soviet, the most highly-placed people who knew her well. They even came from Chita to say farewell to her. They spoke very well. Then music started to play and the relatives threw a clump of earth into the grave first.

Thus the personal bonds between the coworkers and the deceased overcame the Soviet intentions to make the funeral into a rite that emphasized state ideals. Rather than being remembered as a worker who dedicated hi(s)her life to the state, the deceased was remembered as a person with many friends from all walks of life. The colleagues and acquaintances respected and honored the memory of the dead not because they were representatives of Soviet institutions, but because they recognized the good qualities of the deceased. This sort of communal involvement was especially important in the Russian funeral, as noted above, because the more well-wishers a person had, the more likely the soul would be at peace. Given the stress of the situation, most people welcomed state "interference" if it represented true assistance and highlighted the association between the living and the dead and respect for hi(s)her memory.

For the same reason, people often shared food from the funeral meal with their coworkers. Olga R. discussed such a situation: "The following also happens: we are colleagues, our colleague's mom died. We are not so close that we would go to the funeral, but she comes, brings candy and asks 'remember my mom.'" Elena I. also mentioned this practice: "Some bring things if there are leftovers. We have one teacher whose husband died and on the anniversary of his death she brings things to work. She lives alone, her children don't live with her. She either makes a pie or candy." Her mother Elvira A. elaborated: "People work for many years together, they have already become really close, and they mark all joys and sadness, they help each other." Coworkers, then, represented part of the extended family, both for the survivors and for the deceased. They were not part of the Soviet system, from this point of view, but stood outside of it, a defense against it, like the family circle. Soviet

---

reaction. However, none of the people in my informant pool reported that such a person spoke at the funerals of their loved ones. Rather, these were people who knew and worked with the deceased, which made a significant difference in my informants' opinions.

attempts to highlight one's role as a worker, dedicated to the state, were thus belied by these personal connections.[15]

Although many of the tasks related to the burial itself were dealt with by the deceased's employer, they did not get involved in the funeral meal in the home, for which family and friends were responsible. As a result, people were assigned various tasks, as Elvira P. reported: "Everyone made something, we each had our assignment. Someone made *bliny*, his daughter herself made *kut'ia*, I made borscht." Because the initial funeral meal was the largest, and also the most stressful, female relatives and friends gathered to prepare it. The smaller *pominki* thereafter might have been limited to the immediate family. However, in the case of the other elaborate meal on the fortieth day after death, friends and family might also once again have been recruited to help. The communal recognition benefited both the dead and the living. They provided the proper remembrance needed for the dead to be at rest. Communal involvement also provided the living with the support needed to survive the initial pressure of the loss as well as continued recognition of the length of the grieving process. When friends and family gathered for these *pominki*, they fostered the sense of unity and inter-dependence that was essential to all of the Russian life-cycle rituals, from the nineteenth century to the present day.

Western and Soviet Elements in the Funeral Ritual

Because the funeral was the most conservative of the three rituals under consideration, it is not surprising that it exhibited the fewest influences from non-Russian traditions. The only Western tradition that was introduced into the Russian funeral was the use of flowers and wreaths to commemorate the dead, which was not a village custom. Merridale (2000, 84) found evidence that this practice was already present in urban funerals for public figures before the revolution. Participants in Soviet funerary rites expanded the use of wreaths and flowers to all burials before the time period under discussion here. However, the flowers and the fine fabrics used in the coffins (also not customary in the village) do suggest that even in the funeral the Soviet authorities introduced practices associated with conspicuous consumption. Because such items were difficult to obtain, they were somewhat analogous to the clothing, flowers, and rings in weddings and baby goods in the birth ritual. Although consumerist practices were much more restricted than in the

---

[15] The one exception might have been funerals of war veterans from World War II and Afghanistan, who seem to have been identified much more closely with their sacrifice for the state, both in the funeral and by mourners. However, as in the case of the wedding ritual, where people placed flowers at the eternal flame, there was also a deeper connection here between the country and those who had given their lives for the *rodina* 'motherland', rather than solely for the socialist system.

other two rituals, the funeral did have elements that appealed to the materialism of the middle class the Soviet Union was attempting to foster.

The Soviet elements were also much less apparent than in the birth or
wedding rites. While the revolution brought about some changes in the rite,
namely restrictions on public religious rituals, the funeral maintained much
of its folk (and religious) character, as we have seen. However, as in the other
rituals we have discussed, the Soviet authorities attempted to emphasize the
power of the state over the individual and family. They created a funerary rite
which was analogous to a manufacturing process and highlighted secular reason and science over spirituality and nature. We will discuss these issues
within the urban Soviet Russian funeral in turn.

Institutional Power and Egalitarianism

Ritual theorists created rites that enabled state representatives to control the
process in an effort to indoctrinate participants into their roles as citizens
within the Soviet family as conceptualized by the state. They attempted to
demonstrate that the state had power over the participants throughout the
process and determined the nature of their social and familial identity. Ritual
celebrants, namely medical personnel and ZAGS workers, also strove to gain
some power themselves through the ritual in the face of a system that emphasized egalitarianism and submission to the state system. Despite its attempts
to neutralize social distinctions, the Soviet Union actually created strict hierarchies within its official institutions and indeed within the larger society. As a
result, people received two very distinct messages about their role in society.
Official ideology held that socialist Russia was characterized by classlessness,
so that each person was equal to another. However, in an effort to foster governmental stability, the Soviet state created a hierarchical system in which individuals were subject to the whims of the state and its representatives. Those
same representatives may have resented the system just as much as their fellow citizens, but they conformed to their positional norms nevertheless. Only
when they stepped outside of this system and became a "normal" person
were they able to emerge from the stratified and bureaucratic status of their
ranks. When they bonded in this way to fellow citizens, the system shifted to
one based on personal, individual connections.

We have already seen that this type of communal involvement in the funeral, partly inherited from the folk tradition, was enhanced by the state's
decision to focus on the person's role as a worker. When colleagues assisted
with the funeral, either in an official capacity (e.g., as a funeral representative
from work) or in an unofficial one (e.g., as pall bearers), they became part of
the community of mourners. In that role they were not seen as official state
representatives, but rather as simply friends of the deceased. Despite this fact,
the Soviet government introduced a series of requirements in the interment
process that, intentional or not, once again demonstrated to its citizens that

the state ultimately had power over the individual.[16] For example, a doctor had to be called to the house to issue a death certificate, as Natasha T. described: "You have to call the ambulance, a doctor must come to certify the death, to issue a certificate." This requirement meant that an outsider and official representative of the system entered into the family circle at a time of grief and crisis. However, without that certificate, the family could not proceed with arrangements, and in some cases, could not obtain essential items for the funeral, particularly when goods were rationed or simply unavailable. People obviously wanted to honor the dead and perform the burial and funeral ceremonies properly. As a result, the state ultimately was able to assert its influence over its citizens by insisting that a state official come into the family home after a death. Certification of the death, of course, also protected the populace against foul play. However, the death certificate itself was required to obtain items needed for the funeral which were held in government stores. Recall that when a couple filed intent-to-marry documents at the ZAGS, they also received a certificate which allowed them to buy items they would need for setting up their household. Certainly the government hoped to demonstrate that it was providing for families by issuing these certificates, but it also signified its control over the appropriate ritual procedures. Given the difficulty of dealing with salespeople in state stores, who were known for their surliness and for holding back goods for those with *blat*, most people could not have been favorably inclined to deal with them when in mourning.

The death certificate was not the only indicator in the funeral of the hierarchy of Soviet society. Merridale (2000, 140–41) argues that organizing a funeral at the ZAGS was, like much of Soviet life, "a bureaucratic business, the mourners had to do what they were told. They stood at yet another little window and awaited their instructions." While she (279) notes that "the form filling, the demands for documents, the lines, the costs—were not intended to be cruel," they placed additional bureaucratic burdens on the family at a difficult time. The Soviet state generally had been tainted by charges of indifference to its citizens and of interference in family life. It is not surprising, therefore, that citizens were likely to interpret funerary requirements in a similar way.

Every Soviet citizen had to deal with the ZAGS regulations when planning a funeral. However, if a person died in a state institution, namely the hospital, then the family was subject to even more interference in personal decisions. According to one doctor, during the Soviet period every person who died in a hospital had to undergo an autopsy:

> Then a person who was dying was subject to an autopsy. And it was
> very difficult to refuse it. Even at the very end of the Soviet period

---

[16] Some of these acts, as I observed earlier, are true of the institutions in any contemporary civil society. That does not change the fact that the Soviet populace perceived them through the lens of an official bureaucratic culture that they resented.

exceptions were made only for Muslims, because they really made a stink and there was aggression.

She went on to say that even this accord was not a guarantee for freedom from government intrusions into the funeral: "I often went to Central Asia during Soviet times, there were religious areas there where mullahs would not bury someone without a certificate of autopsy results. If a person died in a hospital, until you show the autopsy results, the mullah wouldn't perform the ritual." We can see that, in certain cases, regardless of its citizens' wishes or the government's promises, the medical establishment insisted on an autopsy. Thus non-Orthodox people were subject not only to "Orthodox" traditions in the Soviet funeral (as noted above), but also to other practices that may have been inimical to their faith. Certainly, we could conclude that the demand for an autopsy was designed to illustrate the belief in science over religion (discussed in more detail below). The state potentially interfered in a family's religious life to demonstrate that it was more powerful than its citizens and their religious faith, a key tenet in Soviet ideology. Regardless of the source of this behavior, however, this monolithic bureaucracy required that people conform to its demands or not proceed with the rituals they deemed essential.

The cemeteries themselves were state institutions, and, as a result, people were subject to governmental interference and bureaucracy when dealing with them. Marina K. noted that people were buried only in the appropriate regional cemetery: "It depends on what region they live in." This pattern paralleled practices in weddings and childbirth, because both the ZAGS where people married and the maternity hospital where women delivered were determined by where they lived. Thus, even if a family had been primarily interred in one cemetery, government officials could change the boundary lines, and all other relatives would be buried elsewhere. In some cases, of course, these decisions were based on the lack of physical space. Because an older cemetery had become full, there was no choice but to inter people in another location. In others, Kremleva (1993, 35) contends, relatives could not be buried together as a result of the state's attempts to eliminate residual religious commemoration of the dead at the cemetery itself. If family members were buried at various cemeteries, individuals could not easily go to each gravesite to have the requisite *pominki*, particularly since, as Merridale (2000, 279) remarks, they were often far from the center of town.

Such officially instituted rules also limited people's options within the cemetery itself. Government cemeteries had established regulations about setting up *ogradki* 'fences' around the graves (designed to mark off land for later family burials) and where a person could be buried within the grounds. For example, Elvira A. described the situation when she buried her mother:

When we were burying [her], they didn't allow us anything, not to leave a spot, nothing. People were upset, because their mother could

not be buried next to their father. A child could not be buried with its
parents.... When we buried my mom, everything was in succession
[i.e., the next available plot in line was used]. When my mom died, I
wanted to bury her next to granddad, at that time they didn't allow it,
there was no spot. And we were forced to bury her in another
place.... I still regret that they are in different places.[17]

Some informants noted that *blat* 'connections' played a role in defeating this
system, as Valentin P. said: "There are lots of people with connections there
[in the cemetery where his father-in-law is buried]. There are those who
should get the plots, they give them to people with connections." While certainly every state interferes in one's private life to some extent, as I have
noted, in the case of the Soviet Union during this period, people had no alternative, because the government controlled the ritual processes of birth, marriage, and funerals.

Certainly Soviet restrictions on holding religious funerals were also an indication of the state's power over its citizens. While atheists were indifferent
to this proscription, others felt that they were not having a proper ceremony
for the dead without a full religious service. In fact, Merridale (2000, 264)
notes that sixty percent of people in the post-war years wanted a religious funeral, but due to the shortage of priests, they had to rely on friends who knew
prayers to satisfy this need. Therefore, they invited in *posidelki* 'sitters' to read
prayers or had funeral masses read for the deceased at local churches (if available), even if a priest did not perform a graveside service. They also, as we
have seen, performed religious rites at home, such as sprinkling a cross of dirt
on the body, lighting candles and the like. By performing these 'secret' religious rites, Soviet Russian faithful were able to undermine the state's intentions with regard to official atheism and more importantly for our purposes,
control of its citizens' hearts and minds. For many, religious rites were required to honor the souls of the dead and to ensure that they made the necessary transfer to the afterlife. They also, as we have seen, helped the living
grieve their loss over time. For both these reasons, they persisted throughout
the Soviet period in some form, albeit typically without an *otpevanie* over the
body, either in the church or at the grave.

Ritual theorists were particularly ineffectual at redesigning the funeral
ceremony when compared to their successes in weddings and in birth rituals.
The state only made inroads in establishing a set of rigid rules which demonstrated social hierarchies. Interestingly, the state did make an attempt to

---

[17] Certainly, cemeteries in other countries also have rules about how graves should
look, but they are private concerns and if one does not agree with the restrictions,
there are other places for burial. In the Soviet Union, because people were buried according to the neighborhood in which they lived, they had to conform (or use *blat*
'connections') to try to override the state's rules.

transform the graveside ceremony itself, by instituting a practice of connecting the funeral not to the person's family life, but to hi(s)her work life, as my informants mentioned (corroborated in both Lane 1981, 83 and Merridale 2000, 264). Ugrinovich (1975, 137) writes that the funeral should emphasize the idea that "'everything remains with people [there is no afterlife],' that a person's true immortality is composed of his actions, of his actual legacy, which is embodied in material and spiritual values, in the people he raised." The service itself highlighted the connections between the worker and the state as a primary function of life. The organization where the deceased worked was responsible for helping with funeral arrangements, such as transportation and sending wreaths. Similarly, the person most likely to speak at the graveside was a coworker or union representative. Merridale (141) reports that many of her informants were unhappy with funerals because of this focus on Soviet ideology in the service. My informants, however, did not express such opinions to me about the Soviet-era service, even though they were quite dismissive of the wedding ceremony as performed by government officials during this period. I think the key to understanding this discrepancy, among the people I spoke to at least, is that the many aspects of the graveside service itself were performed by people known to the deceased. Thus relatives and friends, be they from work or from the neighborhood, assumed a personal face that the wedding celebrant could not, since she represented a state institution. While the state may have wished for these people to wear the mantle of officialdom, the funeral allowed them to step outside of the official hierarchy and claim a personal relationship to the family of the deceased, to become a "normal" person, in Yurchak's sense of the term.

In the case of all three rituals under consideration here ritual specialists designed celebrations intended to spread state ideology. However, all three rituals, to varying degrees, remained communal events that highlighted individual and familial concerns above state ones. The funeral is no exception; however, the ritual theorists made the fewest inroads into funerary rites and, as a result, were least effective at establishing the preeminence of the state over its citizens within this ritual. This failure to remake the funeral as they had weddings and birth was the result of two factors we have already discussed. First, the Soviet theorists were uneasy when dealing with funerals generally. They were never able to envision what it meant to redefine the family through death, as they had through birth and marriage. Second, the efforts the Soviet Union made to transform the ritual only emphasized social bonds more. The ceremony, and coworkers' involvement in it, transformed people from state representatives to part of a larger community of mourners. In essence, death could not be controlled in the same way that the other two life-cycle events could be. Thus, despite earnest efforts to standardize and rationalize the end of life, they were unable to overcome its association with the irrational world and nature.

Rationalizing Death

In the previous two chapters, we examined how both birth and weddings were transformed into a type of manufacturing process characterized by rigid schedules. My informants likened the formal portions of these rites to a conveyor belt in a factory. This approach to ritual emerged not only from the glorification of automation, but also from a faith in science over nature and reason over emotion and spirituality. All these factors combined to produce rituals that were intended to convey the socialist worldview of rational, scientific materialism to the participants. It was comparatively easy to turn birth into a scientifically-based, "manufacturing" process. A pregnant woman's body could be effectively controlled through medical treatments. For example, doctors and midwives had at their disposal drugs and technology to speed up or retard labor and delivery. Marriage was also conducive to such rationalization. Wedding dates were set by ZAGS officials and were limited to certain days and times. The ceremony itself was standardized and was timed almost to the second, for maximal efficiency on popular weekend days. While it is true that theorists and state officials faced challenges in these rituals, they were able to inject their ideals regarding reason (e.g., the remade socialist family was the core of a stable state) and manufacturing (e.g., the key to family stability was rational control of its unruly, emotional citizens) into the rites as they were practiced. Funerals, however, resist both scientific rationale and industrialization analogies by their very nature.

Death is the ultimate challenge to an overwhelming belief in the efficacy of science. Like most medical doctors, Soviet Russian physicians tried to extend life, both in patient treatment and through research. They viewed the body, Stites (1989, 153) argues, as a machine which would respond to proper adjustments and repair and continue working. This conception of the body as a machine, however, did not end when a person died. The dead body itself served as one important source of scientific enlightenment in the search to defeat mortality. Trice (1998, 244) discusses how the dead were often subject to autopsies to which the family had not agreed, particularly in the Bolshevik period, although some of my informants mentioned this issue in the post-war period as well. However, the doctors ultimately needed to recognize that they could not defeat death. Perhaps for this very reason most people preferred to die at home. Once the medical establishment could no longer effect any results on the body, patients were discharged (had they been hospitalized) and went home to die. Patients, of course, may also have preferred this state of affairs and may have requested it, but there is no doubt that the hospital during this period was associated primarily with treatment of those who could benefit from treatment, and those who would not went elsewhere.

Recall that funerals most closely parallel childbirth in their design and function. They serve to shift two distinct constituencies into a new status. In birth, the child must become "human," while its mother and father must make the transfer into their new social roles as parents. Thus, a single ritual act serves to "humanize" a child and also allows a parent to assume hi(s)her new responsibility within the family and community. Funerals also serve to remake the dead into "non-humans," i.e., to remove them from humanity through transfer to the afterlife. Similarly, mourners must remake their identity as a family and community without a valued member. They must grieve through the funerary rite, but also perform it correctly to ensure that the soul is at peace. Such functions flouted established Soviet ideology regarding science and reason as superior to nature, emotion and spirituality. Ugrinovich (1975, 137) claims that Soviet rituals served to "reinforce new socialist norms of family behavior, emphasize the equality of spouses and mutual love and respect as the basis of family life and show the unity of family and social interests." Simply put, the funeral did not advance socialist goals for the rational function of family life in society in the same way that birth and wedding rituals did.

Ritual theorists, nevertheless, understood that the funeral should help people mourn. Ugrinovich (1975, 143) states that "Soviet [funerary] ritual allows one to feel ties to the society, the collective. Participants express sympathy and support and take on part of the burden." We have seen that people did sense and willingly embrace these bonds between people as part of the funeral rite. However, we cannot conclude that this resulted from perceived ties to the collective, if by collective we only mean socialist worker community. In fact, my informants viewed the members of the "collective," e.g., co-workers, as part of a community distinct from work and official institutions. In some cases, in fact, this communal ethos was a reaction against a society which did not provide adequately for its members. It emerged not from a desire to unite with the socialist collective for ideological reasons, but rather, given the limitations on provisions and the monetary outlay required for such ceremonies, the ritual could not be properly performed without the help of family and friends. Ugrinovich's statement, however, reveals one of the dilemmas that the ritual theorists faced. His definition of the purpose of the funeral rite is based on a rational state goal, e.g., strengthening the collective. While he does mention sympathy, he actually is trying to show that funerals served a logical purpose, namely to prevent citizens from "breaking down" under the weight of emotion, which was certainly not in the interests of socialist society at large. They never reconciled the disconnect between their argument for the rational basis for ritual and the emotional core of this rite.

The second problem that ritual theorists faced was indeed its religious content. They were largely unsuccessful in divorcing belief from practice. In his discussion of funerals, Ugrinovich (1975, 136) argues that a socialist funeral does not relate to questions of the "eternal soul and life after death." Rather, the key to Soviet funerals was understanding that they focused on the deceased's earthly legacy. While I do not deny that there were atheists in the Soviet Union who accepted this ideal, most of the people I spoke to tied funerals to religious faith. For that reason, as Olga L. noted: "In Soviet times if people went to church, it was associated precisely with funerals." In essence, the arguments of ritual theorists about the reinterpretation of religious practices were only successful in weddings and, in a more limited way, in birth (the rite of baptism persisted among a portion of the populace, as we have seen). However, people continued to view funerary acts as Orthodox rites essential for the soul of the dead in the afterlife, because ritual specialists were unable to redefine them based on reason and science alone. Therefore, to take just one example, their convoluted arguments that the Orthodox phrase *vechnaia pamiat'* 'eternal memory' related only to one's memory on earth and not to one's life in heaven, fell on deaf ears.

The difficulties ritual theorists faced does not mean that they (or Soviet authorities) abandoned all attempts to rationalize funerals based on official ideology about scientific materials and manufacturing models. They hoped to overcome religious beliefs about death through the institution of cremation to replace burial, as we have discussed. If cremation had become widespread, it could have supplanted the religious commemorative rites on the grave and could have symbolized a new scientific and rational approach to death. To achieve this end, Trice (1998, 349) argues, they needed to move the funeral out of the feminized space of the home, where folk and Orthodox rituals thrived: "For cremationists this meant removing the body from what they perceived as the pernicious influence of the female-gendered private sphere through revival of the pre-revolutionary concept of 'fire burial'...." However, Trice (344–45) concludes that the majority of efforts to establish cremation in the Soviet Union failed:

> Soviet cremationists' inability to reach the Russian people, to forge that path into the backwoods in order to dispel the allegedly irrational beliefs and practices impeding Russia's historical progress, may have been their greatest disappointment. Their difficulties in this respect were shaped in part by the economic and political imperatives of their time, for on the one hand they had to compete with Mother Earth, the "cheapest" medium for burial once the Bolsheviks nationalized all cemeteries, while on the other hand, they felt compelled to combat earth burial in accordance with the new regime's anti-religious policies. In place of older, secular and sacred ideas about the integral relationship between the human body and identity, both in this world and the next, cremationists offered people medical, scientific definitions that failed to resonate with their daily experiences and long-term expectations.

In his description of the problems related to the institution of cremation, we can see that the regime faced the same issues I described above with regard to remaking the funeral in general. By relying on "medical, scientific definitions" they could not make inroads into a rite based not on reason and science, but on religious faith and emotional need. More importantly, they could not even truly solve the conundrum themselves and devoted less time and effort to remaking funerals.

Cremation was not the only funerary practice designed to institutionalize a rational, secular view of death. As much as possible, ritual theorists and state authorities tried to "control" death, at least after it had occurred. Medical authorities never, for example, advocated for euthanasia, which would certainly have been a "rational" approach to setting timetables for death. However, once the person had died, ritual celebrants applied the manufacturing analogy we have seen in the other life-cycle rituals. For example, cemetery plots were assigned according to a "rational" pattern, so that families were required to take the next available grave, even if other family members were buried in another spot in the cemetery. Similarly, they were not allowed, without a great deal of effort (or *blat*), to retain any space for future burials by placing fences around the grave. The ZAGS process itself, which Merridale (2000, 140–41) describes as a "bureaucratic business," in which people had to stand in line to obtain the proper forms, pay necessary fees, and get permission to bury people, became a burden for the bereaved. While this might have been a "rational" way to ensure that records were kept properly, it was not at all sensitive to citizens' emotional needs during a period of mourning.

One drawback in the creation of a "scientific and rational" funeral ritual was the lack of governmental institutions to provide goods and services for this rite. Houses of culture and wedding palaces served as beautiful backdrops to celebrate weddings that simultaneously allowed officials to standardize and rationalize the ritual. The *roddom* provided medical treatment throughout the pregnancy and delivery which promoted the normalization of the entire process. While people may have complained about the quality of some of these services, there is little doubt that they took advantage of them, and in some cases even welcomed them, as we have seen. People entered into family life with some governmental support, which in turn enabled the state to pass on some of its own values to its citizens. However, because the Soviet state could not envision a way to cope with death, services for the dying and funerary businesses were unknown. There was no government-run system of funeral homes which could provide caskets, a place for the viewing, interment arrangements and the like. Beyond official registration of deaths at the ZAGS (and providing certificates for funerary goods), civil control of cemeteries, and construction of some crematoria, the state established no official institutions that could serve to remake death rites. Without such a centralized funeral home network, authorities could neither force nor persuade people to accept Soviet ideology about death and burial. Theorists could not come to terms with how to restructure the funeral without reference to faith and emotion. Nor could they rationalize it in the same way that they had birth and marriage rituals. Thus, except for a few desultory attempts, they largely abandoned their aim to restructure this rite.

No hospice movement existed in Soviet Russia either, so that families were responsible for the care and treatment of seriously ill relatives. Doctors, of course, did make house calls for treatment and examinations, but family members had to meet the day-to-day needs of the bedridden and the dying. This practice necessarily led to a stronger sense of community responsibility for the dead within the funeral rite. In addition, family, friends, and co-workers performed all the duties necessary for arranging for the interment and the *pominki*, a fact which brings us once again to the relationship between the family and state within life-cycle rites.

The Family and the State

Soviet-era conceptions of the family as the heart of socialist society came into the limelight in both childbirth and wedding rites. These rituals were based on the idea that the family needed first, to be remade, and second, to foster stability within socialist society. State authorities and ritual celebrants claimed that they alone could establish the family unit legally and socially, would provide for it and therefore ultimately would control it. To some extent, the Soviet government succeeded in these efforts. People accepted certain fundamental socialist values about family life and the state's role within it. They conformed to requirements for having a healthy baby by submitting to treatment at state medical institutions. They did not abandon marriage, but adapted readily to the civil ceremony and incorporated it into their conception of what a wedding should entail. One key to these successes was the provision of essential goods and services by governmental institutions, namely the *roddom* and the ZAGS (or the wedding palace). Such institutions relied on propaganda campaigns to convince people of their centrality to childbirth and marriage rites. They provided certificates for goods required to start a family or have a child. They functioned as the formal stage for life-altering ritual events, which many Russian citizens consequently decided were essential for proper celebration. The funeral, however, lacked an institutional backdrop which functioned to convey socialist ideology. By its very nature, it could not share the essential premise that ritual served to forge a stable socialist family. Most people also resisted any rational or scientific reinterpretation of its religious and folk content and instead relied on these beliefs and social networks to perform and define the funerary rite.

In spite of the success of maternity hospitals and wedding palaces in convincing people to accept some aspects of state ideology, not all citizens complied without resistance. We have already seen that the efforts by Soviet officialdom did not lead to stronger bonds between citizens and the government. Rather, ritual actors relied on personal connections and their families for support, which formed a type of social community network that provided more than the government could for its citizens. Indeed, within these communities, Soviet Russians developed independent and varied conceptions of family identity that contradicted ideology and potentially threatened social stability. The funeral was no exception in this regard. When the family was in the midst of a crisis after a death, the Soviet system did little to support people. While the government failed to provide essential goods and services, to some extent, in all three rituals, it failed most acutely in the funeral. Some informants noted that they had received special certificates necessary to obtain coffins and the fabric to upholster them. But they alone were of no particular use in the face of all the funeral arrangements that needed to be made. In fact, they resulted in additional bureaucratic hassles, since they entailed waiting in line, dealing with shortages and difficult shopkeepers. Others reported that people could not place headstones in a timely fashion, due to delays in production. For example, Natalia S. mentioned this problem: "Usually they put up a fence even earlier [than a year]. It is easier to put them up [than headstones]. You have to gather the money. There is a waiting list for a headstone." Given that the headstone is the most important "gift" to the deceased, these delays increased anxiety and frustration for relatives. In some cases, cemeteries made things even more difficult for survivors. By not complying with mourners' wishes, unless they were most insistent, cemetery officials compounded the pain of its citizens. Nina S. explained: "I put up a fence after the ninth day, because I was afraid that they would take the spot. I went every day, finally they put up stakes and told me not to come back."

Every civil society, of course, has its requirements that place burdens on its citizens. What is exceptional in this case is that Soviet citizens perceived their bureaucracy as a system designed, intentionally or not, to control individual and family needs and to inhibit proper ritual performance. Another significant factor that contributed to this perception was that the state was responsible for all three rituals entirely. It was not as if, as in the United States, for example, one had to obtain a marriage license from the state and then could marry where and when one wished. Rather, the state controlled not only the legal certificates necessary to name, marry, and bury, but also the ceremonies themselves. It even tried to insert itself into the family's private celebration in various ways, e.g., professional *tamady*, Komsomol weddings, civil graveside ceremonies, and public naming ceremonies.

The lack of institutions to organize burial and the impediments erected by the minimal services that did exist were not the only issues my informants faced when arranging a funeral. The state stores consistently had shortages in the foodstuffs required for mourners at the *pominki*. Unlike other celebrations, the funeral meal required certain dishes, and if the ingredients were not available, then the deceased might not be properly commemorated. Elvira P. described the situation at one funeral she attended during Soviet times: "There was a problem with food, therefore everyone helped as they could. Someone could get chickens or meat, et cetera. That is, it was still those times when everything was scarce." Thus, the Soviet Union could not guarantee that its citizens, living or dead, would be properly provided for, an issue that has recurred throughout the discussion of life-cycle rituals and their celebrations. Despite its claims to support the populace, the government failed to furnish essential goods and services, from those as mundane as food for a celebration, to an item as serious as the headstone. This fact always produced dissent among the Russian population during the Soviet period, particularly among women, who did the bulk of the shopping. Shortages of goods were a trial during a wedding or when having a child, but one that was offset by the joy that such celebrations entailed. A funeral did not produce positive emotions to assuage the fear that one was not preparing a proper feast for the dead. The funeral was designed to ensure that the dead would be at peace (and to help the living grieve), but the government's hindrances to the ceremonial rites threatened both of these aims.

The end result was that the funeral required the most communal support of all three rituals. Not only was the family grieving, but the demands of the ritual were such that people faced a difficult financial situation while in crisis. Thus, relatives and friends were charged with furnishing money and goods for the rite (burial site, coffin, fabric, flowers, etc.) and for the meals themselves. While they clearly provided for a newborn and newlyweds as well, those celebrations could be more modest and still be "successful." A family could also plan ahead over many months in preparation for marriage or childbirth. A bride might also wear a rented or borrowed gown to save on expenses, but a corpse cannot be buried in a cardboard box to cut costs. Deaths often occurred unexpectedly and required an elaborate meal and additional outlay for the items necessary for burial. While some people did mention that they had saved up for funerals, it was still a trial to ensure that they had accumulated enough to avoid placing a burden on their surviving relatives. Furthermore, the immediate family had to provide for the dead and for guests at a time when they themselves were suffering from a loss. The ritual process drained the entire family, as Valentin P. noted: "It is hard on relatives, because close relatives sit there twenty-four hours a day." Without help from others in the community, they would not have been able to manage. Natasha T. summarized this interdependence as follows: "All the same, for us everything is maintained by good relations, by good people, friends and acquaintances." With little support from the government or its representatives, people had no choice but to depend on each other. While one government institution, a person's place of employment, did help with arrangements, these coworkers did not represent state functionaries in people's minds. Rather their actions were perceived to emerge from personal connections, even if those who participated were "state officials" in some sense. The Soviet system created a situation in all these rituals, but particularly in the funeral, that encouraged communal ties, rather than dependence on the state.

These communal forces continued to define death, the afterlife, and the responsibilities of the family to the deceased in the funeral. The Soviet theorists had little recourse in remaking the funeral, because they could neither refer to the afterlife nor create a funeral that did not contain symbols related to life after death. As a consequence, ritual specialists made few inroads in the development of a new funeral rite overall, but they did manage to involve the community as they had hoped. Because it could not effectively or logically cope with funerary rituals, at least for the average person, the state had essentially ceded its responsibility for funerals beyond some changes to the graveside service and the cemetery. Overt religious images or symbols were typically not placed on graves, but were replaced by Soviet iconography, such as red stars or the hammer and sickle. Instead of icons, people arranged for photographs of the deceased to be engraved, carved, or painted on the headstones. Beyond these minimal changes, however, the community, not the state, determined how a family should proceed after death and what its new conception of itself should be without the absent member. Soviet ritual specialists believed that ritual consists of what Humphrey and Laidlaw (1994, 193) describe as an "all-explanatory hidden code." In contrast, Humphrey and Laidlaw (260) argue that actors bring their own meanings to the equation and do not necessarily interpret the code as intended. While the Soviet Union managed, at least publicly, to turn the ritual into one that emphasized one's life as a worker and dedication to the state, they could not absolutely convince people to accept the idea that eternity for the deceased meant only a memory of one's earthly life. Rather than relying on weakly-defined Soviet ideology, the Soviet Russian populace defined death primarily on the basis of folk and religious conceptions about it. Using these frameworks, they also established appropriate funeral rites and determined behavior for participants during the ritual and beyond. Most people negotiated identity primarily through these channels alone and not, as they did in childbirth and wedding rites, through a combination of folk, religious, and state norms.

Negotiating Identity in the Funeral Ritual

Recall that Bourdieu highlights the fact that rites of passage (or institution, as he calls them), serve to divide not only the ritual actors from their previous state, e.g., from unmarried to married, from non-parent to parent, from wife to widow, but also from all others that are not members of the group. He (1991, 118) contends that "by solemnly marking the passage over a line which establishes a fundamental division in the social order, rites draw the attention of the observer to the passage (whence the expression 'rites of passage'), whereas the important thing is the line." The funeral, as we have seen, promotes transfer to a new status for both the dead and for survivors. Certainly, the dead are moved to the "non-human" world, and mourners must learn to cope with life without them. More importantly, there is a line, a demarcation between those who have lost loved ones and those who have not. The funeral then establishes what it means to be "dead" and also to be a survivor. Unlike the other two rituals, where the rite of passage marks a distinct social role based primarily on gender and family identity, e.g., parent or spouse, there is no distinct fixed status (beyond widow/widower) for survivors based on these two factors. All who knew the deceased are potentially affected. Certainly, those closest to him/her are faced with a greater adjustment than casual acquaintances are, so that kinship and close friendship still figure into the ritual performance. However, one's status as mourner does not highlight gender distinctions to the same degree that it did in the other two rituals, at least within the Soviet Russian cultural context. We will begin our discussion of the negotiation of identity within the funeral ritual with a focus on the survivors and how the ritual, with its varied sources of *habitus*, served to establish a new social reality. We will also consider whether the funeral rite reflects the same degree of resistance among ritual actors as the other two life-cycle rituals did.

The sources for interpretation of one's role in the funeral were distinct from those in the other rituals we have discussed. In weddings and births, people drew from consumerist and Soviet ideas but also from folk ideas inherited from nineteenth-century Russia. Because the Western borrowings were minimal, the main issue in the Soviet Russian funeral was the conflict between Soviet ideology about death and belief in the afterlife, and folk and Orthodox practices.[18] The latter system emphasized the funeral as a means to properly transfer the soul to a peaceful afterlife, while the former held that the afterlife only entailed people's memory on earth. Orthodoxy held that without a proper burial ritual, the soul would not be at peace, which the Soviet theorists had rejected in favor of a more rational and scientific approach to death. At the same time, funerals helped survivors deal with their grief, by highlighting their continued connection with both the dead and with their own communal networks, a practice that both Soviet and folk religious belief systems endorsed.

Based on the descriptions of the Soviet Russian funerals above, we can conclude that the survivor's role could be characterized as a commemorator and representative of the dead in the living world. Mourning acts served two purposes: they promoted the memory of the dead on earth and they ensured that the soul would be at peace, since memorials were necessary to their well-being in the afterlife. A mourner was thus obliged to perform rites that en-

---

[18] While the majority of my informants who were believers were Orthodox, those who were Jewish or Muslim also retained religious elements from their tradition in their funerals, e.g., burial within twenty-four hours for Jews or the presence of an imam in the Muslim tradition. However, we will focus on Orthodoxy in our discussion, given the overwhelming presence of ritual acts derived from it in the typical funeral rite among those I interviewed.

couraged memorializing the dead among family and friends and even further afield. Therefore, family (and friends, but primarily the former) arranged regular *pominki*; asked for memorial masses to be said for the deceased and lit candles at church in hi(s)her name (if not areligious); acted upon the dead's requests (e.g., by providing goods and food to the dead or to others in the dead's name); kept the grave clean and neat; and provided necessary gravesite decorations and headstones. Finally, they encouraged communal grieving at regular intervals, which helped all of those who had experienced the loss, and also fostered community identity and support.

While it is true that all family members could initiate or participate in these commemorative acts, gender differences emerged even in the funeral to some extent. As we have seen, women primarily instigated or performed memorial rites. They did the cooking for commemorative meals and "for" the dead themselves. They were likely to initiate cleaning of the graves or setting up of *ogradki* or headstones, although they generally invoked the help of male relatives for these purposes. As we have discussed, Russian women were expected to tend the graves and indeed to intercede with the dead as part of their role in life-cycle rituals in the nineteenth century. Women were perceived to be best suited to ritual transition, a concept that persisted throughout the Soviet period, so that women served in professions dealing with such transfers or performed ritual acts to promote transition unofficially, e.g., by washing and dressing the body. Given that women maintained the closest relationship with the church during the Soviet period, it is not surprising that they also arranged for religious commemorations.[19] Men, who represented the public, secular world, generally would not risk engagement with or were not drawn into Orthodoxy. While women too could lose public status or be threatened by an ongoing, overt relationship with the church, they did maintain closer ties to faith because they had been assigned the role of culture bearer within this society. In order for life-cycle rituals to be performed correctly, religious acts were sometimes required, and particularly in the funeral, it was a woman's job to perform them or organize them. To take one example, recall the role of older women as *posidelki* who read prayers for the deceased. Thus, while any person could commemorate the dead, the rite itself favored women as the public representatives for the deceased. On the one hand, these requirements placed additional burdens on women, because they were ultimately responsible for the soul's peace. On the other, they enabled women to grieve more openly and consciously than men, who were limited by both the stoicism expected of them and by their exclusion from many routine commemorative practices.

Funerals, however, not only served to establish the roles of those who remained behind on earth. The funeral ritual also removed a person from the

---

[19] Even today in the post-Soviet period, women greatly outnumber men at formal church services or in visits to churches to pray or light candles at all hours of the day.

world of the living and defined what it meant to be "non-human." First and foremost, the dead should maintain a relationship to survivors by interceding for them or protecting them from harm. Although people recognized that the dead could be a threat to the living, the ongoing relationship between those on earth and those in the afterlife through dreams usually remained a positive one. More importantly, the dead had to be content with their lives in the otherworld, where it seemed that they continued to live much as they had on earth. Mourners thereby provided them with the goods and even the cash they might need in the afterlife during the funeral and afterward. Similarly the dead had an obligation to inform survivors if they were unhappy through dreams, so that relatives could make amends in a timely way.

We can conclude from these descriptions that for the average Soviet Russian, individual identities negotiated through the funeral for the living and the dead were indeed almost entirely drawn from religious faith and folk beliefs. We have seen that the folk, and indeed the religious, traditions were a threat to official Soviet ideals and that citizens used them as a tool, on occasion, to resist state policy. Verdery (1996, 20) writes that

> because socialism's leaders managed only partially and fitfully to win a positive and supporting attitude from their citizens—that is to be seen as legitimate—the regimes were constantly undermined by internal resistance and hidden forms of sabotage *at all system levels* [italics original].

It is difficult to ascertain whether her assertion applied in the case of the funerary rite, primarily because theorists were less successful in defining official ideology regarding it. We do know that the Soviet Union espoused a policy of atheism and designed its official rituals to establish control over the family by sending "acceptable" messages about family life. The writings of the ritual specialists make this goal clear. Rudnev (1979, 22), for example, says that "tradition … is necessary for citizens of a socialist world. Without it we cannot raise the new members of society." In his argument for the introduction of Soviet rituals, Ugrinovich (1975, 137) concludes that life-cycle rituals "[m]ost importantly, indicate the unity of the interests of the family and society, the interest of society in the harmonious development of each family." But we also must recognize that they could not effectively make the funeral conform to these goals, because they were at a loss as to how to remake the rite itself.

However, despite these impediments, we can make some conclusions about the degree of resistance within the funerary rite of the Soviet period. In fact, I contend that this ritual is indeed consonant with the other two we have examined. It exhibits both acceptance of certain Soviet-era values, and a stubborn retention of material that contradicted state ideology, material that was necessary for the negotiation of identity independent of the state's values. The religious and folk content in funerals served as a direct rebuttal of official atheistic policy for most people. Even if they were not fervent believers, people conceived of a spirit of some kind that lived on after death. Orthodox and other commemorative acts, such as *pominki*, enabled mourners to perform the role required of them in the Russian folk religious tradition. They thereby also ensured that the dead were content. If they had not performed these rites, they would neither have been able to grieve properly nor would the dead have been honored as was required. Although the Soviet ritual specialists managed to eliminate the religious portions of the funeral in public, they had little or no control over people outside of the public eye, where these practices thrived as a form of resistance to state policy. People reconciled the ban on public religious rites by either performing them secretly (albeit in a much more restricted way) or by subsuming them under the more acceptable folk tradition, which paralleled Orthodox beliefs. In either case, citizens were asserting that they did not accept the weakly reimagined funeral the ritual theorists espoused, but knew better how the ritual must be performed.

To some extent, however, the ritual theorists achieved the same goal of emphasizing collective responsibility in socialist society as they had in the wedding and birth rituals. In fact, the communal functions of funeral observances became even more important during the Soviet period than they had been in the nineteenth century, because neither the church nor the state, to a large extent, was responsible for the deceased at all. Only the family could ensure the proper ritual transfer, and thus the folk and religious acts performed by relatives and friends became the heart of the ritual. Because the Soviet state provided neither an adequate alternative ritual nor support for the family in the interment itself, my informants viewed the communal aspects of the funeral as most important not only to the soul of the deceased, but to the mourners.

Of all three rituals, funerals most effectively strengthened the ties between people and conformed to the Soviet goals for a stable family life and a united collective. Theorists attempted to institute a rite that would recognize a person's contribution to socialist society and would incorporate the desire for commemoration of the dead, by retaining Orthodox expressions such as *vechnaia pamiat'* 'eternal memory', all the while hoping for a successful reinterpretation of its meaning. However, the family and friends who celebrated the funeral rite truly established the core symbolism of the performance and took their cues not primarily from Soviet ideology, but from religious practices and folk belief. They did not reject out of hand the importance of the recognition of a person's devotion to society, work, and family in the Soviet funeral, but they did not limit their interpretations of funeral rites to these characteristics alone. Rather, they also drew on Russian folk and religious traditions in their burial practices, which retained much of their original significance.

Merridale (2000, 341) suggests that the funeral became impoverished under Soviet rule. While she may be correct in relation to the burial itself, my informants did not express such reservations, because they managed to perform the most important rituals to establish their roles as bereaved survivors, and for the dead. Thus it would seem that the public ceremonies (both funerals and weddings) generally might be classified as impoverished, but once the community (not the state) was the driving force, the rituals were much more rewarding for participants. However, ritual actors also resented the fact that the state vowed to provide for the family in life-cycle rites and elsewhere, but did not follow through on its promises. Therefore, citizens did not uniformly praise the state for the communal ethos that characterized life-cycle rituals in Soviet Russia. Rather, they often condemned the system, because without the communal efforts of friends and family, rituals could not be celebrated as citizens deemed necessary. As a result, the state could never totally convince its citizens to accept official ideology wholeheartedly, but was confronted with a populace that relied on a variety of sources to establish its own conception of family roles through life-cycle rituals.

Perestroika and the fall of the Soviet Union brought about significant change in Russia. The upheavals of this period were not limited to the economy and to the government, of course, but extended into socio-cultural life as well. Not surprisingly, practices in all three rituals began to change, sometimes radically. These changes reflect an alternative view of the family and its relationship to the government, society, and community at large among the populace. As a result, people continue to use rituals to negotiate conceptions of familial and social roles, but the essence of these roles has changed since 1991. Certain practices may have remained the same, but their interpretations will vary from these behaviors under Soviet rule. In addition, some common ritual acts from the Soviet era have been abandoned and still others have been introduced. Changes have arisen not only as part of shifts in Soviet values since Gorbachev's tenure as leader, but as a consequence of the new social structure that took hold after the socialist government was transformed. However, folklore resists change. Just as folk and religious material was preserved in all three rituals throughout the Soviet period, despite attacks and revisions by the state, some *Soviet* "folk" traditions have in turn been slow to die out, as we will see in our examination of post-Soviet life-cycle rituals in the next chapter.

Chapter 6

Life-Cycle Rituals during Late *Perestroika* and in the Post-Soviet World

The 1990s saw the end of the Soviet Union and its reformation as the Russian Federation. With this change came upheaval in all aspects of daily life and a redefinition of social identity. As a result, the rituals themselves have also changed, because the norms of gender and familial roles have altered to some extent. We have established that ritual actors rely on shifting, and sometimes contradictory, ideas to negotiate their identities within the social hierarchy. All the while, they waver between resistance and accommodation to a wide variety of socio-cultural norms. While one might expect that the Soviet influences in rituals would naturally die out, given the shift in society, that has not proven to be the case. This fact is not surprising, given that the Soviet practices are indeed now part of the collective folk memory. Just as pre-revolutionary beliefs played a role in the development of "Soviet" rituals, so too have Soviet ideas contributed to the post-Soviet worldview and to ritual practice. Those creating post-Soviet rituals were, after all, products of the Soviet system. Only the youngest generation does not recall the Soviet experience at all, and it has yet to have its chance to make a lasting mark on established cultural institutions such as maternity hospitals and the ZAGS. As a result, certain Soviet features have been preserved, while both Russian folk traditions and consumerist practices have been strengthened. This combination, one we saw throughout the previous forty years, has resulted in a conflicting series of messages about the individual's social role, one that parallels the general confusion in the post-Soviet era as a whole.

The initial reaction to the transition from socialist state to democratic one was generally positive, as Shtulhofer and Sandfort (2005, 2) conclude:

> Immediately after the "Great Transformation," the prevailing mood was one of high optimism. There was relief that the old regime was finally dead and the hopes of rapid Westernization—by which people usually meant Western prosperity and lifestyles. The cheers were hardly silenced when numerous problems caused by the complex task of simultaneous transformation of political, economic, and social structures surfaced.... The growing distrust in state institutions and

dissatisfaction with the politicians replaced the initial enthusiasm that the process of transition had inaugurated.

In the early stages of the "Great Transformation," Soviet Russian citizens had embraced the notion that the Soviet system had "destroyed" the family and corrupted gender roles within it. The media, politicians, and indeed many citizens called for a return to the traditional family structure. Kay (2002, 58–59) argues that

> [f]rom the early 1990s onwards, a wealth of press articles, media broadcasts and references have been devoted to the issue of reestablishing "correct" gender identities in post-Soviet women and men and to returning a "natural" balance of characteristics, behaviour and division of roles along gender lines. In this context the Soviet experience of "emancipation" is characterized as unequivocally negative for women, their families and society in general.

As a result of this perception of the "ruined family" and the pernicious influence of Soviet feminism on gender roles, Johnson and Robinson (2007b, 5) say that there were widespread calls for "re-feminization and re-masculinization" in the post-Soviet world. They characterize the above reactions as part of a "neotraditional gender ideology," which

> is resonant with those that we more typically describe as traditional (that is, pre-communist regime) because it embraces privatizing and domesticating women's lives. But it is *neo*traditional because it responds to the impact of communism—a communism that was problematic for women and for gender. Communism was problematic because its ideological claims about equality were never realized, and women continued to be constrained by a gender ideology that framed women as feminine/female in private and in public, but also male in public (where male wasn't gender).

Gorbachev himself, as discussed in chapter 1, supported the return of women to the domestic sphere and pledged to dedicate governmental resources "to make it possible for women to return to their purely womanly mission" (Kay 55).

However, the situation has been complicated by economics and the reduction in state services in support of the family. As Kalabikhina (2004, 187), in her focus group study of post-Soviet gender, concludes, "Popular calls for *bringing women back to the families* [italics original] are often painted in rather patriotic colors: they are made to sound like noble attempts to save the nation (in demographic terms) and families (in the social sense) from decay." However, she goes on to say, politicians and social theorists overlook the fact

that thirteen percent of families are single parent households, ninety-five percent of which are headed by women, who cannot simply "return" to the family hearth. Similarly, they do not address the issue that in the economic
climate of post-Soviet Russia, both adults in two-parent families must work to
survive. Thus, over time, there has been increased longing for the perceived
stability of the Soviet-era family.

Zdravomyslova and Temkina (2005, 111) describe the complexity of gender and family identity within the post-Soviet context: "In many strata nostalgia for the patrimonial and state-determined traditions of the soviet model is
growing. At the same time an ever larger discursive space is being conquered
by models of femininity and masculinity which appeal to liberal neotradition-
alism in their conceptions of gendered citizenship." As a result of these competing ideologies, Rands Lyon (2007, 26) asserts that

> the post-Soviet gender culture is characterized by a multiplicity of
> competing gender role models, including both "traditional" and
> "Soviet," and is influenced by a freer flowing traffic in ideas and im-
> ages from around the globe. I find empirical evidence of women
> negotiating gender—shifting in and out of different gender gears—
> within this neotraditionalist gender culture … within certain limits,
> women are actively experimenting with the combination of gender
> models that suits them best. Moreover, their experimentation is itself
> hinged on the more rigid role of men as providers…. For both men
> and women, regardless of their support for neotraditional values,
> they negotiate their roles, make sacrifices, and experiment with new
> modes of work, in order to address both personal and family needs.

We have established that people created identity based on various models
about social position within the family and society through their ritual practice. Rands Lyon's research suggests that the same situation exists in the post-
Soviet period as well, although the fulcrum between oppositional value
systems has shifted. The distinction, as we will see, is that rites now focus not
on the conflict between the Soviet state and its citizen's desires, but between
the Russian tradition (which at this point includes Soviet practices) and the
recently-introduced Western democratic and capitalist models.

Childbirth, marriage, and funeral rituals all illustrate the social shifts that
have occurred over the last fifteen years and the fundamental conflicts between (Soviet) Russian and capitalist traditions in this social structure. Ironically, in some ways Soviet and capitalist ideals previously meshed better than
they do in the post-Soviet world. Both Western and Soviet rituals of the period conveyed messages about institutional control over the individual, a
conveyor-belt approach, and the value of consumer comforts to family life.
While the sources of the messages may have been different (socialist ideology
versus capitalist economy), they were nevertheless consonant with each other

and managed to coexist well during the Soviet era. The post-Soviet experience, though, pits these ideologies against each other. The Soviet and Russian traditions are jointly aligned *against* the consumerist ones. The life-cycle rituals now reflect feelings of cultural dissonance, and people must negotiate two radically different positions to establish familial and social roles, one based on the Russian worldview and one based on capitalist ideology and traditions related to it. Lissyutkina (1993, 280–81) summarizes the current situation with regard to these three "cultural value systems":

> The first system is the remains of the communist ideology: as disillusion, chaos, and famine grow, these remains became the object of nostalgic idealization. Second, there is an appeal to the traditional conceptions and values of prerevolutionary Russia, as an attempt to tie together the broken thread and connect to the past over a period of seventy-five years. And third, there are Western values based on the ideas of democracy, individualism, private enterprise, and private property.

Therefore, practice theory once again will be a valuable tool in our analysis of ritual, because, as Bell notes (1997, 76), "practice theorists are concerned with analyzing large processes of historical and cultural change, often developing more nuanced versions of Geertz's model of the interaction of human action, needs, and experiences, on the one hand, with traditional cultural structures, organizational patterns, and symbolic systems, on the other." In the post-Soviet world, these three cultural systems interact with ritual actors' needs and experiences in a markedly different way than in the previous decades, as we will see. At the same time, the shift from a socialist to a capitalist society necessitates an understanding of the crisis such transitions engender. Scott examines just such a radical shift in his study of resistance in Malay society. He concludes (1985, 184):

> What we observe in Sedaka and elsewhere on the Muda Plain is an emerging capitalist agrarian class which has been steadily shedding its ties to laborers and tenants but which acts in a largely precapitalist normative atmosphere that makes it extremely difficult to justify the actions it has taken. They are, in this sense, capitalists who are obliged to explain themselves—to justify their conduct publicly— without the benefit of the elaborated doctrines of a Malaysian Adam Smith.... The historically given, negotiated, moral context of village life is one in which, if only ideologically, the cards are stacked against the newer forms of capitalist behavior. This moral context consists of a set of expectations and preferences about relations between the well-to-do and the poor.

Within urban Russian society, of course, the transition is not one to a capitalist agrarian class, but his description applies to the situation that people now face. Citizens have reacted to the reality of the transition by applying their own "set of expectations and preferences between the well-to-do and the poor," one based on their experience with the role of the family (and gender) in the Soviet system and Russian folk tradition. We will examine each ritual in turn to illustrate how people negotiate these various systems in their family lives.

Childbirth in the Post-Soviet World

The most obvious change in childbirth in Russian post-Soviet life is the adoption of an overwhelming array of additional Western technologies and approaches to birth. Certainly the birth process, as we have discussed, had already incorporated some features of Western medicine during the Soviet period. However, the access to Western equipment and drugs medicalized the process still further. Nine of the fourteen women who gave birth in the 1990s reported the use of drugs, either to stimulate or to retard labor. While labor intensifiers existed during the Soviet period, it is striking that so many mentioned the use of stimulants, whereas only a small portion did in the earlier informant pool. In addition, women (particularly after the year 2000) began to describe the use of intravenous drips when they arrived at the hospital, and anesthesia and fetal monitors later on, all of which make it more difficult to walk during labor and to find a comfortable position in which to deliver. As Irina S. stated about her 1994 delivery: "I was in the ward literally for an hour, they brought me in right away and put in an IV. They love them, maybe it's possible to do without them, but they did it just in case, in order to protect themselves, everything was according to plan. I don't know what they gave me the first time [for a previous birth]." She does note that both times she received light anesthesia at the peak of labor. However, these procedures were not instituted at every *roddom* at the same time. Elvira P., for example, who delivered her son in 1997 in the same city, did not receive anesthesia, because she did not ask for it: "If there is no mention of the topic, they don't do it [give anesthesia], if you ask, then they do it, but I didn't ask." However, Marina L., who gave birth in 1995 in a small city near Samara, reported (as did those from previous decades) that it is not acceptable practice to give anesthesia during labor. Thus, it would appear that some of the maternity hospitals, in smaller cities, were more conservative. However, by the end of the decade, a great majority of women received anesthesia as a matter of course. Doctors interviewed also reported an increase in the number of cesarean sections, indicating that technological intervention was on the rise in birth generally.

Another interesting phenomenon is that of the seventeen births in the post-Soviet portion of the study, twelve of them involved some kind of prenatal hospitalization.[1] The majority of the mothers were between the ages of nineteen and twenty-five and were physically healthy otherwise. Yet doctors insisted on having them spend from two weeks to a month in the hospital. The phenomenon of more frequent hospitalization is partially the result of the new medical technology available to the doctors. They can perform more tests and have more accurate information about any possible change in the pregnancy, from low protein in the blood to water retention. One obstetrician, Elena L., described this situation:

> It has changed fundamentally during the last ten years, since *pere-stroika* happened, because before in every field, medicine was closed, we didn't know how they treated people abroad, what medical achievements there were, scientific workers might have gone somewhere, read something, but that was such a small percent that it doesn't count. As soon as the political changes began in our country, right then we began to understand what was going on in other countries. We became familiar with medicines that are used worldwide, we learned about new technologies about which we had no conception before.

Physicians are responding not only to the technology at their disposal, but also to the decreased birthrate in Russia (an estimated 9.7 births per 1000 population in 2005 (http://reference.allrefer.com/country-guide-study/russia/russia65.html) and concern about infant mortality (in 2002 there was an incidence of 18 deaths per 1000 live births in Russia, which was down slightly from the 1990 average of 21 deaths per 1000; population growth was –0.06, and the total fertility rate was an average of 1.25 children (http://globalis.gvu.unu.edu/country.cfm?country=RU). They recognize a general decline in health in the country as well. The obstetrician Natalia R. reported

> There are many illnesses that do not prevent pregnancy, but complicate it. That is, blood pressure, often there are edemas, that is, pathological weight gain, often occurs ... personal illnesses. For example, kidney, heart disease. And then many women now have harmful habits, which also complicate the pregnancy ... and then as a result we get sick children.

Due to all these factors doctors were more likely to hospitalize mothers. Medical institutions thereby became even more involved in pregnancy than during the Soviet period. However, control over the individual (at least the

---

[1] Note that in the case of Olga S.'s two pregnancies, the doctors wanted to put her into the hospital, but she refused. Thus only one woman was not advised to undergo bed rest and prenatal hospital care.

mother) in the post-Soviet world is much more strict in many ways due to technological advances.

These behaviors would perhaps contradict the developments in society as a whole, but I would argue that they are to be expected for several reasons. During *perestroika* medical institutions were also in a crisis. They were being transformed from agents of the Soviet state into independent entities. That transition produced the same stress for them and the people employed in them as it did for the average person. The doctors themselves report that their working lives have become much harder than during the Soviet period. For example, Natalia R. described a situation in the hospital where she worked in which "a lot of equipment was assigned to our region, it was not completely installed, the documents were forged by Moscow. And now a big court case has been brought, but I think that it will come to nothing. The equipment just doesn't exist." Her colleague, Evgenia Z., added that the situation is so bad that they even have to ask for swaddling clothes for the babies they deliver: "We even ask for swaddling clothes, a minimal amount, a tiny amount. Once we had several thousand swaddling bands, but now hundreds are disappearing. And winter is ahead. I yell SOS at every staff meeting. They just don't get it." The economic crisis not only affected the workplace, but also the everyday financial lives of the medical personnel, many of whom reported problems living on their salaries. Finally, they expressed dismay over the state of the profession, that young doctors and midwives were more concerned with money than with their patients' health.

As a result of these crises and shifts in technology, doctors responded by becoming more involved in their patients' care. My data show that Western medicine is reinterpreted through a system that is still Soviet in its essential structure. We have already noted that the doctor was not a neutral figure, but one that represented the state and also social norms. When those social norms were threatened, doctors took it upon themselves to ensure that their role was preserved. The freedoms in the society and the increase in options reflecting individual choice in medical care have affected them as well. They now have the option to treat people as they see fit, with fewer controls by a monolithic medical establishment. At the same time, patients also responded to the greater freedom in society and took it upon themselves to assert their own will, which made the doctors nervous, since they realized their official position has been compromised. Most of the medical personnel reported that their current patients do not listen to them, indicating (whether true or not) that they feel less power now than before. For example, a midwife, Vera S., said that the increase in anesthesia was precisely due to the fact that women talked to each other: "Nevertheless women trade information with each other. We have a 'sarafan' radio, where women give each other information, they even might not listen to the doctor, but to each other." Another midwife, Tatiana K., expressed a similar opinion:

When you say to them that they shouldn't smoke during pregnancy, it's dangerous, they answer "my friend gave birth and everything was fine." They don't understand that the child can adapt in there and come out normal, but it can happen that they will give birth to something terrible to describe. That is, our moral lessons are not important for her.

Natalia I. reported that when she started practicing medicine in 1974

[p]atients did not have this information, there was more trust.... A person who knows more, they look at things with skepticism and check on them in one way or another. They might listen, then consult several times, clarify if it is true, and only then might agree with what is being proposed to them.

An American would applaud this attitude among patients, since it indicates individual responsibility and choice. However, the Russian doctors expressed dismay with the reliance on other people's opinions, whether medically based (from books) or from friends and family, because it contradicts the worldview about their status inherited from Soviet medical training.

In addition, the general perception (both because of the increase in general medical problems and because of the view that Soviet times were better) is that women are weaker now than their forebears. Nearly every medical specialist I interviewed mentioned this change; for example, Tatiana V. commented: "Now women have gone much weaker, their body is not as strong, once there were some illnesses, but now there are just lots of weak women." Thus the physicians try to maximize control over their patients by using all the techniques they have at their disposal, from medical technology to folk belief, just as they did in the Soviet period. The difference is that their social roles are now more compromised, so that they try to consolidate as much of their public power as they can. While there may be more freedom of choice on the surface, the maternity hospital as an institution has not responded in kind. Most women experienced the same type of restrictions and problems that their mothers did. As Liuba S. reported about her grandchild's birth, which was traumatic for her daughter and resulted in prolonged care for the child: "We went to a private maternity hospital, thought it would be better, but it turned out to be the same."

While they are trying to limit the patient's freedom of choice, the private medical system is actually fostering it to some extent. Russian women are no longer bound to their local doctor or maternity hospital. They may choose whom they want to treat their pregnancy and also where they would like to give birth. Elvira P. reported that she was assigned to her doctor, but could have chosen any doctor: "In principle I could have picked the doctor I wanted. But upon meeting the doctor I was assigned to, I liked her." Similarly, she described how one can give birth in any of the city's maternity hospitals: "They let us pick the maternity hospital, so you have to agree with the hospital ahead of time and if they have space at your due date, they fill out a form and the clinic writes out an order for treatment at that maternity hospital." Choice, of course, is not a guarantee of better care. One mother, Irina S., chose to have her second child close to home, despite the fact that her doctor advised her against it. She had been hospitalized in a larger *roddom* in the city, but did not like the atmosphere, as she put it, of "conveyor birth." Her doctor overlooked the fact that she had internal bleeding, as a result of which she ended up in intensive care. Thanks to her mother's (who is a doctor) insistence, she was checked by another physician, who operated on her to stop the bleeding. Thus, despite the better technology and the greater options, many informants felt betrayed by the capitalist-model private medical system which had promised so much, but did not, in their view, result in any differences from the problems characteristic of health care in the Soviet period.

The introduction of a capitalist medical model has led to a larger number of options for those who can afford them. Medical institutions have established a series of private (for-pay) wards that allow people to have access to services absent in public (state-subsidized) wards. The state-subsidized wards are still comparatively inexpensive; the private wards are much more costly and since medical insurance is still not widespread, people bear the costs themselves. These services include: having a birth partner present at the delivery; visitor access to the wards; (semi-) private rooms and delivery rooms; twenty-four-hour access to the child (in one's room or in a nursery next door).[2] Natasha M. described her delivery in such a ward as follows:

> I was scared to give birth and my mom agreed with a doctor, there was a for-pay department there, the first in the city, for the first time there was a for-pay ward, then it cost 3200 rubles. That was considered a lot of money and mom sacrificed for it, saying of course [you'll go] there.... There are five chairs standing there [in the state-subsidized ward] and five people giving birth, and I didn't want that, because [I wanted] complete attention only on me the whole time. I had a private room, they brought me there, everything was clean, it was nice.... Both Alesha [the father] and mom could be present[3] ... the baby was with me all the time.

---

[2] In most public wards the child is also now with the mother. In addition, the child is now routinely placed on the mother's chest or stomach after birth for anywhere from half an hour to two hours, to allow the child to nurse and to foster the maternal bond.

[3] In the end neither was present, since she did not call them before she delivered. She said that the pain would have made her kill the father anyway, which was just as well!

Elvira P. also described such a situation for when she delivered her son. Because her aunt worked in the hospital, she was allowed to do things others were not, as though she were in a private ward: "My visitors used their privileges. They didn't come in, but [the nurses] brought them the baby to see. But usually they wouldn't." Irina S. said that when she delivered in a public ward, she was faced with more restrictions than those that paid. She could have visitors, but not in the room: "Only [they couldn't come] into the ward. There is simply a hall for conversation, a vestibule. You can go down there." However, she went on to say that she could not bring the baby with her, but that those who had paid were allowed free access to the ward: "Once again, if you pay, they let you into the ward. And then one asks, 'what's the difference?' That is, you paid and you go into this ward in the same shoes and clothes. They say that you can't, you can bring in infection, but if you pay, then you can do anything."

In the public wards, ritual abasement and stringent controls are still the norm in both the intake procedures and during delivery. Olga L., who gave birth in a public ward in Voronezh in 1999, described the morning after her birth as follows:

> You have to wash, after all, everything is bloody, and in general you lie in that, actually in filth, no one even comes to change anything, and you have to go wash, there is only one place where you can do this, the third floor, and you have to get in line. When it is still hard to stand, everything hurts, and there are both the toilet and a place to wash, it's all one place, only two people [at a time], what's more there are no dividers.

She also reported that the intake nurse yelled at her for not performing the preparatory procedures, such as shaving and an enema, at home. Most women now do so to avoid embarrassment, so that now instead of humiliating people by performing the procedures, they are able to humiliate them for 1) not doing them or 2) doing them improperly. One informant said that she shaved, but not to the nurse's satisfaction, so that she was reshaved upon admittance. Maria S. said that when she complained about pain, she was threatened:

> The midwife started to sew me up [she had tears as a result of the birth]. It started to really hurt, I got nasty and asked what she was doing, because it hurt me. She told me that if I was going to act up, then she would call the male doctors, they wouldn't stand on ceremony. That had a sobering effect on me, when I was in the hospital before my delivery, I could say anything and everything was forgiven, no matter what I did, but here that's it, they put me in my place.

Similarly, Ekaterina Z. reported that, like women in previous decades, she was not allowed to give birth when she was ready, because it was night: "I waited until it [a contraction] ended, and went to the doctor, but it was night-time. Everyone wanted to sleep, no one wanted to deal with me. The doctor said that I would deliver in the morning and sent me to lie down." While not every woman who gave birth in a public ward had such problems, it is clear that the old traditions die hard. The medical personnel have created a dual system that includes one standard of treatment for public wards and one for private. Families are aware of this discrepancy and try to improve their care in public wards by using connections, as Elvira P. did, or by offering some extra cash to the medical personnel before the birth.

Individual choice and advanced medical birthing technology are available for those that have money. If a family does not have the means to access the private ideal, then they have fewer choices. This results in a two-tiered system that is not much different from that of the Soviet period, where personal connections (*blat*) were used to get better medical care. The distinction now is that the capitalist medical system is pitted against the native (Soviet Russian) one. This conflict is the logical continuation of the Soviet Russian idealization of the consumerist models we have discussed. However, it is complicated by the fact that there is nostalgia for the Soviet past, as Boym (1994, 284) has discussed. Both the doctors and the patients recognize the conflict in the current system, the shift in society that promotes capitalist ideals, but they also regret the loss of Soviet professionalism and dedication in the medical profession. Thus they highlight the positive features of the Soviet system in the face of current problems, challenges that have emerged in the face of Westernization. One could indeed argue that the best of the Soviet system (guaranteed free care by dedicated professionals using all means available to them) has been lost and that all that remains of the Soviet system is the bureaucratic officiousness. While this is clearly an oversimplification of a complicated situation, my informants expressed such opinions about health care generally, not just about maternity care.

Certainly, a focus-group study performed by Kalabikhina (2004) in various cities of the former Soviet Union supports this claim. The lack of adequate medical care was a particular concern of the majority of those interviewed: "Dissatisfaction with the quality of free medical service … widely spread official and unofficial charges for medical service, the need for the patients to purchase and bring medicines and bandages along to the clinic in spite of guaranteed free medical service" (194). In addition, her interviewees (204) reported discontent with the private system as well:

> Respondents have countless complaints about medical services; virtually everything costs money; patients have to take along to the hospital their own drugs, bandages, food, and even bed linen in some places; and most services (except emergency surgery) are on a charge

basis. High prices do not always imply high quality … "before doctors were more responsible for health of children than now." … They
note that medicines are available in drug stores but they are very
expensive.… Virtually all gynecological services (including anes-
thetic, drugs, gloves, other materials and examination itself) have a
price tag as well.

They repeatedly mentioned dismissive and difficult medical personnel, who
demand nearly all one's pension or salary for treatment. These opinions reflect the nostalgia for the Soviet past and the disharmony between the new
system and the old.

As a result, the family continues to play a major role in the rite. For those
who cannot afford a private ward (all but three of my informants), the family
must help for the same reasons that they did during the Soviet period. They
are involved at all stages, both during pregnancy, when offering the doctor an
additional payment to ensure quality care, and after delivery, when mother
and child are still kept in isolation. In cases where there are complications, as
in Irina S.'s case, they may also have to help with the actual treatment: "Especially when I was in intensive care. They had to run around to different
places, for some reason there were no medicines, now we have everything, if
there is money. They found the money, but the medicines weren't available in
Gorodok. Some type of strong antibiotics were needed." Similarly, because
women were both isolated in the *roddom* and did not buy items for the children before birth, the *vstrecha* at the hospital showcases the familial role as
provider. The family continues to bring the first set of clothing for the baby
and then returns the mother and child back to a home equipped for the newborn with goods they have provided. Similarly, grandmothers also continue
to visit to help with the newborn and to provide childcare.

The Soviet Union wanted to be the primary provider for the family, but
nevertheless had created a system in which it was difficult for a young family
to survive without the help of relatives. The post-Soviet government in fact
sends messages that the family is extremely important (by allowing three
years maternity leave, for example; eighteen months paid, as opposed to the
three months paid during the Soviet period), but the consumer economy has
inverted the conflict once experienced in the Soviet Union. The goods are
available, but the money to buy them is not, at least not without financial help
from relatives. The system in the *roddom* generally still fosters a feeling that
the institution is more powerful than the family, that it controls the mother
and child, at least those in public wards (where the majority of my informants
gave birth). In addition to the older rules inherited from the Soviet period
(such as isolation, preparatory procedures including an enema and shaving,
and official presentation of the child by a medical worker at the *vstrecha* upon
release from the hospital), patients gained an additional set of restrictions
from the Western medical model, including increased use of medication dur-

ing the birth process and restrictions on food and drink intake during labor. Add to that a higher incidence of cesarean sections and prenatal hospitalization and it becomes clear that the institution is still trying to put itself in a position of power over the mother and child, to convey the message that the institution produces the child, not the parents, not natural processes. Yet the end result is that both the system and the financial situation still promote family involvement in the child's life, as we have seen.

Community involvement is but one remnant of the Russian folk tradition that survived throughout the Soviet period to the present. While technological advances and wealth are being highlighted in the birth process, my informants report a strengthening of the folk system generally. In birth, the resurgent village tradition occurs mainly in two areas: the reemergence of *gadanie* 'fortune telling' and of religious practices. Like many of the women in the previous decades, these women knew that the shape of the stomach could predict the sex of the child. As Ekaterina Z. reported, "If it is a girl, then the stomach is rounder, if a boy, the stomach sticks out at an angle, and if it is a girl, then a little stripe appears across the stomach, [and] I had a stripe." In addition to this common belief, one informant also said that if there is hair on the stomach, it will be a boy. Another had access to a card that predicted the sex of one's child by the date of conception and blood type. Yet a third described how an old woman told her fortune using cards and said she would have a boy. The prevalence of these methods to predict the sex of the child, interestingly, comes at a time when ultrasound is the norm, so that there is also a technological means to perform this task. Once again we see a social conflict between folk knowledge and medical technology. For example, Natasha M., who had her fortune read on cards, went in for her ultrasound and was distressed to find that it showed that she was having a girl. It turned out that the folk method was more accurate in this case, since she had a boy.

A general perception currently exists (both among average people and among folklore specialists) that folk life suffered during the Soviet period, and that it is flourishing in post-Soviet Russia, because it is no longer taboo. When asked about fortune telling, women who delivered in previous decades said that they did not participate in it (beyond the common knowledge about the shape of the stomach). For example, Tatiana K. reported, "That [fortune telling] has appeared now. Now they determine, boy, girl." At the same time that capitalism and technology seem to bring with them a promise for a "better" life, the folk material holds secrets that outperform the contemporary way. When Natasha M. described how the folk method correctly predicted her child's sex, she proudly referred to how Russian tradition had trumped the modern ultrasound technology. One mother, Irina S., said that her advice to mothers was "I would turn to the experience of old people. It seems to me that they did things more correctly. Combining modern achievements together [with the old ways] to determine the proper means of some kind."

Such opinions illustrate the conflict between two worldviews, the traditional Russian one and the modern, technological one.

By reasserting Russian traditions, people are saying that Russia remains powerful in the face of a significant social crisis and loss of influence on the international stage. They can compete with the capitalist and technologically advanced powers and their symbols using their grandmothers' knowledge. They are also reacting to the popular conception that folklore was a casualty of the Soviet Union. While this perception is not entirely accurate, as we have seen, this idea has played an important role in the revival of folk practices.[4] Folklore then serves as a means to overcome a difficult past and rejoin with the "authentic" Russian tradition that had been lost. While we saw this phenomenon in the Soviet period, in the post-Soviet era, the return to tradition is both a rejection of Soviet-era policies and a way to cope with the loss of international identity. This attitude, of course, encapsulates the dilemma of contemporary Russia. While there is nostalgia for the Soviet past, it also was a time fraught with conflict and loss. Similarly, the capitalist and democratic systems that seemed so ideal in the abstract and from a distance have brought with them suffering and economic problems, which have threatened Russia's status as a superpower and thus socio-cultural identity as well.

One area where the Soviet government actually had made great inroads in changing tradition was in the elimination of religious practice, as Timasheff (1946, 226) notes. However, he (240) does make clear, as we have seen, that the state was "unable to create new patterns, but directed society towards the revival of pre-Revolutionary institutions" during the Stalinist period. One institution that was revived (or resisted change) was indeed folk belief. Given the conflation, during Soviet times, of religious belief and folk life, it is not surprising that there has been a resurgence in the former as well. Half of my informants reported christening their children, a much larger percentage than those in the Soviet period. Olga L., whose husband is not a believer, fought to baptize her son; after all, she said, "it won't do any harm." As discussed above, some Soviet Russians did secretly baptize their children, but now the Orthodox (and other faiths) are being reconnected to birth practices. In addition, the connection between the Virgin Mary and birth so prevalent in the nineteenth-century village has returned to some extent. One woman said she thought her prayers to the Virgin Mary helped her conceive, while another had an icon of the Virgin Mary with her to ease her delivery. Several women said that they named their children according to the calendar of saints' days as well, which was not mentioned by any of the women who delivered during the Soviet period.

---

[4] Folklorists investigating this process in Russia today call such revivals, i.e., the renewed interest in and practice of lore that was not handed down by one's forebears, but derived from other (often published or popular) sources, folklorism.

The flourishing of Orthodoxy is a direct reaction to the official atheism of the Soviet period. Despite the nostalgia for Soviet society that most adults express, they also recognize some problems with that society, among them repression of religion. There are certainly still atheists in Russia, including people of all ages I interviewed. However, the Russian Orthodox Church is associated with two powerful entities in the Russian imagination: the imperial past and village life. At a time when Russia has lost its superpower status, the burgeoning church is an icon of imperial power, one that reminds Russians of an era when their nation was at its most dominant. In addition, the village, as Olson (2004, 123; 138ff.) has shown, serves as a primary source for Russian identity and wisdom. Rural residents, who were true believers in the church and who often carried their beliefs throughout the Soviet period, are seen as beacons of the return to Russianness after so much native tradition had been lost during the Soviet times. This concept explains why the 1990s saw an abundance of popular books instructing Russians on their traditional folk beliefs from the past, e.g., the series *Delaite eto pravil'no* 'Do it Right', which includes volumes on the wedding, on fasts, on baptism, and on funerals, or *Ot krestin do pominok* 'From Christening to Funeral Remembrances' (Pankeev 1998), to name a few. These books teach not only about religious practice, but about the folk tradition more broadly, which has helped to spread the upsurge in folk material. At the same time, as Belousova (2002) has documented, the post-Soviet era saw the flourishing of the home-birth movement, which relies on much traditional knowledge and on Orthodoxy as part of its philosophy of childbirth. While its proponents may still be on the fringes of society (although many of my informants did mention it at some point, usually with disapproval), it represents a significant change in attitudes that many Russians are experiencing in the post-Soviet world. The founders of this movement are perhaps the most extreme version of the desire to understand one's traditional past and resurrect that which was lost, but their goals are consonant with those of their more conservative fellow citizens.

Thus, we see once again a great deal of conflict within the ritual practice, just as we did in the Soviet period. The capitalist practices generally (not just in medicine) hold the promise of a better life, and yet most people do not see much improvement. In interviews, Kalabikhina's informants (2004, 194) expressed opinions about post-Soviet Russia that led her to conclude that: "misunderstanding of the substance and disbelief in the outcomes and perspectives of economic reforms and privatization formed a perception that the reforms in Russia served the interests of a very small parochial group at the expense of the majority of the population." Life has become more difficult for them, not easier. In addition, most people are pitted against those who can afford the consumer economy, which creates a serious social divide, similar to the one that existed between powerful Communist Party members and the average citizen (Kalabikhina 197).

Likewise, the Soviet system is both reviled and adored. It is difficult for a society that has been told that the Soviet way of life was always better, that they were sacrificing to create something great, to face the collapse of that system and adoption of that of the "enemy." Yet people recognize the problems with the Soviet system and the degree to which the Soviet way of doing things still affects their lives, in many cases unfairly. Mothers, for example, recognize that they have little or no control over their treatment, and they resent it, especially given that they seem to be promised more freedom that does not materialize in the reality of the medical system. At the same time, they resent the fact that some people can buy their way to better care. In the Soviet Union, almost everyone was assured the same quality care (whether or not this was the case, people say it was). Such positive memories result in both affection and nostalgia for the previous way of life. Thus, many non-Soviet Russian traditions (both folk and religious) are being conflated with the remnants of the Soviet system and are perceived to be in opposition to the capitalism and technological medicine of the post-Soviet era.

While there are essential conflicts between these various views of birth, the concepts about family roles suggested by the birth rite have changed little. Within the Soviet Russian system, the mother was the most important figure in a child's life, and she received messages about her role as part of the birth ritual. The child was bestowed by the state on the family officially, but the bond between mother and child was much stronger, something the state actually used to its benefit, since the future of the state was thereby secured. Fathers had little or nothing to do with the initiation into parenthood, because they were excluded from the ritual for the most part. Not surprisingly, child rearing was primarily a woman's job, and this fact has not changed, as Gal and Kligman (2000, 112–13), Kalabikhina (2004, 203) and Khasbulatova (2005, 336) demonstrate in their studies of post-Soviet gender and family life. Although men are now allowed to be present at births in private wards, none of these women actually had their husbands present in the delivery room, even if they could. Marina K. for example, recounted:

> I never wanted my husband to be present during the delivery. I only wished that when I had already given birth to the child that he could come, hug me, kiss me, but only then. But that he would be present during labor I wouldn't want. It seems to me that it is not a sight for men … because if they are forced into it, they would faint and feel bad.

In fact, in her second birth, which occurred eleven years later, she had the option of having her husband present, as she describes:

> Labor and delivery with the husband is a for-pay service and is paid beforehand. But doctors do not advise women to insist on the pres-

ence of the husband if he is not ready for it. And Oleg was not mentally ready for such a procedure.... But he came to see me just after the delivery, when they had just taken me to the ward. After the positive outcome of the delivery, they take the baby to the children's section, and the mom to the ward and let her rest three hours and take a shower, then they bring the baby to the mother in the ward. When Oleg arrived, I was still very tired and weak, and it was important to me to see him. He hugged me, kissed me, and said that I was great and that he loved me a lot.... This time everything was different. It is true that Oleg only saw and held his son the first time the day after the delivery, since visits by relatives are allowed only until 19:00.... They didn't bring me the baby until 20:00.

Most medical personnel among my informants agreed, as Marina said, that it was a bad idea to have husbands present during the delivery, since they often required treatment while their wives were delivering, which distracted the doctors from their main task.[5] Thus parents receive the same basic message as during the Soviet period: child rearing is a woman's responsibility, and men still have little or no role to play in the process.

While there has been a call for men to "return to the family," the fact is both cultural and economic factors prevent them from doing so. Ashwin (2000b, 2) argues that

> [w]omen are no longer guaranteed work outside the home and, at the same time, social benefits are being eroded and motherhood is being redefined as a private institution and responsibility. The corollary of this is that men are expected to reassume the traditional "male" responsibilities which have now been abandoned by the state, but in a context in which real wages are falling and traditionally high-status male industries, such as mining, metallurgy, and the military-industrial complex, have been particularly badly hit by the economic crisis.

Issoupova (2000, 50) describes the situation as follows:

> [T]he new family ideal in which the man plays a key role does not as yet match reality. Women are continually disappointed by men.... This is not surprising, given that the Soviet state had usurped the role of men in the private sphere to such an extent that it had all but ceased to exist. The retreat of the state, meanwhile, though it may

---

[5] Two midwives said they thought it might be a help if a mother or husband was present, since the husband would respect his wife more after seeing what she had gone through. However, they also noted that some men could not stand the strain and are generally of little use.

have contributed to raising women's expectations, has not had an immediate impact on male behaviour.

Kukhterin (2000, 85) contends that post-Soviet men are trying to "define a new role for themselves within the family and as fathers," but that they have no real role models. They are also faced with the fact that they must work much more to support a family than their own fathers did, which results in their prolonged absence from their children's lives (Kukhterin 88). Kiblitskaia (2000, 97–98) describes as well how the capitalist system has also produced a crisis for men's identity. Due to the economic situation in post-Soviet Russia, it is much harder for men to provide for their families as they think they should. If they cannot, they lose authority within the home, because, as she (98) concludes: "male status was socially defined, not naturally given." Rands Lyon concurs that "men are suddenly expected to provide single-handedly for their families in an economic climate that has favored only a small minority and in which a single earner for the family is rarely sufficient to maintain the standard of living, much less to advance it" (2007, 28). Thus, both men and women are faced with the same dilemma as their parents during the Soviet period. Both parents typically must work outside the home to support a family; they resent the lack of state support (financial or otherwise) for families and children; and they must face conflicting gender norms about their roles. For men, this means that they should take on the role of breadwinner as well as the role of patriarch, a role that their wives (and indeed they) have been socialized to reject.

One significant change, however, is a greater emphasis on the woman's role as a mother, and not as a worker. Gal and Kligman (2000, 75) assert that post-socialism is characterized by "assumptions about women's natural place in reproductive work. No one asks men if they 'want' to work, and men's right to work is usually seen as a liberation from market forces." Although most women do return to work after having a child, the majority of women who gave birth in this period took from one and a half to three years of maternity leave (unlike their mothers, who returned to work after a much shorter period). The intensive prenatal care and perception of their "weakness" both convey that women are less powerful than Soviet Russian women. Yet if motherhood is much more of a trial for them, it is also much more the point of their existence. Issoupova (2000, 43) discusses this issue in the post-Soviet Russian press, in which most stories revolve around the demographic crisis and a woman's responsibility to the nation to unselfishly have children for its sake. She (46) concludes that "[n]onetheless, motherhood is still privileged over the notion of parenthood, and a tendency to view motherhood as the destiny of women persists. The pro-natalist bias of the press is also still very much in place...." Elvira P., for example, said she did not know how their mothers returned to work after three months. Her entire life, she said, was dedicated to the child after its birth, she had become a completely different person who lost her individuality. She, like most of the mothers in this group, stayed home for two and a half years and, even after she returned to work, had afternoons off with her son. Thus, while women almost all need to work for a family to survive, they take advantage of monthly government payments until the child is eighteen months old, under a law established in 1995 (Article 13 of the Federal Law Code No. 81-F3) that was designed to increase the birthrate.[6] This trend continued in 1996, when the Ministry of Health enacted a law that would provide state stipends for medical treatment in the early stages of pregnancy as well as additional leave time after delivery for women with several children (Khasbulatova 2005, 337). Many women now also choose their occupations or place of employment on the basis of flexibility for childcare responsibilities or to guarantee themselves the remnants of governmental subsidies. Thereby they avoid the private sector, which often will not provide such benefits due to the expense (Khasbulatova 334; Gal and Kligman 113). Thus employers, legal and political entities, and the media all send the message that a woman may be a professional, but that a more important duty in life is to be with her children for as long as possible. For this reason, I think, the maternity hospitals have changed the policy of not allowing children to be with their mothers. The institution, of course, still plays a powerful role in deciding whether the mother or child are well enough for this opportunity. If they are, however, the mother is with her child soon after birth, caring for him/her in the hospital, a practice that conveys how important motherhood should be for these women.

The birth ritual still emphasizes the position of the institution in the mother's and child's lives and its ability to bestow the child upon the family. While the system no longer creates a new generation of Soviet children, it still socializes citizens. The medical system teaches that the consumer economy is superior. Medical care, like everything else, is dependant on cash (and influence), so that one's social goal should be achieving economic success. The gap between people produces resentment and dismay instead of the better life that was promised after capitalist and democratic ideas were introduced in Russia. The maternity hospital must still indoctrinate mothers into their new roles. Thus ritual humiliation and isolation are still present in the ritual, as

---

[6] While some Soviet Russian women in my informant pool did take longer leaves, often by combining vacations with maternity leave or by simply taking a longer leave of absence, these were not paid leaves. The government thereby showed a woman that her more valuable role was as a worker, rather than as a mother. The new law reestablishes the importance of a woman's contribution to society as a parent, not as a professional. The emphasis on increasing the birthrate (and on a mother's role in child rearing) has continued. In the spring of 2006, as *The New York Times* reported on May 11, Putin called for a plan to improve the demographic situation; "among his proposals were one-time cash grants to mothers upon the birth of a second child, extended maternity leave benefits, and a graduated scale of cash and day-care subsidies as a woman has more children."

they were in the Soviet period. Now, however, women have more access to their children than twenty years ago, which emphasizes their role as mothers first and foremost and their responsibility for the new life they have created. While the same is theoretically true for men, who can now be present at the birth of their children, they are still largely external to the process, defined less by being fathers than by their professional lives. The birth process still unites the family when faced with these institutional and social pressures. At the same time, the resurgence in traditional material reconnects people with folk wisdom, a force that was able to withstand war, repression, and terror during the Soviet period and represents the true strength of the Russian populace. Continuity in tradition and its association to a family's progeny are particularly important when a society has experienced upheaval, since they provide a sense of comfort and strength in the face of Western practices that seem to threaten the Russian way of life.

Weddings in the Post-Soviet World

The wedding has undergone a significant change since the 1980s. The Soviet ritual specialists in the 1970s had already begun the process of instituting a consumer model in the wedding, including the creation of a special ritual space for weddings, the white dress, decorated cars, and the like. The fall of the Soviet Union allowed for both the resurrection and strengthening of traditional (folk and religious) acts and conspicuous consumption within the wedding (see Bersen'eva 2005 for a description of the ideal contemporary wedding in her guidebook for brides). With the increased emphasis on consumerism, weddings have been turned into an industry. Wedding salons now offer a complete range of services for brides akin to those in the Western capitalist countries.

The wedding palaces have also become consumer-oriented. They offer their own video and photography services (and in some cases, cars for hire) and attempt to keep other professionals out of the ZAGS, so that couples are forced to pay for their services. In one sense, this is the logical conclusion of the changes made during the Soviet era. In another, it also restores weddings to the preeminent role they played during the nineteenth century in Russia. The Soviet attitude toward the wedding was that it should be formal, but not formal enough to be characterized as *pokazukha* 'showing off'. If the ceremony were too elaborate, the Soviet ideal of social equality would have been threatened. Thus the Soviet theorists, when devising their wedding ritual, had to walk a fine line to create a ceremony that honored the establishment of a new family, but that did not give too much attention to the couple or their families. As a result, the ceremony, as characterized by my informants, was a bureaucratic process that did not hold much meaning for them. The reception, which highlighted their transition and honored their roles, became the most important part of the wedding.

These wedding services, of course, did not spring up overnight. Couples who married during the late 1980s in the era of *perestroika* had less elaborate weddings than those who married ten years later. Nevertheless, the changes in weddings had already begun in the early 1990s. During *perestroika* in the Soviet Union it was difficult to procure consumer goods, in many cases even more difficult than at the height of the *zastoi* 'stagnation' in the Brezhnev administration. Couples who married then were faced with the same challenges as previous generations in terms of finding suitable clothing and other goods. When comparing her 1992 wedding to that of her friend who married in 2002, Veronika S. said that it was simpler for her friend: "That is because she got married at a normal time, now if there is money, you can buy anything." Marina K., who also married in 1992, described how they could not find rings in any stores, so that her mother-in-law gave them her own wedding rings. In general, she said, things were complicated for those planning a wedding at that time: "It was really difficult with the economic conditions in the country, there was no gold, there was nothing. We were forced to search to get everything. We drove around all the stores specially to buy something for the reception." Elena P., who married in 1990, said that *perestroika* also affected the presents they received: "It was a bad time for presents, there was nothing in the stores … therefore they gave us money for the most part." However, even in these difficult economic times, the wedding was already becoming more consumer-oriented. Informants who married during this period first described ordering bridal bouquets, which previously had been purchased on the day of the wedding from a local florist or on the street. In addition, the reception moved from the family home to cafes or restaurants during this period. Only two couples in my study who married between 1950 and 1989 had a restaurant reception. From *perestroika* until 2003, only six couples had home receptions, while thirteen had receptions in a restaurant.[7] Of those that had receptions at home, four of them were older couples who did not want to have a large formal wedding due to their age. One said that there were no restaurants available when they wanted to marry. Two couples decided to have a home reception to save for the honeymoon. The number of honeymoons has also increased. Whereas few couples took honeymoon trips before the 1990s, they were common among informants who married in the last decade (fourteen of nineteen couples took a trip after their wedding).

Those who married during the last five years had the most elaborate weddings of all, with a wider array of services adopted from the consumer model of marriage. Wedding magazines describe ideal ceremonies and honeymoons and feature such services as hairdressers and cosmetologists who come to the

---

[7] As a result, the number of guests also increased. On average the total went from twenty-five to fifty to from fifty to seventy guests after *perestroika*. That is not to say that there were not smaller weddings among older couples, but the average young couple who married during this period had more guests than their parents did.

home before the wedding, videography and professional photography, limousine (or other luxury car) rentals, and rings made to order. Dresses for both witnesses and brides have become more elaborate (while most grooms still wear dress suits rather than tuxedos). Bridal salons offer not only dresses off the rack, but also dresses made to order in the latest styles. For those who cannot afford such extravagance, but who want the latest fashion, rentals are available.[8] The emphasis on consumption and display seems to be centered on the bride and her physical attributes, not on her character,[9] an ideal that is characteristic of class-based capitalist societies with a chivalric tradition. Upper-class women in particular, in that context, are prized for their delicacy and beauty. This concept of femininity as tied to physical beauty spread, of course, to the *nouveaux riches* and to the middle class, even within the socialist context, as discussed in chapter 4.

However, it is telling that the focus on feminine beauty and sexuality has occurred when the woman's body is perceived to be "weaker" than it was in the Soviet era. The medical professionals made frequent reference to this fact, as discussed in the previous section. It certainly appears that the shift in the perception of the woman's body is related to the concept of Russia's own weakness in the post-Soviet period. Issoupova (2000, 44) notes that "[i]n the Soviet era, Mother Russia was portrayed as a monumental and heroic figure, an exacting standard against which the citizen-children were measured.... In contemporary Russia, by contrast, she is portrayed as suffering, weak, and unattractive, while her child (the future of Russia) is hunted by evil forces." The image of women in the popular press since the early 1990s has contributed to this new perception of women and their bodies (and Russia herself as a metaphor for that body). The shift has been to view women as sexual beings, judged for their physical charms, not for their intellectual acumen, to which many women object (Johnson and Robinson 2007b, 5; Kay 2002, 82; Gal and Kligman 2000, 84). Kay (81) argues that "the promoting of 'femininity' becomes a part of the process of rejecting the Soviet past and all its values, righting the wrongs done to Russian women by the communist regime and moving forwards to a more civilised and westernised society...." Thus, just as the folk revival serves to connect with "Russianness" through a rejection of "Sovietness," the espousal of female sexuality, physical beauty, and indeed weak-

---

[8] Only one bride in this informant pool rented her dress, but it is a service bridal salons offer, thus allowing a person to participate in the consumer excess while saving some money.

[9] That is not to say that conspicuous consumption and excess do not surround both members of the couple in the *vykup* and reception, but that much more attention is given to the bride's physical appearance (and the techniques necessary to look beautiful) than to that of the groom. Several brides described rising at five or six in the morning to get ready, while their husbands said they did not have much to do before the ceremony.

ness is anti-Soviet as well, even though it is diametrically opposed to folk values of womanhood in many ways. The "weakening" of women's bodies as well as their social status in the public sphere has the concomitant effect of making male power even more apparent. Russian men are not only viewed as physically stronger, but have solidified their social positions within the most prestigious and influential sectors of the public sphere, e.g., in business, politics, and industry.

People who married during the post-Soviet period also describe receiving much more expensive gifts, such as washing machines, tape players, food processors, and microwaves, as well as the more usual housewares that people have traditionally given in Russia. Younger couples reported that guests now usually give cash, so that they can buy something large for the house, like a washing machine, or pay for their wedding trip. While Russians have always given cash for weddings, most of those who married since 2000 said that their only gift (or the bulk of the gifts) was cash, which contrasts with couples who married in previous decades, who mainly listed household items.

The ZAGS, as noted above, has become involved in the business end of the wedding process, offering its own services to compete with the wedding salons. Since the ZAGS, like the maternity hospital, is a state institution, people receive the same message as they do in the birth rite: the consumer economy is now a central factor in life as a couple and as a family. In addition, the ZAGS has responded to the desire to make ceremonies more meaningful, e.g., by allowing couples to pick their own music. While celebrants must still pronounce people married in the name of the Russian Federation, they are no longer bound to a set formula in the ceremonies. Galina V., a Vladimir ZAGS director, said:

> We create the scenarios for the ritual itself ourselves, but we have a required part which must not be changed: "in accordance with the law of the Russian Federation on marriage and the family you are now husband and wife." We have to say that phrase in accordance with the law.... When we congratulate people as we give them their documents, there is of course improvisation.... I like that a lot, thinking up something.... We have some new elements, to change something, to perform it so that our ritual is more interesting than in other cities.

That is not to say that every couple experienced such a ceremony. Galina S., who married in 1998, said that her ceremony was "absolutely bureaucratic phrases that don't even get into your head." Similarly, another couple who married that year in Voronezh, Olga and Dmitrii L., made fun of the woman who performed their ceremony as they were telling about it. They spoke with artificially formal voices and used paraphrased official formulaic language to indicate their negative impressions. On the other hand, Natalia T. said that the woman who performed her daughter's wedding ceremony in 2003 gave a moving speech, in contrast to her own wedding in 1975, which she described as "predetermined" and "ordinary":

> I liked the ZAGS ceremony. It was fairly moving. I didn't expect that.... Tania [her daughter] cried, I also shed a tear, and the other mom too.... The woman registrar who conducted it all spoke with feeling, touchingly. The ceremony stuck in my mind.

However, not all Soviet-era problems have been solved. The assembly-line feel still exists, with a constant stream of couples marrying every fifteen minutes on *torzhestvennye dni* 'formal ritual days'. Couples described celebrants who mixed up names, put the wrong dates on documents, and played music that other couples had chosen. However, the state institution of the wedding palace has responded, to some extent, to the freedom of choice in society just as the maternity hospitals have. Like the hospital, the ZAGS also emphasizes the consumer economy, by offering services to compete with private wedding salons. The maternity hospitals responded to social change by trying, if at all possible, to solidify their status within a new capitalist system. The ZAGS, of course, has no competition, since everyone must be married there. However, their role as the preeminent force in the marriage rite was threatened by wedding boutiques, so that they too have tried to maximize their social influence by starting their own wedding 'business'.

Nevertheless, the Soviet bureaucratic requirements can still be a problem, as they are in maternity hospitals. Olga and Alexander D. noted that they had to make a special trip to pay a fifteen-ruble registration fee when the smallest common bill in circulation was a hundred-ruble note. It took two hours to do this small task, which made Olga swear she would never return there (she did relent and come back for the ceremony). In instances such as these, the ZAGS tries to maximize its control over the couple, by asserting its power and by setting rules about what can be done on what days. If the couple wants to marry, then they have to conform, since without the approval of the ZAGS officials, no wedding can occur. Only civil weddings are legal in Russia even today, although a couple can choose to have a second, religious ceremony. Thus there is no impetus for the wedding palaces or the ZAGS to adjust many of their practices, unlike in the *roddom*, which at least has competition from other hospitals. They also try to protect the business side of the ZAGS, as Olga L. reported:

> Our videographer, who was filming on a video camera, was following behind us. The ZAGS employee started to yell at him that you can't go in there, but he got in anyway. They had a little skirmish, and then when she got him out of there all the same, she began to yell at

us. Because I was on edge, I started to cry. Everything ran down my face ... and so we weren't the first [to marry] after lunch, but came second.

Incidents such as these show that despite some changes in the ceremony itself, ZAGS officials continue to espouse the idea that the institution has control over the citizenry it serves. They thus far have retained their social clout despite changes in the society around them.

Soviet Russian families recognized that weddings were a major transition in their children's lives, and as such, merited celebration (at least from the late 1960s on) with as much fanfare as possible. The core of the celebration was the reception at home, which families provided for their children to acknowledge the new bond in society. The major ritual transition thus occurred in the family home and was arranged not by the state, but by friends and relatives, although the ZAGS ceremony opened the door to the transition and was therefore embraced. This ritual pattern has been further strengthened in the post-Soviet world. While the ZAGS ceremony has become more elaborate, it is still not the focus of the rite. Certainly, it still enables people legally and socially to enter into a new, important social role.

Therefore, the events in the family home before the wedding and afterwards at the reception are still the focus of the wedding. It is here as well that the folk traditions have experienced their most dramatic resurgence, just as they have in the childbirth ritual. Both the pre- and post-wedding periods have seen an upswing in folk practices. Some of these were performed during the Soviet period, and have simply been elaborated. Others are truly resurrected traditions that did not remain in the folk consciousness, but that are the result of popular publications on Russian traditions (described above) as well as of the work of professional *tamady* 'masters of ceremonies'.

The *devichnik/mal'chishnik* parties held by men and women to celebrate their departure from single life are a prime example. In the 1970s, as discussed above, the *devichnik/mal'chishnik* had already experienced a resurgence. While these gatherings differed drastically from those in the nineteenth century, they acknowledged the shift from one status to another, the loss of one's single life and reemergence into a new social role. In these years, however, the *mal'chishnik* was much more common than the *devichnik*. Men, who were perceived to be losing their freedom (unlike the bride, who gained status by marrying) needed an event to commemorate their loss. The post-Soviet era, though, has seen a return of the *devichnik* in full force (at least among the young; informants who married in their thirties did not go in for these "young people's" antics, as Galina S. expressed it). Of the nineteen couples who married in this time frame, twelve organized both a *devichnik* and a *mal'chishnik*; one couple had only a *devichnik*; one had only a *mal'chishnik*. None of the older women had a *devichnik*, but one older husband had a *mal'chishnik*. This is a stark contrast to brides in the 1950s–80s, most of whom did not have a *devichnik* when they married, even if their husbands did have a party. If such a gathering is tied to status loss, its resurgence would suggest that the bride is now losing status by marrying. However, I think that an unlikely argument, since most women do not feel that they are losing by marrying, but gaining (despite the Russian woman's double burden of working both in and outside the home). Rather, it appears that the popularity of the *devichnik* is tied both to the revival of the folk tradition generally and to the flowering of wedding traditions in the post-Soviet era.

Thus there are several issues at work which explain why these parties have become so much more prevalent. First, people have responded to the broad rebirth of folk practices. Most felt that they had been lost during the Soviet era, either due to benign neglect or to direct attacks, and their rebirth allows people to feel more authentically "Russian." Second, weddings are not limited by official state ideology and in fact, encourage the consumer economy and excess. Third, the material goods required to celebrate the wedding "properly" are all now available.

Another pre-wedding rite that has become much more elaborate is the *vykup*. While the buying of the bride existed throughout the Soviet period, in the post-Soviet era it has truly flourished. Natalia S. described a typical approach to the *vykup* in this period:

> For the *vykup* I found some stuff on the Internet and gave it to them [her friends], they had already done some things, written a script, written some verses, so that everything would be organized, thought up contests. And they wrote the script of the *vykup* from the first to the ninth floor. Posters hung on each floor, and the guests arrived and they did the task. They had tasks to do on every floor.

Not only has the buying of the bride become much more of an elaborate scenario, it has also become much more humiliating for the groom. This humiliation is also tied to the couple's future happiness, as Andrei P. noted: "They torment you specially. So that married life will seem like honey." In addition to testing the groom's knowledge about his bride and her family, his strength, and his ability to provide for a family, as the *vykup* has always done, it also tests his willingness to sacrifice for his bride. Often he must perform tasks that leave him open to ridicule. Vladimir C., who married in 1992, for example, had to unlock the door of the bride's apartment after getting the key from a two-liter bottle of water without spilling a drop. He and his witness drank the water and retrieved the key. Then, as he was having difficulty unlocking the door, the bride's relatives were teasing him, saying "*iavno ne gotov*" 'clearly he isn't ready'. This tall, athletic man snapped back at them: "*oni derzhat!*" 'They are holding it [the door]', as if to absolve himself of his inability to perform the task.

The groom's failures or successes become the focus of family stories, a way to both praise and ridicule him. A common task is to require the groom to sing in order to enter in the room where his bride is.[10] Marina K. reported that her husband has a tin ear, but that "love, that's a serious thing, and he sang like he had never sung in his life…. On that day he sang the song so well that even his mom looked up and her eyes were full of tears." Similarly, Veronika S. said that her husband was having trouble with the tasks: "And they ask the groom to solve riddles, but he can't guess them, and he screams from beyond the door, 'Veronika, I love you, but they won't let me in!'" Olga L. chided her husband slyly when she recounted the *vykup*, since he could not identify her lip prints, even though they had bought the lipstick together.

If there is any doubt that this is a challenge to the male social role, then one need only watch a *vykup* to see how the groom gets more and more frustrated as the tasks mount and he has to pay (or give goods) at every step, or so it seems. Veronika S. noted that some men resent the *vykup* and will try to get away with not paying by going over a balcony or in a window (on lower floors at least) or by using force. At one wedding, she said, she was one of the friends organizing the buying of the bride, and the groom wanted to show his power over them:

> I was at one wedding, and came away covered in bruises. We demanded something of the groom at every threshold, for the bride's beauty, give us this, for her braid, this, and he and his friends are pushing us aside and breaking through to the doors, only to not have to pay anything. For them it was like a point of pride to show their strength.

Just as in earlier eras, the *vykup* serves several purposes: ritual humiliation; connection to the Russian past through the revival of folk traditions; and the illustration of gender roles in the marriage, particularly the groom's role as a breadwinner.

Both the *devichnik* and the *vykup* are also tied to the role of marriage as an initiation into adulthood. Women gather now to celebrate the shift into married life, a significant reinterpretation of the original purpose of the *devichnik*, and yet also to say farewell to their childhoods, which is much more in keeping with the nineteenth-century ritual practice. In fact, given that most older couples do not bother with either of these practices, it would seem that weddings have taken on the role of adulthood initiation as well as marriage.[11]

---

[10] In some cases the singing is required not at the *vykup*, but at the reception after the bride has been "stolen" and hidden by friends.

[11] One exception was Tatiana D., whose neighbors unexpectedly demanded a *vykup* of cash and wine after they returned from the ZAGS, but it was not formally arranged by the bridal couple.

People throughout the study seemed to indicate that, as adults already (in their late twenties or older), they had no need for these ritual acts. They connected many wedding traditions with the youth of the participants, as a way not just to celebrate the wedding, but to show their entrance into adult life as a married couple. There were brides who did not have a *vykup*, even if they were younger, because the *vykup* is tied to acknowledging both adulthood and the transition into married life. One bride was pregnant with her husband's child when they married: "It seemed to me that buying was somehow stupid in my situation. Who would take me pregnant?" Tatiana S. had lived with her fiancé for a year, so that a *vykup* seemed disingenuous: "We had lived together practically a year before the wedding, and I said that I would have to go to mom's specially, set this all up, at a place I haven't lived for a year. And therefore I suggested that we do without it." In essence, both of these couples had already made the transition into "marriage" and adult relationships, by living and/or sleeping together, so that the *vykup* was not necessary for them, just as it was not for older couples.

From start to finish, folk practices have been revived and strengthened in the weddings of most younger couples. These revivals come from popular sources, such as the Internet or books, but also from the professional *tamada* that most couples now hire (discussed in more detail below). The tour of the city, a nineteenth-century tradition that the Soviets adapted to inculcate the couple's dedication to the state, continues today. While some couples do not now go to the eternal flame or World War II monuments, many of my informants did. In addition, the folk nature of the tour has been strengthened. Each city has a set of established places that couples visit to ensure that they will have a happy married life together. In St. Petersburg, Voronezh, and Kazan, for example, couples should cross at least seven bridges to bring good luck. The groom should carry the bride over at least one of those bridges. In Vladimir, one need not cross bridges, but the groom should carry the bride through the *Zolotye vorota* 'Golden Gate' in the center of town. In addition, at both the ZAGS and/or at the reception, couples have adopted the Western folk tradition of carrying the bride across the threshold. All these are physical representations of the social transition, of course, which, as Turner (1969, 28) notes, are characteristic of ritual. In addition, these practices point to the return of the groom's strength, after he had been powerless during the *vykup*. It also illustrates his role as bearer of both financial and physical burdens, represented by his new wife, whom he holds in his arms.

As part of the tour the couple often visits picturesque locales in or near the city, such as parks, forests, towers, or other elevated spots, all of which offer an excellent backdrop for photography. Given the current trend toward display in the wedding, these scenic areas allow for more memorable shots. In addition, they provide the opportunity for some tricks of perspective that illustrate stereotypical marital gender roles. In one common shot, for example, the bride is shot to look like a miniature person, while, through a trick of perspective, the groom holds her in his hand, as though she is a bridal doll, delicate and fragile. More rarely, the bride holds the groom in her hand as well. Most of those who had the bride holding the groom in her hand described how humorous it was, since she was the "more powerful" figure, in contrast to gender role expectations for the marriage. In other variations, the bride is lifted onto walls or other precarious perches, and is supported by the groom, who stands below her. These shots reinforce messages about the groom's strength and the bride's weakness. Interestingly, these concepts are derived from the Western romantic tradition based on chivalric ideals about male and female relationships. The Russian folk tradition emphasized the bride's contribution to the marriage as a worker, while the current Western one emphasizes her beauty and delicacy. The man, by contrast, performs acts that emphasize his role as breadwinner and his physical strength.

In the birth ritual, we saw the revival of religious belief and practices, both during the pregnancy and after delivery, with an increase in christenings. As in birth, informal religious acts have been restored in the wedding. It is now the norm for most couples to go to a sacred site, for example the Center of Russia Chapel in Novosibirsk (a church reconstructed on the site of one destroyed in order to erect a statue of Stalin), the monastery in Sergeev Posad, or the Kazansky Cathedral in Moscow, to light a candle or get some holy water.[12] However, a formal ceremony in a church is still rare. Only two couples of the nineteen who married in this period actually had a religious ceremony. Two brides wanted one, but their husbands have refused thus far. An additional complication with the wedding in comparison with a baptism, is that both participants must have been christened themselves. Thus an adult would have to take the extra step of being baptized before (s)he could marry in the church. As a result, even believers who remained unchristened during the Soviet period do not seem willing to go through the entire process. Instead, it seems to be enough to acknowledge one's beliefs by only visiting a church, without any official ceremony. Even for those who are not particularly religious, it should be noted that the churches offer a beautiful backdrop for photographs, a fact in keeping with the emphasis on the display in the post-Soviet Russian wedding as well as a return to "Russianness."

While people may not have religious wedding services, this does not mean that religion does not influence ceremonies in other ways. Galina V., the Vladimir ZAGS director, said that

> [n]ow Christian traditions have been very strongly reborn, people have begun to observe the fasts. A very large number of couples get married in church, accordingly we have few couples who have a formal ceremony during Lent.... During the fasts the tempo somehow

---

[12] Obviously these are couples in which both partners are "Orthodox," and not of mixed faiths or who include a non-believer.

slows down, although the summer fasts don't influence the number of weddings much. It is basically the Christmas fast and Lent.

Although it appears that the desire for a summer wedding can outweigh religious concerns, the ZAGS workers recognize the role that religion now plays in scheduling ceremonies. Natalia T.'s daughter, for example, first submitted a request to be married on April 25, but that year it was Good Friday: "And we told her that you wouldn't be able to do a wedding on Good Friday, because you can't eat, drink, or dance. And they register people only on Fridays, that's in a region [of the city] named 'Soviet'.... Therefore twenty-five minus a week would be exactly the eighteenth. So it turned out that she got married on the eighteenth, just like I did." Thus religious observances have affected not only the post-wedding tour of the city, but indeed the times that weddings occur. Religious services may not be required for the couple to be married, but other facets of religious belief do play a role in the post-Soviet wedding.

The reception also features the renewal of folk tradition, mainly because of the *tamada*. *Tamady* have been a tradition at Soviet Russian weddings for most of the twentieth century. They typically were friends or family members who had a lively sense of humor and spoke well in public, i.e., natural hosts. During the 1970s, *tamada* became a profession; they could be hired out from Houses of Culture or local clubs in order to host a wedding. In the post-Soviet world, "master of ceremonies" is a flourishing business. They are able to capitalize not only on the consumer economy and the desire for elaborate weddings, but also on the nostalgia for folk traditions. Most couples I interviewed had met with the *tamada* to find out what services (s)he offered and then chose what games and other amusements they wanted at their reception. Once the plan is set, the *tamada* brings the necessary props for the games and contests, including women's clothes for men's *riazhanie*, "Roma" outfits, and various other objects. Tanya K. described the male cross-dressing at her wedding: "They danced a can-can. One dressed like Alla Pugacheva and sang a song. It was the *tamada* who asked them to do it. She told them how to dress and what to do and if they agreed, then they got dressed up and did it." *Tamady* are generally responsible for entertaining the crowd, playing music, getting people to dance, and to participate in the games. A Russian-language Google search for *tamada* produced over 85,000 hits and shows that they are inextricably involved with the wedding business in general. These sites offer not only traditional services, but also videography and photography, cakes, musical acts, florists, and the like, making them closer to the role of wedding planners in the United States. Thus, the folk tradition is expanding through the new practices surrounding consumerism. The professional *tamada* represents two opposing worlds, the nostalgia for past tradition and the desire to take advantage of the consumer economy.

The games that the *tamada* organizes vary little from those that people included in previous decades. The first group of games are designed to predict the couple's future and help influence it. In the former category, games emphasize the couple's marital roles and family relationships. While some couples did perform tasks in previous decades that would predict who would be the head of the household, in the post-Soviet era they have become much more an integral part of the activities. Couples knew about the tradition of stepping first on the carpet in the ZAGS (parallel to stepping first into the aisle of the church in the pre-revolutionary period); and about biting more off the *karavai* as well as stepping on the groom's foot while receiving the *karavai*, to ensure that the bride would dominate the relationship. Other games make predictions about the couple's children, such as *kolgotki* 'stockings'. In that game the family collects money in blue and pink stockings to predict whether a boy or girl will be born first, as Liuba S. described for her daughter's 2002 wedding: "And we also collected money, I personally ran around, for a boy or a girl in stockings. If the guests want a boy, then they put money in the blue stockings, if a girl, then in the pink. But I gathered more for a boy. And she had a boy." Another common game involves predictions of what jobs the bride and groom will do in the marriage. Irina E., a Moscow pediatrician who married in 2000, described this game as follows:

> There were little slips of paper too, with phrases written on them: I will do the laundry, I will take care of the child, I will wash the floor, I will earn the money. And the groom and bride each take turns picking one and reading it. For us it turned out just as it should have. Dima will earn the money, I will raise the children. I have some domestic tasks, and he has financial ones.[13]

Similarly, the ritual in which brides have to sweep up money (and trash) described earlier (often on the second day) is maintained, but now money is often hung from 'cobwebs' that the bride has to sweep as well. This practice is in keeping with the Russian ritual tradition and not the Western one. While the jobs in these two games may be domestic chores, they emphasize work roles and each person's contribution to the relationship. They stand in stark contrast then to the ideal adopted from the Western chivalric tradition of the bride as a beautiful and helpless figure. Rather, she is expected to contribute in significant ways to family life.

The second type of game ritually abases the couple (or people associated with them, such as relatives or witnesses). For example, the couple's friends

---

[13] It is striking from an American perspective that a professional woman would consider her performance of domestic tasks as the norm. This comment is additional evidence of the distinct gender roles found not only in Russian families, but in the wedding ritual itself.

often "steal" the bride or her shoe through some ruse and someone is required to perform a task to get it back. For example, Olga L. had her shoe stolen, and her husband Dima had to carry her into the room. As he held her, his witness had to drink vodka out of her other shoe (a glass was placed in the heel to hold the liquor). Once he had done so, they returned the shoe. When the bride herself is "stolen," the groom or his witness have to perform an embarrassing task, such as singing a love song, so that their friends will return her. Or the couple has to perform tasks that show their love for each other. There is often an erotic component to these tasks, such as public kissing when people shout *gor'ko* 'bitter' and count to see how long the couple can kiss. In addition, most couples played *spichki*, in which matches are stuck into an apple, and the couple takes turns calling each other endearing terms, while removing a match. The first to not think of a term becomes the butt of the guests' jokes.

The games and contests the *tamada* arranges have seemingly become the center of the reception in the course of the last fifteen years. Several couples reported that the *tamada* was so demanding of their time that they were not able to eat or sit down at their own receptions. However, friends and family still play a large role in the celebration. Not only are they participants in the games, games that can influence the couple's future, but they also devise their own scenarios. Many people described how witnesses and friends gave a play or recited poetry or sayings and read humorous diplomas or certificates about marriage. One interesting fact is that these documents have become more overtly erotic than in the Soviet period. During *glasnost'*, sexual openness became associated with Western democracy and modernity. The wedding has come to represent the degree of "sophistication" of the participants not only in terms of its luxury, but with regard to sexual behavior as well. In short, the bride's physical characteristics and the couple's sexuality in general are now highlighted much more than in the past. This shift produces conflict in many women, according to some theorists, who embrace the fact that the consumer economy has provided them with the goods (clothing, cosmetics, etc.) to escape from what Kay (1997, 82) calls Soviet "austerity and hardship." Yet many resent the fact that they are reduced to sexual beings, whose intellect is of little import in evaluating their social and professional contributions (see Johnson and Robinson 2007; Kay 1997; Lissyutkina 1993 for a discussion of this issue).

These antics not only serve to poke fun at the couple and their families, but also bring them good fortune. The guests' participation is important in wishing the couple well, in providing both material and emotional support as they start their new lives. While the Russian wedding may have become more commercial, it is still intimately tied to the wider social network. Since the reception is the most important part of the wedding, the guests' gift giving and well-wishes are key to a successful transition into marital happiness. While the gifts may be more elaborate, the toasts that accompany them as they are being presented, the sharing of food and the ritual acts all promote a sense of belonging to the community and help the couple make the transition to their new social roles.

The increased consumerism in the wedding ritual has not produced the same degree of social stress that it has in the birth ritual. Weddings, after all, have always required financial outlay. No Soviet family expected a free wedding. Even the ZAGS had registration fees during the Soviet era, so that each step in the wedding cost money. Therefore the increased expense and display in the post-Soviet wedding seem a natural result of wanting to celebrate a wedding properly, as Russians have always done. There is no real divide between the haves and the have-nots, as there is in the maternity hospitals, which seemingly provide "good" care only for the well-to-do. Any couple can have a proper wedding (with their family's help and support).

We have discussed how the wedding couple in Soviet Russia relied on a variety of sources in the negotiation of their identities, some of which were in direct conflict with one another. In the post-Soviet period the conflicts have grown even stronger. Women are faced with three symbolic systems in establishing their role as wives. One that has become even more prominent is the class-based conception, imported from Western countries, that bases the bride's value on her beauty and delicacy. While this image certainly existed in the Soviet period, it has become a major focus in media images of women in post-Soviet Russia. It combines with the emphasis on conspicuous consumption in the wedding, so that much of her beauty is the result of purchasing goods and services, from wedding gowns to make-up artists. In some sense, this phenomenon is a rejection of the "bleakness" of Soviet-era weddings, but also a response to the allure of what Yurchak called the "Imaginary West" (2006, 159) and the shift toward capitalist ideals in attitudes toward the female body and in consumption. While some women object to the view of their bodies as their primary asset, they do not seem to resent the capitalist system in the wedding in the same way that they do in birth, perhaps, as noted above, because weddings are a joyous occasion that has always entailed expense.

At the same time, women are faced with two competing ideals with regard to their social position, both of which are reflected in the wedding. The government (and its post-Soviet maternity policies) tells women that their primary social role is not as a working professional, but as a mother, so that the wedding reception now features games, such as *kolgotki* 'stockings' and *listochki* 'slips of paper', in which women's role as mother and homemaker is highlighted. This is not to say that the folk and Soviet traditions did not view weddings as the entry point into childbearing and homemaking, but that the messages about motherhood were offset by Soviet images of women as professionals or folk messages of balance in familial work roles. Nevertheless, despite the rejection of some Soviet ideology about family life and a resurgence of folk tradition in an attempt to restore their "Russianness," most middle-class people assume that women will work outside the home as a matter of course. Gal and Kligman (2000, 113) note that "even with the advent of the 'stay-at-home wife' as a new status symbol, most women want to continue working for wages, even if their families do not need the money." The equality among the sexes that the Soviets espoused does not seem to be the sole impetus for this phenomenon (although it surely plays a role in couples' assumptions that women will pursue a career), but the fact is that without the income families cannot survive in these difficult economic times. Even if the folk material instructs a woman that her role is to fulfill traditional domestic tasks, she cannot accept only that role. She must also fulfill the ideal of beauty queen that the wedding highlights and she must work outside the home to survive in the current economic climate. Gal and Kligman (113) conclude: "What seem like the same activities are recontextualized; they gain new meanings and consequences as their texts have changed."

The wedding exemplifies this situation. The consumerist messages contained within the Soviet-era wedding have provided the basis for an easy bridge to an overtly consumerist wedding celebration in the post-Soviet period. However, it no longer illustrates the government's support of the family, but even more strongly conveys the image of the family as an independent provider within a capitalist society. It also brings with it a new view of women's bodies, which represents a rejection of Soviet-era ideology about women as well as yet another means to embrace consumerism.

The introduction of capitalism, however, has produced its own crisis in the family. As a result, the populace does not always view capitalism as a positive force. Soviet Russian women were expected to work to match Soviet ideals for gender equality. Post-Soviet Russian women also must work, not to live up to an ideal, but to survive within the new economic environment. While Soviet women also worked to survive, as we have discussed, the transition has brought with it a sense of insecurity that did not exist in the Soviet context. Shtulhofer and Sandfort (2005, 7) conclude that this crisis emerges from the shift in society from a secure, planned economy to a volatile, capitalist model: "Economic and social hardship, rising unemployment (due to the closing of large production units), erosion of family savings, and the breakdown of community ties ... had a direct impact on marital and family dynamics." Kiblitskaia (2000, 66–67) notes that the post-Soviet Muscovite women she interviewed "feel deserted by the state, which no longer guarantees them employment, no longer glorifies and supports their role as mothers, and no longer provides them with a safety net. As a result, they have turned inwards, to concentrate on their families." Zdravomyslova and Temkina (2005, 110) express the dilemma that women face in the post-Soviet world in establishing their social roles as wives and mothers:

The model of the working mother is legitimised by the Soviet tradition, stretching over several generations, of mass women's employment, moral and economic responsibility for family life and natural-ised motherhood.... In the post-Soviet version the duties of the "working mother" are not a civil obligation. The privatisation of motherhood and the removal of parenthood from the sphere of civic duties are combined with personal choice for women. The duty to participate in social production has been replaced by an economic need to provide for one's family, which has necessitated a more active role for women in the sphere of paid work.

In sum, the wedding demonstrates the continuation of a complicated array of expectations for the Russian woman. She must still struggle to balance the social demands of domestic life derived from folk belief, the romantic chival-ric ideal, and the post-Soviet expectation of making a financial contribution.

While certain aspects of daily life have been recontextualized, as Gal and Kligman assert, we cannot conclude absolutely that the systems have been thoroughly remade in all cases. Rather, Kay (2002, 59) contends that many of the conceptions about gender that existed in the Soviet period have actually continued with little challenge. Couples continue to conform to ideas that are inherited from the Soviet era, which seem natural and are not subject to de-bate. Women function in the private sphere as mothers and "guardians of the hearth," while men are public actors who provide for, protect, and support their families and wives. She (1997, 94) argues:

> Nor can women's own responses and thinking on these issues be en-tirely divorced from that [Soviet] legacy, the convictions of which have, in places, survived the ideology which bore them. Moreover, claims that the totalitarian state which interfered with personal and family decisions regarding life-style choices has been swept aside and replaced with a new "democracy" supporting individual freedom and self-determination are belied by the pervasiveness with which "new" but equally restrictive stereotypes are now propounded.

The folk material provides an excellent example of a system that was firmly rooted in the Soviet period and continues to function much as it did then. The folk practices in the wedding still convey the message that women should be primary actors in the domestic sphere. At the same time, they serve, as they have always done, to resist remnants of Soviet ideology and to define "Rus-sianness." In fact, the even greater resurgence of folk beliefs in the wedding indicates that in the post-Soviet period folk tradition is being used to establish a sense of cultural unity in response to what people felt they had lost in the Soviet period. People have tried to reclaim their heritage over the last fifteen years, a fact that is particularly important within a nation that has undergone a social crisis of identity itself.

At first glance, it seems that men have fewer conflicting messages, since the Soviet, Western, and folk material all overlap to convey that he should be a provider for his family. However, men have indeed had trouble adjusting to post-Soviet expectations for their roles in the family. Issoupova (2000, 42) discusses how the press has created an idealized version of the father that calls for the institution of a Western Protestant model of the man as the sole breadwinner, who also takes an active role in child rearing. This role is a direct contrast to the native folk and Orthodox view of paternity, in which a father and husband was responsible for his family's financial stability, but his social acts were primarily directed outward toward the community. As we have seen, this was a pattern that the Soviet Union took advantage of in its own family ideology. Issoupova concludes that it is an "open question" whether men will accept this obligation for themselves, which "highlights one of the key areas of tension in Russia's new pattern of gender relations." In fact, another study on male roles in the family from the Soviet to the post-Soviet period confirms this dilemma. Kukhterin (2000, 88) argues that men and women have different views of their definitions of the male as the head of the household. For women, he is "someone who takes over some of the responsibility for the home"; for men he is "a breadwinner whose word is treated as law." Kukhterin's data (86, 88) suggest that men continue to hold onto the latter definition, working longer hours to bring in more money and preserving their role as public agents by socializing with business contacts after work.

We cannot conclude, however, that men have assumed an absolutist patriarchal stance. As noted above, most assume as a matter of course, despite current ideals regarding the full-time homemaker, that their wives will work. This belief stems not only from the current economic climate, but from Soviet ideology about women workers. Rands Lyon (2007, 32) notes that the men she interviewed want their wives at home all the time, "but none of them felt that they had the right to insist on such an arrangement. Most recognized that their wives' incomes were helpful to their families, but they also respected their wives' desire—and right—to work." Women, indeed, express their desire to work for personal development, self-satisfaction, and independence (Kay 2002, 63–64). However, this state of affairs can cause a crisis in identity for men, who feel that they are not living up to the social standards demanded of them (see Olson 2004, 160ff. for an interesting consideration of the crisis in masculine identity and the renewed interest in the overtly macho Cossack culture). Kiblitskaia (2000, 96), Ashwin (2000b, 2) and Rands Lyon (2007, 28), among others, have argued that men have had a more difficult time adapting to the shift toward a capitalist economy. The state had assumed a portion of the role as provider in the Soviet period, so that men did not entirely support their families. In the current economic climate, most men cannot live up to the expectations for being a sole provider, even if they would wish to. Finally, they are less flexible than their wives, since their identities have been so defined by public and professional roles. Women, who always could rely on the centrality of their role in the family, do not feel the same threat to identity when they shift to a less prestigious career or lose their job (Kalabikhina 2004, 196; Gal and Kligman 2000, 68–69). However, my data indicate that this is an oversimplification of the stress women face when negotiating their social and familial roles in post-Soviet Russia. Many women are unhappy with the state of affairs, which demands such a wide array of divergent expectations from them, while many men have adapted readily to the new capitalist ethos and their family roles within it. At the same time, these same men and women expressed support for "egalitarian decision making" on major family issues. However, they did note that there was a division of labor, to some extent, so that wives had the final word with regard to the children, while husbands made the decisions regarding major household purchases and the car (Rands Lyon 32–33).

The wedding epitomizes, for both men and women, a conflicting series of beliefs about familial roles in post-Soviet society. Women face the same essential conflicts they did in the Soviet period. However, the emphasis on conspicuous consumption and physical beauty is now contrasted to material inherited both from Soviet ideology and folk traditions. People perceive the latter to be native "Russian" elements that are opposed to imported Western ideals. At first glance, men received the same messages from both the folk tradition and Soviet ideology about their mission in professional and public life—as a provider for the family's needs. Nevertheless, they must also grapple with the non-native notion that if they are to become good husbands, they must serve as the *sole* breadwinner, who also plays a central role in child rearing and domestic chores. This is contrasted to native conceptions of the husband as family patriarch, who was not involved in the daily demands of domestic life. Yet he must simultaneously respect Soviet notions about equality between the spouses and his wife's right to work (and indeed in most cases, financial necessity for her to work). The wedding then illustrates the dissonance characteristic of post-Soviet society in microcosm. In the larger world, as in the wedding, "Russian" elements based on revived folk beliefs and Soviet norms are opposed to Western capitalist ideals, and ritual participants must negotiate a complicated series of messages to establish their identities as husbands and wives.

Funerals in the Post-Soviet World

While the funeral had been the most conservative ritual of the three under consideration throughout the Soviet period, even it has also been altered over the last decade. The most prominent change has been the introduction of funeral service businesses. Those who arranged funerals over the last five years typically called in one of these companies to prepare the body, order the casket, and make the necessary funeral arrangements.[14] Natalia S. compared the situation in Soviet times to the current day: "They invite special older women from their courtyard or from some church, they come, wash and dress it [the body]. Now of course there are ritual services, they ask them and they do everything." The service may remove the body from the home to the morgue or they may perform these tasks at home. For example, Tatiana U. described the latter situation: "My dad died at home. We hired a service. They came to the house, dressed him, et cetera. And he was at home for two nights." In more and more cases, the services take the body to the morgue. At this point, the person may be buried directly from the morgue or may be brought home for one night, as was done in the Soviet period if someone died in the hospital. Liudmila B. explained:

> When it [the body] is in the morgue, the embalming happens there, they perform all the procedures and bury from the morgue. All the mourners come to the morgue. Sometimes the car with the deceased comes to the house where he lived, they carry out the coffin so that neighbors can say farewell to him. And then they take it to the cemetery.

Other informants said that it is important for the deceased to spend at least one night at home, even if (s)he was taken to the morgue by the funeral service or died in a hospital. Marina K. reported:

> It is the norm that, when they collect the deceased from the morgue, it is necessary for it to be home one night. They put the coffin at home with the head toward the window, legs toward the doors. They place candles, pour water, on the glass with the water they put a piece of bread. It is thought that its soul is hovering somewhere around. Or they pour vodka. Either way, some water, some vodka.

However, it is clear that there has been a shift, so that death is more removed from the family circle. As Olga D. put it, "[I]n big cities it is already unacceptable for them [funerals] to be at home." While there are many factors involved, including the age of the deceased, family tradition, and financial concerns, funeral businesses have become the norm, rather than the exception, over the last decade.

---

[14] At the same time they also depended on the family. Some who arranged funerals during this time still maintained the Soviet traditions of wakes in the family home which the family and friends organize. I would note, however, that this was generally the norm when senior citizens died. Those who died at a younger age often were prepared for burial by a funeral company.

   Another common change is the shift of the funeral meal to outside the home. For example, Alexander U. said that "now they don't do them [*po-minki*] at home." His wife added that while the *pominki* on the ninth and the fortieth days might still be at home, those on the day of the funeral are often at a *stolovaia* 'cafeteria'. Lidia C. expressed a similar opinion: "For *pominki* the last place of employment responds, gives access to the cafeteria, et cetera. Once again it is easier, because this is ritual food, it was easier to make in a cafeteria in big pots." Elena P. expressed similar sentiments:

> We ordered [the meal]. We had mom's in a cafeteria.... It depends on money. How much money someone has, however much one can manage, that's what one does. If there is someone to cook, after all lots of people come, you have to cook in advance. It is uncomfortable to cook if the deceased is lying in the next room.... It is better not to have it that way.

While this change does make it easier for people, since they do not have to prepare a meal for large numbers of mourners, it also is a significant altera-tion in the attitude toward the funeral. As Elena's comment shows, money is now a primary concern. This rite has become much more closely associated with the consumer economy than in the Soviet period. In some ways these developments make things easier for the family, as these informants have noted, but in other ways the role of finances in the funeral complicates matters, both for the individual and for the society at large.

   The financial situation has caused some concern among my informants, particularly older ones. With inflation and the economic crises in recent years, those who had saved for their funerals to help their children, now think they will not be able to afford them. Klara K., for example, said that she had a good savings account for that purpose, but the currency revaluation and inflation had reduced her life savings to nothing. She was concerned that this would place an undue burden on her family when she died. Many people made reference to the expense surrounding a funeral (a factor also in the Soviet pe-riod certainly). Merridale (2000, 341) also discusses how her informants were worried about the expense of a funeral in post-Soviet Russia. As a result, con-tributing to the funeral fund has become an important role for mourners. While people always helped financially in Soviet Russia, more informants in the post-Soviet period reported that they gave money (and not other kinds of help, such as cooking or making arrangements).

   Like weddings, funerals have always cost money in the Soviet Union. One did not have had to pay for a burial plot, but one did have to pay for the funeral meals and coffin as well as give items or cash to people who prepared the body and dug the grave and the like. However, there seems to be a different attitude toward the funeral expenses in post-Soviet Russia than those in wedding celebrations. This reaction is akin to the one we saw in our discussion of post-socialist childbirth. A two-tiered system has been created for both birth and burial. Families who can afford more have an easier time, since the funeral service and the cafeterias provide support for them that families of more modest means cannot afford. As a result families with lower incomes still have to rely on friends and family to have a proper funeral. Money is a concern at all levels, as Natalia P. noted: "Relatives give money, they help as they can, because the material situation is so bad." Natalia T. expanded on this idea in her comments:

> Now it is a little bit different, you can put everything on strangers. It was not an agency before, but coworkers, those with whom he [the deceased] worked.... Once in Russia, before the 1990s, before commercialization, everything depended on relatives and on friends and acquaintances, absolutely everything ... and now that is still true in many ways. If you have money, you buy everything, but that's a lot of money. The majority of the population does not have that kind of money, and all the same everything depends on good relations, on good people, on friends and acquaintances.

Alexander U. expressed his opinion of the current situation in funerals succinctly: "And now, if you pay, everyone will come, even a whole car lot." People can no longer rely on employers and the state to help with funeral expenses.[15] In the post-Soviet world the situation has become one that emphasizes the divide between people, between those who have thrived in the consumer economy and those who have not.

Seemingly, times of potential crisis (both birth and death) result in a great deal of anger about the current system. In contrast, the wedding is a joyous occasion, which may be modest and still be a proper celebration of the union. Thus it would appear that there is less concern about wedding expenses, since they are promoted not by a crisis, but by individual decisions about how to celebrate. However, in matters of life and death, the attitude of my informants is that post-Soviet society (and in particular the Western consumer economy model it adopted) has betrayed them. They do not have access to the fundamental services needed to ensure that future generations will be born healthy and that past generations will be properly honored. If people cannot afford these things so essential to life, then resentment naturally follows. The association of birth and death with business makes the society as a whole seem much less supportive than in the Soviet period. As Natalia T. noted, many things still depend on good friends and family, communal involvement in ritual is still key. Nevertheless, those who charge for their services are perceived

---

[15] The state still does bury veterans at its own expense. Two informants had state support for the funerals of their relatives who were World War II veterans during this period.

as mercenary for turning a profit from family hardship. The economic and cultural divide between the well-off and families of modest means grows ever wider as a result.

Urban Russians are reacting to the shift to capitalism, as noted above in the introduction to this chapter, in much the same way that Scott's Malay farmers (1985, 184) did. They resent the capitalist system and make reference to established patterns derived from Soviet and folk beliefs. While the cities of the Soviet Union were clearly not agrarian villages, they too were characterized by what Scott calls the "negotiated, moral context," in which the community supported and defined itself through interdependence. Soviet citizenship was based on a concrete set of *dukhovnye tsennosti* 'spiritual values' about the collective, greed, and social equality, which were adopted by large portions of the population. As Yurchak has shown, and as we have demonstrated in this study, the moral code contained within Soviet ideology established a cohesive national identity. Capitalism undermines many of these notions about morality and results in a society in which business and finance are more important than community support. This state of affairs has resulted in resentment about the society's shift toward profiting from its fellow citizens, rather than supporting them in times of need.

Those associated with official institutions in all three life-cycle rituals, as we have discussed, have been characterized by their bureaucratic officiousness. For example, many people cited problems they had with cemeteries that would not allow families to be buried together. The post-Soviet era has at least brought some relief in this area. Elvira A., who complained that her mother could not be buried next to her grandfather in 1984, said that this Vladimir cemetery had begun to allow this practice since the end of the 1990s. At the same time, while some changes in the funeral arrangements allow for more flexibility, as in other rituals, some remnants of the old problems remain. For example, Olga L. asserted that one must have connections in order to be buried in the "best" Voronezh cemetery: "The cemetery in which people want to be buried most of all, because it is accessible, not far ... there everything is decided by *blat*, I would say that eighty percent of the people, if someone has some acquaintances and agrees somehow in general, then the funeral can begin." This apparently is not an isolated problem, since Valentin P. made the same remark about the Novosibirsk cemetery where his father-in-law is buried.

One change that indicates the greater flexibility of society is the reintroduction of religious practice in the funeral rite. Most of my informants mentioned the post-Soviet changes in the area of religion. While, as I have discussed, there were some religious components to funerals during the Soviet period, they were often hidden within the home. In fact, it was the one ritual that retained the greatest number of religious associations, as Olga L. noted: "In Soviet times if people went to church, it was associated precisely with funerals." Certainly a funeral mass at the graveside was generally not an option.

Nor were openly religious items buried with the corpse. However, the religious practices in the funeral were the best preserved. Since the fall of the Soviet Union, funerals have become more and more religious, not surprisingly, given these traditional attitudes. In fact, unlike in baptismal or marriage rites, participants themselves need not be believers to have an Orthodox funeral. Tatiana D. described just such a situation: "When we buried my aunt, she never believed in God, her friends said that we had to invite a priest. And we invited a priest to the house. It is interesting. I myself saw how they perform the funeral mass, right here, before they bury [someone]." The religious funeral rites may occur, as in this case, at the home, or people might take the deceased to the church before burial. In rare instances, the priest may come to the graveside. Alexander U. noted that the priest may say the mass at home and also go to the cemetery. Nina S. described one funeral that she had recently attended which had a full religious service:

> For Evgeny Pavlovich we went to the home, there are many flowers, five wreaths. In his hand he is holding a small icon and at his head two candles are burning. And a lamp is lit. They took him from his house to the house which he built with his own hands near Vladimir.... There they unloaded him from the car in which they were transporting him again, put him on stools, and a religious worker, either a Catholic priest or an Orthodox one, began the prayer for the dead. He read something, then together with another man, they sang something. Then they walked around the coffin with a censer. That was about forty minutes. Then once again they put him into the car, into the hearse, and we went to the church. At the church they put the coffin in the designated place where they say the mass for the dead, once again a funeral service for the dead.

Some aspects of the *otpevanie* ritual had been preserved in families (albeit without a priest present) during the Soviet period, such as sprinkling a cross of dirt on the deceased's chest. However, now the priest openly performs all these rituals, as Ekaterina Z. related:

> The Father reads prayers, censes. The choir sings in response to him. Then he obligatorily says parting words. This depends on who died and who is present. Usually it has a comforting effect on people. I know that the Father puts in a type of note, a prayer of absolution.... The Father blesses earth and then sprinkles it in the shape of a cross.

Other religious markers that informants named include a religious text in the coffin (Bible, prayers, psalter), a band with a prayer on the deceased's forehead, and a lit candle in hi(s)her hands.

Liudmila B., who was born in 1932, said that the resurgence in religious ritual causes some concern for people of her age:

> In general recently they follow our Orthodox traditions more, they try to observe them more, because we lost something somewhere…. Now they are trying to revive them. It is hard. People of our circle, we also don't know everything, can't do everything, sometimes probably do things not how they should be done. But we want to observe tradition, the faith of our people. We ourselves were raised outside of these traditions. We are not fervent atheists, but we were raised that there was no God. We try to know, to learn…. We lived for so many years without all that, and it is so hard to come to it.

Given that it is important for both the repose of the soul and for the living to have a proper burial, these concerns are serious. If one performs the ritual improperly then it fails to achieve its goals. Even if people do not know why they perform these rites, they continue to do them in this way, Liuba S. explained: "Over many years of Soviet rule proper behavior was destroyed, but some things are passed on and in critical moments people tried to perform as they should, as was once bequeathed. Maybe it is not really understood, but that is the way it is done and that's it, they do it that way." The return of religious aspects of the ritual is thus both a comfort and a source of stress. In addition to such concerns, people also expressed dismay that the return of Orthodoxy actually adds to the expense of the funeral. Alexander K., for example, said they did not have a mass, because they did not have the money to pay for a priest. In this sense, the return of the church is connected not only to lost tradition, but also to the consumer economy. For the church to survive, of course, it must have funds, funds provided by donations for funeral masses and prayers among them.

One interesting difference between Soviet and post-Soviet funerals is the limited use of the brass and wind ensemble that played at most Soviet-era funerals. As I have argued, the associations between the state and the deceased were not firmly established. People regarded the role of coworkers as a representation of a personal connection between the dead and the living. They overlooked or ignored the Soviet goal of connecting a person primarily to his working life and to the institution, not to his family. Not surprisingly then, the one true Soviet innovation in the funeral, the brass ensemble, has fallen by the wayside. However, they do still play at the funerals of veterans, to acknowledge their sacrifice for the state, or of public figures, who are intimately associated with the state as an institution, either locally or on a larger scale. As we can see, for those who logically were associated with the Soviet Union (such as veterans) or with the government (such as political leaders), the brass ensemble that makes clear this relationship (and the original intent

of the Soviet-era funeral in this regard) is the one remnant of the Soviet funeral to survive the transition to a republic.

Other religious commemorations of the dead have also been restored.
People not only order masses on various important anniversaries of the death
(such as the ninth and fortieth days), but also visit the grave around Easter
and on *roditel'skie subboty* 'Parents' Saturdays'. For example, Olga R. said that
she had visited the cemetery recently on the Parents' Saturday during the
Pentecost (lit. 'Trinity') holiday in late spring: "It was Trinity Day recently, it
is the custom to go on Trinity, Parent's Day. There were lots of people at the
cemetery. There was a service there, the priest said a prayer, then they put up
little houses, so that you could put up a candle. You could buy icons." While
there is a commercial aspect to the ceremony (the church sold icons and candles), the goal of these events is to once again unite as a family to remember
and honor the dead. Liudmila B. reported that now the government is also involved in promoting such remembrances: "Our city government especially
organizes buses on those [Parents'] days to the cemetery, because the cemetery is outside the city and not everyone has a car." Such public acknowledgements of the bond between religion and the state show the shift in attitudes toward faith broadly. Instead of the state sending the message that the
primary social role of the deceased is as a worker, they now highlight hi(s)her
connection to the family (and to the church) by enabling people to get access
to the graves on religious holidays.

While the government, in this case, is showing more support for familial
traditions in the funeral, a common feature of all three life-cycle rituals is the
perception that the state has betrayed the family in the post-Soviet era. This
shift in the attitude appears inconsistent to previous decades, given the resentment toward the lack of support in the Soviet era of which we have seen
evidence in these rites. However, Gal and Kligman (2000, 69) connect this apparent disconnect to nostalgia for the stable, socialist period in the face of
social upheaval:

> But today, nostalgic memory often constructs the communist-era fam-
> ily as autonomous from the corruption of the state and politics. The
> private household continues to be valued as the place where people
> live their honest, authentic, and meaningful lives. In the communist
> era the danger was understood to be the intrusiveness of the state;
> now it is more often the uncertainty and untrustworthiness of state
> action and the insecurity of markets and employment.

Kalabikhina's informants (2004, 200–01) assert that what they wish for is a
return of "Soviet social guarantees," with particular emphasis on "secure stable jobs and decent wages … future of children, good education for them …
good health for themselves and family members … decent housing … stability in the economy and business, paying off debts … protection by laws."

They make particular reference to the "growing disparity of living standard [sic] between people," an issue of much concern (Kalabikhina 197). The life-cycle rituals themselves highlight the fear of not being able to provide for one's family in times of need. If the family, which is idealized as the "place where people live their honest, authentic, and meaningful lives," is threatened by the current socio-economic system, then the Soviet Union, which provided these services for the populace, is likewise idealized. Boym (2001, 44–49) examines the "restorative nostalgia" for the Soviet Union, which reconstructs "emblems and rituals of home and homeland in an attempt to conquer time" to return to a simpler age.

This type of reflective nostalgia occurs in the rites themselves. Ritual actors are faced with a government that has abandoned idealism in favor of what is viewed as greed and corruption at the expense of the populace they are supposed to protect. Thus, even the social supports the post-socialist government promises fall short (e.g., late and/or minimal pensions or stipends for children, inferior public medical care and the poor quality of public education, drastic inflation in staple foods, utilities, and rents and the like). Kiblitskaia (2000, 66) and Tartakovskaia (2000, 127, 133) argue that both citizens and the press assert that the post-Soviet state has abandoned its obligations to the family and does not support it as the Soviet government did. Issoupova (2000, 43) notes that "many articles imply that the post-communist state has reneged on what still tend to be perceived as its parental responsibilities ... what is usually noted in such articles is the insufficiency of state support, and the consequent fall of the birthrate and increased incidence of child poverty." In the life-cycle rites of crisis, namely birth and death, this conflict between two social experiences is emphasized. People both resent the Soviet system that left them with inadequate religious and folk beliefs and yet wish the current government provided like the Soviet state is perceived to have done.[16] In the wedding, the dissonance is less severe, but does emerge in the definition of male and female roles in the family. As a result, Soviet ideology has merged with the religious and folk traditions as a unified "native" belief system, which stands in stark contrast to the values of the capitalist pluralist society Russia has become.

---

[16] Certainly age plays a role, so that those who remember the Soviet Union, like the majority of those in this study, have a different attitude than those in the youngest generation. Shtulhofer and Sandfort (2005, 4) and Kalabikhina (2004, 197) note that the older generations do long for a return of the Soviet Union, while younger people do not, although they may still wish for the reintroduction of social services the socialist state provided.

Negotiating Identity in Post-Soviet Life-Cycle Rituals

In the post-Soviet world participants in life-cycle ritual have adopted a consumerist perspective. These three rites convey the idea that people should
embrace the consumer ethos in order to be proper members of society. This
message can produce a great deal of conflict, since people cannot participate
fully in the "best" aspects of the system. In weddings this seems to be less of a
problem, because one can tailor the ritual to one's means. However, childbirth
and funerals do not offer that option. People having a child must pay beyond
their means or resort to public health care, which is seen as a poor alternative.
Likewise, citizens must face the costs demanded by funeral services to properly bury a loved one. Without family and community support, be it financial,
as the current economy demands, or domestic (preparing meals and sewing
clothing), then the rituals will not fulfill enough of their desired function. For
this reason, the level of community involvement inherited from the village
and strengthened by Soviet practices has retained its importance in the post-
Soviet world. In the Soviet period people could not obtain what they needed
without connections and help. Now citizens can buy anything they might
need, but are limited in funds, so that a pool of resources from family (and often from their connections) is required to perform a rite. Families certainly
still contribute in kind, that is, they organize the rituals, cook, and provide
non-financial support. Thus, their role is just as strong, if not stronger, in the
post-Soviet era.
     The range of folk traditions has also been revived much more enthusias-
tically over the last fifteen years. Rejuvenation of both the secular and the
religious folk practices serves several purposes. It illustrates the power of the
Russian folk, who were able to survive the trials of the Soviet period somewhat intact. As a result, the nation itself is seen as vibrant, as one that retains
a special quality that distinguishes it from the West. This attitude is particularly important at a time when Western ideas seem to be threatening the
social fabric of the culture. In addition, reconnecting with tradition makes the
rituals more "authentic," more Russian in participants' minds. Olson (2004,
123; 138ff.) examines how people connect performance of folk music and
dance to national identity on a fundamental level. In particular, folk language
and music, as Pesman (2000, 81) discusses, are perceived to be an essential
component of the conception of the Russian "soul." I would argue that folk
ritual also performs similar, if not identical, functions for participants, and we
must now consider the role of the folk revival in rites as part of an ongoing,
broader social process.
     To some extent, revived folk traditions mark the fact that people have
moved beyond the Soviet Union and rejected many of its ideals. They have
survived a difficult period during which everyone suffered, because there
were few goods in the stores to have proper rituals, because people were ex-
iled, because religion was officially taboo. At the same time, there is a pro-

found nostalgia for the Soviet world, such that many informants recall with fondness a simpler time, during which they could count on each other and also were citizens of a nation that was a major player on the world stage. As a result, Soviet-era traditions have not all been lost. Trips to the eternal flame after weddings and brass music at the funerals of veterans honor this period in history. Thus, there is no call, for example, to pull down the wedding palaces or to insist only on religious weddings. In fact, the ZAGS has become even more central to the wedding rite through the incorporation of consumerist trappings. The ceremony at the wedding palace, however mundane it may still be to some, is a Soviet-era tradition that has continued unquestioned and is necessary for a "proper" wedding.

Johnson and Robinson (2007b, 3) conclude that "[m]ore individual freedom enhances the ability to resist being categorized as one particular gender construction. However, if the market and its domination merely replace the domination of the central coercive state, then there may be more choices, but not a substantive change in the gendered order." I would argue that this statement applies to all the familial roles under consideration here and not just to gender identity. Soviet norms and folk traditions may have been tempered, and in some cases replaced, with Western consumerist ideology. Nevertheless ritual actors still create their social roles on the basis of the same information about their positions as parents and children, mourners and deceased, husbands and wives as they did throughout the Soviet period. Practice theorists contend that ritual is, according to Bell (1997, 79), "the means for mediating enduring cultural structures and the current situation. It is through ritual practice that culture molds consciousness in terms of underlying structures and patterns, while current realities simultaneously instigate transformations of those very structures and patterns as well." In post-Soviet Russian life-cycle rites, older symbolic codes evolve through the renegotiation of family roles in the face of an unfamiliar social system based on consumption and plurality. At the same time, these rituals codify established patterns to define Russianness in the face of a social crisis in identity and, as Gal and Kligman (2000, 114) assert, "what appear to be new arrangements and solutions are given legitimacy and authority by linking them to old patterns."

Chapter 7

The Soviet Ritual Complex

The life-cycle rituals we have studied demonstrate the complexity of negotiating family identity in the last four decades of the Soviet Union. They were created, as we have seen, on the basis of three distinct sources: Soviet ideology; folk and religious tradition; and consumerist ideals, scientific practices and philosophical theories adopted from the West. Nevertheless, these three sources meshed to form a coherent system which people relied upon to create and establish their social roles. While one might expect the public ceremonies to highlight only official ideology, we have found that the birth and wedding rites ritual specialists devised included material from all three sources. Funerals, in contrast, generally contained only Soviet and folk/religious practices and were largely unaffected by Western tradition, being the rite most resistant to change of any kind. Through life-cycle rituals, people balanced the desire to be middle class (simply put, the desire for material comforts) as endorsed by the state with communist morality consonant with official state norms. At the same time, people preserved family traditions derived from folk and religious beliefs, practices that were sometimes in direct conflict with the Soviet morality the state rituals espoused. In other cases, these folk acts actually supported the state's goals and ideology for citizens and their families and were incorporated into the system wholeheartedly.

Despite the fact that the rituals are part of the same symbolic system, they are not absolutely parallel. In many ways, birth and funeral rites share a symbolic system that the wedding does not. These two life crisis rites retained their connections to religion and folk belief much more effectively than the wedding. While the birth rite was heavily influenced by medicalization of the pregnancy and delivery, many of the decisions about how medical authorities behaved within this process were derived from folk beliefs, from isolation of the mother and child to removal of the mother's jewelry to prevent the umbilical cord from choking the baby. Nevertheless, the birth ritual also conveyed the Soviet-era conception that women were the center of the family unit and dedicated primarily to child rearing before all else. The funeral rite also preserved the bulk of its symbolic content from the nineteenth century, even if priests no longer performed the ceremonies. However, ritual theorists largely remade the marriage ritual in the decades following World War II.

Although folk practices were retained (or reinstituted), this rite reflected more Soviet-era ideology about gender roles in society and family identity than the other two rituals. This was largely the case because many folk beliefs actually conformed to official ideology. Beyond reconceptualizing the man's role as patriarch and pushing women into the work force, men's and women's roles in marriage were largely consonant with the state's conservative views (and nineteenth-century folk beliefs) about the family. The state never actually re-made family responsibilities by instituting true equality and, in fact, wanted to remove men from the familial sphere to make inroads into government control of the family.

The combination of three distinct traditions produced rituals indicative of significant historical trends in the conceptions of familial and gender roles from the 1950s through the end of the Soviet era. As the ideas about the cen-trality of the family in Soviet society and citizen's roles within the family and society changed, ritual actors adapted their ceremonies to these shifting needs and ideological positions both to remake the system and to conform to its demands. Within this period, women's roles shifted from worker, demon-strating the Bolshevik dedication to equality, to worker-mother/homemaker, the latter becoming more and more important over the years. Men, on the other hand, maintained a fairly consistent position as public figures and breadwinners who were effectively removed from their nineteenth-century family roles as patriarchs.

Because the system had not truly restructured the family and work roles within it, women resented the fact that they had two jobs (one professional and one in the home) and blamed their husbands for not providing adequate support around the house. At the same time, men were seeing their tradi-tional role in society usurped by women in the workplace. They also found that their position in the family had shifted radically, since women generally maintained control of the household economy and day-to-day decisions. A Soviet-era joke refers to this situation; one woman says to another: "I make all the trivial, unimportant decisions—where we will vacation, if we will move to a new apartment, if we will buy a car... My husband makes the really im-portant decisions in the family, you know: Can we build communism in one country? Should the two Germanies reunite?" (cited in both Ries 1997, 73 and Draitser 1999, 180). The ritual specialists had hoped to infuse Soviet morality into the populace through these three ceremonies. They aimed to create a sta-ble socialist family that would provide productive workers for the future and that would not disrupt the current social order through divorces and other family dramas. They did not count on the fact that the Soviet system itself made it especially difficult for families to survive as a unit and, in fact, pro-moted gender and familial conflict.

Women, then, not only retained their traditional role in the family (and even strengthened it), but also made incursions into the male's traditional sphere, both in the family and in the public eye. Shlapentokh (1984, 171) summarizes this situation as follows:

> [T]he disruption of the dominant system of values, the sharp conflict between often mutually exclusive desires, and the gigantic educational and professional advances of women—all this has destroyed the previous fundamentals of relations between the sexes in Soviet society ... conflicts between women and men are now among the most salient aspects of everyday life....

A prime example of this essential conflict appears in a Leningrad study which found that women wanted a modern marriage characterized by equality between partners, while men wanted a traditional family structure (Shlapentokh 1984, 203). In practice, however, it seems that women did dominate the family, as Tolstaia (1990, 4) asserts: "A Russian woman is entirely the mistress of her household, the children belong to her and to her alone, the family often doesn't even ask for male advice." Certainly, there were also families where men assumed the dominant role in the relationship, which most women resented due to their desires for an egalitarian marriage. Conflicts between husbands and wives about gender roles and expectations for them were a major factor in marriages of the Soviet period. While some Soviet Russian women would gladly have given up work outside the home, the economic situation usually made that choice impossible, despite the government's periodic pushes for women to return to the home or cut back their hours to part-time levels to increase the birthrate. In addition, Shlapentokh (1984, 177) notes that women wanted to work for other reasons, including prestige and recognition, the opportunity to communicate with others, and their desire for independence from their husbands. As a result, the rituals could not foster the stability in the family that the state and its representatives had hoped for. The three radically different sources for the rituals conveyed some inherently contradictory messages about gender roles and about family structure. In the end they often led to increased dissonance, not only in the family circle itself, but between the family and the state.

We have applied practice theory to examine how ritual actors used state-devised ceremonies to achieve their own ends to negotiate their social and familial identities. They complied with and even wholeheartedly adopted certain aspects of ideology, but also resisted it when it contradicted their own folk and religious perceptions of family roles. Bell (1997, 82) argues that the practice approach to ritual presupposes that

> ritual is more complex than the mere communication of meanings and values; it is a set of activities that construct particular types of meanings and values in specific ways. Hence, rather than ritual as the vehicle for the *expression* of authority, practice theorists tend to ex-

plore how ritual is a vehicle for the *construction* of relationships of authority and submission. [italics original]

The tripartite system Russians faced led to a ritual complex that helped both to resolve and exacerbate the contradictions inherent in identity within the Soviet Russian family and society. Through these rituals, citizens established their position within the social hierarchy. They thereby enabled the continuity of Soviet ideology about the family, but also helped to reshape it through ritual practice by stubbornly retaining essential beliefs from other sources, e.g., folk practices designed to demonstrate inequality between the marriage partners, the centrality of grandmothers and folk knowledge in child rearing and the existence of the soul in the afterlife. People also relied on folk beliefs to resist the state's attempts to establish dominance over the family unit, by creating it an independent unit with its own traditions and norms. These belief systems ran counter to those that socialist family ideology propounded, but did not totally erase the power of the official system. Women and men accepted the predominance of the state in ritual life, participated in these state rites, and incorporated some fundamental concepts related to family identity into their belief systems. Our study of childbirth, for example, demonstrates how effectively the medical system remade the birth process through a Soviet model that established women's centrality to family and the role of the state in "creating" and supporting a child.

Soviet ideology, in its purest form, conveyed the message that women and men were equal partners in the public and private spheres. The ritual specialists Rudnev (1979, 12–13) and Ugrinovich (1975, 20) argue forcefully that the Soviet revolution provided freedom for women from traditional norms (held by the church) that men were the heads of the household. Rudnev (13) concludes that civil marriage, thus, allows for "equality of the sides entering into marriage," a belief that most people espoused, at least in theory. In addition, he says that these rituals must reflect communist morality, which precludes showiness or excessive wealth. While these opinions encapsulate the party line, in fact the rituals were designed to some extent to feature *pokazukha* 'showiness' and the desire for consumer goods among middle-class citizens. There is no doubt that the rituals were aimed at the "middle-class mentality" and that urban citizens adopted this attitude toward family life. In his description of just such a Leningrad wedding from the 1970s, Rudnev (140) notes that such weddings will be the model for later ceremonies for workers, students and collective farmers, e.g., members of the working class or those without a great deal of cash to spend. In essence, the middle class and its rites became a standard for the society as a whole.

Not only did these rituals embody the inherent (and seemingly contradictory) bond between Soviet and capitalist ideologies, but they also displayed how people attempted to preserve family religious and folk traditions. At first glance, these practices would perhaps have always been in conflict with Soviet and capitalist viewpoints. However, the ritual specialists chose to reinvigorate some folk traditions, if they were consonant with Soviet ideology, by incorporating them into the rites. They justified this step by arguing that folk ritual acts were areligious and actually anti-Orthodox. They also stressed the significance of folk material as a means to convey ancestral wisdom to future generations (see Mar'ianov 1976a, 10–12; Sukhanov 1976, 55–68), to which people seemingly responded. Soviet Russians saw folk belief as essential to their definition of "Russianness," a trend that has even been strengthened in the post-Soviet era.

However, theorists could not simultaneously prevent people from performing folk and religious rites that citizens found to be relevant to their own conceptions of family identity, e.g., the *vykup* 'buying of the bride' and baptism. They could not foresee (or could not prevent) that people would take these rituals and make them their own, that they might either openly reject the Soviet messages or radically reinterpret them. Mourners, for example, might be told that the phrase *vechnaia pamiat'* referred exclusively to one's deeds on earth, but it brought to mind the afterlife. Parents might be instructed that the witnesses at the naming ritual were not godparents, but the ritual model itself suggested this interpretation. The very fact that the Soviet theorists raised these issues indicates that they knew that their fellow citizens would be likely to read religious meaning into the acts. Similarly, while a concern for consumer goods might foster a happy middle class and thus a stable society, they could not anticipate that people would resent the government for not living up to its promises to provide for its citizens. As a result, both the desire for "Western" products and a disdain for government property (theft at the workplace was common) were an accepted fact of everyday life (Verdery 1996, 29; Shlapentokh 1989, 165). These negative perceptions of the government's failures in adequate provision of material items emerged in the life-cycle rituals as well. People relied on their families to provide the essential goods and services needed for a proper celebration, which made families even more central to the ritual process. But the most telling discrepancy between the goals the specialists had for their rituals and the actual results was evident in the family circle.

The Soviet Russian family could represent an oppositional, private space in relation to the public, state-controlled world. In some cases the rituals reflected this essential division between the inner and outer spheres. Within the public ceremonies, people were willing to play their parts, accepting, for instance, state control in the *roddom* and the ZAGS. They may, of course, have done so precisely because there were no alternatives or out of fear of reprisals. But that attitude simplifies a complex socio-cultural phenomenon. Yurchak's study (2006, 18), like this one, attempts

> to examine how people living with that system engaged with, interpreted, and created their reality. The analysis in this book will con-

sider discourse and forms of knowledge that circulated in everyday
Soviet life not as divided into spheres or codes that are fixed and
bounded, but as processes that are never completely known in advance and that are actively produced and reinterpreted.

It was certainly to people's advantage to participate in the public ceremonies
and to be seen to espouse Soviet values, but we cannot conclude that all the
values represented by these performances were anathema to Soviet Russian
citizens. As we have shown, they adopted certain essential values from Soviet
ideology about their roles as parents, spouses, and family members, just as
they rejected others. Thus, the family and its life-cycle rituals were the center
of negotiation about official ideology. They could be the heart of resistance,
and thus a threat to the Soviet state, but they also played a key role in the
perpetuation of core Soviet-era norms about family life and gender roles
within it.

   Despite the centrality of Soviet institutions to the life-cycle rites, the heart
of the rituals were those events that occurred outside of the public sphere,
within the family circle. Within this context people were free to devise their
own rituals, to maintain their own traditions, to foster their conception of national Russian identity, and to truly move through the rite of passage into a
new status. Within these portions of the celebrations, the state (and its agents,
ritual specialists) initially lost control of the ritual. They attempted to regain
their influence over the rites by devising their own versions of wedding
receptions (in lieu of private, family parties), naming ceremonies, and civil funerals (in lieu of religious christening and burial rites). However, once the
state established formal ritual celebrations, it opened the door to the flourishing of older traditions that contradicted spiritual values and communist morality. Theorists could not eliminate the folk and/or religious traditions they
found unseemly, such as the *vykup* or the prayers for the dead. Nor could
they prevent people from reinterpreting official messages built into the ritual
with their own, contradictory ones. For example, the state promoted the notion of a "middle class" which would be rewarded with more comfortable
material lives. People willingly embraced consumer goods, but then complained when their government could not or would not provide these items.
Similarly, while citizens officially endorsed the ideals of equality between the
sexes, they continued to adopt both folk and "bourgeois" messages that the
Soviets viewed as outmoded, e.g., by buying the bride and thus focusing on
the wife as an object and the groom as only a cash cow of sorts. Native folk
and adopted Western material was meshed with Soviet-era norms into a
sometimes dissonant definition of social and familial identity. Nevertheless,
these three distinct models formed the heart of the people's understanding of
their roles as spouses, as parents, and as the bereaved.

   The practice of Soviet Russian life-cycle rituals throughout this period illustrates the persistence of folk belief, which withstands even direct attacks if

its practices remain essential to an understanding of one's place in society. However, they also show the mutability of folk tradition. It adapts to changing circumstances and meshes with material from a variety of sources that are not classically defined as "folk," from medicalized birth to consumerist ideology. We see clear evidence of this process in the post-Soviet world. Capitalism has come to the forefront in the rituals. Excess and display, so longed for in the Soviet times, are now at their center. Not everyone is content with this change to be sure. Many of my informants, particularly in connection with childbirth and the funeral, expressed dismay at the shift toward a consumerist stance. Buraway and Verdery (1999, 12), in their discussion of the post-socialist world, mention that "capitalist institutions provoke their own form of resistance, recalling the radiant past." Boym (2001, 42) also describes the nostalgia for the Soviet era and the desire for a continuity with the past that is characteristic of post-Soviet reality.

As a result of this desire to connect with and preserve the past, Soviet-era rituals have not been totally abandoned. Within the current social framework, people not only miss Soviet-era values, but also have encouraged a revival of the folk and religious traditions of the pre-revolutionary period that the Soviet officials purportedly destroyed. The resurgence in folk and religious behaviors connects people to a sense of national identity and "Russianness," but for a very different reason than in the Soviet period. Then folk practices established an independent familial identity under the threat from a government which had eliminated core social institutions (e.g., the church and patriarchal family life) and spreading propaganda about the "backwardness" of folk belief. In the post-Soviet era, performance of folk rituals illustrates the power of the *narod* 'folk, people', who survived the privations of the Soviet period (including, to name a few, the gulags, the devastation of World War II, and a revolutionary socialist experiment which produced some dubious economic and social effects on the family unit). In addition, in the face of the challenge to Russia's role as a superpower on the international stage, folk beliefs provide a core sense of national identity and strength in a time of uncertainty and perceived weakness. These revivals also counter the perceived threat of social and familial instability within the capitalist, pluralist system citizens now face. Folk and religious traditions, oddly enough, have thus merged with Soviet-era values. People view them as "native" traditions that help to overcome the instability represented by the current state of affairs in the country. In the end the Soviet period is simultaneously beloved as a sort of "golden age" as well as criticized for its attacks on Russian folk and religious beliefs. However, the rituals have not been static. Like the society around them, they have continued to evolve as the needs and values of the people have changed. They have adopted some essential notions of the role of consumerism, at the same time that they have rejuvenated a hyperbolic folk tradition.

Analysis of the life-cycle complex has provided us with an essential tool for an understanding of daily life in Soviet Russia and its changing conceptions of family and gender identity. The content of birth, wedding, and funeral practices from the death of Stalin to the post-Soviet period articulates the dilemmas citizens faced in establishing their social roles. They represent a microcosm of the larger society itself and thus illuminate family structure and its relation to the public sphere. People created their own independent social reality through life-cycle rituals. By promulgating a wide array of official notions of family life, these rites simultaneously maintained and yet undermined socialist ideology. But they also established the family as the center of an "alternate" sphere. This space enabled families to negotiate some independent identities which deconstructed official socialist norms. Soviet Russian citizens were thus free to redefine their roles as parents, spouses, and survivors upon the basis of (occasionally anti-establishment) native folk and religious material as well as borrowed material from the West. Russian citizens have met their needs for the formation of social identity through ritual performance itself by fusing ideas from three distinct roots. Nevertheless, the rituals have united these diverse belief systems into a coherent whole, a whole that demonstrates the complexity of roles within the family and within the public sphere for urban Russians during the Soviet period and beyond.

Interviews

1. Alevtina A., engineer, DOB 1937, native of Vladimir, interviewed 6/9/03 in Vladimir.
2. Alexander D., computer science professor, DOB 1972, native of Tver', interviewed 7/1/04 in Lexington, KY.
3. Alexander K., engineer-inspector, DOB 1945, native of Archangelsk, interviewed 6/12/03 in Novosibirsk.
4. Alexander U., engineer, DOB 1948, native of Kaliningrad, interviewed 6/9/04 in Vladimir.
5. Alexei A., English teacher, DOB 1971, native of Semipalatinsk, interviewed 6/1/04 in Novosibirsk.
6. Andrei M., sales representative, DOB 1968, native of Vladimir, interviewed 6/30/03 in Vladimir.
7. Anna I., seamstress, DOB 1930, native of Chita, interviewed 3/29/01 in Novosibirsk.
8. Anna M., salesperson, DOB 1980, native of Vladimir, interviewed 7/6/03 in Vladimir.
9. Anna V., teacher, DOB 1960, native of Kazan', interviewed 4/18/06 in Lexington, KY.
10. Dmitrii E., programmer, DOB 1977, native of Moscow, interviewed 6/13/04 in Moscow.
11. Dmitrii L., programmer, DOB 1976, native of Voronezh, interviewed 7/14/04 in Lexington, KY.
12. Ekaterina Z., institute researcher, DOB 1978, native of Novosibirsk, interviewed 6/2/04 in Novosibirsk.
13. Elena B., university professor, DOB 1952, native of Novosibirsk, interviewed 5/14/01 and 6/18/03 in Novosibirsk.
14. Elena E., midwife, DOB 1971, native of Novosibirsk, interviewed 9/17/01 in Novosibirsk.
15. Elena I., English teacher, DOB 1961, native of Vladimir, interviewed 7/7/03 in Vladimir.
16. Elena L., doctor (obstetrics/gynecology), DOB 1965, native of Moscow, interviewed 10/4/01 in Moscow.
17. Elena P., kindergarten teacher, DOB 1971, native of Vladimir, interviewed 6/30/03 in Vladimir.
18. Elena S., banker, DOB 1965, native of Novosibirsk, interviewed 4/2/01 in Novosibirsk.

19. Elvira A., engineer, DOB 1938, native of Vladimir, interviewed 7/7/03 in Vladimir.
20. Elvira P., secretary, DOB 1970, native of Tashkent, interviewed 3/23/01 and 5/27/04 in Novosibirsk.
21. Evgenia Z., doctor (obstetrics/gynecology), DOB 1963, native of Khabarovsk, interviewed 11/13/01 in Lexington, KY.
22. Galina S., engineer, DOB 1971, native of Novosibirsk, interviewed 5/28/04 in Novosibirsk.
23. Galina T., private school teacher, DOB 1942, native of Vladimir, interviewed 6/3/03 in Vladimir.
24. Galina V., ZAGS director, DOB unknown, native of Dresden, interviewed 7/11/03 in Vladimir.
25. Iana Iu., senior teacher, DOB 1975, native of St. Petersburg, interviewed 5/19/04 in St. Petersburg.
26. Igor S., physicist, DOB 1950, native of Novosibirsk, interviewed 6/16/03 in Novosibirsk.
27. Irina E., pediatrician, DOB 1977, native of Moscow, interviewed 6/13/04 in Moscow.
28. Irina S., graphic artist, DOB 1969, native of Novosibirsk, interviewed 4/14/01 in Novosibirsk.
29. Irina V., psychotherapist, DOB 1957, native of Moscow, interviewed 7/20/03 in Moscow.
30. Katia K., university professor, DOB 1950, native of Novosibirsk, interviewed 3/12/01 and 6/16/03 in Novosibirsk.
31. Klara K., insurance agent, DOB 1935, native of Ufa, interviewed 3/14/01 in Novosibirsk.
32. Larisa S., midwife, DOB 1971, native of Novosibirsk, interviewed 5/4/01 in Novosibirsk.
33. Larisa T., private school teacher, DOB 1946, native of Dzerzhinsk, interviewed 6/3/03 in Vladimir.
34. Larisa Z., English teacher, DOB 1977, native of Norilsk, interviewed 6/1/04 in Novosibirsk.
35. Lena L., private school teacher, DOB 1957, native of Vladimir, interviewed 6/9/97 in Vladimir.
36. Lena S., midwife, DOB 1964, native of Novosibirsk, interviewed 9/14/01 in Novosibirsk.
37. Lidia C., English teacher, DOB 1956, native of Novosibirsk, inteviewed 4/20/01 and 6/18/03 in Novosibirsk.
38. Lidia S., midwife, DOB 1987, native of Khabarovsk, interviewed 11/13/01 in Lexington, KY.
39. Lilia T., ZAGS director, DOB unknown, native of Novosibirsk, interviewed 6/24/03 in Novosibirsk.
40. Liuba P., civil engineer, DOB 1948, native of Vladimir, interviewed 6/15/97 in Vladimir.

41. Liuba S., art teacher, DOB 1954, native of Petrovskii Zavod, interviewed 5/11/01 and 6/25/03 in Novosibirsk.
42. Liubov' K., printer, DOB 1951, native of Novosibirsk, interviewed 6/12/03 in Novosibirsk.
43. Liudmila B., teacher, DOB 1932, native of Kovrov, interviewed 7/10/03 in Vladimir.
44. Liudmila K., salesperson, DOB 1962, native of Novosibirsk, interviewed 5/11/01 and 6/15/03 in Novosibirsk.
45. Liudmila S., midwife, DOB 1971, native of Moscow, interviewed 10/2/01 in Moscow.
46. Maria S., accountant, DOB 1969, native of Novosibirsk, interviewed 4/4/01 in Novosibirsk.
47. Marina K., director of organizational-analytic department, private firm, DOB 1974, native of Novosibirsk, interviewed 4/21/01 and 6/11/03 in Novosibirsk.
48. Marina L., high school teacher, DOB 1967, native of Samara, interviewed 4/2/98 in Lexington, KY.
49. Marina S., doctor (obstetrician-gynecologist), DOB 1962, native of Novosibirsk, interviewed 5/24/01 in Novosibirsk.
50. Nadezhda B., factory worker, DOB 1951, native of Chelyabinsk, interviewed 2/15/99 in Lexington, KY.
51. Nadezhda P., mathematician-programmer, DOB 1942, native of Novosibirsk, interviewed 4/24/01 and 6/20/03 in Novosibirsk.
52. Natalia I., doctor (obstetrics/gynecology), DOB 1950, native of Novosibirsk, interviewed 9/17/01 in Novosibirsk.
53. Natalia R., doctor (obstetrics/gynecology), DOB 1967, native of Khabarovsk, interviewed 11/13/01 in Lexington, KY.
54. Natalia S., engineer, DOB 1954, native of Vladimir, interviewed 6/9/04 in Vladimir.
55. Natalia T., university professor, DOB 1954, native of Novosibirsk, interviewed 5/28/01 and 6/23/03 in Novosibirsk.
56. Natalia Z., private school director, DOB 1955, native of Novosibirsk, interviewed 5/21/01 in Novosibirsk.
57. Natasha M., beautician, DOB 1974, native of St. Petersburg, interviewed 4/2/98 in Lexington, KY.
58. Natasha R., engineer, DOB 1969, native of Novosibirsk, interviewed 5/28/04 in Novosibirsk.
59. Natasha S., government worker, DOB 1975, native of Novosibirsk, interviewed 6/25/03 in Novosibirsk.
60. Nina S., engineer, DOB 1930, native of Vladimir, interviewed 7/10/03 in Vladimir.
61. Nina V., college professor, DOB 1940, native of St. Petersburg, interviewed 6/15/01 in Lexington, KY.

62. Olga D., computer scientist, DOB 1971, native of Tver', interviewed 7/1/04 in Lexington, KY.
63. Olga K., university professor, DOB 1957, native of Novosibirsk, interviewed 5/7/01 in Novosibirsk.
64. Olga L., graduate student (statistics), DOB 1976, native of Voronezh, interviewed 7/14/04 in Lexington, KY.
65. Olga R., university professor, DOB 1951, native of Novosibirsk, interviewed 5/30/01 and 6/18/03 in Novosibirsk.
66. Olga T., music teacher, DOB 1967, native of Vladimir, interviewed 6/3/03 in Vladimir.
67. Olga V., marketing specialist, DOB 1955, native of Moscow, interviewed 6/21/98 in Moscow.
68. Polina D., English teacher, DOB 1983, native of Moscow, interviewed 6/13/04 in Moscow.
69. Sergei M., mechanic, DOB 1980, native of Vladimir, interviewed 7/6/03 in Vladimir.
70. Svetlana V., midwife, DOB 1969, native of Moscow, interviewed 10/2/01 in Moscow.
71. Taisia V., nurse, DOB 1929, native of Krapiva, interviewed 6/29/97 in Krapiva.
72. Tamara B., doctor (neonatalogist), DOB 1950, native of Novosibirsk, interviewed 5/5/01 in Novosibirsk.
73. Tania K., tax inspector, DOB 1978, native of Novosibirsk, interviewed 5/30/04 in Novosibirsk.
74. Tatiana D., private school teacher, DOB 1953, native of Vladimir, interviewed 6/30/97 and 6/2/03 in Vladimir.
75. Tatiana G., midwife, DOB 1960, native of Khabarovsk, interviewed 11/13/01 in Lexington, KY.
76. Tatiana K., public relations specialist, DOB 1937, native of Moscow, interviewed 4/2/98 in Lexington, KY.
77. Tatiana K., midwife, DOB 1970, native of Khabarovsk, interviewed 11/13/01 in Lexington, KY.
78. Tatiana S., quality control inspector, DOB 1975, native of Novosibirsk, interviewed 6/11/03 in Novosibirsk.
80. Tatiana U., accountant, DOB 1948, native of Vladivostok, interviewed 6/9/04 in Vladimir.
81. Tatiana V., midwife, DOB 1973, native of Novosibirsk, interviewed 9/17/01 in Novosibirsk.
82. Vadim D., programmer, DOB 1969, native of Gomel', interviewed 6/13/04 in Moscow.
83. Valentin P., math/computer science professor, DOB 1940, native of Altai, interviewed 6/20/03 in Novosibirsk.
84. Valentina P., doctor (neonatalogist), DOB 1952, native of Vladimir, interviewed 6/26/97 in Vladimir.

85. Vera S., midwife, DOB 1968, native of Novosibirsk, interviewed 9/14/01 in Novosibirsk.
86. Veronika S., engineer, DOB 1961, native of Novosibirsk, interviewed 6/11/03 in Novosibirsk.

Works Cited

Aasamaa, Iina. 1974. *Kak sebia vesti*. Tallinn: Valgus.

Abu-Lughod, Lila. 1986. *Veiled sentiments: Honor and poetry in a Bedouin society*. Berkeley: University of California Press.

Adon'eva, S. B. 1998. "O ritual'noi funktsii zhenshchiny v russkoi traditsii." *Zhivaia starina*, no. 1: 26–28.

Afanas'ev, A. 1994. *Poeticheskie vozzreniia slavian na prirodu*. Vol. 3. Moscow: Indrik.

Aleksandrov, V. A., I. V. Vlasova, and N. S. Polishchuk, eds. 2003. *Russkie*. Moscow: Nauka.

AllRefer.com, s.v. "Russia: Population: Demographic conditions: Fertility: Abortion." http://reference.allrefer.com/country-guide-study/russia/russia65.html (accessed 15 June 2006).

Anashkina, G. P. 2001. "Traditsii i novatsii v etnicheskoi kul'ture." In Nekliudov 2001, 206–16.

Ananicheva, T. M., and E. A. Samodelova. 1997. *Obriady i obriadovyi fol'klor*. Moscow: Nasledie.

Ashwin, Sarah, ed. 2000a. *Gender, state and society in Soviet and post-Soviet Russia*. London: Routledge.

———. "Introduction." 2000b. In Ashwin 2000a, 1–29.

Attwood, Lynne. 1990. *The new Soviet man and woman*. Bloomington: Indiana University Press.

———. 1996. "The post-Soviet woman in the move to the market: A return to domesticity and dependence?" In Marsh 1996, 255–66.

Baiburin, A. K. 1993. *Ritual v traditsionnoi kul'ture: Strukturno-semanticheskii analiz vostochnoslavianskikh obriadov*. St. Petersburg: Nauka.

———. 1997. "Rodinnyi obriad u slavian i ego mesto v zhiznennom tsikle." *Zhivaia starina*, no. 2: 7–9.

Baiburin, A. K., and G. A. Levinton. 1990. "Pokhorony i svad'ba." In Ivanov and Nevskaia 1990, 64–99.

Balashov, D. M., U. I. Marchenko, and N. I. Kalmykova. 1985. *Russkaia svad'ba*. Moscow: Sovremennik.

Balzer, Marjorie Mandelstam, ed. 1992. *Russian traditional culture*. Armonk, NY: M. E. Sharpe.

Banks, Amanda Carson. 1999. *Birth chairs, midwives, and medicine*. Jackson: University Press of Mississippi.

Baranov, D. A. 2001. "Rodinnyi obriad: Vremia, prostranstvo, dvizhenie." In Nekliudov 2001, 9–30.

Baranskaia, Natalia. 1989. *Nedelia kak nedelia*. Eds. Lora Paperno, Natalie Roklina, and Richard Leed. Columbus, OH: Slavica Publishers.

Barney, Sandra Lee. 2000. *Authorized to heal: Gender, class and the transformation of medicine in Appalachia, 1880–1930*. Chapel Hill: University of North Carolina Press.

Bell, Catherine. 1997. *Ritual: Perspectives and dimensions*. New York: Oxford University Press.

Belousov, A. F., I. S. Veselova, and S. Iu. Nekliudov. 2003. *Sovremennyi gorodskoi fol'klor*. Moscow: Rossiiskii gosudarstvennyi gumanitarnyi universitet.

Belousova, E. A. 1998. "Nash malysh: Sotsializatsiia novorozhdennogo v sovremennoi gorodskoi kul'ture." *Zhivaia starina*, no. 2: 24–25.

———. 1999. "Predstavleniia i verovaniia, sviazannye s rozhdeniem rebenka: Sovremennaia gorodskaia kul'tura." Kandidatskaia dissertatsiia, Rossiiskii gosudarstvennyi gumanitarnyi universitet.

———. 2002. "Preservation of national childbirth traditions in the Russian homebirth community." *Slavic and East European Folklore Journal* 7 (2): 50–77.

———. 2003. "Sredstva i sposoby sotsializatsii materi v rodil'nom dome." In Belousov et al. 2003, 340–69.

Bersen'eva, K. G., ed. 2005. *Svad'ba ot traditsii k sovremennosti*. Moscow: Tsentropoligraf.

Bourdieu, Pierre. 1991. *Language and symbolic power*. Ed. John Thompson. Trans. Gino Raymond and Matthew Adamson. Cambridge, MA: Harvard University Press.

———. 1977. *Outline of a theory of practice*. Trans. Richard Nice. Cambridge: Cambridge University Press.

———. 1990. *The logic of practice*. Trans. Richard Nice. Stanford, CA: Stanford University Press.

Boym, Svetlana. 1994. *Common places: Mythologies of everyday life in Russia*. Cambridge, MA: Harvard University Press.

———. 2001. *The future of nostalgia*. New York: Basic Books.

Bronfenbrenner, Urie. 1970. *Two worlds of childhood: U.S. and U.S.S.R.* New York: Russell Sage Foundation.

Bronner, Simon J. 1998. *Following tradition: Folklore in the discourse of American culture*. Logan: Utah State University Press.

Buckley, Mary. 1996. "Why be a shock worker or Stakhanovite?" In Marsh 1996, 199–213.

———. ed. 1997. *Post-Soviet women: From the Baltic to Central Asia*. Cambridge: Cambridge University Press.

Burawoy, Michael, and Katherine Verdery, eds. 1999. *Uncertain transitions: Ethnographies of change in the postsocialist world*. Lanham, MD: Rowman and Littlefield.

—————. 1999. "Introduction." In Burawoy and Verdery 1999, 1–17.

Burns, Tom, and Charles D. Laughlin. "Ritual and Social Power." In D'Aquili et al. 1979, 249–79.

Bushnell, John. 1980. "The 'new Soviet man' turns pessimist." In Cohen et al. 1980, 179–99.

Cheevers, C. J. "Putin urges plan to reverse slide in birth rate." *New York Times*, 11 May 2006. http://www.nytimes.com/2006/05/11/world/europe/11russia.html?ex=1305000000&en=2c8d1952038c2b83&ei=5088&partner=rssnyt&emc=rss (accessed 11 May 2006).

Chistiakov, V. A. 1982. "Predstavleniia o doroge v zagrobnyi mir v russkikh pokhoronnykh prichitaniiakh XIX–XX vv." In Sokolova 1982, 114–27.

Chizhikova, L. N. 1989. "Svadebnaia obriadnost' sel'skogo naseleniia Kurskoi gubernii v XIX–nachale XX v." In Gromyko and Listova 1989, 171–98.

Clements, Barbara Evans, Barbara Alpern Engel, and Christine D. Worobec, eds. 1991. *Russia's women: Accommodation, resistance, transformation*. Berkeley: University of California Press.

Cohen, Stephen F., Alexander Rabinowich, and Robert Sharlet, eds. 1980. *The Soviet Union since Stalin*. Bloomington: Indiana University Press.

Comaroff, Jean. 1985. *Body of power, spirit of resistance: The culture and history of a South African people*. Chicago: University of Chicago Press.

Crone, Anna Lisa, and Catherine V. Chvany, eds. 1996. *New studies in Russian language and literature*. Columbus, OH: Slavica Publishers.

D'Aquili, Eugene, Charles D. Laughlin, and John McManus, eds. 1979. *The spectrum of ritual: A biogenetic structural analysis*. New York: Columbia University Press.

Davis, Christopher M. 1990. "Economics of Soviet public health, 1928–1932." In Solomon and Hutchinson 1990, 146–72.

Davis-Floyd, Robbie. 1992. *Birth as an American rite of passage*. Berkeley: University of California Press.

Dobrovol'skaia, V. E. 2001. "Institut povival'nykh babok i rodil'no-krestil'naia obriadnost'." In Nekliudov 2001, 92–106.

Draitser, Emil. 1999. *Making war, not love: Gender and sexuality in Russian humor*. New York: St. Martin's Press.

Duffy, Diane. 2000. "Social identity and its influence on women's roles in East-Central Europe." *International Feminist Journal of Politics* 2 (2): 214–43.

Du Plessix-Gray, Francine. 1990. *Soviet women: Walking the tightrope*. New York: Doubleday.

Dunham, Vera. 1976. *In Stalin's time*. Cambridge: Cambridge University Press.

Edmondson, Linda. 1996. "Equality and difference in women's history: Where does Russia fit in?" In Marsh 1996, 94–108.

El'shtein, N. V. 1986. *Dialog o meditsine*. Tallinn: Vargus.

Farnsworth, Beatrice, and Lynne Viola, eds. 1992. *Russian peasant women*. Oxford: Oxford University Press.

Fawn, Rick, and Stephen White, eds. 2002. *Russia after communism*. London: Frank Cass.

Field, Deborah A. 1998. "Irreconcilable differences: Divorce and conceptions of private life in the Khrushchev era." *Russian Review* 57 (4): 599–613.

Filtzer, Donald. 1996. "Industrial working conditions and the political economy of female labour during perestroika." In Marsh 1996, 214–27.

Firsov, B. M., and I. G. Kiseleva, eds. 1993. *Byt velikorusskikh krest'ian-zemlepashtsev: Opisanie materialov etnograficheskogo biuro kniazia V. N. Tenisheva*. St. Petersburg: Izdatel'stvo Evropeiskogo doma.

Foster, Helen Bradley, and Donald Clay Johnson, eds. 2003. *Wedding dress across cultures*. Oxford: Berg.

Foucault, Michel. 1984. *The Foucault Reader*. Ed. Paul Rabinow. New York: Pantheon Books.

Funk, Nannette, and Magda Miller, eds. 1993. *Gender politics and post-communism: Reflections from Eastern Europe and the former Soviet Union*. New York: Routledge.

Gal, Susan, and Gail Kligman. 2000. *The politics of gender after socialism*. Princeton, NJ: Princeton University Press.

Goldberg A., V. Kamenetskii, and L. Akinfieva. 1982. "Preodelet' trudnosti podsteragaiushchiie sem'iu." In Vasil'eva 1982, 63–70.

Gennep, Arnold van. 1960. *The rites of passage*. Trans. Monika B. Vizedom and Gabrielle L. Caffee. Chicago: University of Chicago Press.

Glickman, Rose L. 1991. "The peasant woman as healer." In Clements et al. 1991, 148–62.

Globalis, an interactive world map. http://globalis.gvu.unu.edu/country/cfm?country=RU (for information on global health statistics, accessed 15 June 2006).

Goldman, Wendy Z. 1993. *Women, the state, and revolution: Soviet family policy and social life, 1917–1936*. Cambridge: Cambridge University Press.

————. 2002. *Women at the gates: Gender and industry in Stalin's Russia*. Cambridge: Cambridge University Press.

Gromyko, M. M., and T. A. Listova, eds. 1989. *Russkie: Semeinyi i obshchestvennyi byt*. Moscow: Nauka.

Gura, A. V. 1997. *Simvolika zhivotnykh v slavianskoi narodnoi traditsii*. Moscow: Indrik.

Guseva, S. M. 1989. "Problemy traditsionnosti sovremennoi russkoi svad'by." In Gromyko and Listova 1989, 221–29.

Gvozdikova, L. S., and T. T. Shapovalova. 1982. "*Dev'ia krasota*." In Sokolova 1982, 264–76.

Hobsbawm, Eric. 1983a. "Introduction: Inventing traditions." In Hobsbawm and Ranger 1983, 1–14.

Hobsbawm, Eric. 1983b. "Mass-producing traditions: Europe, 1870–1914." In Hobsbawm and Ranger 1983, 263–307.

Hobsbawm, Eric, and Terence Ranger. 1983. *The invention of tradition*. Cambridge: Cambridge University Press.

Humphrey, Caroline, and James Laidlaw. 1994. *The archetypal actions of ritual*. Oxford: Clarendon Press.

Hyer, Janet. 1996. "Managing the female organism: Doctors and the medicalization of women's paid work in Soviet Russia during the 1920s." In Marsh 1996, 111–20.

Iankova, Z. A. 1972. *Semeinnye struktury sotsial'nykh rolei zhenshchin v razvitom sotsialisticheskom obshchestve i model' sem'i*. Paper given at the Soviet Sociological Association 12th International Seminar on the Study of the Family. Moscow.

———. 1975. "Razvitie lichnosti zhenshchiny v sovetskom obshchestve." *Sotsiologicheskie issledovaniia*, no. 4: 42–51.

Ilic, Melanie. 1986. "Generals without armies, commanders without troops: Gorbachev's 'protection' of female workers." In Marsh 1996, 228–40.

Ingram, Anne. 1998. "The not quite dearly departed: Funerary rituals and beliefs about the dead in Ukrainian culture." PhD diss., University of Virginia.

Issoupova, Olga. 2000. "From duty to pleasure? Motherhood in Soviet and post-Soviet Russia." In Ashwin 2000, 30–54.

Ivanov V. V., and L. G. Nevskaia, eds. 1990. *Issledovaniia v oblasti balto-slavianskoi dukhovnoi kul'tury: Pogrebal'nyi obriad*. Moscow: Nauka.

Johnson, Janet E., and Jean C. Robinson. 2007a. *Living gender after communism*. Bloomington: Indiana University Press.

———. "Living Gender." 2007b. In Johnson and Robinson 2007, 1–21.

Junler, Peter. 1980. "The Soviet Family in Post-Stalinist Russia." In Cohen et al. 1980, 227–51.

Kabakova, G. I. 2001. *Antropologiia zhenskogo tela v slavianskoi traditsii*. Moscow: Ladomir.

Kalabikhina, E. 2004. *Gendernye voprosy v Rossii v kontse XX veka: Fokus-gruppovoe issledovanie v gorodskoi i sel'skoi mestnosti*. Moscow: Akisflat.

Kargin, A. S., ed. 2000. *Russkaia svad'ba, tom 1*. Moscow: Gosudarstvennyi respublikanskii tsentr russkogo fol'klora.

———. *Russkaia svad'ba, tom 2*. 2001. Moscow: Gosudarstvennyi respublikanskii tsentr russkogo fol'klora.

Kay, Rebecca. 2002. "A liberation from emancipation? Changing discourses on women's employment in Soviet and post-Soviet Russia." In Fawn and White 2002, 51–72.

———. 1997. "Perceptions of Russian womanhood." In Buckley 1997, 77–98.

Kharchev, A. G. 1979. *Brak i sem'ia v SSSR*. Moscow: Mysl'.

———. 1979. *Nravstvennost' i sem'ia*. Moscow: Znanie.

Khasbulatova, O. A. 2005. *Rossiiskaia gendernaia politika v XX stoletii: Mify i realii.* Ivanovo: Izdatel'stvo Ivanovskogo gosudarstvennogo universiteta.

Kiblitskaia, Marina. 2000. "'Once we were kings': Male experiences of loss of status at work in post-communist Russia." In Ashwin 2000, 90–104.

Kolpakova N. P., ed. 1973. *Lirika russkoi svad'by.* Leningrad: Nauka.

Krasovskaia, Iu. 1980. "Okh, kak eta svad'ba pela i pliasala…" *Klub i khudozhestvennaia samodeiatel'nost'*, no. 14: 23–24.

Kremleva, I. A. 1993. "Pokhoronno-pominal'nye obriady u russkikh: Traditsii i sovremennost'." In Simchenko and Tishkov 1993, 8–47.

—. 2003. "Pokhoronno-pominal'nye obychai i obriady." In Aleksandrov et al. 2003, 517–32.

Krugliakova, T. A. 2001. "Byt i fol'klor dorodovogo otdeleniia." In Nekliudov 2001, 217–35.

Kukhterin, Sergei. 2000. "Fathers and patriarchs in communist and post-communist Russia." In Ashwin 2000, 71–89.

Kuznetsova, V. P., and K. K. Loginov. 2001. *Russkaia svad'ba Zaonezh'ia.* Petrozavodsk: Petrozavodsk State University.

Lakoff, George, and Mark Johnson. 1999. *Philosophy in the flesh: The embodied mind and its challenge to western thought.* New York: Basic Books.

Lane, Christel. 1981. *The rites of rulers.* Cambridge: Cambridge University Press.

Leitsadu, I. 1982. "Kak igraiut na svad'bakh?" *Kul'turno-prosvetitel'naia rabota*, no. 10: 50–53.

—. 1983. "Tamada na svad'be." *Kul'turno-prosvetitel'naia rabota*, no. 5: 57–61.

Levi-Strauss, Claude. 1981. *The naked man: Introduction to a science of mythology.* Vol. 4. London: Jonathan Cape.

Lisavtsev, E. 1966. *Novye sovetskie traditsii.* Moscow: Sovetskaia Rossiia.

Lissyutkina, Larissa. 1993. "Soviet women at the crossroads of perestroika." In Funk and Miller 1993, 274–86.

Listova, T. A. 1989. "Russkie obriady, obychai i pover'ia sviazannye s povival'noi babkoi (vtoraia polovina XIX–20-e gody XX v.)." In Gromyko and Listova 1989, 142–71.

—. 1992. "Russian rituals, customs, and beliefs associated with the midwife (1850–1930)." In Balzer 1992, 122–45.

—. 1993. "Pokhoronno-pominal'nye obychai i obriady russkikh smolenskoi, pskovskoi i kostromskoi oblastei (konets XX v.)." In Simchenko and Tishkov 1993, 48–83.

—. 2003. "Narodnaia religioznaia kontseptsiia zarozhdeniia i nachala zhizni." In Aleksandrov et al. 2003, 685–701.

—. 2003. "Obriady i obychai, sviazannye s rozhdeniem detei. Pervyi god zhizni." In Aleksandrov et al. 2003, 500–17.

—. 1993. "Svad'ba na Smolenshchine." In Polishchuk and Makashina 1993, 7–45.

Lobanov, M. A. 2004. "The priest in the village wedding (ethnographic notes)." In *Folklorica* 9 (2): 14–31.

Mahler, Elsa. 1960. *Die russischen dörflichen Hochzeitsbräuche*. Berlin: Freie Universität Berlin.

———. 1935. *Die russische Totenklage: Ihre rituelle und dichterische Deutung*. Leipzig: Veröffenlichungen des slawischen Instituts.

Makashina, T. S. 2003. "Svadebnyi obriad." In Aleksandrov et al. 2003, 466–99.

Mar'ianov, V. 1976a. "Estafeta dukhovnogo bogatstva." In Mar'ianov 1976b, 3–16.

———., ed. 1976b. *Prazdniki, obriady i traditsii*. Moscow: Molodaia gvardiia.

Marody, Mira. 1993. "Why I am not a feminist." *Social Research* 60 (4): 853–64.

Marsh, Rosalind, ed. 1996. *Women in Russia and Ukraine*. Cambridge: Cambridge University Press.

Maslova, G. S. 1984. *Narodnaia odezhda v vostochnoslaviaskikh traditsionnykh obychaiakh i obriadakh XIX–nachala XX vekov*. Moscow: Nauka.

Matlin, M. G. 2003. "Svadebnyi obriad." In Belousov et al. 2003, 370–90.

Matossian, Mary. 1992. "The peasant way of life." In Farnsworth and Viola 1992, 11–40.

McManus, John. 1979. "Ritual and human social cognition." In D'Aquili et al. 1979, 216–48.

Mee, Janice, and Irina Safronova. 2003. "An historical perspective of English and Soviet bridalwear between 1917 and 1960." In Foster and Johnson 2003, 141–56.

Merridale, Catherine. 2000. *Night of stone: Death and memory in twentieth-century Russia*. New York: Viking.

Michaelson, Karen, ed. 1998. *Childbirth in America: Anthropological perspectives*. South Hadley, MA: Bergin and Garvey.

Minyonok, Yelena. 2007. "Visit to the Cemetery." In Rouhier-Willoughby et al.

Molyneux, Maxine, and Anastaia Posadskaia. 1991. "Interview with Anastasia Posadskaia (25 September 1990)." In "Shifting territories: Feminism and Europe," special issue, *Feminist Review*, no. 39: 133–40.

Moyle, Natalie K. 1996. "Mermaids (*rusalki*) and Russian beliefs about women." In Crone and Chvany 1996, 221–38.

Naumenko, G. M. 2001. *Narodnaia mudrost' i znaniia o rebenke*. Moscow: Tsentrpoligraf.

Nekliudov, S. Iu., ed. 2001. *Rodiny, deti, povitukhi v traditsiiakh narodnoi kul'tury*. Moscow: Rossiiskii gosudarstvennyi gumanitarnyi universitet.

Nosova, G. A. 1993. "Russkii traditsionnyi pokhoronyi obriad: sovremennye formy." In Simchenko and Tishkov 1993, 84–122.

———. 1999. *Traditsionnye obriady russkikh (krestiny, pokhorony, pominki)*. Moscow: Koordinatsionno-metodicheskii tsentr "Narody i kul'tury," Institut etnologii i antropologii RAN.

Olson, Laura. 2004. *Performing Russia: Folk revival and Russian identity*. New York: Routledge.

Ortner, Sherry B. 1989. *High religion: A cultural and political history of Sherpa Buddhism*. Princeton, NJ: Princeton University Press.

Pankeev, I. A. 1998. *Ot krestin do pominok*. Moscow: Eksmo.

Petrone, Karen. 2000. *Life has become more joyous, comrades: Celebrations in the time of Stalin*. Bloomington: Indiana University Press.

Polishchuk, N. S., and T. S. Makashina, eds. 1993. *Svadebnye obriady narodov Rossii i blizhnego zarubezh'ia*. Moscow: Akademiia nauk.

Rabow-Edling, Susanna. 2006. *Slavophile thought and the politics of cultural nationalism*. Albany: State University of New York Press.

Ramer, Samuel C. 1992. "Childbirth and culture: Midwifery in the nineteenth-century Russian countryside." In Farnsworth and Viola 1992, 107–20.

———. 1990. "Feldshers and rural health care in the early Soviet period." In Solomon and Hutchinson 1990, 121–45.

Rands Lyon, Tania. 2007. "Housewife fantasies: Family realities in the new Russia." In Johnson and Robinson 2007, 25–39.

Ransel, David L. 1991. "Infant-care cultures in the Russian empire." In Clements et al. 1991, 113–32.

———. 2000. *Village mothers: Three generations of change in Russia and Tataria*. Bloomington: Indiana University Press.

Razumova, I. A. 2001. *Potaennoe znanie sovremennoi russkoi sem'i*. Moscow: Indrik.

Reeder, Roberta. 1975. *Down along the Mother Volga: An anthology of Russian folk lyrics*. Philadelphia: University of Pennsylvania Press.

Ries, Nancy. 1997. *Russian talk: Culture and conversation during perestroika*. Ithaca, NY: Cornell University Press.

Rivkin-Fish, Michele. 1997. "Reproducing Russia: Women's health and moral education in the construction of a post-Soviet society." PhD diss., Princeton University.

———. 2005. *Women's health in post-Soviet Russia: The politics of intervention*. Bloomington: Indiana University Press.

Rouhier-Willoughby, Jeanmarie. 2003a. "'Ne posylai menia na chuzhuiu storonu': Traurnye aspekty severno-russkoi svad'by glazami amerikanskogo issledovatelia (po zapisiam 19-ogo veka)." *Sibirskii filologicheskii zhurnal*, no. 2: 13–23.

———. 2003b. "Russian birth customs: Ancient traditions in modern guise." *Slavic and East European Journal* 47 (2): 227–50.

Rouhier-Willoughby, Jeanmarie, Yelena Minyonok, and Vera Kuznetsova. 2007. *The Russian Folk Religious Imagination*. http://www.rch.uky.edu/RFRI/.

Rudnev, V. A. 1979. *Sovetskie prazdniki, obriady, ritualy*. Leningrad: Lenizdat.

Ryan, Michael. 1978. *The organization of Soviet medical care*. Oxford: Blackwell.

———. 1990. *Doctors and the state in the Soviet Union*. New York: St. Martin's Press.

Sacks, Michael Paul. 1976. *Women's work in Soviet Russia: Continuity in the midst of change*. New York: Praeger.

Sahlins, Marshall. 1976. *Culture and practical reason*. Chicago: University of Chicago Press.

———. 1981. *Historical metaphors and mythical realities*. Ann Arbor: University of Michigan Press.

———. 1985. *Islands of history*. Chicago: University of Chicago Press.

Sargeant, Elena. 1996. "The 'women question' and problems of maternity in post-Soviet Russia." In Marsh 1996, 269–85.

Scott, James C. 1985. *Weapons of the weak: Everyday forms of peasant resistance*. New Haven: Yale University Press.

Serykh, V. D. 1986. *Voinskie ritualy*. Moscow: Voennoe izdatel'stvo.

Sedakova, O. A. 2004. *Poetika obriada: Pogrebal'naia obriadnost' vostochnykh i iuzhnykh slavian*. Moscow: Indrik.

Shening-Parshina, M. M., and A. N. Shibaeva. 1967. *Sanitarnoe prosveshchenie po okhrane zdorov'ia zhenshchin*. Moscow: Institut sanitarnogo prosveshcheniia.

Shevchenko, V. F. 2003. "Pokhoronnie i pominal'nye ritualy." In Belousov et al., 391–406.

Shlapentokh, Vladimir. 1984. *Love, marriage and friendship in the Soviet Union: Ideals and practices*. New York: Praeger.

———. 1989. *Public and private life of the Soviet people: Changing values in post-Stalinist Russia*. New York: Oxford University Press.

Shmelova M. N. 1989. "Traditsionnye bytovye sviazi sovremennoi gorodskoi sem'i u russkikh (po materialam tsentral'nykh oblastei RSFSR)." In Gromyko and Listova 1989, 63–84.

Shtulhofer, Aleksandar, and Theo Sandfort. 2005. *Sexuality and gender in postcommunist Eastern Europe and Russia*. New York: Haworth.

———. 2005. "Introduction: Sexuality and gender in times of transition." In Shtulhofer and Sandfort 2005, 1–25.

Simchenko, Iu. B., and V. A. Tishkov, eds. 1993. *Pokhoronno-pominal'nye obychai i obriady*. Moscow: Rossiiskaia akademiia nauk, Institut etnologii i antropologii imeni N. N. Miklukho-Maklaia.

Sims, Martha C., and Martine Stephens. 2005. *Living folklore: An introduction to the study of people and their traditions*. Logan: Utah State University Press.

Sokolov, Iurii M. 1950. *Russian folklore*. Trans. Catherine R. Smith. New York: Macmillan.

Sokolova, V. K., ed. 1982. *Obriady i obriadovyi fol'klor*. Moscow: Nauka.

Solomon, Susan Gross, and John F. Hutchinson, eds. 1990. *Health and society in revolutionary Russia*. Bloomington: Indiana University Press.

Stites, Richard. 1989. *Revolutionary dreams: Utopian vision and experimental life in the Russian revolution*. New York: Oxford University Press.

———. 1978. *The women's liberation movement in Russia: Feminism, nihilism, and Bolshevism, 1860–1930*. Princeton, NJ: Princeton University Press.

Sukhanov, I. V. 1976. *Obychai, traditsii, i preemstvennost' pokolenii.* Moscow: Politizdat.

Surkhasko, Iu. Iu. 1985. *Semeinye obriady i verovaniia karel konets XIX–nachalo XX v.* Leningrad: Nauka.

Szabo, Amy. 2006. "Looking from within and without: Interpretations of socialist legacy for women in the former Yugoslavia." Paper presented at the Midwest Slavic Conference, Ohio State University, March 2006.

Tartakovskaia, Irina. 2000. "The changing representation of gender roles in the Soviet and post-Soviet press." In Ashwin 2000, 118–36.

Tian-Shanskaia, O. S. 1993. *Village life in late tsarist Russia.* Ed. David L. Ransel. Bloomington: Indiana University Press.

Timasheff, Nicholas S. 1946. *The great retreat: The growth and decline of communism in Russia.* New York: E. P. Dutton.

Tolstaia, Tatiana. 1990. "Notes from the underground." *New York Review of Books* 37 (9) (May 31): 3–9.

Tolstoi, N. I. 1990. "Perevorachivanie predmetov v slavianskom pogrebal'nom obriade." In Ivanov and Nevskaia 1990, 119–28.

———. 1995. *Iazyk i narodnaia kul'tura. Ocherki po slavianskoi mifologii i etnolingvistike.* Moscow: Indrik.

———. 1995. "Iazyk i kul'tura." In Tolstoi 1995, 15–26.

———. 1995. "Iz 'grammatiki' slavianskikh obriadov." In Tolstoi 1995, 63–77.

———. 1995. "Votorichnaia funktsiia obriadogo simvola." In Tolstoi 1995, 167–84.

Tolz, Vera, and Stephanie Booth, eds. 2005. *Nation and gender in contemporary Europe.* Manchester: Manchester University Press.

Trice, Thomas R. 1998, "The 'body politic': Russian funerals and the politics of representation, 1841–1921." PhD diss., University of Illinois at Urbana-Champaign.

Tumarkin, Nina. 1994. *The living and the dead.* New York: Basic Books.

Turner, Victor. 1969. *The ritual process: Structure and anti-structure.* Ithaca, NY: Cornell University Press.

Tuve, Jeannette E. 1984. *The first Russian women physicians.* Newtonville, MA: Oriental Research Partners.

Ugrinovich, D. M. 1975. *Obriady: Za i protiv.* Moscow: Politizdat.

Vasil'eva, E. 1982. *Sovremennaia sem'ia.* Moscow: Finansy i statistika.

Verdery, Katherine. 1996. *What was socialism and what comes next.* Princeton, NJ: Princeton University Press.

Vlaskina, T. Iu. 2001. "Mifologicheskii tekst rodin." In Nekluidov 2001, 61–78.

Voznesenskaia, Iulia. 1986. *Women's Decameron.* Trans. W. B. Linton. London: Quarter.

Warner, Elizabeth A. 2000. "Russian peasant beliefs and practices concerning death and the supernatural collected in Novosokol'niki region, Pskov province, Russia, 1995. Part II: Death in Natural Circumstances." In *Folklore* 111 (2). http://search.epnet.com/direct.asp?an=3990535&db=aph

Weemer, Matthew. "Russians given day off work to make babies." *The Guardian*, 14 August 2007. http://www.guardian.co.uk/worldlatest/story/0,,-6849496,00.html (accessed 14 August 2007).

Weissman, Neil B. 1990. "Origins of Soviet health administration: Narkom-zdrav, 1918–1928." In Solomon and Hutchinson 1990, 97–120.

Whitaker, Elizabeth Dixon. 2000. *Measuring mamma's milk: Fascism and the medicalization of maternity in Italy*. Ann Arbor: University of Michigan Press.

Wolff, Larry. 1994. *Inventing Eastern Europe: The map of civilization on the mind of the Enlightenment*. Stanford, CA: Stanford University Press.

Worobec, Christine D. 1991. "Accommodation and resistance." In Clements et al. 1991, 17–28.

————. 1995. *Peasant Russia*. DeKalb: Northern Illinois University Press.

Yurchak, Aleksei. 2006. *Everything was forever, until it was no more: The last Soviet generation*. Princeton, NJ: Princeton University Press.

Zabylin M. 1880/1990. *Russkii narod: Ego obychai, obriady, predaniia, sueveriia i poeziia*. Moscow: Kniga Printshop.

Zagradskaia, S. 1980. "Svad'be-stsenarii." *Klub i khudozhestvennaia samodeia-tel'nost'*, no. 14: 22.

————. 1981. "Obriad, kakim emu byt' segodnia?" *Kul'turno-prosvetitel'naia rabota*, no. 7: 22–24.

Zdravomyslova, Elena, and Anna Temkina. 2005. "Gender citizenship in Soviet and post-Soviet societies." In Tolz and Booth 2005, 96–113.

Zelenin, D. K. 1927/1991. *Vostochnoslavianskaia etnografiia*. Ed. K. V. Chistov. Trans. K. D. Tsivina. Moscow: Nauka.

Zhekulina, V. I. 1982. "Istoricheskie izmeneniia v svadebnom obriade i poezii (po materialam Novgorodskoi oblasti)." In Sokolova, 237–53.

Zhirnova, G. V. 1980. *Brak i svad'ba russkikh gorozhan v proshlom i nastoiashchem*. Moscow: Nauka.

Zorin, N. V. 1981. *Russkaia svad'ba v srednem Povolzh'e*. Kazan: Kazan State University.

————. 2001. *Russkii svadebnyi ritual*. Moscow: Nauka.

Index